John Camden Hotten

The slang dictionary

John Camden Hotten

The slang dictionary

ISBN/EAN: 9783742876461

Manufactured in Europe, USA, Canada, Australia, Japa

Cover: Foto ©Andreas Hilbeck / pixelio.de

Manufactured and distributed by brebook publishing software (www.brebook.com)

John Camden Hotten

The slang dictionary

THE
SLANG DICTIONARY;

OR,

THE VULGAR WORDS, STREET PHRASES,

AND "FAST" EXPRESSIONS OF

HIGH AND LOW

SOCIETY.

MANY WITH THEIR ETYMOLOGY,
AND A FEW WITH THEIR HISTORY TRACED.

"Rabble-charming words, which carry so much wild-fire wrapt up in them."

The "Wedge" and the "Wooden Spoon."—See p. 272.

LONDON:
JOHN CAMDEN HOTTEN, PICCADILLY.
1869.

PREFACE.

WITH this work is incorporated *The Dictionary of Modern Slang, Cant, and Vulgar Words*, issued by "a London Antiquary" in 1859. The first edition of that work contained about 3000 words; the second, issued twelve months later, gave upwards of 5000. Both editions were reviewed by the critical press with an approval seldom accorded to small works of the kind. During the four years that have elapsed, the compiler has gone over the field of unrecognised English once more. The entire subject has been re-surveyed, out-lying terms and phrases have been brought in, new street-words have been added, and better illustrations of old colloquial expressions given. The result is the volume before the reader, which offers, for his amusement or instruction, nearly 10,000 words and phrases commonly deemed "vulgar," but which are used by the highest and lowest, the best, the wisest, as well as the worst and most ignorant of society.

Any apology for an inquiry like the present is believed to be unnecessary. The philologist and the historian usually find in such material the best evidences of a people's progress or decline It may not be out of place to say here—and I am sure he would not have objected—

that the late Mr Buckle took the greatest interest in the subject, and that in a few instances I am indebted to that gentleman for the probable etymologies of some of the terms given in the Dictionary. "Many of these words and phrases," he used to say, "are but serving their apprenticeship, and will eventually become the active strength of our language."

The widespread interest taken in the subject of English vulgar speech has surprised me. From almost every capital in Europe I have received communications asking further particulars, or informing me that scraps of their language have become mixed with our street-talk; and from India, China, the Cape, Australia, and North and South America I have received letters of advice or inquiry upon the subject. In German magazines numerous articles have appeared upon my former book; and, at Turin, Professor Ascoli has published a lengthy work upon the Lingua Franca words in the speech of our lower orders, which the *Dictionary of Modern Slang* was the first to detect and make known. The Professor looks to the Lombard merchants, who flocked to London in the days of Elizabeth and James I., as the source from whence we derive this curious element in our vulgar speech. I am sorry to inform him that we have to thank the less dignified organ-grinders, as they are termed, for the introduction of this Italian peculiarity in our street-language.

PREFACE.

The short history of Cant and Slang, which precedes the Dictionary, was first published in 1859, and has not since been re-written, although the Dictionary, which follows, has been more than trebled in size, and consequently contains many more illustrations of the different classes of colloquial speech than are given in the introduction. For the general style and aim of this preliminary performance, the compiler feels it necessary to offer some apology.

The more vulgar and less known Cant or secret terms of the London thieves are given in the Dictionary at the foot of each page. The compiler scarcely knew what to do with some of the more repulsive of these words—those explanatory of thieving, &c., and which continually occur in the language of low life. Their very existence is a lamentable fact; and the dry, unpoetic way they explain criminal intentions and actions is miserable in the extreme. Crime is an awkward thing to deal with, and, as in the case of our own Legislature, when trying successfully to regulate the punishment, and at the same time provide for the reformation of criminal offenders, he found the matter a singularly difficult one to manage. Slang is generally pithy and amusing, whereas Cant, like our lower orders in their thoughts and actions, is unrelieved by any feeling approaching to the poetic or the refined.

A few Slang and Cant words will be observed in the plural. The compiler endeavoured, as far as possible, to give the singular number; but in the case of some of the terms he found this impossible, as he never heard them used in any other form than the plural.

The reader will please bear in mind that this is a Dictionary of *modern* Slang,—a list of colloquial words and phrases in *present* use,—whether of ancient or modern formation. Whenever *Ancient* or *Ancient English* is appended to a Slang or Cant word, it is meant to signify that the expression was in respectable use in or previous to the reign of Queen Elizabeth. *Ancient Cant* indicates that the term was used as a Cant word in or previous to the same reign. *Old* or *Old English,* affixed to a vulgar word, signifies that it was in general use as a proper expression in or previous to the reign of Charles II. *Old Cant* indicates that the term was in use as a Cant word during or before the same reign.

Obsolete Slang terms are not given; no notice, therefore, has been taken of the numerous expressions that occur in the play-books and other popular literature of the past three hundred years, which have served their day, and now form no part of our tongue. Only the *living* language of the time has been dealt with.

Not long since the compiler purchased *The History of a Manchester Cadger: Narrated in his own Language,* price 1d. He was certainly somewhat surprised on opening the pamphlet to find that it consisted of eight pages of his own little book, reprinted with a few errors, and without any acknowledgment of the source from whence it was taken. He could from his heart recommend the Manchester Cadger to reprint the Ten Commandments, and study one of them, now that he has somewhat improved his fortune by the first pilfer. It is said that 40,000 copies have been sold of the *History*. H.I.H. the Prince Lucien Bonaparte very recently discovered one of his privately-printed little books, *The Song of Solomon, in the Lancashire Dialect*, being hawked around the same city in the form of a twopenny edition.

The compiler will be thankful for any corrections, additional examples, or words omitted. He has occupied many spare hours in the formation of this Dictionary of unrecognised English, and he wishes in future editions to make it as perfect as possible.

Based upon the present performance, a work of a similar but more extended character is in progress. It will give an appropriate extract from books, serials, broadsheets, or any other source which may afford material illustrative of the actual employment of the several Slang, Cant, and Vulgar terms in English printed literature. It is believed that the work will be of considerable value to the philologist. Further particulars may be obtained of the publisher, who will also receive subscribers' names.

In conclusion, the compiler begs to express his obligations to those correspondents who have from time to time assisted him with their valuable suggestions.

J. C. H.

Piccadilly, 1st June 1864.

⁎ *The Prefaces to the compiler's previous work are added, as it is believed that they will not prove uninteresting to the reader.*

PREFACE TO THE FIRST EDITION

OF THE

DICTIONARY OF MODERN SLANG, ETC.

IF any gentleman of a studious turn of mind, who may have acquired the habit of carrying pencils and note-books, would for one year reside in Monmouth Court, Seven Dials; six months in Orchard Street, Westminster; three months in Mint Street, Borough; and consent to undergo another three months on the extremely popular but very much disliked treadmill, (*vulgo* the "Everlasting Staircase,") finishing, I will propose, by a six months' tramp, in the character of a cadger and beggar, over England, I have not the least doubt but that he would be able to write an interesting work on the languages, secret and vulgar, of the lower orders.

In the matter of SLANG, our studious friend would have to divide his time betwixt observation and research. Conversations on the outsides of omnibuses, on steamboat piers, or at railway termini, would demand his most attentive hearing; so would the knots of semi-decayed cabmen, standing about in bundles of worn-out great coats and haybands, betwixt watering-pails, and conversing in a dialect every third word of which is without home or respectable relations. He would also have to station himself for hours near gatherings of ragged boys playing or fighting, but ever and anon contributing to the note-book a pure street-term. He would have to "hang about" lobbies, mark the refined word-droppings of magniloquent flunkeys, "run after" all the popular preachers, go to the Inns of Court, be up all night and about all day—in fact, be a ubiquitarian, with a note-book and pencil in hand.

As for research, he would have to turn over each page of our popular literature, wander through all the weekly serials, wade through the newspapers, fashionable and unfashionable, and subscribe to Mudie's, and scour the novels. This done, and if he has been an observant man, I will engage to say that he has made a choice gathering, and that we may reasonably expect an interesting little book.

I give this outline of preparatory study to shew the reason the task has never been undertaken before. People in the present chase after respectability don't care to turn blackguards, and exchange cards with the Whitechapel Pecker, or the Sharp's-alley Chicken, for the sake of a few vulgar, although curious words; and we may rest assured that it is quite impossible to write any account of vulgar or low language, and remain seated on damask in one's own drawing-room. But a fortunate circumstance attended the compiler of the present work, and he has neither been required to reside in Seven Dials, visit the treadmill, nor wander over the country in the character of a vagabond or a cadger.

In collecting old ballads, penny histories, and other printed street narratives, as materials for a *History of Cheap or Popular Literature*, he frequently had occasion to purchase in Seven Dials and the Borough a few old songs or dying speeches, from the chaunters and patterers who abound in those neighbourhoods. With some of these men (their names would not in the least interest the reader, and would only serve the purpose of making this Preface look like a vulgar page from the London Directory) an arrangement was made that they should collect the Cant and Slang words used by the different wandering tribes of London and the country. Some of these chaunters are men of respectable education, (although filling a vagabond's calling,) and can write good hands, and express themselves fluently, if not with orthographical correctness. To prevent deception and mistakes, the words and phrases sent in were checked off by other chaunters and tramps. Assistance was also sought and obtained, through an intelligent printer in Seven Dials, from the costermongers in London, and the pedlars and hucksters who traverse the country. In this manner the greater number of Cant words were procured, very valuable help being continually derived from *Mayhew's London Labour and the London Poor*, a work which had gone over much of the same ground. The Slang and vulgar expressions were gleaned from every source which appeared to offer any materials; indeed the references attached to words in the Dictionary frequently indicate the channels which afforded them.

Although in the Introduction I have divided Cant from Slang, and treated the subjects separately, yet in the Dictionary I have only, in a few instances, pointed out which are Slang, or which are Cant terms. The task would have been a difficult one. Many words which were once Cant are Slang now. The words PRIG and COVE are instances in point. Once Cant and secret terms, they are now only street vulgarisms.

The etymologies attempted are only given as contributions to the subject, and the derivation of no vulgar term is guaranteed. The origin of many street-words will, perhaps, never be discovered, having commenced with a knot of illiterate persons, and spread amongst a public that cared not a fig for the history of the word, so long as it came to their tongues to give a vulgar piquancy to a joke, or relish to an exceedingly familiar conversation. The references and authorities given in italics frequently shew only the direction or probable source of the etymology. The author, to avoid tedious verbiage, was obliged, in so small a work, to be curt in his notes and suggestions.

He has to explain also that a few words will probably be noticed in the Slang and Cant Dictionary that are questionable as coming under either of those designations· These have been admitted because they were originally either vulgar terms, or the compiler had something novel to say concerning them. The makers of our large dictionaries have been exceedingly crotchety in their choice of what they considered respectable words. It is amusing to know that Richardson used the word HUMBUG to explain the sense of other words, but omitted it in the alphabetical arrangement as not sufficiently respectable and ancient. The word SLANG, too, he served in the same way.

Filthy and obscene words have been carefully excluded, although street-talk, unlicensed and unwritten, abounds in these.

> "Immodest words admit of no defence,
> For want of decency is want of sense."

It appears from the calculations of philologists, that there are 38,000 words in the English language, including derivations. I believe I have, for the first time, in consecutive order, added at least 3000 words to the previous stock,—vulgar and often very objectionable, but still terms in everyday use, and employed by thousands. It is not generally known, that the polite Lord Chesterfield once desired Dr Johnson to compile a Slang Dictionary; indeed, it was Chesterfield, some say, who first used the word HUMBUG.

Words, like peculiar styles of dress, get into public favour, and come and go in fashion. When great favourites and universal they truly become "household words," although generally considered Slang, when their origin or antecedents are inquired into.

A few errors of the press, I am sorry to say, may be noticed; but, considering the novelty of the subject, and the fact that no fixed orthography of vulgar speech exists, it will, I hope, be deemed a not uninteresting essay on a new and very singular branch of human inquiry; for, as Mayhew remarks, "the whole subject of Cant and Slang is, to the philologist, replete with interest of the most profound character."

THE COMPILER WILL BE MUCH OBLIGED BY THE RECEIPT OF ANY CANT, SLANG, OR VULGAR WORDS NOT MENTIONED IN THE DICTIONARY. THE PROBABLE ORIGIN, OR ETYMOLOGY, OF ANY FASHIONABLE OR UNFASHIONABLE VULGARISM, WILL ALSO BE RECEIVED BY HIM WITH THANKS.

PICCADILLY, *June* 30, 1859.

PREFACE TO THE SECOND EDITION

OF THE

DICTIONARY OF MODERN SLANG, ETC.

The First Edition of this work had a rapid sale, and within a few weeks after it was published, the entire issue passed from the publisher's shelves into the hands of the public. A Second Edition, although urgently called for, was not immediately attempted. The First had been found incomplete, and faulty in many respects, and the author determined thoroughly to revise and recast before again going to press. The present Edition, therefore, will be found much more complete than the First; indeed, I may say that it has been entirely re-written, and that, whereas the First contained but 3000 words, this gives nearly 5000, with a mass of fresh illustrations, and extended articles on the more important Slang terms—HUMBUG, for instance. The notices of a *Lingua Franca* element in the language of London vagabonds are peculiar to this Edition.

My best thanks are due to several correspondents for valuable hints and suggestions as to the probable etymologies of various colloquial expressions.

One literary journal of high repute recommended a division of Cant from Slang; but the annoyance of two indices in a small work appeared to me to more than counterbalance the benefit of a stricter philological classification, so I have for the present adhered to the old arrangement; indeed, to separate Cant from Slang would be almost impossible.

PICCADILLY, *March* 15, 1860.

CONTENTS.

THE HISTORY OF CANT, OR THE SECRET LANGUAGE OF VAGABONDS.

	PAGE
Black and Coloured VAGABONDS—Vagabonds all over Europe—Vagabonds Universal,	1–3
Etymology of CANT—Cant used in old times—Difference between Cant and Slang,	3–5
The GIPSIES—Gipsies taught English Vagabonds—The Gipsy-Vagabond alliance—The Origin of Cant—Vulgar words from the Gipsy—Gipsy element in the English language—The poet Moore on the origin of Cant—Borrow on the Gipsy language—The inventor of Canting not hanged,	5–11
Old CANT words still used—Old Cant words with modern meanings—The words "*Rum*" and "*Queer*" explained—Old Cant words entirely obsolete,	11–14
THE OLDEST "ROGUE'S DICTIONARY,"	14–20
"Jaw-breakers," or hard words, used as Cant—Were Highwaymen educated men?—Vagabonds used Foreign words as Cant—The Lingua Franca, or Bastard Italian—Cant derived from Jews and Showmen—Classic words used as English Cant—Old English words used as Cant—Old English words not fashionable now—Our old Authors very vulgar persons—Was Shakspeare a pugilist?—Old Dramatists used Cant words—Curious systems of Cant,	20–26

ACCOUNT OF THE HIEROGLYPHICS USED BY VAGABONDS.

MENDICANT FREEMASONRY—Hieroglyphics of Vagabonds—Maps used by Beggars—Account of a Cadger's Map—Explanation of the Hieroglyphics—Did the Gipsies invent them?—The Murderer's Signal on the Gallows,	27–32

CONTENTS.

A SHORT HISTORY OF SLANG, OR THE VULGAR LANGUAGE OF FAST LIFE.

	PAGE
Slang at Babylon and Nineveh—Old English Slang—Slang in the time of Cromwell, and in the Court of Charles II.—Swift and Arbuthnot fond of Slang—The origin of *"Cabbage"*—"The Real Simon Pure"—Tom Brown and Ned Ward—Did Dr Johnson compile a Slang Dictionary?—John Bee's absurd etymology of *Slang*—The true origin of the term—Derived from the Gipsies—Burns and his fat friend, Grose—Slang used by all classes, High and Low—Slang in Parliament, and amongst our friends—New words not so reprehensible as old words burdened with strange meanings—The poor Foreigner's perplexity—Long and windy Slang words—Vulgar corruptions,	33-42
FASHIONABLE SLANG,	42
PARLIAMENTARY SLANG,	45
MILITARY AND DANDY SLANG,	47
UNIVERSITY SLANG,	48
RELIGIOUS SLANG,	49
LEGAL SLANG, or Slang amongst the Lawyers,	52
LITERARY SLANG—*Punch* on "Slang and Sanscrit,"	53
THEATRICAL SLANG, or Slang both before and behind the curtain,	56
CIVIC SLANG,	57
SLANG TERMS FOR MONEY—Her Majesty's coin is insulted by one hundred and thirty distinct Slang terms—Old Slang terms for money—The classical origin of Slang money-terms—The terms used by the Ancient Romans vulgarisms in the Nineteenth Century,	58-61
SHOPKEEPERS' SLANG,	61
WORKMEN'S SLANG, or Slang in the workshop—Many Slang terms for money derived from operatives,	62
SLANG APOLOGIES FOR OATHS, or sham exclamations for passion and temper—Slang swearing,	63
SLANG TERMS FOR DRUNKENNESS, and the graduated scale of fuddlement and intoxication,	64

CONTENTS.

DICTIONARY OF MODERN SLANG, CANT, AND VULGAR WORDS; *many with their etymologies traced, together with illustrations, and references to authorities,* . . . 65–274

SOME ACCOUNT OF THE BACK SLANG, the secret language of Costermongers—The principle of the Back Slang—Boys and girls soon acquire it—The Back Slang unknown to the Police—Costermongers' terms for money—Arithmetic amongst the Costermongers, ... 275–279

GLOSSARY OF THE BACK SLANG, ... 280–284

SOME ACCOUNT OF THE RHYMING SLANG, the secret language of Chaunters and Patterers—The origin of the Rhyming Slang—Spoken principally by Vagabond Poets, Patterers, and Cheap Jacks—Patterers "well up" in Street Slang—Curious Slang Letter from a Chaunter, ... 285–288

GLOSSARY OF THE RHYMING SLANG, ... 289–292

THE BIBLIOGRAPHY OF SLANG, CANT, AND VULGAR LANGUAGE, or a list of the books which have been consulted in the compilation of this work, comprising nearly every known treatise upon the subject, ... 293–305

THE SLANG DICTIONARY.

THE HISTORY OF CANT

OR

THE SECRET LANGUAGE OF VAGABONDS.

CANT and SLANG are universal and world-wide.
Nearly every nation on the face of the globe, polite and barbarous, may be divided into two portions, the stationary and the wandering, the civilised and the uncivilised, the respectable and the scoundrel,—those who have fixed abodes and avail themselves of the refinements of civilisation, and those who go from place to place picking up a precarious livelihood by petty sales, begging, or theft. This peculiarity is to be observed amongst the heathen tribes of the southern hemisphere, as well as in the oldest and most refined countries of Europe. As Mayhew very pertinently remarks, "It would appear, that not only are all races divisible into wanderers and settlers, but that each civilised or settled tribe has generally some wandering horde intermingled with and in a measure preying upon it." In South Africa, the naked and miserable Hottentots are pestered by the still more abject *Sonquas;* and it may be some satisfaction for us to know that our old enemies at the Cape, the Kaffirs, are troubled with a tribe of rascals called *Fingoes,*—the former term, we are informed by travellers, signifying beggars, and the latter wanderers and outcasts. In South America, and among the islands of the Pacific, matters are pretty much the same. Sleek and fat rascals, with not much inclination towards honesty, fatten, or rather fasten, like body insects, upon other rascals, who would be equally sleek and fat but for their vagabond dependents. Luckily for respectable persons, however, vagabonds, both at home and abroad, shew certain outward peculiarities which distinguish them from

A

the great mass of lawful people off whom they feed and fatten. Personal observation, and a little research into books, enable me to mark these external traits. The wandering races are remarkable for the development of the bones of the face, as the jaws, cheek-bones, &c., high-crowned, stubborn-shaped heads, quick, restless eyes,* and hands nervously itching to be doing;† for their love of gambling,—staking their very existence upon a single cast; for sensuality of all kinds; *and for their use of a* CANT *language with which to conceal their designs and plunderings.*

The secret jargon, or rude speech, of the vagabonds who hang upon the Hottentots is termed *Cuze-cat*. In Finland, the fellows who steal seal-skins, pick the pockets of bear-skin overcoats, and talk Cant, are termed Lappes. In France, the secret language of highwaymen, housebreakers, and pickpockets is named *Argot*. The brigands and more romantic rascals of Spain term their private tongue Germania,‡ or Robbers' Language. Rothwälsch,§ or foreign-beggar-talk, is synonymous with Cant and thieves' talk in Germany. The vulgar dialect of Malta, and the Scala towns of the Levant—imported into this country and incorporated with English cant—is known as the *Lingua Franca*, or bastard Italian. And the crowds of lazy beggars that infest the streets of Naples and Rome, and the brigands that Albert Smith used to describe near Pompeii—stopping a railway train, and deliberately rifling the pockets and baggage of the passengers—their

---

* "Swarms of vagabonds, whose eyes were so sharp as Lynx."—*Bullein's Simples and Surgery*, 1562.

† *Mayhew* has a curious idea upon the habitual restlessness of the nomadic tribes— *i.e.*, "Whether it be that in the mere act of wandering there is a greater determination of blood to the surface of the body, and, consequently, a less quantity sent to the brain."—*London Labour*, vol. i., p. 2.

‡ *Germania*, probably from the Gipsies, who were supposed to come from Germany into Spain.

§ *Rothwälsch*, from *Roter*, beggar, vagabond, and *wälsch*, foreign. See Dictionary of Gipsy language in *Pott's Zigeuner in Europa und Asien*, vol. ii., Halle, 1844. The Italian cant is called *Fourbesque*, and the Portuguese, *Calao*. See *Francisque-Michel, Dictionnaire d'Argot*, Paris, 1856.

secret language is termed *Gergo*. In England, as we all know, it is called *Cant*—often improperly *Slang*.

Most nations, then, may boast, or rather lament, a vulgar tongue—formed principally from the national language—the hereditary property of thieves, tramps, and beggars,—the pests of civilised communities. The formation of these secret tongues vary, of course, with the circumstances surrounding the speakers. A writer in *Notes and Queries** has well remarked, that "the investigation of the origin and principles of Cant and Slang language opens a curious field of inquiry, replete with considerable interest to the philologist and the philosopher. It affords a remarkable instance of lingual contrivance, which, without the introduction of much arbitrary matter, has developed a system of communicating ideas, having all the advantages of a foreign language."

An inquiry into the etymology of foreign vulgar secret tongues, and their analogy with that spoken in England, would be curious and interesting in the extreme; but neither present space nor personal acquirements permit of the task, and therefore the writer confines himself to a short account of the origin of English Cant.

The terms CANT and CANTING were doubtless derived from *chaunt* or *chaunting*,—the "whining tone, or modulation of voice adopted by beggars, with intent to coax, wheedle, or cajole by pretensions of wretchedness."† For the origin of the other application of the word CANT, pulpit hypocrisy, we are indebted to a pleasant page in the *Spectator*, (No. 147:)—"*Cant* is by some people derived from one Andrew Cant, who, they say, was a Presbyterian minister in some illiterate part of Scotland, who, by exercise and use, had obtained the faculty, *alias* gift, of talking in the pulpit in such a dialect that 'tis said he was

---

* Mr Thos. Lawrence, who promised an *Etymological Cant and Slang Dictionary.* Where is the book ?   † *Richardson's Dictionary.*

understood by none but his own congregation,— and not by all of them. Since Master *Cant's* time it has been understood in a larger sense, and signifies all exclamations, whinings, unusual tones, and, in fine, all praying and preaching like the unlearned of the Presbyterians." This anecdote is curious, if it is not correct. It was the custom in Addison's time to have a fling at the true-blue Presbyterians, and the mention made by Whitelocke of Andrew Cant, a fanatical Scotch preacher, and the squib upon the same worthy, in *Scotch Presbyterian Eloquence Displayed*, may probably have started the whimsical etymology. As far as we are concerned, however, in the present inquiry, CANT was derived from *chaunt*, a beggar's whine; CHAUNTING being the recognised term amongst beggars to this day for begging orations and street whinings; and CHAUNTER, a street talker and tramp, the very term still used by strollers and patterers. The use of the word CANT, amongst beggars, must certainly have commenced at a very early date, for we find "TO CANTE, to speake," in Harman's list of Rogues' Words in the year 1566; and Harrison about the same time,* in speaking of beggars and Gipsies, says, "they have devised a language among themselves which they name CANTING, but others Pedlars' Frenche."

Now the word CANT in its old sense, and SLANG† in its modern application, although used by good writers and persons of education as synonymes, are in reality quite distinct and separate terms. CANT, apart from religious hypocrisy, refers to the old secret language, by allegory or distinct terms, of Gipsies, thieves, tramps, and beggars. SLANG represents that evanescent, vulgar language, ever changing with fashion and taste, which has princi-

---

* *Description of England*, prefixed to *Holinshed's Chronicle*.

† The word SLANG, as will be seen in the chapter upon that subject, is purely a Gipsy term, although now-a-days it refers to low or vulgar language of any kind, other than cant. SLANG and GIBBERISH in the Gipsy language are synonymous; but, as English adoptions, have meanings very different from that given to them in their original.

pally come into vogue during the last seventy or eighty years, spoken by persons in every grade of life, rich and poor, honest and dishonest.* CANT is old; SLANG is always modern and changing. To illustrate the difference: a thief in *Cant* language would term a horse a PRANCER or a PRAD; while in *Slang*, a man of fashion would speak of it as a BIT OF BLOOD, or a SPANKER, or a NEAT TIT. A handkerchief, too, would be a BILLY, a FOGLE, or a KENT RAG, in the secret language of low characters; whilst amongst vulgar persons, or those who aped their speech, it would be called a RAG, a WIPE, or a CLOUT. CANT was formed for purposes of secrecy. SLANG is indulged in from a desire to appear familiar with life, gaiety, town-humour, and with the transient nicknames and street jokes of the day. Both Cant and Slang, I am aware, are often huddled together as synonymes; but they are distinct terms, and as such should be used.

To the Gipsies beggars and thieves are undoubtedly indebted for their Cant language. The Gipsies landed in this country early in the reign of Henry VIII. They were at first treated as conjurors and magicians,—indeed, they were hailed by the populace with as much applause as a company of English theatricals usually receive on arriving in a distant colony. They came here with all their old Eastern arts of palmistry, fortune-telling, doubling money by incantation and burial,—shreds of pagan idolatry; and they brought with them, also, the dishonesty of the lower caste of Asiatics, and the vagabondism they had acquired since leaving their ancient dwelling-places in the East many centuries before. They possessed, also, a *language* quite distinct from anything that had been heard in England, and they claimed the title of Egyptians, and as such, when their thievish wandering propensities became a public nuisance, were cautioned

* "The vulgar tongue consists of two parts: the first is the CANT Language; the second, those burlesque phrases, quaint allusions, and nicknames for persons, things, and places, which, from long uninterrupted usage, are made classical by prescription."
—*Grose's Dictionary of the Vulgar Tongue*, 1st edition, 1785.

and proscribed in a royal proclamation by Henry VIII.* The Gipsies were not long in the country before they found native imitators. Vagabondism is peculiarly catching. The idle, the vagrant, and the criminal outcasts of society, caught an idea from the so-called Egyptians—soon corrupted to Gipsies. They learned from them how to tramp, sleep under hedges and trees, to tell fortunes, and find stolen property for a consideration—frequently, as the saying runs, before it was lost. They also learned the value and application of a *secret tongue;* indeed, all the accompaniments of maunding and imposture, except thieving and begging, which were well known in this country long before the Gipsies paid it a visit,—perhaps the only negative good that can be said in their favour.

Harman, in 1566, wrote a singular, not to say droll, book, entitled, *A Caveat for commen Cvrsetors, vulgarly called Vagabones, newly augmented and inlarged*, wherein the history and various descriptions of rogues and vagabonds are given, together with their canting tongue. This book, the earliest of the kind, gives the singular fact that within a dozen years after the landing of the Gipsies, companies of English vagrants were formed, places of meeting appointed, districts for plunder and begging operations marked out, and rules agreed to for their common management. In some cases Gipsies joined the English gangs; in others, English vagrants joined the Gipsies. The fellowship was found convenient and profitable, as both parties were aliens to the laws and customs of the country, living in a great measure in the open air, apart from the lawful public, and often meeting each other on the same by-path, or in the same retired valley ;—but seldom intermarrying, or entirely adopting each other's habits. The common people, too, soon began to consider them as of one family,—all rogues, and from Egypt. The secret language spoken by the Gipsies, principally Hindoo, and extremely bar-

* "Outlandish people calling themselves *Egyptians*." 1530.

barous to English ears, was found incomprehensible and very difficult to learn. The Gipsies, also, found the same difficulty with the English language. A rude, rough, and most singular compromise was made, and a mixture of Gipsy, Old English, newly-coined words, and cribbings from any foreign, and therefore secret language, mixed and jumbled together, formed what has ever since been known as the CANTING LANGUAGE, or PEDLARS' FRENCH; or, during the past century, ST GILES'S GREEK.

Such was the origin of CANT; and in illustration of its blending with the Gipsy or Cingari tongue, dusky and Oriental from the sunny plains of Central Asia, I am enabled to give the accompanying list of Gipsy, and often Hindoo, words, with, in many instances, their English adoptions:—

Gipsy.	English.
BAMBOOZLE, to perplex or mislead by hiding. *Modern Gipsy.*	BAMBOOZLE, to delude, cheat, or make a fool of any one.
BOSH, rubbish, nonsense, offal. *Gipsy and Persian.*	BOSH, stupidity, foolishness.
CHEESE, thing or article, "That's the CHEESE," or thing. *Gipsy and Hindoo.*	CHEESE, or CHEESY, a first-rate or very good article.
CHIVE, the tongue. *Gipsy.*	CHIVE, or CHIVEY, a shout, or loud-tongued.
CUTA, a gold coin. *Danubian Gipsy.*	COUTER, a sovereign, twenty shillings.
DADE, or DADI, a father. *Gipsy.*	DADDY, nursery term for father.*
DISTARABIN, a prison. *Gipsy.*	STURABIN, a prison.
GAD, or GADSI, a wife. *Gipsy.*	GAD, a female scold; a woman who tramps over the country with a beggar or hawker.
GIBBERISH, the language of Gipsies, synonymous with SLANG. *Gipsy.*	GIBBERISH, rapid and unmeaning speech.

* In those instances, indicated by a *, it is impossible to say whether or not we are indebted to the Gipsies for the terms. DAD, in *Welsh,* also signifies a father. CUR is stated to be a mere term of reproach, like "Dog," which in all European languages has been applied in an abusive sense. Objections may also be raised against GAD and MAUND.

VULGAR WORDS FROM THE GIPSY.

Gipsy.	English.
ISCHUR, Schur, or Chur, a thief. *Gipsy and Hindoo.*	CUR, a mean or dishonest man.
LAB, a word. *Gipsy.*	LOBS, words.
LOWE, or Lowr, money. *Gipsy and Wallachian.*	LOWRE, money. *Ancient Cant.*
MAMI, a grandmother. *Gipsy.*	MAMMY, or Mamma, a mother, formerly sometimes used for grandmother.
MANG, or Maung, to beg. *Gipsy and Hindoo.*	MAUND, to beg.
MORT, a free woman,—one for common use amongst the male Gipsies, so appointed by Gipsy custom. *Gipsy.*	MORT, or Mott, a prostitute.
MU, the mouth. *Gipsy and Hindoo.*	MOO, or Mun, the mouth.
MULL, to spoil or destroy. *Gipsy.*	MULL, to spoil, or bungle.
PAL, a brother. *Gipsy.*	PAL, a partner, or relation.
PANÉ, water. *Gipsy. Hindoo,* pawnee.	PARNEY, rain.
RIG, a performance. *Gipsy.*	RIG, a frolic, or "spree."
ROMANY, speech or language. *Spanish Gipsy.*	ROMANY, the Gipsy language.
ROME, or Romm, a man. *Gipsy and Coptic.*	RUM, a good man, or thing. In the Robbers' language of Spain, (partly Gipsy,) rum signifies a harlot.
ROMEE, a woman. *Gipsy.*	RUMY, a good woman or girl.
SLANG, the language spoken by Gipsies. *Gipsy.*	SLANG, low, vulgar, unauthorised language.
TAWNO, little. *Gipsy.*	TANNY, Teeny, little.
TSCHIB, or Jibb, the tongue. *Gipsy and Hindoo.*	JIBB, the tongue; Jabber,[*] quick-tongued, or fast talk.

Here, then, we have the remarkable fact of several words of pure Gipsy and Asiatic origin going the round of Europe, passing into this country before the Reformation, and coming down to us through numerous generations purely in the mouths of the people. They have seldom been written or used in books, and simply as vulgarisms have they reached our time. Only a few

[*] Jabber, I am reminded, may be only another form of gabber, gab, very common in Old English, from the *Anglo-Saxon,* gæbban.

are now Cant, and some are household words. The word JOCKEY, as applied to a dealer or rider of horses, came from the Gipsy, and means in that language a whip. Our standard dictionaries give, of course, none but conjectural etymologies. Another word, BAMBOOZLE, has been a sore difficulty with lexicographers. It is not in the old dictionaries, although extensively used in familiar or popular language for the last two centuries; in fact, the very word that Swift, Butler, L'Estrange, and Arbuthnot would pick out at once as a telling and most serviceable term. It is, as we have seen, from the Gipsy; and here I must state that it was Boucher who first drew attention to the fact, although in his remarks on the dusky tongue he has made a ridiculous mistake by concluding it to be identical with its offspring, CANT. Other parallel instances, with but slight variations from the old Gipsy meanings, could be mentioned; but sufficient examples have been adduced to shew that Marsden, the great Oriental scholar in the last century, when he declared before the Society of Antiquaries that the Cant of English thieves and beggars had nothing to do with the language spoken by the despised Gipsies, was in error. Had the Gipsy tongue been analysed and committed to writing three centuries ago, there is every probability that many scores of words now in common use could be at once traced to its source. Instances continually occur now-a-days of street vulgarisms ascending to the drawing-rooms of respectable society. Why, then, may not the Gipsy-vagabond alliance three centuries ago have contributed its quota of common words to popular speech?

I feel confident there is a Gipsy element in the English language hitherto unrecognised; slender it may be, but not, therefore, unimportant.

"Indeed," says Moore the poet, in a humorous little book, *Tom Crib's Memorial to Congress*, 1819, "the Gipsy language, with the exception of such terms as relate to their own peculiar customs, differs but little from the regular Flash or Cant language." But this was magnifying the importance of the alliance. Moore knew nothing of the Gipsy tongue other than the few Cant words put into the mouths of the beggars in *Beaumont and Fletcher's Comedy of the Beggar's Bush*, and *Ben Jonson's Masque of the Gipsies Metamorphosed*,—hence his confounding Cant with Gipsy speech, and appealing to the Glossary of Cant for so-called "Gipsy" words at the end of the *Life of Bamfylde Moore Carew*, to bear him out in his assertion. Still his remark bears much truth, and proof would have been found long ago if any scholar had taken the trouble to examine the "barbarous jargon of Cant," and to have compared it with Gipsy speech. As George Borrow, in his *Account of the Gipsies in Spain*, eloquently concludes his second volume, speaking of the connexion of the Gipsies with Europeans:—"Yet from this temporary association were produced two results: European fraud became sharpened by coming into contact with Asiatic craft; whilst European tongues, by imperceptible degrees, became recruited with various words, (some of them wonderfully expressive,) many of which have long been stumbling-blocks to the philologist, who, whilst stigmatising them as words of mere vulgar invention, or of unknown origin, has been far from dreaming that a little more research or reflection would have proved their affinity to the Sclavonic, Persian, or Romaic, or perhaps to the mysterious object of his veneration, the Sanscrit, the sacred tongue of the palm-covered regions of Ind; words originally introduced into Europe by objects too miserable to occupy for a moment his lettered attention,—the despised denizens of the tents of Roma."

But the Gipsies, their speech, their character—bad enough, as all the world testifies—their history, and their religious belief, have been totally disregarded, and their poor persons buffeted and jostled about until it is a wonder that any trace of origin or national speech exists in them. On the Continent they received better attention at the hands of learned men. Their language was taken down, their history traced, and their extraordinary customs and practice of living in the open air, and eating raw or putrid meat, explained. They ate reptiles and told fortunes because they had learnt to do so through their forefathers centuries back in Hindostan; and they devoured carrion because the Hindoo proverb—"*That which God kills is better than that killed by man*"*—was still in their remembrance. Grellman, a learned German, was their principal historian, and to him we are almost entirely indebted for the little we know of their language.† The first European settlement of the Gipsies was in the provinces adjoining the Danube, Moldau and Theiss, where M. Cogalniceano, in his *Essai sur les Cigains de la Moldo-Valachie*, estimates them at 200,000. Not a few of our ancient and modern Cant and Slang terms are Wallachian and Greek words, brought in by these wanderers from the East. See COUTER, DRUM, BOUNG, (*Harman*,) LOWR, &c.

GIPSY, then, started, and partially merged into CANT; and the old story told by Harrison and others, that the first inventor of canting was hanged for his pains, would seem to be a fable, for jargon as it is, it was, doubtless, of gradual formation, like all other languages or systems of speech. The Gipsies at the present day all know the *old Cant* words, as well as their own tongue, —or rather what remains of it. As Borrow states, "The dialect of the English Gipsies is mixed with English words."‡ Those of the tribe who frequent fairs, and mix with English tramps, readily learn the new words, as they are adopted by what Harman calls "the fraternity of vagabonds." Indeed, the old CANT is a common language to vagrants of all descriptions and origin scattered over the British Isles.

* This very proverb was mentioned by a young Gipsy to *Crabb*, a few years ago.—*Gipsies' Advocate*, p. 14.
† I except, of course, the numerous writers who have followed Grellman, and based their researches upon his labours.
‡ *Gipsies in Spain*, vol. i., p. 18.

Ancient English CANT has considerably altered since the first dictionary was compiled by Harman in 1566. A great many words are unknown in the present tramps' and thieves' vernacular. Some of them, however, bear still their old definitions, while others have adopted fresh meanings,—to escape detection, I suppose. "ABRAHAM-MAN" is yet seen in our modern SHAM ABRAHAM, or PLAY THE OLD SOLDIER—*i. e.*, to feign sickness or distress. "AUTUM" is still a church or chapel amongst Gipsies; and "BECK," a constable, is our modern Cant and Slang BEEK, a policeman or magistrate. "BENE," or BONE, stands for *good* in Seven Dials and the back streets of Westminster; and "BOWSE" is our modern BOOZE, to drink or fuddle. A "BOWSING KEN" was the old Cant term for a public-house; and BOOZING KEN, in modern Cant, has precisely the same meaning. "BUFE" was then the term for a dog, now it is BUFFER,—frequently applied to men. "CASSAN" is both old and modern Cant for cheese; the same may be said of "CHATTES" or CHATTS, the gallows. "COFE," or COVE, is still the vulgar synonyme for a man. "DRAWERS" was hose, or "hosen,"—now applied to the lining for trousers. "DUDES" was Cant for clothes; we now say DUDDS. "FLAG" is still a fourpenny-piece; and "FYLCHE" means to rob. "KEN" is a house, and "LICK" means to thrash; "PRANCER" is yet known amongst rogues as a horse; and "to PRIG," amongst high and low, is to steal. Three centuries ago, if one beggar said anything disagreeable to another, the person annoyed would say, "STOW YOU," or hold your peace; low people now say, STOW IT, equivalent to "be quiet." "TRINE" is still to hang; "WYN" yet stands for a penny. And many other words, as will be seen in the Dictionary, still retain their ancient meaning.

As specimens of those words which have altered their original Cant signification, I may instance "CHETE," now written CHEAT. CHETE was in ancient cant what *chop* is in the Canton-Chinese, —an almost inseparable adjunct. Everything was termed a

CHETE, and qualified by a substantive-adjective, which shewed what kind of a CHETE was meant; for instance, "CRASHING-CHETES" were teeth; a "MOFFLING-CHETE," a napkin; a "GRUNTING-CHETE," a pig, &c., &c. CHEAT now-a-days means to defraud or swindle, and lexicographers have tortured etymology for an original—but without success. *Escheats* and *escheatours* have been named, but with great doubts; indeed, Stevens, the learned commentator on Shakspeare, acknowledged that he "did not recollect to have met with the word *cheat* in our ancient writers."* CHEAT, to defraud, then, is no other than an old Cant term somewhat altered in its meaning,† and as such it should be described in the next etymological dictionary. Another instance of a change in the meaning of the old Cant, but the retention of the word, is seen in "CLY," formerly to take or steal, now a pocket; —remembering a certain class of low characters, a curious connexion between the two meanings will be discovered. "MAKE" was a halfpenny; we now say MAG,—MAKE being modern Cant for appropriating,—" convey the wise it call." "MILLING" stood for stealing, it is now a pugilistic term for fighting or beating. "NAB" was a head,—low people now say NOB, the former meaning, in modern Cant, to steal or seize. "PEK" was meat,—we still say PECKISH, when hungry. "PRYGGES, *dronken Tinkers or beastly people*," as old Harman wrote, would scarcely be understood now; a PRIG, in the 19th century, is a pickpocket or thief. "QUIER," or QUEER, like *cheat*, was a very common prefix, and meant bad or wicked,—it now means odd, curious, or strange; but to the ancient Cant we are indebted for the word, which etymologists should remember.‡ "ROME," or RUM, formerly

---

* Shaks. Henry IV., part ii., act ii., scene 4.

† It is easy to see how *cheat* became synonymous with "fraud," when we remember that it was one of the most common words of the greatest class of cheats in the country.

‡ I am reminded by an eminent philologist that the origin of QUEER is seen in the German QUER, crooked,—hence "odd." I agree with this etymology, but still have reason to believe that the word was *first* used in this country in a Cant sense. Is it

meant good, or of the first quality, and was extensively used like *cheat* and *queer*,—indeed as an adjective it was the opposite of the latter. RUM now means curious, and is synonymous with *queer*; thus,—a "RUMMY old fellow," or a "QUEER old man." Here again we see the origin of an every-day word, scouted by lexicographers and snubbed by respectable persons, but still a word of frequent and popular use. "YANNAM" meant bread; PANNUM is the word now. Other instances could be pointed out, but they will be observed in the Dictionary.

Several words are entirely obsolete. "ALYBBEG" no longer means a bed, nor "ASKEW" a cup. "BOOGET,"* now-a-days, would not be understood for a basket; neither would "GAN" pass current for mouth. "FULLAMS" was the old Cant term for false or loaded dice, and although used by Shakspeare in this sense, is now unknown and obsolete. Indeed, as Tom Moore somewhere remarks, the present Greeks of St Giles's, themselves, would be thoroughly puzzled by many of the ancient canting songs,—taking, for example, the first verse of an old favourite—

> "Bing out, bien Morts, and toure and toure,
> Bing out, bien Morts, and toure;
> For all your duds are bing'd awast;
> The bien cove hath the loure." †

But I think I cannot do better than present to the reader at once an entire copy of the first Canting Dictionary ever compiled. As before mentioned, it was the work of one Thomas Harman, a gentleman who lived in the days of Queen Elizabeth. Some

---

mentioned anywhere as a respectable term before 1500? If not, it had a vulgar or Cant introduction into this country.

* BOOGET properly signifies a leathern wallet, and is probably derived from the low Latin BULGA. A tinker's budget is from the same source.

† Which, literally translated, means—

> "Go out, good girls, and look and see,
> Go out, good girls, and see;
> For all your clothes are carried away,
> And the good man has the money."

writers have remarked that Decker* was the first to compile a Dictionary of the vagabonds' tongue; whilst Borrow,† and Thomas Moore, the poet, stated that Richard Head performed that service in his *Life of an English Rogue*, published in the year 1680. All these statements are equally incorrect, for the first attempt was made more than a century before the latter work was issued. The quaint spelling and old-fashioned phraseology are preserved, and the reader will quickly detect many vulgar street words, old acquaintances, dressed in antique garb.‡

ABRAHAM-MEN be those that fayn themselves to have beene mad, and have bene kept either in Bethelem, or in some other pryson a good time.
ALYBBEG, a bedde.
ASKEW, a cuppe.
AUTEM, a churche.
AUTEM MORTES, married women as chaste as a cowe.
BAUDYE BASKETS bee women who goe with baskets and capcases on their armes, wherein they have laces, pinnes, nedles, whyte inkel, and round sylke gyrdels of all colours.
BECK, [Beek,] a constable.
BELLY-CHETE, apron.
BENE, good. *Benar*, better.
BENSHIP, very good.
BLETING CHETE, a calfe or sheepe.
BOOGET, a travelling tinker's baskete.
BORDE, a shilling.
BOUNG, a purse. [*Friesic*, pong; *Wallachian*, punga; see note, page 11.] The oldest form of this word is in Ulphilas, PUGGS; it exists also in the *Greek*, πουγγή.
BOWSE, drink.
BOWSING-KEN, an alehouse.
BUFE, [buffer, a man,] a dogge.
BYNGE A WASTE, go you hence.

---

* Who wrote about the year 1610.
† *Gipsies in Spain*, vol. i., p. 18. Borrow further commits himself by remarking that "Head's Vocabulary has always been accepted as the speech of the English Gipsies." Nothing of the kind. Head professed to have lived with the Gipsies, but in reality filched his words from Decker and Brome.
‡ The modern meanings of a few of the old Cant words are given within brackets.

CACKLING-CHETE, a coke, [cock,] or capon.
CASSAN, [cassam,] cheese.
CASTERS, a cloake.
CATETH, "the vpright Cofe *cateth* to the Roge," [probably a shortening or misprint of *Canteth*.]
CHATTES, the gallowes.
CHETE, [see what has been previously said about this word.]
CLY, [a pocket,] to take, receive, or have.
COFE, [cove,] a person.
COMMISSION, [mish,] a shirt.
COUNTERFET CRANKE, these that do counterfet the Cranke be yong knaves and yonge harlots, that deeply dissemble the falling sickness.
CRANKE, [cranky, foolish,] falling evil, [or wasting sickness.]
CRASHING-CHETES, teeth.
CUFFEN, a manne. [A *cuif* in Northumberland and Scotland signifies a lout or awkward fellow.]
DARKEMANS, the night.
DELL, a yonge wench.
DEWSE-A-VYLE, the countrey.
DOCK, to deflower.
DOXES, harlots.
DRAWERS, hosen.
DUDES, [or dudds,] clothes.
FAMBLES, handes.
FAMBLING-CHETE, a ring on one's hand.
FLAGG, a groat.
FRATER, a beggar wyth a false paper.
FRESHE-WATER-MARINERS, these kind of caterpillers counterfet great losses on the sea :—their shippes were drowned in the playne of Salisbury.
FYLCHE, to robbe : *Fylch-man*, [a robber.]
GAGE, a quart pot.
GAN, a mouth.
GENTRY COFE, a noble or gentle man.
GENTRY-COFES-KEN, a noble or gentle man's house.
GENTRY MORT, a noble or gentle woman.
GERRY, excrement.
GLASYERS, eyes.
GLYMMAR, fyer.
GRANNAM, corne.

GRUNTING-CHETE, a pygge.
GYB, a writing.
GYGER, [jigger,] a dore.
HEARING-CHETES, eares.
JARKE, a seale.
JARKEMAN, one who make writings and set seales for [counterfeit] licences and passports.
KEN, a house.
KYNCHEN CO, [or *cove*,] a young boye trained up, like a "*Kynching Morte.*" [From the German diminutive *Kindschen*.]
KYNCHING MORTE, is a little gyrle, carried at their mothers' backe in a slate, or sheete, who brings them up sauagely.
LAG, water.
LAG OF DUDES a bucke [or basket] of clothes.
LAGE, to washe.
LAP, butter, mylke, or whey.
LIGHTMANS, the day.
LOWING-CHETE, a cowe.
LOWRE, money. [From the *Wallachian Gipsy* word LOWE, coined money. See M. Cogalniceano's *Essai sur les Cigains de la Moldo-Valachie*.]
LUBBARES,—" sturdy *Lubbares*," country bumpkins, or men of a low degree.
LYB-BEG, a bed.
LYCKE, [lick,] to beate.
LYP, to lie down.
LYPKEN, a house to lye in.
MAKE, [mag,] a halfpenny.
MARGERI PRATER, a hen.
MILLING, to steale, [by sending a child in at a window.]
MOFFLING-CHETE, a napkin.
MORTES, [motts,] harlots.
MYLL, to robbe.
MYNT, gold.
NAB, [nob,] a heade.
NABCHET, a hat or cap.
NASE, dronken.
NOSEGENT, a nunne.
PALLYARD, a borne beggar, [who counterfeits sickness, or incurable sores. They are mostly Welshmen, Harman says.]
PARAM, mylke.

B

PATRICO, a priest.
PATRICOS KINCHEN, a pygge, [a satirical hit at the church, *Patrico* meaning a parson or priest, and *Kinchen* his little boy or girl.]
PEK, [peckish,] meat.
POPPELARS, porrage.
PRAT, a buttocke.
PRATLING-CHETE, a toung.
PRAUNCER, a horse.
PRIGGER OF PRAUNCERS be horse-stealers, for to prigge signifieth in their language to steale, and a Prauncer is a horse, so being put together, the matter was playn. [Thus writes old Thomas Harman, who concludes his description of this order of "pryggers," by very quietly saying, "I had the best gelding stolen out of my pasture, that I had amongst others, whyle this book was first a printing."]
PRYGGES, dronken Tinkers, or beastly people.
QUACKING-CHETE, a drake or duck.
QUAROMES, a body.
QUIER, [queer,] badde. [*See* what has been previously said about this word.]
QUYER CRAMPRINGES, boltes or fetters.
QUIER CUFFIN, the iustice of peace.
QUYER-KYN, a pryson house.
RED SHANKE, a drake or ducke.
ROGER, a goose.
ROME, goode, [now curious, noted, or remarkable in any way. *Rum* is the modern orthography.]
ROME BOUSE, [rum booze,] wyne.
ROME MORT, the Queene, [Elizabeth.]
ROME VYLE, [or Rum-ville,] London.
RUFF PECK, baken, [short bread, common in old times at farm-houses.]
RUFFMANS, the woods or bushes.
SALOMON, an alter or masse.
SKYPPER, a barne.
SLATE, a sheete or shetes.
SMELLING-CHETE, a nose.
SMELLING-CHETE, a garden or orchard.
SNOWT FAYRE, [said of a woman who has a pretty face or is comely.]
STALL, [to initiate a beggar or rogue into the rights and privileges of the canting order. Harman relates that when an upright man, or initiated first-class rogue, "mete any beggar, whether he be sturdy or impotent, he will demand of him whether ever he was '*stalled to the roge*' or no. If he say he was, he will know of whom, and his name yt stalled him. And if he be not learnedly able to shew him the whole circumstance

thereof, he will spoyle him of his money, either of his best garment, if it be worth any money, and haue him to the bowsing-ken: which is, to some typpling-house next adjoyninge, and layth there to gage the best thing that he hath for twenty pence or two shillings: this man obeyeth for feare of beatinge. Then dooth this upright man call for a gage of bowse, which is a quarte potte of drink, and powres the same vpon his peld pate, adding these words,—I, G. P., do stalle thee, W. T., to the Roge, and that from henceforth it shall be lawfull for thee to cant, that is, to aske or begge for thi liuing in al places." Something like this treatment is the popular idea of freemasonry, and what schoolboys term "freeing."]

STAMPES, legges.
STAMPERS, shoes.
STAULING-KEN, a house that will receyue stollen wares.
STAWLINGE-KENS, tippling-houses.
STOW YOU, [stow it,] hold your peace.
STRIKE, to steale.
STROMMELL, strawe.
SWADDER, or *Pedler*, [a man who hawks goods.]
THE HIGH PAD, the highway.
THE RUFFIAN CLY THEE, the devil take thee.
TOGEMANS, [togg,] a cloake.
TOGMAN, a coate.
TO BOWSE, to drinke.
TO CANTE, to speake.
TO CLY THE GERKE, to be whipped.
TO COUCH A HOGSHEAD, to lie down and slepe.
TO CUTTE, to say. [*Cut it, cut it short*, &c., are modern slang phrases.]
TO CUT BENE WHYDDES, to speake or give good words.
TO CUTTE QUYER WHYDDES, to giue euil words or euil language.
TO CUT BENLE, to speak gentle.
TO DUP YE GYGER, [jigger,] to open the dore.
TO FYLCHE, to robbe.
TO HEUE A BOUGH, to robbe or rifle a boweth, [booth.]
TO MAUNDE, to aske or require.
TO MILL A KEN, to robbe a house.
TO NYGLE, [coition.]
TO NYP A BOUNG, [nip, to steal,] to cut a purse.
TO SKOWER THE CRAMPRINGES, to weare boltes or fetters.
TO STALL, to make or ordain.
TO THE RUFFIAN, to the Devil.

TO TOWRE, to see.
TRYNING, [trine,] hanging.
TYB OF THE BUTERY, a goose.
WALKING MORTE, womene, [who pass for widows.]
WAPPING [coition.]
WHYDDES, wordes.
WYN, a penny. [A correspondent of *Notes and Queries* suggests the connexion of this word with the *Welch* GWYN, white—*i. e.*, the white silver penny. See other examples under BLUNT, in the Dictionary; cf. also the *Armorican*, "GWENNEK," a penny.]
YANNAM, bread.

Turning our attention more to the Cant of modern times, in connexion with the old, we find that words have been drawn into the thieves' vocabulary from every conceivable source. Hard or infrequent words, vulgarly termed *crack-jaw*, or *jaw-breakers*, were very often used and considered as Cant terms. And here it should be mentioned that at the present day the most inconsistent and far-fetched terms are often used for secret purposes, when they are known to be caviare to the million. It is really laughable to know that such words as *incongruous, insipid, interloper, intriguing, indecorum, forestall, equip, hush, grapple*, &c., &c., were current Cant words a century and a half ago; but such was the case, as any one may see in the *Dictionary of Canting Words* at the end of *Bacchus and Venus*,* 1737. They are inserted not as jokes or squibs, but as selections from the veritable pocket dictionaries of the Jack Sheppards and Dick Turpins of the day. If they were safely used as unknown and cabalistic terms amongst the commonalty, the fact would form a very curious illustration of the ignorance of our poor ancestors. One piece of information is conveyed to us—*i.e.*, that the "knights" or "gentlemen of the road," using these polite words in those days of highwaymen, were really well-educated men,—which heretofore has always

---

* This is a curious volume, and is worth from one to two guineas. The Canting Dictionary was afterwards reprinted, word for word, with the title of *The Scoundrel's Dictionary*, in 1751. It was originally published, without date, about the year 1710 by B. E., under the title of a *Dictionary of the Canting Crew*.

been a hard point of belief, notwithstanding old novels and operas.

Amongst those Cant words which have either altered their meaning, or have become extinct, I may cite LADY, formerly the Cant for "a very crooked, deformed, and ill-shapen woman;"* and HARMAN, "a pair of stocks, or a constable." The former is a pleasant piece of satire, whilst the latter indicates a singular method of revenge. HARMAN was the first author who specially wrote against English vagabonds, and for his trouble his name became synonymous with a pair of stocks, or a policeman of the olden time.

Apart from the Gipsy element, we find that Cant abounds in terms from foreign languages, and that it exhibits the growth of most recognised and completely-formed tongues,—the gathering of words from foreign sources. In the reign of Elizabeth and of King James I., several Dutch, Spanish, and Flemish words were introduced by soldiers who had served in the Low Countries, and sailors who had returned from the Spanish Main, who, like "mine ancient Pistol," were fond of garnishing their speech with outlandish phrases. Many of these were soon picked up and adopted by vagabonds and tramps in their Cant language. The Anglo-Norman and the Anglo-Saxon, the Scotch, the French, the Italian, and even the classic languages of ancient Italy and Greece, have contributed to its list of words, besides the various provincial dialects of England. Indeed, as Mayhew remarks, English Cant seems to be formed on the same basis as the *Argot* of the French and the *Roth-Spræc* of the Germans,—partly metaphorical, and partly by the introduction of such corrupted foreign terms as are likely to be unknown to the society amid which the Cant speakers exist. ARGOT is the London thieves' word for their secret language; it is, of course, from the French, but that matters not so long as it is incomprehensible to the police and

* *Bacchus and Venus.* 1737.

the mob. BOOZE, or BOUSE, I am reminded by a friendly correspondent, comes from the Dutch BUYSEN. DOMINE, a parson, is from the Spanish. DONNA AND FEELES, a woman and children, is from the Latin; and DON, a clever fellow, has been filched from the Lingua Franca, or bastard Italian, although it sounds like an odd mixture of Spanish and French; whilst DUDDS, the vulgar term for clothes, may have been pilfered either from the Gaelic or the Dutch. FEELE, a daughter, from the French; and FROW, a girl or wife, from the German—are common tramps' terms. So are GENT, silver, from the French *Argent;* and VIAL, a country town, also from the French. HORRID-HORN, a fool, is believed to be from the Erse; and GLOAK, a man, from the Scotch. As stated before, the Dictionary will supply numerous other instances.

The Celtic languages have contributed many Cant and vulgar words to our popular vocabulary. These have come to us through the Gaelic or Irish languages, so closely allied in their material as to be merely dialects of a primitive common tongue. This element may be from the Celtic population, which, from its ancient position as slaves or servants to the Anglo-Saxon conquerors, has contributed so largely to the lowest class of our population, and therefore to our Slang, provincial, or colloquial words; or it may be an importation from Irish immigrants, who have undoubtedly contributed very largely to our criminal population.

There is one source, however, of secret street terms, which in the first edition of this work was entirely overlooked,—indeed, it was unknown to the editor until pointed out by a friendly correspondent,—the *Lingua Franca,* or bastard Italian, spoken at Genoa, Trieste, Malta, Constantinople, Smyrna, Alexandria, and all Mediterranean seaport towns. The ingredients of this imported Cant are many. Its foundation is Italian, with a mixture of modern Greek, German, (from the Austrian ports,) Spanish, Turkish, and French. It has been introduced to the notice of the London wandering tribes by the sailors, foreign and English, who trade to and from the Mediterranean seaports, by the swarms of organ-players from all parts of Italy, and by the makers of images from Rome and Florence,—all of whom, in dense thoroughfares, mingle with our lower orders. It would occupy too much space here to give a list of these words. They are all noted in the Dictionary.

"There are several Hebrew terms in our Cant language, obtained, it would appear, from the intercourse of the thieves with the Jew *fences*, (receivers of stolen goods ;) many of the Cant terms, again, are Sanscrit, got from the Gipsies ; many Latin, got by the beggars from the Catholic prayers before the Reformation ; and many, again, Italian, got from the wandering musicians and others ; indeed, the showmen have but lately introduced a number of Italian phrases into their Cant language."* The Hindostanee also contributes several words, and these have been introduced by the Lascar sailors, who come over here in the East Indiamen, and lodge during their stay in the low tramps' lodging-houses at the east end of London. Speaking of the learned tongues, I may mention that, precarious and abandoned as the vagabond's existence is, many persons of classical or refined education have from time to time joined the ranks,—occasionally from inclination, as in the popular instance of Bamfylde Moore Carew, but generally through indiscretion and loss of character.† This will in some measure account for numerous classical and learned words figuring as Cant terms in the vulgar Dictionary.

In the early part of the last century, when highwaymen were by all accounts so plentiful, a great many new words were added to the canting vocabulary, whilst several old terms fell into disuse.

---

* Mayhew's *London Labour and the London Poor*, vol. iii., No. 43, Oct. 4, 1851.

† Mayhew (vol. i., p. 217) speaks of a low lodging-house "in which there were at one time five university men, three surgeons, and several sorts of broken-down clerks." But old Harman's saying, that "a wylde Roge is he that is *borne* a roge," will perhaps explain this seeming anomaly.

CANT, for instance, as applied to thieves' talk, was supplanted by the word FLASH. In the North of England, the Cant employed by tramps and thieves is known as "the GAMMY." It is mainly from the old Gipsy corrupted. In the large towns of Ireland and Scotland this secret language is also spoken. All those words derived from "the GAMMY" are inserted in the Dictionary as from the "North Country."

A singular feature, however, in vulgar language, is the retention and the revival of sterling old English words, long since laid up in ancient manuscripts, or the subject of dispute among learned antiquaries. Disraeli somewhere says, "The purest source of *neology* is in the revival of *old words*"—

"Words that wise Bacon or brave Rawleigh spake;"

and Dr Latham honours our subject by remarking that "the thieves of London are the conservators of Anglo-Saxonisms." Mayhew, too, in his interesting work, *London Labour and the London Poor*, admits that many Cant and Slang phrases are merely old English terms which have become obsolete through the caprices of fashion. And the reader who looks into the Dictionary of the vagabond's lingo, will see at a glance that these gentlemen were quite correct, and that we are compelled to acknowledge the singular truth that a great many old words, once respectable, and in the mouths of kings and fine ladies, are now only so many signals for shrugs and shudders amongst exceedingly polite people. A young gentleman from Belgravia, who had lost his watch or his pocket-handkerchief, would scarcely remark to his mamma that it had been BONED—yet BONE, in old times, meant, amongst high and low, to steal. And a young lady living in the precincts of dingy but aristocratic May-Fair, although enraptured with a Jenny Lind or a Ristori, would hardly think of turning back in the box to inform papa that she (Ristori or Lind) "made no BONES of it"—yet the phrase was most respectable and well-to-do before it met with a change of circumstances. "A CRACK article," however first-rate, would, as far as speech is concerned, have greatly displeased Dr Johnson and Mr Walker—yet both CRACK, in the sense of excellent, and CRACK UP, to boast or praise, were not considered vulgarisms in the time of Henry VIII. DODGE, a cunning trick, is from the Anglo-Saxon; and ancient nobles used to "get each other's DANDER UP" before appealing to their swords,—quite FLABERGASTING (also a respectable old word) the half score of lookers-on with the thumps and cuts of their heavy weapons. GALLAVANTING, waiting upon the ladies, was as polite in expression as in action; whilst a clergyman at Paule's Crosse thought nothing of bidding a noisy hearer "hold his GAB," or "shut up his GOB." GADDING, roaming about in an idle and trapesing manner, was used in an old translation of the Bible; and "to do anything GINGERLY" was to do it with great care. Persons of modern tastes will be shocked to know that the great Lord Bacon spoke of the lower part of a man's face as his GILLS.

Shakspeare, or, as the French say, "the divine William," also used many words which are now counted as dreadfully vulgar. "CLEAN gone," in the sense of out of sight, or entirely away; "you took me all A-MORT," or confounded me; "it won't FADGE," or suit, are phrases taken at random from the great dramatist's works. A London costermonger, or inhabitant of the streets, instead of saying, "I'll make him yield," or "give in," in a fight or contest, would say, "I'll make him BUCKLE under." Shakspeare, in his *Henry the Fourth*, (Part ii., act i., scene 1,) has the word; and Mr Halliwell, one of the greatest and most industrious of living antiquaries, informs us that "the commentators do not supply another example." How strange, then, that the Bard of Avon and the Cockney costermongers should be joint partners and sole proprietors of the vulgarism! If Shakspeare was not a pugilist, he certainly anticipated the terms of the prize ring—or they were respectable words before the prize ring was thought of—for he has PAY, to beat or thrash, and PEPPER, with a similar meaning; also FANCY, in the sense of pets and favourites,—pugilists are often termed *the* FANCY. The cant word PRIG, from the Saxon, *priccan*, to filch, is also Shakspearian; so indeed is PIECE, a contemptuous term for a young woman. Shakspeare was not the only vulgar dramatist of his time. Ben Jonson, Beaumont and Fletcher, Brome, and other play-writers, occasionally put Cant words into the mouths of their low characters, or employed old words which have since degenerated into vulgarisms. CRUSTY, poor tempered; "two of a KIDNEY," two of a sort; LARK, a piece of fun; LUG, to pull; BUNG, to give or pass; PICKLE, a sad plight; FRUMP, to mock, are a few specimens casually picked from the works of the old histrionic writers.

One old English mode of canting, simple and effective when familiarised by practice, was the inserting a consonant betwixt each syllable: thus, taking *g*, "How do you do?" would be "How*g* do*g* you*g* do*g*?" The name very properly given to this disagreeable nonsense, we are informed by Grose, was *Gibberish*.

Another Cant has recently* been attempted by transposing the initial letters of words, so that a mutton chop becomes a *c*utton *m*op, a pint of stout a *s*tint of *p*out; but it is satisfactory to know that it has gained no ground. This is called *Marrowskying*, or *Medical Greek*, from its use by medical students at the hospitals. Albert Smith terms it the *Gower Street Dialect*.

The *Language of Ziph*, I may add, is another rude mode of disguising English, in use among the students at Winchester College. Some notices of this method of conveying secret information, with an extensive Glossary of the Words, Phrases, Customs, &c., peculiar to the College, may be found in Mr Mansfield's recently-published *School Life at Winchester College*.

* "Before 1848," a correspondent writes.

ACCOUNT

OF THE

HIEROGLYPHICS USED BY VAGABONDS.

ONE of the most singular chapters in a *History of Vagabondism* would certainly be "An Account of the Hieroglyphic Signs used by Tramps and Thieves." The reader may be startled to know that, in addition to a sacred language, the wandering tribes of this country have private marks and symbolic signs with which to score their successes, failures, and advice to succeeding beggars; in fact, that the country is really dotted over with beggars' finger-posts and guide-stones. The assertion, however strange it may appear, is no fiction. The subject was not long since brought under the attention of the Government by Mr Rawlinson.* "There is," he says in his report, "a sort of blackguards' literature, and the initiated understand each other by Slang [Cant] terms, by pantomimic signs, *and by* HIEROGLYPHICS. *The vagrant's mark may be seen in Havant, on corners of streets, on door-posts, on house-steps. Simple as these chalk-lines appear, they inform the succeeding vagrants of all they require to know; and a few white scratches may say, ' Be importunate,' or ' Pass on.'*"

Another very curious account was taken from a provincial newspaper, published in 1849, and forwarded to *Notes and Queries*,† under the head of MENDICANT FREEMASONRY. "Persons," remarks the writer, "indiscreet enough to open their purses to the relief of the beggar tribe, would do well to take a readily-learned lesson as to the folly of that misguided bene-

---

* *Mr Rawlinson's Report to the General Board of Health, Parish of Havant, Hampshire.* † Vol. v., p. 210.

volence which encourages and perpetuates vagabondism. Every door or passage is pregnant with instruction as to the error committed by the patron of beggars; as the beggar-marks shew that a system of freemasonry is followed, by which a beggar knows whether it will be worth his while to call into a passage or knock at a door. Let any one examine the entrances to the passages in any town, and there he will find chalk marks, unintelligible to him, but significant enough to beggars. If a thousand towns are examined, the same marks will be found at every passage entrance. The passage mark is a cypher with a twisted tail: in some cases the tail projects into the passage, in others outwardly; thus seeming to indicate whether the houses down the passage are worth calling at or not. Almost every door has its marks: these are varied. In some cases there is a cross on the brick work, in others a cypher: the figures 1, 2, 3, are also used. Every person may for himself test the accuracy of these statements by the examination of the brick-work near his own doorway—thus demonstrating that mendicity is a regular trade, carried out upon a system calculated to save time, and realise the largest profits." These remarks refer mainly to provincial towns, London being looked upon as the tramps' home, and therefore too FLY, or experienced, to be duped by such means.

The only other notice of the hieroglyphics of vagabonds that I have met with is in Mayhew's *London Labour and the London Poor*.* Mayhew obtained his information from two tramps, who stated that hawkers employ these signs as well as beggars. One tramp thus described the method of WORKING† a small town. "Two hawkers (PALS†) go together, but separate when they enter a village, one taking one side of the road, and selling different things; and so as to inform each other as to the character of the people at whose houses they call, *they chalk certain marks on their door-posts*." Another informant stated that "if

---

* Vol. i., pp. 218 and 247.   † See Dictionary.

a PATTERER* has been CRABBED (that is, offended) at any of the CRIBS, (houses,) *he mostly chalks a signal at or near the door.*"

Another use is also made of these hieroglyphics. Charts of successful begging neighbourhoods are rudely drawn, and symbolical signs attached to each house to shew whether benevolent or adverse.† "In many cases there is over the kitchen mantel piece" of a tramps' lodging-house "*a map of the district*, dotted here and there with memorandums of failure or success."‡ A correct facsimile of one of these singular maps has been placed as a frontispiece. It was obtained from the patterers and tramps who supplied a great many words for this work, and who have been employed by me for some time in collecting Old Ballads, Christmas Carols, Dying Speeches, and Last Lamentations, as materials for a *History of Popular Literature*. The reader will no doubt be amused with the drawing. The locality depicted is near Maidstone, in Kent; and I am informed that it was probably sketched by a wandering SCREEVER§ in payment for a night's lodging. The English practice of marking everything, and scratching names on public property, extends itself to the tribe of vagabonds. On the map, as may be seen in the left-hand corner, some TRAVELLER§ has drawn a favourite or noted female, singularly nicknamed *Three-quarter Sarah*. What were

---

* See Dictionary.

† Sometimes, as appears from the following, the names of persons and houses are written instead. "In almost every one of the padding-kens, or low lodging-houses in the country, there is a list of walks pasted up over the kitchen mantel-piece. Now at St Albans, for instance, at the ———, and at other places, there is a paper stuck up in each of the kitchens. This paper is headed 'WALKS OUT OF THIS TOWN,' and underneath it is set down the names of the villages in the neighbourhood at which a beggar may call when out on his walk, and they are so arranged as to allow the cadger to make a round of about six miles each day, and return the same night. In many of these papers there are sometimes twenty walks set down. No villages that are in any way "gammy" [bad] are ever mentioned in these papers, and the cadger, if he feels inclined to stop for a few days in the town, will be told by the lodging-house keeper, or the other cadgers that he may meet there, what gentlemen's seats or private houses are of any account on the walk that he means to take. The names of the good houses are not set down in the paper for fear of the police."—*Mayhew*, vol. i., p. 418.   ‡ Mayhew, vol. i., p. 218.   § See Dictionary.

the peculiar accomplishments of this lady to demand so uncommon a name, the reader will be at a loss to discover; but a patterer says it probably refers to a shuffling dance of that name, common in tramps' lodging-houses, and in which "¾ Sarah" may have been a proficient. Above her, three beggars or hawkers have reckoned their day's earnings, amounting to 13s.; and on the right a tolerably correct sketch of a low hawker, or costermonger, is drawn. "To Dover, the *nigh* way," is the exact phraseology; and "hup here," a fair specimen of the self-acquired education of the tribe of cadgers. No key or explanation to the hieroglyphics was given in the original, because it would have been superfluous, when every inmate of the lodging-house knew the marks from their cradle—or rather their mother's back.

Should there be no map, in most lodging-houses there is an old man who is guide to every "WALK" in the vicinity, and who can tell on every round each house that is "good for a cold tatur." The hieroglyphics that are used are:—

✗   NO GOOD; too poor, and know too much.

♃   STOP,—If you have what they want, they will buy. They are pretty "*fly*," (knowing.)

⊃⊢   GO IN THIS DIRECTION, it is better than the other road. Nothing that way.

◇   BONE, (good.) Safe for a "cold tatur," if for nothing else. "*Cheese your patter*" (don't talk much) here.

▽   COOPER'D, (spoilt,) by too many tramps calling there.

☐   GAMMY (unfavourable,) like to have you taken up. Mind the dog.

⊙   FLUMMUXED, (dangerous,) sure of a month in "*quod*," (prison.)

⊕   RELIGIOUS, but tidy on the whole.

Where did these signs come from, and when were they first used? are questions which I have asked myself again and again, whilst endeavouring to discover their history. Knowing the character of the Gipsies, and ascertaining from a tramp that they are well acquainted with the hieroglyphics, "and have been as long ago as ever he could remember," I have little hesitation in ascribing the invention to them. And strange it would be if some modern Belzoni, or Champollion, discovered in these beggars' marks fragments of ancient Egyptian or Hindoo hieroglyphical writing! But this, of course, is a simple vagary of the imagination.

That the Gipsies were in the habit of leaving memorials of the road they had taken, and the successes that had befallen them, there can be no doubt. In an old book, *The Triumph of Wit*, 1724, there is a passage which appears to have been copied from some older work, and it runs thus:—" The Gipsies set out twice a year, and scatter all over England, each parcel having their appointed stages, that they may not interfere, nor hinder each other; and for that purpose, when they set forward in the country, *they stick up boughs in the way of divers kinds, according as it is agreed among them, that one company may know which way another is gone, and so take another road.*" The works of Hoyland and Borrow supply other instances.

I cannot close this subject without drawing attention to the extraordinary fact, that actually on the threshold of the gibbet the sign of the vagabond is to be met with! "The murderer's signal is even exhibited from the gallows; as a red handkerchief held in the hand of the felon about to be executed is a token that he dies without having betrayed any professional secrets."*

Since the first edition of this work was published, the author has received from various parts of England numerous evidences of the still active use of beggars' marks and mendicant hieroglyphics. One gentleman writes from Great Yarmouth to say

---

* *Mr Rawlinson's Report to the General Board of Health, Parish of Havant, Hampshire.*

that only a short time since, whilst residing in Norwich, he used frequently to see them on the houses and street corners in the suburbs. From another gentleman, a clergyman, I learn that he has so far made himself acquainted with the meanings of the signs employed, that by himself marking the characters ☐ (*Gammy*) and ⊙ (*Flummuxed*) on the gate posts of his parsonage, he enjoys a singular immunity from alms-seekers and cadgers on the tramp.

In a popular constable's *Guide*, giving the practice of justices in petty sessions, I have recently met with the following interesting paragraph, corroborating what has just been said on the hieroglyphics used by vagabonds:—

"Gipsies follow their brethren by numerous marks, such as strewing handfuls of grass in the day time at a four lane or cross roads; the grass being strewn down the road the gang have taken; also, by a cross being made on the ground with a stick or knife—the longest end of the cross denotes the route taken. In the night time a CLEFT STICK is placed in the fence at the cross roads, *with an arm pointing down the road* their comrades have taken. The marks are always placed on the left-hand side, so that the stragglers can easily and readily find them." *

From the cleft stick here alluded to, we learn the origin and use of ⊃⊷, the third hieroglyphic in the vagabond's private list.

* Snowden's *Magistrate's Assistant*, 1852, p. 444.

> "*All ridiculous words make their first entry into a language by familiar phrases; I dare not answer for these that they will not in time be looked upon as a part of our tongue.*"—Addison's *Spectator*.

A SHORT HISTORY OF SLANG,

OR

THE VULGAR LANGUAGE OF FAST LIFE.

SLANG is the language of street humour, of fast, high, and low life. CANT, as was stated in the chapter upon that subject, is the vulgar language of secrecy. They are both universal and ancient, and appear to have been the peculiar concomitants of gay, vulgar, or worthless persons in every part of the world at every period of time. Indeed, if we are to believe implicitly the saying of *the* wise man, that "there is nothing new under the sun," the "fast" men of buried Nineveh, with their knotty and door-matty-looking beards, may have cracked Slang jokes on the steps of Sennacherib's palace; and the stocks and stones of ancient Egypt, and the bricks of venerable and used-up Babylon, may, for aught we know, be covered with Slang hieroglyphics, unknown to modern antiquaries, which have long been stumbling-blocks to the philologist; so impossible is it at this day to say what was then authorised, or what vulgar language. Slang is as old as speech and the congregating together of people in cities. It is the result of crowding, and excitement, and artificial life. Even to the Classics it was not unknown, as witness the pages of Aristophanes and Plautus, Terence and Athenæus. Martial, the epigrammatist, is full of Slang. When an uninvited guest accompanied his friend, the Slang of the day styled him his UMBRA; when a man was trussed, neck and heels, it called him jocosely QUADRUPUS.

Old English Slang was coarser, and depended more upon downright vulgarity than our modern Slang. It was a jesting speech, or humorous indulgence for the thoughtless moment, or the drunken hour, and it acted as a vent-peg for a fit of temper or irritability; but it did not interlard and permeate every description of conversation as now. It was confined to nicknames and improper subjects, and encroached but to a very small extent upon the domain of authorised speech. Indeed, it was exceedingly limited when compared with the vast territory of Slang in such general favour and complete circulation at the present day. Still, although not an alarming encumbrance, as in our time, Slang certainly did exist in this country centuries ago, as we may see if we look down the page of any respectable History of England. Cromwell was familiarly called OLD NOLL,—just the same as Bonaparte was termed BONEY, and Wellington CONKEY, or NOSEY, only a few years ago. His Legislature, too, was spoken of in a high-flavoured way as the BAREBONES, or RUMP Parliament, and his followers were nicknamed ROUNDHEADS, and the peculiar religious sects of his protectorate were styled PURITANS and QUAKERS.* The Civil-War pamphlets, and the satirical hits of the Cavaliers and the Commonwealth men, originated numerous Slang words and vulgar similes in full use at the present moment. Here is a field of inquiry for the Philological Society, indeed I may say a territory, for there are thirty thousand of these partisan tracts. Later still, in the court of Charles II., the naughty ladies and the gay lords, with Rochester at their head, talked Slang; and very naughty Slang it was too! Fops, in those days, when "over head and ears" in debt, and in

---

* This term, with a singular literal downrightness, which would be remarkable in any other people than the French, is translated by them as the sect of *Trembleurs*.

continual fear of arrest, termed their enemies, the bailiffs, PHILISTINES* or MOABITES. At a later period, when collars were worn detached from shirts, in order to save the expense of washing—an object it would seem with needy "swells" in all ages—they obtained the name of JACOBITES. One half of the coarse wit in Butler's *Hudibras* lurks in the vulgar words and phrases which he was so fond of employing. They were more homely and forcible than the mild and elegant sentences of Cowley, and the people, therefore, hurrahed them, and pronounced Butler one of themselves,—or, as we should say, in a joyful moment, "a jolly good fellow." Orator Henley preached and prayed in Slang, and first charmed and then swayed the dirty mobs in Lincoln's-Inn-Fields by vulgarisms. Burly Grose mentions Henley, with the remark that we owe a great many Slang phrases to him. Swift, and old Sir Roger L'Estrange, and Arbuthnot, were all fond of vulgar or Slang language; indeed, we may see from a Slang word used by the latter how curious is the gradual adoption of vulgar terms in our standard dictionaries. The worthy doctor, in order to annihilate (or, as we should say, with a fitting respect to the subject under consideration, SMASH) an opponent, thought proper on an occasion to use the word CABBAGE, not in the ancient and esculentary sense of a flatulent vegetable of the kitchen garden, but in the at once Slang sense of purloining or cribbing. Johnson soon met with the word, looked at it, examined it, weighed it, and shook his head, but out of respect to a brother doctor inserted it in his dictionary, labelling it, however, prominently "*Cant;*" whilst Walker and Webster, years after, when *to cabbage* was *to pilfer* all over England, placed the term in their dictionaries as an ancient and very respectable word. Another Slang term, GULL, to cheat, or delude, sometimes varied to GULLY, is stated to be connected with the Dean of St Patrick's. GULL, a dupe, or a fool, is often used by

---

* Swift alludes to this term in his *Art of Polite Conversation*, p. 14. 1738.

our old dramatists, and is generally believed to have given rise to the verb; but a curious little edition of *Bamfylde Moore Carew*, published in 1827, says that to GULL, or GULLY, is derived from the well-known *Gulliver*, the hero of the famous *Travels*. How crammed with Slang are the dramatic works of the last century! The writers of the comedies and farces in those days must have lived in the streets, and written their plays in the public-houses, so filled are they with vulgarisms and unauthorised words. The popular phrases, "I owe you one," "That's one for his nob," and "Keep moving, dad," arose in this way.* The second of these sayings was, doubtless, taken from the card-table, for at cribbage the player who holds the knave of the suit turned up counts "one for his nob," and the dealer who turns up a knave counts "two for his heels."

In Mrs Centlivre's admirable comedy of *A Bold Stroke for a Wife*, we see the origin of that popular street phrase, THE REAL SIMON PURE. Simon Pure is the Quaker name adopted by Colonel Feignwell as a trick to obtain the hand of Mistress Anne Lovely in marriage. The veritable Quaker, the "real Simon Pure," recommended by Aminadab Holdfast, of Bristol, as a fit sojourner with Obadiah Prim, arrives at last, to the discomfiture of the Colonel, who, to maintain his position and gain time, concocts a letter in which the real Quaker is spoken of as a housebreaker who had travelled in the "leather conveniency" from Bristol, and adopted the garb and name of the western Quaker in order to pass off as the "REAL SIMON PURE," but only for the purpose of robbing the house and cutting the throat of the perplexed Obadiah. The scene in which the two Simon Pures, the *real* and the *counterfeit*, meet, is one of the best in the comedy.

Tom Brown, of "facetious memory," as his friends were wont to say, and Ned Ward, who wrote humorous books, and when tired drew beer for his customers at his alehouse in Long

---

* See *Notes and Queries*, vol. L, p. 185. 1850.

Acre,* were both great producers of Slang in the last century, and to them we owe many popular current phrases and household words.

Written Slang was checked, rather than advanced, by the pens of Addison, Johnson, and Goldsmith; although John Bee, the bottle-holder and historiographer of the pugilistic band of brothers in the youthful days of flat-nosed Tom Crib, has gravely stated that Johnson, when young and rakish, contributed to an early volume of the *Gentleman's Magazine* a few pages, by way of specimen, of a Slang dictionary, the result, Mr Bee says, "of his midnight ramblings!"† And Goldsmith, I must not forget to remark, certainly coined a few words, although, as a rule, his pen was pure and graceful, and adverse to neologisms. The word FUDGE, it has been stated, was first used by him in literary composition,‡ although it originated with one Captain Fudge, a notorious fibber, nearly a century before. Street phrases, nicknames, and vulgar words were continually being added to the great stock of popular Slang up to the commencement of the present century, when it received numerous additions from pugilism, horse-racing, and "fast" life generally, which suddenly came into great public favour, and was at its height when the Prince Regent was in his rakish minority. Slang in those days was generally termed FLASH language. So popular was it with the "bloods" of high life, that it constituted the best paying literary capital for certain authors and dramatists. Pierce Egan issued *Boxiana*, and *Life in London*, six portly octavo volumes, crammed with Slang; and Moncrieff wrote the most popular farce of the day, *Tom and Jerry*, (adapted from the latter work,) which, to use newspaper Slang, "took the town by storm," and, with its then fashionable vulgarisms, made the fortune of the old Adelphi

---

* He afterwards kept a tavern at Wapping, mentioned by Pope in the *Dunciad*.

† *Sportsman's Dictionary*, 1825, p. 15. I have searched the venerable magazine in vain for this Slang glossary.

‡ This is incorrect. See under FUDGE in the Dictionary.

Theatre, and was, without exception, the most wonderful instance of a continuous theatrical RUN in ancient or modern times. This, also, was brimful of Slang. Other authors helped to popularise and extend Slang down to our own time, when it has taken a somewhat different turn, dropping many of the Cant and old vulgar words, and assuming a certain quaint and fashionable phraseology—Frenchy, familiar, utilitarian, and jovial. There can be no doubt but that common speech is greatly influenced by fashion, fresh manners, and that general change of ideas which steals over a people once in a generation. But before I proceed further into the region of *Slang*, it will be well to say something on the etymology of the word.

The word SLANG is only mentioned by two lexicographers— Webster and Ogilvie.* Johnson, Walker, and the older compilers of dictionaries, give *slang* the preterite of *sling*, but not a word about SLANG in the sense of low, vulgar, or unrecognised language. The origin of the word has often been asked for in literary journals and books, but only one man, as far as I can learn, has ever hazarded an etymology—Jonathan Bee, the vulgar chronicler of the prize-ring.† With a recklessness peculiar to pugilism, Bee stated that SLANG was derived from " the *slangs* or fetters worn by prisoners, having acquired that name from the manner in which they were worn, as they required a sling of string to keep them off the ground." Bee had just been nettled at Pierce Egan producing a new edition of Grose's *Dictionary of the Vulgar Tongue*, and was determined to excel him in a vulgar dictionary of his own, which should be more racy, more pugilistic, and more original. How far he succeeded in this latter particular, his ridiculous etymology of Slang will shew. SLANG is not an English word; it is the Gipsy term for their secret language, and

---

* This introduction was written in 1859, before the new edition of *Worcester*, and Nuttall's recent work were published.

† Introduction to Bee's *Sportsman's Dictionary*, 1825.

its synonyme is GIBBERISH—another word which was believed to have had no distinct origin.* Grose—stout and burly Captain Grose—whom we may characterise as the greatest antiquary, joker, and porter-drinker of his day, was the first lexicographer to recognise the word SLANG. It occurs in his *Classical Dictionary of the Vulgar Tongue*, of 1785, with the signification that it implies "Cant or vulgar language." Grose, I may remark in passing, was a great favourite with the poet Burns, and so pleased him by his extensive powers of story-telling and grog-imbibing, that the companionable and humour-loving Scotch bard wrote for his fat friend—or, to use his own words, "the fine, fat, fodgel wight"—the immortal poem of "Tam O'Shanter."

Without troubling the reader with a long account of the transformation into an English term of the word SLANG, I may remark in passing that it is easily seen how we obtained it from the Gipsies. Hucksters and beggars on tramp, or at fairs and races, associate and frequently join in any rough enterprise with the Gipsies.† The word would be continually heard by them, and would in this manner soon become CANT;‡ and, when carried by "fast" or vulgar fashionables from the society of thieves and low characters to their own drawing-rooms, would as quickly become SLANG, and the representative term for all vulgar or Slang language.

---

* The Gipsies use the word Slang as the Anglican synonyme for Romany, the continental (or rather Spanish) term for the Cingari or Gipsy tongue. Crabb, who wrote the *Gipsies' Advocate* in 1831, thus mentions the word:—"This language [Gipsy] *called by themselves* SLANG, or GIBBERISH, invented, as they think, by their forefathers for secret purposes, is not merely the language of one or a few of these wandering tribes, which are found in the European nations, but is adopted by the vast numbers who inhabit the earth."

† See what the Druid says, in *Silk and Scarlet, Post and Paddock*, and his other sporting works, about the card-sellers, booth-men, horse-holders, cocksby-men, and other well-known frequenters of race-courses.

‡ The word SLANG assumed various meanings amongst costermongers, beggars, and vagabonds of all orders. It was, and is still, used to express "cheating by false weights," "a raree show," "retiring by a back door," "a watch-chain," their "secret language," &c.

Any sudden excitement, peculiar circumstance, or popular literary production, is quite sufficient to originate and set agoing a score of Slang words. Nearly every election or public agitation throws out offshoots of the excitement, or scintillations of the humour in the shape of Slang terms—vulgar at first, but at length adopted as semi-respectable from the force of habit and custom. There is scarcely a condition or calling in life that does not possess its own peculiar Slang. The professions, legal and medical, have each familiar and unauthorised terms for peculiar circumstances and things, and I am quite certain that the clerical calling, or "*the cloth*," is not entirely free from this peculiarity. Every workshop, warehouse, factory, and mill throughout the country has its Slang, and so have the public schools of Eton, Harrow, and Westminster, and the great Universities of Oxford and Cambridge. Sea Slang constitutes the principal charm of a sailor's "yarn;" and our soldiers and officers have each their peculiar nicknames and terms for things and subjects proper and improper. A writer in *Household Words* (No. 183) has gone so far as to remark, that a person "shall not read one single parliamentary debate, as reported in a first-class newspaper, without meeting scores of Slang words;" and "that from Mr Speaker in his chair, to the Cabinet Ministers whispering behind it—from mover to seconder, from true-blue Protectionist to extremest Radical—Mr Barry's New House echoes and re-echoes with Slang." Really it seems as if our boasted English tongue were a very paltry and ill-provided contrivance after all; or can it be that we are the most vulgar of people?

The universality of Slang is extraordinary. Let any person for a short time narrowly examine the conversation of their dearest and nearest friends, ay, censor-like, even slice and analyse their own supposed correct talk, and they shall be amazed at the numerous unauthorised, and what we can only call vulgar, words they continually employ. It is not the number of new words that we are ever introducing that is so reprehensible, there is not so much harm in this practice (frequently termed in books "the licence of expression") if neologisms are really required, but it is the continually encumbering of *old* words with fresh and strange meanings. Look at those simple and useful verbs, *do, cut, go,* and *take,* and see how they are hampered and overloaded, and then let us ask ourselves how is it possible for a French or German gentleman, be he ever so well educated, to avoid continually blundering and floundering amongst our *little* words when trying to make himself understood in an ordinary conversation? He may have studied our language the required time, and have gone through the usual amount of "grinding," and practised the common allotment of patience, but all to no purpose as far as accuracy is concerned. I am aware that most new words are generally regarded as Slang, although afterwards they may become useful and respectable additions to our standard dictionaries. JABBER and HOAX were Slang and Cant terms in Swift's time; so indeed were MOB and SHAM.* Words directly from the Latin and Greek, and Carlyleisms, are allowed by an indulgent public to pass and take their places in books. Sound contributes many Slang words—a source that etymologists too frequently overlook. Nothing pleases an ignorant person so much as a high-sounding term "full of fury." How melodious and drumlike are those vulgar coruscations RUMBUMPTIOUS, SLANTINGDICULAR, SPLENDIFEROUS,† RUMBUSTIOUS, and FERRICADOUZER. What a "pull" the sharp-nosed lodging-house-keeper thinks she has over her victims if she can but hurl such testimonies of a liberal

---

* North, in his *Examen,* p. 574, says, "I may note that the rabble first changed their title, and were called the MOB in the assemblies of this [Green Ribbon] club. It was their beasts of burden, and called first *mobile vulgus,* but fell naturally into the contraction of one syllable, and ever since is become proper English." In the same work, p. 231, the disgraceful origin of SHAM is given.

† It is somewhat singular that Drayton, the poet of Queen Elizabeth's time, should have coined a similar word, SPLENDIDIOUS. The Latin, *Splendidus,* however, was probably what he meant to employ.

education at them when they are disputing her charges, and threatening to ABSQUATULATE! In the United States the vulgar-genteel even excel the poor "stuck-up" Cockneys in their formation of a native fashionable language. How charming to a refined ear are ABSKIZE, CATAWAMPOUSLY, EXFLUNCTIFY, OBSCUTE, KESLOSH, KESOUSE, KESWOLLOP, and KEWHOLLUX! Vulgar words representing action and brisk movement often owe their origin to sound. Mispronunciation, too, is another great source of vulgar or Slang words—RAMSHACKLE, SHACKLY, NARY-ONE for neither or neither one, OTTOMY or ATOMY for anatomy, RENCH for rinse, are specimens. The commonalty dislike frequently-occurring words difficult of pronunciation, and so we have the street abridgments of BIMEBY for by and by, CAZE for because, GIN for given, HANKERCHER for handkerchief, RUMATIZ for rheumatism, BACKY for tobacco, and many others, not perhaps Slang, but certainly all vulgarisms. Archbishop Whately, in his interesting *Remains of Bishop Copleston,* has inserted a leaf from the Bishop's note-book on the popular corruption of names, mentioning among others KICKSHAWS, as from the French, *quelques choses;* BEEFEATER, the lubberly guardian of royalty in a procession, and the supposed devourer of enormous beefsteaks, as but a vulgar pronunciation of the French, *buffetier;* and GEORGE and CANNON, the sign of a public-house, as nothing but a corruption (although so soon!) of the popular premier of the last generation, *George Canning.* Literature has its Slang terms; and the desire on the part of writers to say funny and startling things in a novel and curious way (the late *Household Words,*[*] for instance) contributes many unauthorised words to the great stock of Slang.

Fashionable or *Upper-class Slang* is of several varieties. There is the Belgravian, military and naval, parliamentary, dandy, and

---

[*] It is rather singular that this popular journal should have contained a long article on *Slang* a short time ago.

the reunion and visiting Slang. English officers, civilians, and their families, who have resided long in India, have contributed many terms from the Hindostanee to our language. Several of these, such as CHIT, a letter, or TIFFIN, lunch, are fast losing their Slang character, and becoming regularly-recognised English words. JUNGLE, as a term for a forest or wilderness, is now an English phrase; a few years past, however, it was merely the Hindostanee JUNKUL. The extension of trade in China, and the English settlement at Hong Kong, have introduced among us several examples of Canton Jargon, that exceedingly curious Anglo-Chinese dialect spoken in the seaports of the Celestial Empire. While these words have been carried as it were into the families of the upper and middle classes, persons in a humbler rank of life, through the sailors, soldiers, Lascar and Chinese beggars that haunt the metropolis, have also adopted many Anglo-Indian and Anglo-Chinese phrases. As this Dictionary would have been incomplete without them, they are all carefully recorded in its columns. Concerning the Slang of the fashionable world, a writer in *Household Words* curiously, but not altogether truthfully, remarks, that it is mostly imported from France; and that an unmeaning gibberish of Gallicisms runs through English fashionable conversation, and fashionable novels, and accounts of fashionable parties in the fashionable newspapers. Yet, ludicrously enough, immediately the fashionable magnates of England seize on any French idiom, the French themselves not only universally abandon it to us, but positively repudiate it altogether from their idiomatic vocabulary. If you were to tell a well-bred Frenchman that such and such an aristocratic marriage was on the *tapis*, he would stare with astonishment, and look down on the carpet in the startled endeavour to find a marriage in so unusual a place. If you were to talk to him of the *beau monde*, he would imagine you meant the world which God made, not half-a-dozen streets and squares between Hyde Park

Corner and Chelsea Bun House. The *thé dansante** would be completely inexplicable to him. If you were to point out to him the Dowager Lady Grimgriffin acting as *chaperon* to Lady Amanda Creamville, he would imagine you were referring to the *petit Chaperon rouge*—to little Red-Riding Hood. He might just understand what was meant by *vis-à-vis, entremets,* and some others of the flying horde of frivolous little foreign slangisms hovering about fashionable cookery and fashionable furniture; but three-fourths of them would seem to him as barbarous French provincialisms, or, at best, but as antiquated and obsolete expressions, picked out of the letters of Mademoiselle Scuderi, or the tales of Crebillon the "younger." Servants, too, appropriate the scraps of French conversation which fall from their masters' guests at the dinner table, and forthwith in the world of flunkeydom the word "know" is disused, and the lady's-maid, in doubt on a particular point, asks John whether or no he SAVEYS it?* What, too, can be more abominable than that heartless piece of fashionable newspaper Slang, regularly employed when speaking of the successful courtship of young people in the fashionable world:—

M ARRIAGE IN HIGH LIFE.—We understand that a marriage is ARRANGED (!) betwixt the Lady, &c. &c., and the Honourable, &c. &c.

ARRANGED! Is that cold-blooded Smithfield or Mark-Lane term for a sale or a purchase the proper word to express the hopeful, joyous, golden union of young and trustful hearts? Which is the proper way to pronounce the names of great people, and what the correct authority? Lord Cowper, we are often assured, is Lord *Cooper*—on this principle Lord Cowley would certainly be Lord *Cooley*—and Mr Carew, we are told, should be Mr

---

* The writer is quite correct in instancing this piece of fashionable twaddle. The mongrel formation is exceedingly amusing to a polite Parisian.

† Savez-vous cela?

Carey, Ponsonby should be *Punsunby*, Eyre should be *Aire*, Cholmondeley should be *Chumley*, St John *Singen*, Majoribanks *Marshbanks*, and Powell should always be *Poel*. I don't know that these lofty persons have as much cause to complain of the illiberality of fate in giving them disagreeable names as did the celebrated Psyche, (as she was termed by Tom Moore,) whose original name, through her husband, was *Teague*, but which was afterwards altered to Tighe. The pronunciation of proper names has long been an anomaly in the conversation of the upper classes of this country. Hodge and Podge, the clodhoppers of Shakspeare's time, talked in their mug-houses of the great Lords *Darbie*, *Barkelie*, and *Bartie*. In Pall Mall and May Fair these personages are spoken of in exactly the same manner at the present day, whilst in the City, and amongst the *middle* classes, we only hear of Derby, Berkley, &c., — the correct pronunciations, if the spelling is worth aught. A costermonger is ignorant of such a place as Birmingham, but understands you in a moment if you talk of *Brummagem*. Why do not Pall Mall join with the costermongers in this pronunciation? It is the ancient one.*

Parliamentary Slang, excepting a few peculiar terms connected with "*the* House," (scarcely Slang, I suppose,) is mainly composed of fashionable, literary, and learned Slang. When members, however, get excited, and wish to be forcible, they are often not very particular which of the street terms they select, providing it carries, as good old Dr South said, plenty of "wild-fire" in it. Sir Hugh Cairns very lately spoke of "that homely but expressive phrase, DODGE." Out of "the House," several Slang terms are used in connexion with Parliament or members of Parliament. If Lord Palmerston is known by name to the

---

* At page 24 of a curious old Civil-War tract, entitled, *The Oxonian Antippodes*, by I. B., Gent., 1644, the town is called BRUMMIDGHAM, and this was the general rendering in the printed literature of the seventeenth century.

tribes of the Caucasus and Asia Minor as a great foreign diplomatist, when the name of our Queen Victoria is an unknown title to the inhabitants of those parts—as was stated in the *Times* a short time ago—I have only to remark that amongst the costers and the wild inhabitants of the streets he is better known as PAM. I have often heard the cabmen on the "ranks" in Piccadilly remark of the late Chancellor of the Exchequer, when he has been going from his residence at Grosvenor Gate to Derby House in St James's Square, "Hollo, there! de yer see old DIZZY doing a stump?" A PLUMPER is a single vote at an election—not a SPLIT-TICKET; and electors who have occupied a house, no matter how small, and boiled a pot in it, thus qualifying themselves for voting, are termed POT-WALLOPERS. A quiet WALK OVER is a re-election without opposition and much cost. A CAUCUS meeting refers to the private assembling of politicians before an election, when candidates are chosen, and measures of action agreed upon. The term comes from America. A JOB, in political phraseology, is a government office or contract obtained by secret influence or favouritism. Only the other day the *Times* spoke of "the patriotic member of Parliament POTTED OUT in a dusty little lodging somewhere about Bury Street." The term QUOCKERWODGER, although referring to a wooden toy figure which jerks its limbs about when pulled by a string, has been supplemented with a political meaning. A pseudo-politician, one whose strings of action are pulled by somebody else, is now often termed a QUOCKERWODGER. The term RAT, too, in allusion to rats deserting vessels about to sink, has long been employed towards those turncoat politicians who change their party for interest. Who that occasionally passes near the Houses of Parliament has not often noticed stout or careful M.P.s walk briskly through the Hall, and on the curb-stone in front, with umbrella or walking cane uplifted, shout to the cabmen on the rank, FOUR-WHEELER! The term is a useful one, but I am afraid we must consider it Slang, until it is stamped with the mint mark of lexicographical authority.*

Military, or *Officers' Slang*, is on a par, and of a character, with *Dandy Slang*. Inconvenient friends, or elderly and lecturing relatives, are pronounced DREADFUL BORES. Four-wheeled cabs are called BOUNDERS; and a member of the Four-in-hand Club, driving to Epsom on the Derby Day, would, using fashionable phraseology, speak of it as TOOLING HIS DRAG DOWN TO THE DERBY. A vehicle, if not a DRAG (or dwag) is a TRAP, or a CASK; and if the TURN OUT happens to be in other than a trim condition, it is pronounced at once as not DOWN THE ROAD. Your City swell would say it is not UP TO THE MARK; whilst the costermonger would call it WERY DICKEY. In the army a barrack or military station is known as a LOBSTER-BOX; to "cram" for an examination is to MUG-UP; to reject from the examination is to SPIN; and that part of the barrack occupied by subalterns is frequently spoken of as the ROOKERY. In dandy or swell Slang, any celebrity, from Paul Bedford, to the Pope of Rome, is a SWELL. Wrinkled-faced old professors, who hold dress and fashionable tailors in abhorrence, are called AWFUL SWELLS,—if they happen to be very learned or clever. I may remark that in this upper-class Slang, a title is termed a HANDLE; trousers, INEXPRESSIBLES; or, when of a large pattern, or the inflated Zouave cut, HOWLING BAGS; a superior appearance, EXTENSIVE; a four-wheeled cab, a BIRDCAGE; a dance, a HOP; dining at another man's table, "sitting under his MAHOGANY;" anything flashy or showy, LOUD; the peculiar make or cut of a coat, its BUILD; full dress, FULL-FIG; wearing clothes which re-

---

* From an early period politics and partyism have attracted unto themselves quaint Slang terms. Horace Walpole quotes a party nickname of February 1742, as a Slang word of the day:—"The Tories declare against any further prosecution, if Tories there are, for now one hears of nothing but the BROAD-BOTTOM; it is the reigning Cant word, and means the taking all parties and people, indifferently, into the Ministry." Thus BROAD-BOTTOM in those days was Slang for *coalition*.

present the very extreme of fashion, "dressing to DEATH;" a reunion, a SPREAD; a friend, (or a "good fellow,") a TRUMP; a difficulty, a SCREW LOOSE; and everything that is unpleasant, "from bad sherry to a writ from a tailor," JEUCED INFERNAL. The military phrase, "to send a man to COVENTRY," or permit no person to speak to him, although an ancient saying, must still be considered Slang.

The *Universities of Oxford and Cambridge*, and the great public schools, are the hotbeds of fashionable Slang. Growing boys and high-spirited young fellows detest restraint of all kinds, and prefer making a dash at life in a Slang phraseology of their own, to all the set forms and syntactical rules of *Alma Mater*. Many of the most expressive words in a common chit-chat, or free-and-easy conversation, are old university vulgarisms. CUT, in the sense of dropping an acquaintance, was originally a Cambridge form of speech; and HOAX, to deceive or ridicule, we are informed by Grose, was many years since an Oxford term. Among the words that fast society has borrowed from our great scholastic (I was going to say *establishments*, but I remember the linen-drapers' horrid and habitual use of the word) institutions, I find CRIB, a house or apartments; DEAD-MEN, empty wine bottles; DRAWING TEETH,* wrenching off knockers; FIZZING, first-rate, or splendid; GOVERNOR, or RELIEVING-OFFICER, the general term for a male parent; PLUCKED, defeated or turned back; QUIZ, to scrutinise, or a prying old fellow; and ROW, a noisy disturbance. The Slang words in use at Oxford and Cambridge would alone fill a volume. As examples I may instance SCOUT, which at Oxford refers to an undergraduate's valet, whilst the same menial at Cambridge is termed a GYP,—popularly derived by the Cantabs from the Greek, GYPS, ($γὺψ$,) a vulture; SCULL, the head, or master of a college; BATTLES, the Oxford

---

* This is more especially an amusement with medical students, and is comparatively unknown out of London.

term for rations, changed at Cambridge into COMMONS. The
term DICKEY, a half shirt, I am told, originated with the students
of Trinity College, Dublin, who at first styled it a TOMMY, from
the Greek, τομή, a section. CRIB, a literal translation, is now
universal; GRIND refers to "working up" for an examination,
also, to a walk, or "constitutional;" HIVITE is a student of St
Begh's (St Bee's) College, Cumberland; to JAPAN, in this Slang
speech, is to ordain; MORTAR-BOARD is a square college cap; SIM,
a student of a Methodistical turn—in allusion to the Rev. Charles
Simeon; SLOGGERS, at Cambridge, refers to the second division of
race boats, known at Oxford as TORPIDS; SPORT is to shew or
exhibit; TROTTER is the jocose term for a tailor's man who goes
round for orders; and TUFTS are wealthy students who dine with
the DONS, and are distinguished by golden *tufts*, or tassels, in
their caps. There are many terms in use at Oxford not known
at Cambridge; and such Slang names as COACH, GULF, HARRY-
SOPH, POKER, or POST-MORTEM, common enough at Cambridge,
are seldom or never heard at the great sister university. For
numerous other examples of college Slang the reader is referred
to the Dictionary.

Religious Slang, strange as the compound may appear, exists
with other descriptions of vulgar speech at the present day.
Punch, a short time since, in one of those half-humorous, half-
serious articles in which he is so fond of lecturing any national
abuse or popular folly, remarked that Slang had "long since
penetrated into the Forum, and now we meet it in the Senate,
and even the pulpit itself is no longer free from its intrusion."
I would not, for one moment, wish to infer that the practice is
general. On the contrary, and in justice to the clergy, it must
be said that the principal disseminators of pure English throughout the country are the ministers of our Established Church.
Yet it cannot be denied but that a great deal of Slang phraseology and disagreeable vulgarism have gradually crept into the

very pulpits which should give forth as pure speech as doctrine.

Dean Conybeare, in his able *Essay on Church Parties*,* has noticed this wretched addition to our pulpit speech. As stated in his Essay, the practice appears to confine itself mainly to the exaggerated forms of the High and Low Church—the Tractarians and the "Recordites." † By way of illustration, the Dean cites the evening parties, or social meetings, common amongst the wealthier lay members of the Recordite (exaggerated Evangelical) Churches, where the principal topics discussed—one or more favourite clergymen being present in a quasi-official manner—are "the merits and demerits of different preachers, the approaching restoration of the Jews, the date of the Millennium, the progress of the 'Tractarian heresy,' and the anticipated 'perversion' of High-Church neighbours." These subjects are canvassed in a dialect differing considerably from common English. The words FAITHFUL, TAINTED, ACCEPTABLE, DECIDED, LEGAL, and many others, are used in a technical sense. We hear that Mr A. has been more OWNED than Mr B.; and that Mr C. has more SEALS ‡ than Mr D. Again, the word GRACIOUS is invested with a meaning as extensive as that attached by young ladies to *nice*. Thus, we hear of a "GRACIOUS sermon," a "GRACIOUS meeting," a "GRACIOUS child," and even a "GRACIOUS whipping." The word DARK has also a new and peculiar usage. It is applied to every person, book, or place, not impregnated with Recordite principles. We once were witnesses of a ludicrous misunderstanding resulting from this phraseology. "What did you mean," said A. to B., "by telling me that —— was such a very DARK village? I rode over there to-day, and found the street particularly broad and

---

* *Edinburgh Review*, October 1853.

† A term derived from the *Record Newspaper*, the exponent of this singular section of the Low, or so-called Evangelical Church.

‡ A preacher is said, in this phraseology, to be OWNED when he makes many converts, and his converts are called his SEALS.

cheerful, and there is not a tree in the place." "*The gospel is not preached there*," was B.'s laconic reply. The conclusion of one of these singular evening parties is generally marked by an "*exposition*"—an unseasonable sermon of nearly one hour's duration, circumscribed by no text, and delivered from the table by one of the clerical visitors with a view to "improve the occasion." In the same Essay, the religious Slang terms for the two great divisions of the Established Church receive some explanation. The old-fashioned High-Church party—rich and "stagnant," noted for its "sluggish mediocrity, hatred of zeal, dread of innovation, abuse of Dissent, blundering and languid utterance"—is called the HIGH AND DRY; whilst the corresponding division, known as the Low Church—equally stagnant with the former, but poorer, and more lazily inclined (from absence of education) to Dissent—receives the nickname of the LOW AND SLOW. Already have these terms become so familiar that they are shortened, in ordinary conversation, to the DRY and the SLOW. The so-called "Broad Church," I should remark, is often spoken of as the BROAD AND SHALLOW.

What can be more objectionable than the irreverent and offensive manner in which many of the Dissenting ministers continually pronounce the names of the Deity—God and Lord? God, instead of pronouncing in the plain and beautiful simple old English way, G-O-D, they drawl out into GORDE or GAUDE; and Lord, instead of speaking in the proper way, they desecrate into LOARD or LOERD,—lingering on the *u*, or the *r*, as the case may be, until an honest hearer feels disgusted, and almost inclined to run the gantlet of beadles and deacons, and pull the vulgar preacher from his pulpit. I have observed that many young preachers strive hard to acquire this peculiar pronunciation, in imitation of the older ministers. What can more properly, then, be called Slang, or, indeed, the most objectionable of Slang, than this studious endeavour to pronounce the most sacred names in a uniformly vulgar and unbecoming manner If the old-fashioned preacher whistled Cant through his nose, the modern vulgar reverend whines Slang from the more natural organ. These vagaries of speech will, perhaps, by an apologist, be termed "pulpit peculiarities," and the writer dared to intermeddle with a subject that is or should be removed from his criticisms. The terms used by the mob towards the Church, however illiberal and satirically vulgar, are within his province in such an inquiry as the present. A clergyman, in vulgar language, is spoken of as a CHOKER, a CUSHION-THUMPER, a DOMINIE, an EARWIG, a GOSPEL-GRINDER, a GRAY-COAT PARSON; if he is a lessee of the great tithes, ONE IN TEN, PADRE; if spoken of by an Anglo-Indian, a ROOK, a SPOUTER, a WHITE-CHOKER, or a WARMING-PAN RECTOR, if he only holds the living *pro tempore*, or is simply keeping the place warm for his successor. If a Tractarian, his outer garment is rudely spoken of as a PYGOSTOLE, or M.B. (MARK OF THE BEAST) COAT. His profession is termed THE CLOTH, and his practice TUB-THUMPING. Should he belong to the Dissenting body, he is probably styled a PANTILER, or a PSALM-SMITER, or, perhaps, a SWADDLER. His chapel, too, is spoken of as a SCHISM SHOP. A Roman Catholic, I may remark, is coarsely named a BRISKET-BEATER.

Particular as lawyers generally are about the meaning of words, they have not prevented an unauthorised phraseology from arising, which we may term *Legal Slang*. So forcibly did this truth impress a late writer, that he wrote in a popular journal, "You may hear Slang every day in term from barristers in their robes, at every mess-table, at every bar-mess, at every college commons, and in every club dining-room." Swift, in his *Art of Polite Conversation*, (p. 15,) published a century and a half ago, states that VARDI was the Slang in his time for "verdict." A few of the most common and well-known terms used out of doors, with reference to legal matters, are COOK, to hash or make up a balance-sheet; DIPPED, mortgaged; DUN, to solicit payment; FULLIED, to be "*fully* committed for trial;" LAND-SHARK, a sailor's definition of a lawyer; LIMB OF THE LAW, a milder term for the same "professional;" MONKEY WITH A LONG TAIL, a mortgage—phrase used in the well-known case for libel, Smith *v.* Jones; MOUTHPIECE, the coster's term for his counsel; "to go through the RING," to take advantage of the Insolvency Act; SMASH, to become bankrupt; SNIPE, an attorney with a long bill; and WHITEWASHED, said of any debtor who has taken the benefit of the Insolvent Act. Lawyers, from their connexion with the police courts, and transactions with persons in every grade of society, have ample opportunities for acquiring street Slang, which, in cross-questioning and wrangling, they frequently avail themselves of.

It has been said there exists a *Literary Slang,* or "the *Slang of Criticism*—dramatic, artistic, and scientific. Such words as 'æsthetic,' 'transcendental,' the 'harmonies,' the 'unities,' a 'myth:' such phrases as 'an exquisite *morceau* on the big drum,' a 'scholarlike rendering of John the Baptist's great toe,' 'keeping harmony,' 'middle distance,' 'aerial perspective,' 'delicate handling,' 'nervous chiaroscuro,' and the like." More than one literary journal that I could name are fond of employing such terms in their art-criticisms; but it is questionable, after all, whether they are not allowable as the generous inflections and bendings of a bountiful language, for the purpose of expressing fresh phases of thought, and ideas not yet provided with representative words.* The well-known and ever-acceptable *Punch,* with his fresh and choice little pictorial bits by Leech, often employs a Slang term to give point to a joke, or humour to a

---

* "All our newspapers contain more or less colloquial words; in fact, there seems no other way of expressing certain ideas connected with passing events of every-day life with the requisite force and piquancy. In the English newspapers the same thing is observable, and certain of them contain more of the class denominated Slang words than our own."—*Bartlett's Americanisms,* p. 10, 1859.

line of satire. A short time since (4th May 1859) he gave an original etymology of the schoolboy-ism SLOG. SLOG, said the classical and studious *Punch*, is derived from the Greek word SLOGO, to baste, to wallop, to slaughter. And it was not long ago that he amused his readers with two columns on *Slang* and *Sanscrit*:—

"The allegory which pervades the conversation of all Eastern nations," remarked the philosophical *Punch*, "is the foundation of Western Slang; and the increased number of students of the Oriental languages, especially since Sanscrit and Arabic have been made subjects for the Indian Civil Service examinations, may have contributed to supply the English language with a large portion of its new dialect. While, however, the spirit of allegory comes from the East, there is so great a difference between the brevity of Western expression and the more cumbrous diction of the Oriental, that the origin of a phrase becomes difficult to trace. Thus, for instance, whilst the Turkish merchant might address his friend somewhat as follows— 'That which seems good to my father is to his servant as the perfumed breath of the west wind in the calm night of the Arabian summer;' the Western negotiator observes more briefly, 'ALL SERENE!'"

But the vulgar term, BRICK, *Punch* remarks, in illustration,

"must be allowed to be an exception, its Greek derivation being universally admitted, corresponding so exactly as it does in its rectangular form and compactness to the perfection of manhood, according to the views of Plato and Simonides; but any deviation from the simple expression, in which locality is indicated,—as, for instance, 'a genuine Bath,'—decidedly breathes the Oriental spirit."

It is singular that what *Punch* says unwittingly and in humour respecting the Slang expression, BOSH, should be quite true. BOSH, remarks *Punch*, after speaking of it as belonging to the stock of words pilfered from the Turks, "is one whose innate force and beauty the slangographer is reluctantly compelled to admit. It is the only word which seems a proper appellation for a great deal which we are obliged to hear and to read every day of our life." BOSH, nonsense or stupidity, is derived from the

Gipsy and the Persian. The universality of Slang, I may here remark, is proved by its continual use in the pages of *Punch*. Whoever thinks, unless belonging to a past generation, of asking a friend to explain the stray vulgar words employed by the *London Charivari* ?

The *Athenæum*, the most learned and censor-like of all the "weeklies," often indulges in a Slang word, when force of expression or a little humour is desired, or when the writer wishes to say something which is better said in Slang, or so-called vulgar speech, than in the authorised language of Dr Johnson or Lindley Murray. It was but the other day that a writer in its pages employed an old and favourite word, used always when we were highly pleased with any article at school—STUNNING. Bartlett, the compiler of the *Dictionary of Americanisms*, continually cites the *Athenæum* as using Slang and vulgar expressions ; but the magazine the American refers to is not the excellent literary journal which is so esteemed at the present day—it was a smaller, and now defunct "weekly." Many other highly respectable journals often use Slang words and phrases. The *Times* (or, in Slang, the THUNDERER) frequently employs unauthorised terms ; and, following a "leader"* of the purest and most eloquent composition, may sometimes be seen another "article"* on a totally different subject, containing, perhaps, a score or more of exceedingly questionable words. Among the words and phrases which may be included under the head of Literary Slang are, BALAAM, matter kept constantly in type about monstrous productions of nature, to fill up spaces in newspapers ; BALAAM-BOX, the term given in *Blackwood* to the repository for rejected articles ; and SLATE, to pelt with abuse, or CUT UP in a review. The Slang names given to newspapers are curious ;—thus, the *Morning*

---

* The terms *leader* and *article* can scarcely be called Slang, yet it would be desirable to know upon what authority they were first employed in their present peculiar sense.

Advertiser is known as the TAP-TUB, the TIZER, and the GIN AND GOSPEL GAZETTE. The *Morning Post* has obtained the suggestive *sobriquet* of JEAMES ; whilst the *Morning Herald* has long been caricatured as MRS HARRIS, and the *Standard* as MRS GAMP.*

The *Stage*, of course, has its Slang—"both before and behind the curtain," as a journalist remarks. The stage-manager is familiarly termed DADDY ; and an actor by profession, or a "professional," is called a PRO. A man who is occasionally hired at a trifling remuneration to come upon the stage as one of a crowd, or when a number of actors are wanted to give effect, is named a SUP,—an abbreviation of "supernumerary." A SURF is a third-rate actor who frequently pursues another calling ; and the band, or orchestra between the pit and the stage, is generally spoken of as the MENAGERY. A BEN is a benefit : and SAL is the Slang abbreviation of "salary." Should no wages be forthcoming on the Saturday night, it is said that the GHOST DOESN'T WALK. The travelling or provincial theatricals, who perform in any large room that can be rented in a country village, are called BARN-STORMERS. A LENGTH is forty-two lines of any dramatic composition ; and a RUN is the good or bad success of a performance. A SADDLE is the additional charge made by a manager to an actor or actress upon their benefit night. To MUG UP is to paint one's face, or arrange the person to represent a particular character ; to CORPSE, or to STICK, is to balk, or put the other actors out in their parts by forgetting yours. A performance is spoken of as either a GOOSER or a SCREAMER, should it be a failure or a great success ;—if the latter, it is not infrequently termed a HIT. To STAR IT is to perform as the centre of attraction, with none but subordinates and indifferent actors in the same performance. The expressive term CLAP-TRAP, high-sounding nonsense, is nothing but an ancient theatrical term, and

---

* For some account of the origin of these nicknames see under MRS HARRIS in the Dictionary.

signified a TRAP to catch a CLAP by way of applause. "Up amongst the GODS," refers to being among the spectators in the gallery,—termed in French Slang PARADIS.

There exists, too, in the great territory of vulgar speech what may not inappropriately be termed *Civic Slang*. It consists of mercantile and Stock-Exchange terms, and the Slang of good living and wealth. A turkey hung with sausages is facetiously styled AN ALDERMAN IN CHAINS; and a half-crown, perhaps from its rotundity, is often termed an ALDERMAN. A BEAR is a speculator on the Exchange; and a BULL, although of another order, follows a like profession. There is something very humorous and applicable in the Slang term LAME DUCK, a defaulter in stock-jobbing speculations. The allusion to his "waddling out of the Alley," as they say, is excellent. BREAKING SHINS, in City Slang, is borrowing money; a rotten or unsound scheme is spoken of as FISHY; "RIGGING the market" means playing tricks with it; and STAG was a common term during the railway mania for a speculator without capital, a seller of "scrip" in "Diddlesex Junction" and other equally safe lines. In Lombard Street a MONKEY is £500, a PLUM £100,000, and a MARYGOLD is one million sterling. But before I proceed further in a sketch of the different kinds of Slang, I cannot do better than speak here of the extraordinary number of Cant and Slang terms in use to represent money—from farthings to bank-notes the value of fortunes. *Her Majesty's coin, collectively or in the piece, is insulted by no less than one hundred and thirty distinct Slang words*, from the humble BROWN (a halfpenny) to FLIMSIES, or LONG-TAILED ONES, (bank-notes.)

"Money," it has been well remarked, "the bare, simple word itself, has a sonorous, significant ring in its sound," and might have sufficed, one would have imagined, for all ordinary purposes. But a vulgar or "fast" society has thought differently, and so we have the Slang synonymes—BEANS, BLUNT, (*i. e.*, specie,—not *stiff* or *rags*, bank-notes,) BRADS, BRASS, BUSTLE, COPPERS, (copper money, or mixed pence,) CHINK, CHINKERS, CHIPS, CORKS, DIBBS, DINARLY, DIMMOCK, DUST, FEATHERS, GENT, (silver,—from *argent*,) HADDOCK, (a purse of money,) HORSE NAILS, LOAVER, LOUR, (the oldest Cant term for money,) MOPUSSES, NEEDFUL, NOBBINGS, (money collected in a hat by street-performers,) OCHRE, (gold,) PEWTER, PALM OIL, POSH, QUEEN'S PICTURES, QUIDS, RAGS, (banknotes,) READY, or READY GILT, REDGE, (gold,) RHINO, ROWDY, SHINERS, (sovereigns,) SKIN, (a purse of money,) STIFF, (paper, or bill of acceptance,) STUFF, STUMPY, TIN, (silver,) WEDGE, (silver,) and YELLOW-BOYS, (sovereigns ;)—just forty-three vulgar equivalents for the simple word *money*. So attentive is Slang speech to financial matters, that there are seven terms for bad, or "bogus" coin, (as our friends, the Americans, call it :) a CASE is a counterfeit five-shilling piece ; HALF A CASE represents half that sum ; GRAYS are halfpence made double for gambling purposes ; QUEERSOFT is counterfeit or lead coin ; SCHOFEL refers to coated or spurious coin ; SHEEN is bad money of any description ; and SINKERS bears the same and not inappropriate meaning. FLYING THE KITE, or obtaining money on bills and promissory-notes, is closely connected with the allegorical expression of RAISING THE WIND, which is a well-known phrase for procuring money by immediate sale, pledging, or by a forced loan. In winter or in summer any elderly gentleman who may have prospered in life is pronounced WARM ; whilst an equivalent is immediately at hand in the phrase " his pockets are well LINED." Each separate piece of money has its own Slang term, and often half a score of synonymes. To begin with that extremely humble coin, a *farthing*: first we have FADGE, then FIDDLER, then GIG, and lastly QUARTEREEN. A *halfpenny* is a BROWN or a MADZA SALTEE, (Cant,) or a MAG, or a POSH, or a RAP,—whence the popular phrase, "I don't care a RAP." The useful and universal *penny* has for Slang equivalents a COPPER, a SALTEE, (Cant,) and a WINN. *Twopence* is a DEUCE, and *threepence* is either a THRUMS or a THRUPS. *Fourpence*, or a *groat*, may in vulgar speech be termed a BIT, a FLAG, or a JOEY. *Sixpence* is well represented in street talk, and some of the slangisms are very comical —for instance, BANDY, BENDER, CRIPPLE, and DOWNER; then we have FYE-BUCK, HALF A HOG, KICK, (thus "two and a KICK," or 2s. 6d.,) LORD OF THE MANOR, PIG, POT, (the price of a *pot* of beer —thus a half-a-crown is a "five POT piece,") SNID, SPRAT, SOW'S BABY, TANNER, TESTER, TIZZY,—sixteen vulgar words to one coin. *Sevenpence* being an uncommon amount has only one Slang synonyme, SETTER. The same remark applies to *eightpence* and *ninepence*, the former being only represented by OTTER, and the latter by the Cant phrase NOBBA-SALTEE. *Tenpence* is DACHA-SALTEE, and *elevenpence* DACHA-ONE,—both Cant expressions. *One shilling* boasts eleven Slang equivalents; thus we have BEONG, BOB, BREAKY-LEG, DEANER, GEN, (either from *argent*, silver, or the back Slang,) HOG, LEVY, PEG, STAG, TEVISS, and TWELVER. *One shilling and sixpence* is a KY-BOSH. *Half-a-crown* is known as an ALDERMAN, HALF A BULL, HALF A TUSHEROON, and a MADZA CAROON; whilst a *crown* piece, or *five shillings*, may be called either a BULL, or a CAROON, or a CARTWHEEL, or a COACHWHEEL, or a THICK-UN, or a TUSHEROON. The next advance in Slang money is *ten shillings*, or *half-a-sovereign*, which may be either pronounced as HALF A BEAN, HALF A COUTER, a MADZA POONA, or HALF A QUID. A *sovereign*, or *twenty shillings*, is a BEAN, CANARY, COUTER, FOONT, GOLDFINCH, JAMES, POONA, PORTRAIT, QUID, a THICK-UN, or a YELLOW-BOY. *Guineas* are nearly obsolete, yet the terms NEDS, and HALF NEDS, are still in use. Bank-notes are FLIMSIES, LONG-TAILED ONES, or SOFT. A FINUF is a five-pound note. One hundred pounds, (or any other "round sum,") quietly handed over as payment for services performed, is curiously termed "a COOL hundred." Thus ends, with several omissions, this long list of Slang terms for the coins of the realm, which for copiousness, I will engage to say, is not equalled by any other vulgar or unauthorised language in Europe.

The antiquity of many of these Slang names is remarkable. WINN was the vulgar term for a penny in the days of Queen Elizabeth; and TESTER, a sixpence, (formerly a shilling,) was the correct name in the days of Henry VIII. The reader, too, will have remarked the frequency of animals' names as Slang terms for money. Little, as a modern writer has remarked, do the persons using these phrases know of their remote and somewhat classical origin, which may, indeed, be traced to the period antecedent to that when monarchs monopolised the surface of coined money with their own image and superscriptions. They are identical with the very name of money among the early Romans, which was *pecunia*, from *pecus*, a flock. The collections of coin-dealers amply shew that the figure of a HOG was anciently placed on a small silver coin; and that that of a BULL decorated larger ones of the same metal. These coins were frequently deeply crossed on the reverse; this was for the convenience of easily breaking them into two or more pieces, should the bargain for which they were employed require it, and the parties making it had no smaller change handy to complete the transaction. Thus we find that the HALF BULL of the itinerant street-seller, or "traveller,"* so far from being a phrase of modern invention, as is generally supposed, is in point of fact referable to an era extremely remote. We may learn from Erizzo, in his *Discorso*, a further illustration of the proverb "that there is nothing new under the sun;" for he says that the Roman boys at the time of Hadrian tossed up their coppers and cried, "Head or ship;" of which tradition our "*heads or tails*" and "*man or woman*" is certainly a less-refined version. We thence gather, however, that the prow of a vessel would appear to have been the more ordinary device of the reverse of the brass coin of that ancient period.

* See Dictionary.

There are many other Cant words directly from a classic source, as will be seen in the Dictionary.

Shopkeepers' Slang is perhaps the most offensive of all Slang. It is not a casual eyesore, as newspaper Slang, neither is it an occasional discomfort to the ear, as in the case of some vulgar byword of the street; but it is a perpetual nuisance, and stares you in the face on tradesmen's invoices, on labels in the shop-windows, and placards on the hoardings, in posters against the house next to your own door—if it happens to be empty for a few weeks—and in bills thrust into your hand, as you peaceably walk through the streets. Under your door, and down your area, Slang hand-bills are dropped by some PUSHING tradesman; and for the thousandth time you are called upon to learn that an ALARMING SACRIFICE is taking place in the next street; that prices are DOWN AGAIN; that, in consequence of some other tradesman not DRIVING a ROARING TRADE, being, in fact, SOLD UP, and for the time being a resident in BURDON'S HOTEL, (Whitecross-Street Prison,) the PUSHING tradesman wishes to sell out at AWFULLY LOW PRICES, "to the kind patrons, and numerous customers," &c. &c., "that have on every occasion," &c. &c. In this Slang any occupation or calling is termed a LINE,—thus, the "building LINE." A tailor usurps to himself a good deal of Slang. Amongst operatives he is called a SNIP, or a STEEL-BAR DRIVER; by the world, a NINTH PART OF A MAN; and by the young collegian, or "fast" man, a SUFFERER. If he takes army contracts, it is SANK WORK; if he is a SLOP tailor, he is a SPRINGER UP, and his garments are BLOWN TOGETHER. Perquisites with him are SPIFFS, and remnants of cloth PEAKING, or CABBAGE. The per-centage he allows to his assistants (or COUNTER JUMPERS) on the sale of old-fashioned articles is termed TINGE. If he pays his workmen in goods, or gives them tickets upon other tradesmen, with whom he shares the profit, he is soon known as a TOMMY MASTER. If his business succeeds, it TAKES;

if neglected, it becomes SHAKY, and GOES TO POT; if he is deceived by a creditor, (a not by any means unusual circumstance,) he is LET IN, or, as it is sometimes varied, TAKEN IN. I need scarcely remark that any credit he may give is termed TICK.

Operatives' or Workmen's Slang, in quality, is but slightly removed from tradesmen's Slang. When belonging to the same shop or factory, they GRAFT there, and are BROTHER CHIPS. They generally dine at SLAP-BANG SHOPS, and are often paid at TOMMY SHOPS. At the nearest PUB, or public-house, they generally have a SCORE CHALKED UP against them, which has to be WIPED OFF regularly on the Saturday night. When out of work, they borrow a word from the flunkey vocabulary, and describe themselves as being OUT OF COLLAR. They term each other FLINTS and DUNGS, if they are "society" or "non-society" men. Their salary is a SCREW, and to be discharged is to GET THE SACK. When they quit work, they KNOCK OFF; and when out of employ, they ask if any HANDS are wanted. FAT is the vulgar synonyme for perquisites; ELBOW-GREASE signifies labour; and SAINT MONDAY is the favourite day of the week. Names of animals figure plentifully in the workman's vocabulary; thus we have GOOSE, a tailor's smoothing-iron; SHEEP'S-FOOT, an iron hammer; SOW, a receptacle for molten iron, whilst the metal poured from it is termed PIG. I have often thought that many of the Slang terms for money originally came from the worshop, thus—BRADS, from the ironmonger; CHIPS, from the carpenter; DUST, from the goldsmith; FEATHERS, from the upholsterer; HORSE-NAILS, from the farrier; HADDOCK, from the fishmonger; and TANNER, from the leather-dresser. The subject is curious. Allow me to call the attention of numismatists to it.

There yet remain several distinct divisions of Slang to be examined:—the Slang of the *stable*, or *jockey* Slang; the Slang of the *prize ring*; the Slang of *servitude*, or *flunkeydom*; vulgar, or *street* Slang; the Slang of *softened oaths*; and the

Slang of *intoxication*. I shall only examine the last two. If society, as has been remarked, is a sham, from the vulgar foundation of commonalty to the crowning summit of royalty, especially do we perceive the justness of the remark in the Slang makeshifts for oaths, and sham exclamations for passion and temper. These apologies for feeling are a disgrace to our vernacular, although it is some satisfaction to know that they serve the purpose of reducing the stock of national profanity. "YOU BE BLOWED," or "I'll BE BLOWED IF," &c., is an exclamation often heard in the streets. BLAZES, or "like BLAZES," came probably from the army. BLAST, too, although in general vulgar use, may have had a like origin; so may the phrase, "I wish I may be SHOT, if," &c. BLOW ME TIGHT, is a very windy and common exclamation. The same may be said of STRIKE ME LUCKY, NEVER TRUST ME, and SO HELP ME DAVY; the latter derived from the truer old phrase, I'LL TAKE MY DAVY ON 'T—*i.e.*, my *affidavit*, DAVY being a corruption of that word. BY GOLLY, GOL DARN IT, and SO HELP ME BOB, are evident shams for profane oaths. NATION is but a softening of *damnation;* and OD, whether used in OD DRAT IT, or OD'S BLOOD, is but an apology for the name of the Deity. MARRY, a term of asseveration in common use, was originally, in Popish times, a mode of swearing by the *Virgin Mary;* q. d., *by Mary*.—So also MARROW-BONES, for the knees. I'll bring him down upon his *marrow-bones—i. e.*, I'll make him bend his knees as he does to the *Virgin Mary*. The Irish phrase, BAD SCRAN TO YER! is equivalent to wishing a person bad food. "I'm SNIGGERED if you will," and "I'm JIGGERED," are other stupid forms of mild swearing,—fearful of committing an open profanity, yet slily nibbling at the sin. Both DEUCE and DICKENS are vulgar old synonymes for the devil; and ZOUNDS is an abbreviation of GOD'S WOUNDS,—a very ancient Catholic oath.

In a casual survey of the territory of Slang, it is curious to observe how well represented are the familiar wants and failings of life. First, there is money, with one hundred and twenty Slang terms and synonymes; then comes drink, from small beer to champagne; and next, as a very natural sequence, *intoxication*, and fuddlement generally, with some half a hundred vulgar terms, graduating the scale of drunkenness from a slight inebriation, to the soaky state of gutterdom and stretcherdom,—I pray the reader to forgive the expressions. The Slang synonymes for mild intoxication are certainly very choice,—they are BEERY, BEMUSED, BOOZY, BOSKY, BUFFY, CORNED, FOGGY, FOU, FRESH, HAZY, ELEVATED, KISKY, LUSHY, MOONY, MUGGY, MUZZY, ON, SCREWED, STEWED, TIGHT, and WINEY. A higher or more intense state of beastliness is represented by the expressions, PODGY, BEARGERED, BLUED, CUT, PRIMED, LUMPY, PLOUGHED, MUDDLED, OBFUSCATED, SWIPEY, THREE SHEETS IN THE WIND, and TOP-HEAVY. But the climax of fuddlement is only obtained when the DISGUISED individual CAN'T SEE A HOLE IN A LADDER, or when he is all MOPS AND BROOMS, or OFF HIS NUT, or with his MAIN-BRACE WELL SPLICED, or with the SUN IN HIS EYES, or when he has LAPPED THE GUTTER, and got the GRAVEL RASH, or on the RAN-TAN, or on the RE-RAW, or when he is SEWED UP, or regularly SCAMMERED, —then, and not till then, is he entitled, in vulgar society, to the title of LUSHINGTON, or recommended to PUT IN THE PIN.

SLANG DERIVATIONS.

Slang derivations are generally indirect, turning upon metaphor and fanciful allusions, and other than direct etymological connexion. Such allusions and fancies are essentially temporary or local; they rapidly pass out of the public mind: the word remains, while the key to its origin is lost.

A DICTIONARY

OF

MODERN SLANG, CANT, AND VULGAR WORDS;

MANY WITH THEIR ETYMOLOGIES TRACED.

A 1, first-rate, the very best; "she's a prime girl, she is; she is A 1."— *Sam Slick.* The highest classification of ships at Lloyd's; common term in the United States; also at Liverpool and other English seaports. Another, even more intensive, form is, "first-class, letter A, No. 1.

ABIGAIL, a lady's-maid; derived from old comedies.

ABOUT RIGHT, "to do the thing ABOUT RIGHT," *i.e.*, to do it properly, soundly, correctly; "he guv it 'im ABOUT RIGHT," *i.e.*, he beat him severely.

ABRAM-MAN, a vagabond, such as were driven to beg about the country after the dissolution of the monasteries.—See BESS O' BEDLAM, *infra.* They are well described under the title of *Bedlam Beggars.*—*Shakspeare's K. Lear* ii. 3.

> "And these, what name or title e'er they bear,
> Jarkman, or Patrico, Cranke, or Clapper-dudgeon,
> Frater, or ABRAM-MAN; I speak to all
> That stand in fair election for the title
> Of king of beggars."—*Beaumont and Fletcher's Begg. Bush.* ii. 1.

It appears to have been the practice in former days to allow certain inmates of Bethlehem Hospital to have fixed days "to go begging;" hence impostors were said to "SHAM ABRAHAM" (the Abraham Ward in Bedlam having for its inmates these mendicant lunatics) when they pretended they were licensed beggars in behalf of the hospital.—See review of 2d edition of this work in *The Bookseller*, May 26, 1860.

ABANDANNAD, "an ABANDANNAD (abandoned) boy," is one who picks pockets of bandanna handkerchiefs.—*Westminster.*

E

ABRAM-SHAM, or SHAM-ABRAHAM, to feign sickness or distress. From ABRAM-MAN, the *ancient Cant* term for a begging impostor, or one who pretended to have been mad.—*Burton's Anatomy of Melancholy*, vol. i. p. 360. When Abraham Newland was Cashier of the Bank of England, and signed their notes, it was sung:—

"I have heard people say
That SHAM ABRAHAM you may,
But you mustn't SHAM ABRAHAM Newland."

ABSQUATULATE, to run away, or abscond; a hybrid *American* expression, from the Latin *ab*, and "squat," to settle.

ACRES, a coward.

ADAM'S ALE, water.—*English.* The *Scotch* term is ADAM'S WINE.

"ADMIRAL OF THE RED," a person whose very red face evinces a fondness for strong potations.

AFFYGRAPHY. "It fits to an AFFYGRAPHY," *i.e.*, to a nicety—to a T.

AFTERNOON FARMER, one who wastes his best opportunity, and drives off the large end of his work to the little end of his time.

AGGERAWATOR, (corruption of *Aggravator*,) the greasy lock of hair in vogue among costermongers and other street folk, worn twisted from the temple back towards the ear. They are also, from a supposed resemblance in form, termed NEWGATE KNOCKERS, which *see*.—*Sala's Gaslight*, &c.

AKEYBO, a slang phrase used in the following manner:—"He beats AKEYBO, and AKEYBO beat the devil."

ALBERTOPOLIS, a facetious appellation given by the Londoners to the Kensington Gore district.

ALDERMAN, a half-crown—possibly from its rotundity.

ALDERMAN, a turkey; "ALDERMAN IN CHAINS," a turkey hung with sausages.

ALL, equal, a term used in various games; thus, if both parties have scored six points each, the marker cries, "Six ALL!"

"ALL OF A HUGH!" all on one side; falling with a thump; the word HUGH being pronounced with a grunt.—*Suffolk*.

"ALL MY EYE," answer of astonishment to an improbable story; "ALL MY EYE AND BETTY MARTIN," a vulgar phrase with similar meaning, said to be the commencement of a Popish prayer to St Martin, "Oh, mihi, beate Martine," and fallen into discredit at the Reformation.

ALL OUT, "by far;"—"he was ALL OUT the best of the lot." *Old*—frequently used by *Burton* in his *Anatomy of Melancholy*.

ALL-OVERISH, neither sick nor well, the premonitory symptoms of illness.

ALL-ROUNDER, the fashionable shirt collar of the present time worn meeting in front.

ALL SERENE, an ejaculation of acquiescence.—*See* SERENE.

ALLS, tap-droppings, refuse spirits sold at a cheap rate in gin-palaces.—*See* LOVEAGE.

ALL THERE, in strict fashion, first-rate, "up to the mark;" a vulgar person would speak of a spruce, showily-dressed female as being ALL-THERE. An artisan would use the same phrase to express the capabilities of a skilful fellow-workman. Sometimes ALL THE WAY THERE. A modern song has—

> "Says little Tom Sayers, 'If the blues do not stay us,
> I'll lead him a dance for the Island;
> He shall see how we fight here in my land!
> We're ALL THE WAY THERE in the Island.
> Although he's so tall, he
> Shall yet feel my mawley
> Ere I give up the "Belt" of the Island.'"

"ALL TO PIECES," utterly, excessively; "he beat him ALL TO PIECES," *i.e.*, excelled or surpassed him exceedingly.

"ALL TO SMASH," or "GONE TO PIECES," bankrupt, or smashed to pieces.—*Somersetshire.*

ALMIGHTY DOLLAR, an *American* expression for the "power of money," first introduced by Washington Irving in 1837.*

AMINADAB, a quaker; from old comedies.

ANDREW MILLAR, a ship of war.—*Sea.*

AN'T, or AIN'T, the vulgar abbreviation of "am not," or "are not."

ANOINTED, used in a bad sense, to express eminent rascality in any one; "an ANOINTED scoundrel," as if he were the king of scoundrels.—*Irish.*

ANOINTING, a good beating.

ANONYMA, a lady of the *demi-monde*—or worse—a pretty horse-breaker.—*Times.* INCOGNITA was the term at first.

ANY HOW, in any way, or at any rate, bad: "he went on ANY HOW," *i.e.*, badly or indifferently.

ANTISCRIPTURAL, oaths, foul language.

"APARTMENTS TO LET," said of one who has a somewhat empty head.

APOSTLE'S GROVE, the London district known as St John's Wood.

APOSTLES, THE TWELVE, the last twelve names on the Poll, or "Ordinary Degree" List at the Cambridge Examinations, when it was arranged in order of merit, and not alphabetically, and in classes, as at present; so called from there being *post alios*, after the others.†—*See* POLL.

---

* The *idea* of this phrase, at any rate, is far older than the time of *Irving*. Ben Jonson's *Epistle to Elizabeth, Countess of Rutland,* commences thus:—

> "Whilst that for which all virtue now is sold,
> And almost every vice, *almightie gold.*"

† The last of all was called ST PAUL, (or Saint Poll,) as being the least of the apostles, and "not meet to be called an apostle," (*see* 1 Cor. xv. 9.) As in the "Honour" list, (*see* Gulf,) students who had failed only slightly in one or more subjects were occasionally allowed their degrees, and these were termed ELEGANT EXTRACTS.—*Camb. Univ. Slang.*

APPLE-PIE BED, a trick played at schools on new comers, or on any boy disliked by the rest. One of the sheets is removed, and the other is doubled in the middle, so that both edges are brought to the top, and look as if both sheets were there; but the unhappy occupant is prevented getting more than half way down, and his night's rest is in all probability spoiled.

APPLE-CART, "down with his APPLE-CART," *i.e.*, upset him.—*North.*

APPLE-PIE ORDER, in exact or very nice order.

ARTICLE, derisive term for a weak specimen of humanity.

ARY, corruption of "ever a," "e'er a;" ARY ONE, *i.e.*, e'er a one.

"AS YOU WERE," a military phrase in drilling; used in a Slang sense to one who is going on too fast in his assertions, and wants recalling to moderation.

ATOMY, a diminutive or deformed person. From ANATOMY.

ATTACK, to carve, or commence operations on; "ATTACK that beef, and oblige!"

ATTIC, the head; "queer in the ATTIC," intoxicated.—*Pugilistic.*

AUNT SALLY, a favourite game on race-courses and at fairs, consisting of a wooden head mounted on a stick, firmly fixed in the ground; in the nose of which, or rather in that part of the facial arrangement of AUNT SALLY which is generally considered incomplete without a nasal projection, a tobacco pipe is inserted. The fun consists in standing at a distance and demolishing AUNT SALLY'S pipe-clay projection with short bludgeons, very similar to the half of a broom-handle. The Duke of Beaufort is a "crack hand" at smashing pipe noses; and his performances a few years ago on Brighton race-course are yet fresh in remembrance. Aunt Sally proprietors are indebted to the noble duke for having brought the game into fashionable notoriety.

AVAST, a sailor's phrase for stop, shut up, go away,—apparently connected with the old *Cant*, BYNGE A WASTE; or from the *Italian*, BASTA, hold! enough.

AWAKE, or FLY, knowing, thoroughly understanding, not ignorant of. The phrase WIDE AWAKE carries the same meaning in ordinary conversation.

AWFUL, (or, with the Cockneys, ORFUL,) a senseless expletive, used to intensify a description of anything good or bad; "what an AWFUL fine woman!" *i.e.*, how handsome, or showy!

AREA-SNEAK, a boy thief who commits depredations upon kitchens and cellars.—*See* CROW.

ARGOT, a term used amongst London thieves for their secret or Cant language. *French* term for Slang.

AUTUMN, a Slang term for an execution by hanging. When the drop was introduced instead of the old gallows, cart, and ladder, and a man was for the first time "turned-off" in the present fashion, the mob were so pleased with the invention that they spoke of the operation as at AUTUMN, or the FALL OF THE LEAF, (*sc.*, the drop,) with the man about to be hanged.

AXE, to ask.—*Saxon*, ACSIAN.

AYAH, a lady's-maid or nurse.—*Anglo-Indian.*

BABES, the lowest order of KNOCK-OUTS, (which *see*,) who are prevailed upon not to give opposing biddings at auctions, in consideration of their receiving a small sum, (from one shilling to half-a-crown,) and a certain quantity of beer. BABES exist in Baltimore, U.S., where they are known as blackguards and "rowdies."

BACK, to support, or "lay" money on a particular horse in a race. The term is very generally used in the "ring," as well as on the "turf."

BACK OUT, to retreat from a difficulty; the reverse of GO AHEAD. Metaphor borrowed from the stables.

"BACK SLANG IT," to go out the back way.

BACK-HANDER, a blow on the face with the back of the hand, a back-handed tip. Also a drink out of turn, as when a greedy person delays the decanter to get a second glass.

BACKER, one who bets, or "lays" his money, on a favourite horse; a one-sided supporter in a contest. *Sporting*, and very general.

BACON, "to save one's BACON," to escape.

BAD, "to go to the BAD," to deteriorate in character, be ruined. *Virgil* has an exactly similar phrase, *in pejus ruere*.

BADMINTON, blood,—properly a peculiar kind of claret-cup invented at the Duke of Beaufort's seat of that name. BADMINTON proper is made of claret, sugar, spice, and cucumber peel iced, and is used by the Prize Ring as a synonyme for *blood* out of compliment to a well-known patron.

BAFFATY, calico. Used in the drapery trade.

BAGMAN, a commercial traveller.

BAGS, trousers. Trousers of an extensive pattern, or exaggerated fashionable cut, have lately been termed HOWLING-BAGS, but only when the style has been very "*loud*." The word is probably an abbreviation for b-mbags. "To have the BAGS off," to be of age and one's own master, to have plenty of money. "BAGS OF MYSTERY" is another phrase in frequent use.

BAKE, "he's only HALF BAKED," *i.e.*, soft, inexperienced.

BAKER'S DOZEN. This consists of thirteen or fourteen; the surplus number, called the *inbread*, being thrown in for fear of incurring the penalty for short weight. To "give a man a BAKER'S DOZEN," in a Slang sense, means to give him an extra good beating or pummelling.

BALAAM, printers' Slang for matter kept in type about monstrous productions of nature, &c., to fill up spaces in newspapers that would otherwise be vacant. The term BALAAM-BOX has long been used in *Blackwood* as the name of the depository for rejected articles. Evidently from Numbers xxii. 30, and denoting the "speech of an ass," or any story difficult of deglutition, not contained in Scripture.

BACK JUMP, a back window.—*Prison term.*

BALD-FACED STAG, a term of derision applied to a person with a bald head. Also, still more coarsely, "BLADDER-OF-LARD." Another name is "Marquis of Granby," which *see*.

BALE UP! the Australian bushrangers' "Stand and deliver!" now imported into the streets of London as a synonyme for "Stop!"

BALLAMBANGJANG. The Straits of BALLAMBANGJANG, though unnoticed by geographers, are frequently mentioned in sailors' yarns as being so narrow, and the rocks on each side so crowded with trees inhabited by monkeys, that the ship's yards cannot be squared, on account of the monkeys' tails getting jammed into, and choking up, the brace blocks.—*Sea*.

BALMY, insane.

BALMY, sleep; "have a dose of the BALMY"—go to sleep.

BAMBOOING, a beating—from the instrument employed.

BAMBOOZLE, to deceive, make fun of, or cheat a person; abbreviated to BAM, which is used also as a substantive—a deception, a sham, a "sell." *Swift* says BAMBOOZLE was invented by a nobleman in the reign of Charles II.; but this I conceive to be an error. The probability is that a nobleman first *used* it in polite society. The term is derived from the *Gipsies*.

BANDED, hungry.

BANDY, or CRIPPLE, a sixpence, so called from this coin being generally bent or crooked; old term for flimsy or bad cloth, temp. Q. Elizabeth.

BANG, to excel or surpass; BANGING, great or thumping.

BANG-UP, first-rate.

BANK, to put in a place of safety. "BANK the rag," *i.e.*, secure the note.

BANTLING, a child; stated in *Bacchus and Venus*, 1737, and by *Grose*, to be a Cant term.

BANYAN-DAY, a day on which no meat is served out for rations; probably derived from the BANIANS, a Hindoo caste, who abstain from animal food.—*Sea*.

BAR, or BARRING, excepting; in common use in the betting-ring; "I bet against the field BAR two." The Irish use of BARRIN' is very similar.

BARBER'S CAT, said of a half-starved, sickly-looking person, in connexion with an expression too coarse to print.

BARKER, a man employed to cry at the doors of "gaffs," shows, and puffing shops, to entice people inside.

BARNACLES, a pair of spectacles; corruption of BINOCULI. Derived by some from the barnacle,* a kind of conical shell adhering to ships' bottoms. Hence a marine term for goggles, which they resemble in shape, and for which they are used by sailors in case of ophthalmic derangement.

* *Lepas Anatifera.*

BALL, prison allowance, viz., six ounces of meat.

BARKING-IRON, a pistol. Term used by footpads.

BARNEY, a LARK, SPREE, rough enjoyment; "get up a BARNEY," to have a "lark." Also, a deception, a "CROSS."

BARNEY, a mob, a crowd.

BARN-STORMERS, theatrical performers who travel the country and act in barns, selecting short and frantic pieces to suit the rustic taste.—*Theatrical.*

BARRIKIN, jargon, speech, or discourse; "we can't tumble to that BARRIKIN," *i.e.*, we don't understand what he says. *Miege* calls it "a sort of stuff;" *Old French*, BARACAN.

BASH, to beat, thrash; "BASHING a donna," beating a woman; originally a provincial word, and chiefly applied to the practice of beating walnut trees, when in bud, with long poles, to increase their productiveness. Hence the West country proverb—

> "A woman, a whelp, and a walnut tree,
> The more you BASH 'em, the better they be."

BASTE, to beat, properly to pour gravy on roasting meat to keep it from burning. Also, a sewing term.

BASTILE, the workhouse. General name for "the Union" amongst the lower orders of the *North*. Formerly used to denote a prison, or "lock-up;" but its abbreviated form, STEEL, is now the favourite expression with the lower orders.

BAT, "on his own BAT," on his own account.—*See* HOOK.

BATS, a pair of bad boots.

BATTER, wear and tear; "can't stand the BATTER," *i.e.*, not equal to the task; "on the BATTER," literally "on the streets," or given up to roistering and debauchery.

BATTLES, the students' term at Oxford for rations. At Cambridge, COMMONS. *Qy.* BATTELLS.

BATTY, wages, perquisites. Derived from BATTA, an extra pay given to soldiers while serving in *India.*

BATTY-FANG, to beat; BATTY-FANGING, a beating; also BATTER-FANG. Used metaphorically as early as 1630.

> "So *batter-fanged* and belabour'd with tongue mettle, that he was weary of his life."—*Taylor's Works,* 1630.

BAZAAR, a shop or counter. *Gipsy* and *Hindoo*, a market.

BEACH-COMBER, a fellow who prowls about the sea-shore to plunder wrecks, and pick up waifs and strays of any kind.—*Sea.*

BEAK, a magistrate, judge, or policeman; "to baffle the BEAK," to get remanded. *Ancient Cant,* BECK. *Saxon,* BEAG, a necklace or gold collar—emblem of authority. Sir John Fielding was called the BLIND-BEAK in the last century. Query, if connected with the Italian BECCO, which means a (bird's) *beak*, and also a *blockhead ?* See, however, under WALKER! for another derivation.

BEAKER-HUNTER, a stealer of poultry.

BEANS, money; "a haddock of BEANS," a purse of money; formerly, BEAN meant a guinea; *French*, BIENS, property; also used as a synonyme for BRICK, which *see*.

BEAR, one who contracts to deliver or sell a certain quantity of stock in the public funds on a forthcoming day at a stated place, but who does not possess it, trusting to a decline in public securities to enable him to fulfil the agreement and realise a profit.—*See* BULL. Both words are Slang terms on the Stock Exchange, and are frequently used in the business columns of newspapers.

> "He who sells that of which he is not possessed is proverbially said to sell the skin before he has caught the BEAR. It was the practice of stock-jobbers, in the year 1720, to enter into a contract for transferring South Sea stock at a future time for a certain price; but he who contracted to sell had frequently no stock to transfer, nor did he who bought intend to receive any in consequence of his bargain; the seller was, therefore, called a BEAR, in allusion to the proverb, and the buyer a BULL, perhaps only as a similar distinction. The contract was merely a wager, to be determined by the rise or fall of stock; if it rose, the seller paid the difference to the buyer, proportioned to the sum determined by the same computation to the seller."—*Dr Warton on Pope*.

BEARGERED, to be drunk.

BEAT, the allotted range traversed by a policeman on duty.

BEAT, or BEAT-HOLLOW, to surpass or excel; also "BEAT into fits."

BEAT, "DEAD-BEAT," wholly worn out, done for.

BEATER-CASES, boots. *Nearly obsolete*.

BEAVER, old street term for a hat; GOSS is the modern word, BEAVER, except in the country, having fallen into disuse.

BE-BLOWED, a windy exclamation equivalent to an oath.—*See* BLOW-ME.

BED-POST, "in the twinkling of a BED-POST," in a moment, or very quickly. Originally BED-STAFF, a stick placed vertically in the frame of a bed to keep the bedding in its place.—*Shadwell's Virtuoso*, 1676, act i., scene 1. This was used sometimes as a defensive weapon.

BED-FAGOT, a contemptuous term for a bed-fellow.—*See* FAGOT.

BEDFORDSHIRE, bed; when a person says, "I'm off for BEDFORDSHIRE," he means that he is going to bed.

BEE, "to have a BEE in one's bonnet," *i.e.*, to be not exactly sane.

BEEBEE, a lady.—*Anglo-Indian*.

BEEF-HEADED, stupid.

BEEFY, unduly thick or fat, commonly said of women's ancles.—*See* MULLINGAR.

BEERY, intoxicated, or fuddled with beer.

BEESWAX, poor soft cheese.

BEETLE-CRUSHER, or SQUASHER, a large flat foot. The expression was first used in one of Mr Leech's caricatures in *Punch*.

BEGGAR'S VELVET, downy particles which accumulate under furniture from the negligence of house-maids. Otherwise called SLUT'S-WOOL.

BELCHER, a handkerchief.—*See* under BILLY for description.

BELL, a song. Tramps' term.

BELLOWS, the lungs. BELLOWSER, a blow in the "wind," or pit of the stomach; taking one's breath away.

"BELLOWS TO MEND," said of a person out of breath.

BELLY-TIMBER, food, or "grub."

BELLY-VENGEANCE, small sour beer, apt to cause gastralgia.

BEMUSE, to fuddle one's-self with drink, "BEMUSING himself with beer," &c.—*Sala's Gaslight and Daylight*, p. 308.

BEN, a benefit.—*Theatrical*.

BEND, "that's above my BEND," *i.e.*, beyond my power, too expensive, or too difficult for me to perform.

BENDER, a sixpence,—from its liability to bend.

BENDER, the arm; "over the BENDER," synonymous with "over the left."—*See* OVER. Also an ironical exclamation similar to WALKER!

BENDIGO, a rough fur cap worn in the midland counties, named after a noted pugilist of that name.

BENE, good.—*Ancient Cant;* BENAR was the comparative.—*See* BONE. Latin.

BENEDICT, a married man.

BENJAMIN, a coat. Formerly termed a JOSEPH, in allusion, perhaps, to Joseph's coat of many colours.—*See* UPPER-BENJAMIN.

BEN JOLTRAM, brown bread and skimmed milk; a Norfolk term for a ploughboy's breakfast.

BENJY, a waistcoat,—the diminutive of BENJAMIN.

BEONG, a shilling.—*See* SALTEE.—*Lingua Franca*.

BESS.—*See* BROWN-BESS.

BESS-O'-BEDLAM, a lunatic vagrant.—*Norfolk*.

BEST, to get the better or "best" of a man in any way—not necessarily to cheat—to have the best of a bargain. BESTED, taken in, or defrauded. BESTER, a low betting cheat.

BETTER, more; "how far is it to town?" "Oh, BETTER 'n a mile."—*Saxon* and *Old English*, now a vulgarism.

BETTING ROUND. *See* BOOK, and BOOK-MAKING.

B. FLATS, bugs.—*Compare* F. SHARPS.

BIBLE-CARRIER, a person who sells songs without singing them.—*Seven Dials*.

BIG, "to look BIG," to assume an inflated address, or manner; "to talk BIG," *i.e.*, boastingly, or with an "extensive" air.

"BIG-BIRD, TO GET THE," *i.e.*, to be hissed, as actors occasionally are by the "gods."—*Theat. Slang*.

BELLOWSED, or LAGGED, transported.

BEN CULL, a friend, or "pal."—*Millbank Penitentiary*.

BETTY, a skeleton key, or picklock.—*Old Prison Cant*.

BIG-HOUSE, the work-house,—a phrase used by the very poor.

BIG-WIG, a person in authority or office.

BILBO, a sword; abbrev. of "BILBOA blade." Spanish swords were anciently very celebrated, especially those of Toledo, Bilboa, &c.

BILK, a cheat, or a swindler. Formerly in general use, now confined to the streets, where it is very common. *Gothic*, BILAICAN.

BILK, to defraud, or obtain goods, &c., without paying for them; "to BILK the schoolmaster," to get information or experience without paying for it.

BILLINGSGATE, (when applied to speech,) foul and coarse language. Not many years since, one of the London notorieties was to hear the fishwomen at Billingsgate abuse each other. The anecdote of Dr Johnson and the Billingsgate virago is well known.

BILLY, a silk pocket-handkerchief.—*Scotch.*—*See* WIPE.

⁎ A list of the Slang terms descriptive of the various patterns of handkerchiefs, pocket and neck, is here subjoined:—

> BELCHER, darkish blue ground, large round white spots, with a spot in the centre of darker blue than the ground. This was adopted by Jim Belcher, the pugilist, and soon became popular amongst "the fancy."
> BIRD'S-EYE WIPE, same as preceding.
> BLOOD-RED FANCY, red.
> BLUE BILLY, blue ground with white spots.
> CREAM FANCY, any pattern on a white ground.
> GREEN KING'S MAN, any pattern on a green ground.
> RANDAL'S MAN, green, with white spots; named after Jack Randal, pugilist.
> WATER'S MAN, sky coloured.
> YELLOW FANCY, yellow, with white spots.
> YELLOW MAN, all yellow.

BILLY-BARLOW, a street clown; sometimes termed a JIM CROW, or SALTIMBANCO,—so called from the hero of a Slang song.—*Bulwer's Paul Clifford.*—Billy was a real person, semi-idiotic, and, though in dirt and rags, fancied himself a swell of the first water. Occasionally he came out with real witticisms. He was a well-known street character about the east end of London, and died in Whitechapel Workhouse.—(P.)

BILLY-COCK, a hat of the Jim Crow or "wide-awake" description, principally worn by carters.

BINGY, a term largely used in the butter trade to denote bad ropy butter; nearly equivalent to VINNIED.

BINGO, brandy.—*Bulwer's Paul Clifford.*

BIRD-CAGE, a four-wheeled cab.

BILLY, a policeman's staff.

BILLY, stolen metal of any kind.

BILLY-HUNTING, buying old metal.—*See* BILLY-FENCER.

BILLY-FENCER, a marine-store dealer.

BIT, fourpence; in America 12½ cents are called a BIT, and a defaced 20 cent piece is termed a LONG BIT. A BIT is the smallest coin in Jamaica, equal to 6d.

BIT, money. Charles Bannister, the witty singer and actor, one day meeting a Bow-Street runner with a man in custody, asked what the prisoner had done; and being told that he had stolen a bridle, and had been detected in the act of selling it, said, "Ah! then, he wanted to touch the BIT."

BITCH, tea; "a BITCH party," a tea-drinking.—*Oxford.*

BITE, a cheat; "a Yorkshire BITE," a cheating fellow from that county.—*North;* also *old Slang*—used by *Pope.* Swift says it originated with a nobleman in his day.

BITE, to cheat; "to be BITTEN," to be taken in or imposed upon. Originally a Gipsy term.*—*See Bacchus and Venus.*

BITTERS, "to do BITTERS," to drink beer.—*Oxford.*

BITTOCK, a distance of very undecided length. If a north countryman be asked the distance to a place, he will most probably reply, "a mile and a BITTOCK;" and the latter may be considered any distance from one hundred yards to ten miles!

B. K. S. Military officers in *mufti,* when out on a spree, and not wishing their profession to be known, speak of their barracks as the B. K. S.

BIVVY, or GATTER, beer; "shant of BIVVY," a pot or quart of beer. In Suffolk, the afternoon refreshment of reapers is called BEVER. It is also an old English term.

"He is none of those same ordinary eaters, that will devour three breakfasts, and as many dinners, without any prejudice to their BEVERS, drinkings, or suppers."—*Beaumont and Fletcher's Woman Hater,* i. 3.

Both words are probably from the *Italian,* BEVERE, BERE. *Latin,* BIBERE. *English,* BEVERAGE.

"BLACK AND WHITE," handwriting, or print.

BLACK-A-VISED, having a very dark complexion.

BLACKBIRD-CATCHING, *sea* Slang for the slave-trade.

BLACK DIAMONDS, coals; talented persons of dingy or unpolished exterior; rough jewels.

BLACK-LEG, a rascal, swindler, or card cheat. The derivation of this term was solemnly argued before the full court of Queen's Bench, upon a motion for a new trial for libel, but was not decided by the learned tribunal. Probably it is from the custom of sporting and turf men wearing black *top-boots.* Hence BLACK-LEG came to be the phrase for a professional sporting man.

---

* CROSS-BITER, for a cheat, continually occurs in writers of the sixteenth century. N. Bailey has CROSS-BITE, a disappointment, probably the primary sense; and BITE is very probably a contraction of this.—*See Nares's Glossary,* s. v.

BIT, a purse, or any sum of money.—*Prison Cant.*

BIT-FAKER, or TURNER OUT, a coiner of bad money.

BLACKBERRY-SWAGGER, a person who hawks tapes, boot-laces, &c.

BLACK-SHEEP, a "bad lot," "*mauvais sujet;*" also a workman who refuses to join in a strike.

BLACK-STRAP, port wine.

BLACKGUARD, a low, or dirty fellow.

> "A Cant word amongst the vulgar, by which is implied a dirty fellow of the meanest kind, Dr Johnson says, and he cites only the modern authority of Swift. But the introduction of this word into our language belongs not to the vulgar, and is more than a century prior to the time of Swift. Mr Malone agrees with me in exhibiting the two first of the following examples:—The *black-guard* is evidently designed to imply a fit attendant on the devil. Mr Gifford, however, in his late edition of Ben Jonson's works, assigns an origin of the name different from what the old examples which I have cited seem to countenance. It has been formed, he says, from those 'mean and dirty dependants, in great houses, who were selected to carry coals to the kitchen, halls, &c. To this smutty regiment, who attended the progresses, and rode in the carts with the pots and kettles, which, with every other article of furniture, were then moved from palace to palace, the people, in derision, gave the name of *black guards;* a term since become sufficiently familiar, and never properly explained.'—*Ben Jonson*, i. 169, vii. 250."—*Todd's Johnson's Dictionary.*

BLADE, a man—in ancient times the term for a soldier; "knowing BLADE," a wide-awake, sharp, or cunning man.

BLADDER-OF-LARD, a coarse, satirical nickname for a bald-headed person.

BLARNEY, flattery, exaggeration. A castle in the county of Cork. It is said that whoever kisses a certain stool in this castle will be able to persuade others of whatever he or she pleases. The name of the castle is derived from BLADH, a blossom, *i.e.*, the flowery or fertile demesne. BLADH is also flattery; hence the connexion.—*Irish.*

BLAST, to curse. Originally a *Military* expression.

BLAZES, a low synonyme for the infernal regions. Also as applied to the brilliant habiliments of flunkeys.—*See Pickwick Papers.*

BLEST, a vow; "BLEST if I'll do it," *i.e.*, I am determined not to do it; euphemism for CURST.

BLEED, to victimise, or extract money from a person, to sponge on, to make suffer vindictively.

BLEW, or BLOW, to inform, or peach.

BLEWED, got rid of, disposed of, spent; "I BLEWED all my blunt last night," I spent all my money.

BLIND, a pretence, or make-believe.

BLIND-HALF-HUNDRED, the fiftieth regiment of foot; so called through their great sufferings from ophthalmia, when serving in Egypt.

BLIND-HOOKEY, a gambling game at cards; called also WILFUL MURDER.

BLIND-MAN'S-HOLIDAY, night, darkness.

BLINKER, a blackened eye.—*Norwich Slang.* BLINKERS, spectacles.

BLINK-FENCER, a person who sells spectacles.

BLOAK, or BLOKE, a man; "the BLOAK with a jasey," the man with a wig, *i.e.*, the Judge. *Gipsy* and *Hindoo*, LOKE. *North*, BLOACHER, any large animal.

BLOATER.—*See* MILD.

BLOCK, the head. "To BLOCK a hat," is to knock a man's hat down over his eyes.—*See* BONNET.

BLOCK ORNAMENTS, the small dark-coloured pieces of meat exposed on the cheap butchers' blocks or counters,—debateable points to all the sharp-visaged argumentative old women in low neighbourhoods.

BLOOD, a fast or high-mettled man. Nearly obsolete in the sense in which it was used in George the Fourth's time.

BLOOD-RED FANCY, a particular kind of handkerchief worn by pugilists and frequenters of prize fights.—*See* BILLY.

BLOODY-JEMMY, an uncooked sheep's head.—*See* SANGUINARY JAMES.

"BLOW A CLOUD," to smoke a cigar or pipe—a phrase in use two centuries ago.

BLOW ME, or BLOW ME TIGHT, a vow, a ridiculous and unmeaning ejaculation, inferring an appeal to the ejaculator; "I'm BLOWED if you will" is a common expression among the lower orders; "BLOW ME UP" was the term a century ago.—*See Parker's Adventures*, 1781.—The expression BE-BLOWED is now more general. Tom Hood used to tell a story:—

> "I was once asked to contribute to a new journal, not exactly gratuitously, but at a very small advance upon nothing—and avowedly because the work had been planned according to that estimate. However, I accepted the terms conditionally—that is to say, provided the principle could be properly carried out. Accordingly, I wrote to my butcher, baker, and other tradesmen, informing them that it was necessary, for the sake of cheap literature and the interest of the reading public, that they should furnish me with their several commodities at a very trifling per-centage above cost price. It will be sufficient to quote the answer of the butcher:—'Sir,—Respectin' your note, Cheap literater BE BLOWED! Butchers must live as well as other pepel—and if so be you or the readin' publick wants to have meat at prime cost, you must buy your own beastesses, and kill yourselves.—I remane, etc.,
> "'JOHN STOKES.'"

BLOW OUT, or TUCK IN, a feast.

BLOW UP, to make a noise, or scold; formerly a Cant expression used amongst thieves, now a recognised and respectable phrase. BLOWING UP, a jobation, a scolding.

BLOB, (from BLAB,) to talk. Beggars are of two kinds,—those who SCREEVE, (introduce themselves with a FAKEMENT, or false document,) and those who BLOB, or state their case in their own truly "unvarnished" language.

BLOW, to expose, or inform; "BLOW the gaff," to inform against a person.

> "'As for that,' says Will, 'I could tell it well enough, if I had it, but I must not be seen anywhere among my old acquaintances, for I am BLOWN, and they will all betray me.'"—*History of Colonel Jack*, 1723.

In *America*, "to BLOW" is Slang for to taunt.

BLOWER, a girl; a contemptuous name in opposition to JOMER.

BLOWEN, a showy or flaunting female. In *Wilts*, a BLOWEN is a blossom. *Germ.* BLUHEN, to bloom. In *German*, also, BUHLEN is to court, and BUHLE, a sweetheart.

"O du *blühende* Mädchen viel schöne Willkomm!"—*German Song.*

Possibly, however, the street term BLOWEN may mean one whose reputation has been BLOWN UPON, or damaged.

BLUBBER, to cry in a childish manner.—*Ancient.* A correspondent says, "probably from hanging the lip."

BLUE, said of talk that is smutty or indecent. When the conversation has assumed an entirely opposite character, it is then said to be BROWN, or Quakerish.

BLUE, a policeman; "disguised in BLUE and liquor."—*Boots at the Swan.* "THE GENTLEMAN IN BLUE AND WHITE"—*i.e.*, a policeman—was frequently called upon for a song at the pleasant camp-fire meetings on Wimbledon Common, during the volunteer encampment there in 1863.

BLUE, or BLEW, to pawn or pledge.

BLUE, confounded or surprised; "to look BLUE," to be astonished or disappointed.

BLUE BILLY, the handkerchief (blue ground with white spots) worn and used at prize fights. Before a "SET TO," it is common to take it from the neck and tie it round the leg as a garter, or round the waist, to "keep in the wind." Also, the refuse ammoniacal lime from gas factories.

BLUE-BLANKET, a rough overcoat made of coarse pilot cloth.

BLUE-BOTTLE, a policeman. It is singular that this well-known Slang term for a London constable should have been used by *Shakspeare.* In Part ii. of *King Henry IV.*, act v., scene 4, Doll Tearsheet calls the beadle, who is dragging her in, a "thin man in a censer, a BLUE-BOTTLE rogue."

BLUED, or BLEWED, tipsy, or drunk.

BLUE DEVILS, the apparitions supposed to be seen by habitual drunkards

BLUE MOON, an unlimited period.

BLUE MURDER, a desperate or alarming cry.—*French*, MORTBLEU.

BLUE RUIN, gin.

BLUES, a fit of despondency.—*See* BLUE DEVILS.

BLUFF, an excuse; more frequently used as an adjective, in the sense of rough, coarse, plain-spoken.

BLUFF, to turn aside, stop, or excuse.

BLUDGER, a low thief, who does not hesitate to use violence.—*Prison Cant.*

BLUE-PIGEON-FLYER, a journeyman plumber, glazier, or other workman, who, under the plea of repairing houses, strips off the lead, and makes away with it. Sometimes they get off with it by wrapping it round their bodies.

BLUEY, lead.—*German*, BLEI.

BLUNT, money. It has been said that this term is from the *French* BLOND, sandy or golden colour, and that a parallel may be found in BROWN or BROWNS, the slang for halfpence. Far-fetched as this etymology may be, it is doubtless correct, as it is borne out by the analogy of similar expressions. Cf. BLANQUILLO, a word used in Morocco and Southern Spain for a small Moorish coin. The "asper" ($\mathring{a}\sigma\pi\rho o\nu$) of Constantinople is called by the Turks AKCHEH, *i.e.*, "little white." *See* also WINN, (Harman,) above, p. 20.

BLURT OUT, to speak from impulse, and without reflection.—*Shakspeare.*

BOARD-OF-GREEN-CLOTH, a facetious synonyme for a card-table.

BOB, a shilling. Formerly BOBSTICK, which may have been the original. BOB-A-NOB, a shilling a-head. *Query*, if connected with Sir Rob. Walpole, as JOEY is with Joseph Hume?

BOB, "s' help my BOB," a street oath, equivalent to "so help me God." Other words are used in street language for a similarly evasive purpose, *i.e.*, CAT, GREENS, TATUR, &c., all equally profane and disgusting.

BOB IT, drop it, give it up.

BOBBERY, a squabble, tumult.—*Anglo-Indian.*

BOBBISH, very well, clever, spruce. "How are you doing?" "Oh! pretty BOBBISH."—*Old.*

BOBBY, a policeman. Both BOBBY and PEELER were nicknames given to the new police, in allusion to the Christian and surnames of the late *Sir Robert Peel*, who was the prime mover in effecting their introduction and improvement. The term BOBBY is, however, older than the *Saturday Reviewer* imagines. The official square-keeper, who is always armed with a cane to drive away idle and disorderly urchins, has, time out of mind, been called by the said urchins, BOBBY *the Beadle*. BOBBY is also, I may remark, an old English word for striking or hitting, a quality not unknown to policemen.—*See Halliwell's Dictionary.*

BODKIN, a small, or young person, sitting in the centre, between two others, in a carriage, is said "to ride bodkin." Amongst sporting men, applied to a person who takes his turn between the sheets on alternate nights, when the hotel has twice as many visitors as it can comfortably lodge.

BODY-SNATCHER, a bailiff or runner: SNATCH, the trick by which the bailiff captures the delinquent.

BODY-SNATCHER, a cat-stealer.

BOG-ORANGES, potatoes.

BOG, or BOG-HOUSE, a privy as distinguished from a water-closet.—*School term.* In the Inns of Court, I am informed, the term is very common.

BOG-TROTTER, satirical name for an Irishman.—*Miege.* Camden, however, speaking of the "debateable land" on the borders of England and Scotland, says, "both these dales breed notable BOG-TROTTERS."

BOLUS, an apothecary.

BOILERS, or BROMPTON BOILERS, the Slang name given to the New Kensington Museum and School of Art, in allusion to the peculiar form of the buildings, and the fact of their being mainly composed of, and covered with, sheet iron.—*See* PEPPER-BOXES.

BOLT, to run away, decamp, or abscond.

BOLT, to swallow without chewing.

BOMBAY DUCKS; in the East India Company's army the Bombay regiments were so designated. The name is now given to a dried fish, (*bummelow*,) much eaten by natives and Europeans in Western India.—*Anglo-Indian.*

BONE, to steal or appropriate what does not belong to you. BONED, seized apprehended.—*Old.*

BONE-PICKER, a footman.

BONES, TO RATTLE THE BONES, to play at dice; also called ST HUGH'S BONES.

BONES, "he made no BONES of it," he did not hesitate, *i.e.*, undertook and finished the work without difficulty, "found no BONES in the jelly."—*Ancient, vide Cotgrave.*

BONIFACE, landlord of a tavern or inn.

BONNET, a gambling cheat. "A man who sits at a gaming-table, and appears to be playing against the table; when a stranger enters, the BONNET generally wins."—*Times,* Nov. 17, 1856. Also, a pretence, or make-believe, a sham bidder at auctions, one who metaphorically blinds or BONNETS others.—*See* the following.

BONNET, to strike a man's cap or hat over his eyes.

BONNETER, one who induces another to gamble.

BOOBY-TRAP, a favourite amusement of boys at school. It consists in placing a pitcher of water on the top of a door set ajar for the purpose; the person whom they wish to drench is then enticed to pass through the door, and receives the pitcher and its contents on his unlucky head. Books are sometimes used.

BOOK, an arrangement of bets for and against, chronicled in a pocket-book made for that purpose; "making a BOOK upon it," a common phrase to denote the general arrangement of a person's bets on a race. "That does not suit my BOOK," *i.e.*, does not accord with my other arrangements. The principle of MAKING A BOOK, or BETTING ROUND, as it is sometimes termed, is to lay out a previously-determined sum against every horse in the race, or as many as possible; and should the BOOKMAKER GET ROUND, *i.e.*, succeed in laying against as many horses as will more than balance the odds laid, he is certain to be a winner.—*See* HEDGE.

BOOKED, caught, fixed, disposed of.—Term in *Book-keeping.*

BONE, good, excellent. ◊, the vagabond's hieroglyphic for BONE, or good, chalked by them on houses and street corners, as a hint to succeeding beggars. *French,* BON.

BONE-GRUBBER, a person who hunts dust-holes, gutters, and all likely spots for refuse bones, which he sells at the rag-shops, or to the bone-grinders.

BOOKS, a pack of cards. Term used by professional card-players.—*See* DEVIL'S BOOKS.

BOOK-HOLDER, a prompter.—*Theatrical.*

BOOM, "to top one's BOOM off," to be off, or start in a certain direction.—*Sea.*

BOOM-PASSENGER, a sailor's Slang term for a convict on board ship.—*Sea.*

BOOZE, drink. *Ancient Cant,* BOWSE. BOOZE, or SUCK-CASA, a public-house.

BOOZE, to drink, or more properly, to use another Slang term, to "lush," viz., to drink continually, until drunk, or nearly so. The term is an old one. *Harman,* in Queen Elizabeth's days, speaks of "BOUSING (or boozing) and belly-cheere." The term was good English in the fourteenth century, and came from the *Dutch,* BUYZEN, to tipple.

BOOZING-KEN, a beer-shop, a low public-house.—*Ancient.*

BOOZY, intoxicated or fuddled.

BORE, a troublesome friend or acquaintance, a nuisance, anything which wearies or annoys, so called from his unvaried and pertinacious pushing. The *Gradus ad Cantabrigiam* suggests the derivation of BORE from the *Greek* Βάροs, a burden. *Shakspeare* uses it, *King Henry VIII.* i. 1—

"——— at this instant
He BORES me with some trick."

Grose speaks of this word as being much in fashion about the year 1780-81, and states that it vanished of a sudden, without leaving a trace behind. Not so, burly Grose, the term is still in favour, and is as piquant and expressive as ever. Of the modern sense of the word BORE, the Prince Consort made an amusing and effective use in his masterly address to the British Association, at Aberdeen, September 14, 1859. He said, (as reported by the *Times:*)—

"I will not weary you by further examples, with which most of you are better acquainted than I am myself, but merely express my satisfaction that there should exist bodies of men who will bring the well-considered and understood wants of science before the public and the Government, who will even hand round the begging-box, and expose themselves to refusals and rebuffs, to which all beggars all liable, with the certainty besides of being considered great BORES. Please to recollect that this species of "bore" is a most useful animal, well adapted for the ends for which nature intended him. He alone, by constantly returning to the charge, and repeating the same truths and the same requests, succeeds in awakening attention to the cause which he advocates, and obtains that hearing which is granted him at last for self-protection, as the minor evil compared to his importunity, but which is requisite to make his cause understood."

BORE, (*Pugilistic,*) to press a man to the ropes of the ring by superior weight.

BOSH, nonsense, stupidity.—*Gipsy* and *Persian.* Also pure *Turkish,* BOSH LAKERDI, empty talk. A person, in the *Saturday Review,* has stated that BOSH is coeval with Morier's novel, *Hadji Baba,* which was published in 1828; but this is a blunder. The term was used in this country as early as 1760, and may be found in the *Student,* vol. ii., p. 217. A correspondent asserts that this colloquial expression is from the *German* BOSH, or BOSSCH, answering to our word "swipes."

BOSKY, inebriated.—*Household Words*, No. 183.

BOSS-EYED, a person with one eye, or rather with one eye injured.

BOTANY BAY, Worcester Coll. Oxon, so called from its remote situation.

BOTHER, (from the *Hibernicism* POTHER,) trouble, or annoyance. Grose has a singular derivation, BOTHER, or BOTH-EARED, from two persons talking at the same time, or to both ears. BLOTHER, an old word, signifying to chatter idly.—*See Halliwell.*

BOTHER, to teaze, to annoy.

BOTHERATION! trouble, annoyance; "BOTHERATION to it," "confound it," or "deuce take it"—an exclamation when irritated.

BOTTLE-HOLDER, an assistant to a "Second," (*Pugilistic ;*) an abettor; also, the bridegroom's man at a wedding. Slang term for Lord Palmerston, derived from a speech he made some years ago when foreign secretary, in which he described himself as acting the part of a judicious "BOTTLE-HOLDER" among the foreign powers. A lately-invented instrument to hold a bottle has thus received the name of a PALMERSTON.

BOTTOM, stamina in a horse or man. Power to stand fatigue; endurance to receive a good beating, and still fight on. "A fellow of PLUCK, sound WIND, and good BOTTOM is fit to fight anything."

BOTTS, the colic or bellyache.—*Stable Slang.* Burns uses it. *See Death and Dr Hornbook.*

BOTTY, conceited, swaggering.—*Stable.*

BOUNCE, impudence. A showy swindler.

BOUNCE, to boast, cheat, or bully.—*Old Cant.* Also to lie.

BOUNCEABLE, prone to bouncing or boasting.

BOUNCING-BEN, a learned man.

BOUNDER, a four-wheeled cab. *Lucus a non lucendo?* Also a University term for a TRAP.

"The man who drives has a well-appointed 'BOUNDER' of his own, to the splashboard of which is affixed a mysterious box, containing clamps and cords, straps and buckles, with a view to breakages and other accidents."
—*Hints to Freshman*, 1842.

BOW-CATCHER, or KISS-CURL, a small curl twisted on the cheeks or temples of young—and often old—girls, adhering to the face as if gummed or pasted. Evidently a corruption of BEAU-CATCHER. In old times this was called a *lovelock*, when it was the mark at which all the Puritan and ranting preachers levelled their pulpit pop-guns, loaded with sharp and virulent abuse. Hall and Prynne looked upon

---

BOSH, a fiddle. BOSH-FAKER, a violin-player. Terms only used by the lower orders.

BOS-KEN, a farm-house. *Ancient.—See* KEN.

BOSMAN, a farmer; "faking a BOSMAN on the main toby," robbing a farmer on the highway. Boss, a master.—*American.* Both terms from the Dutch, BOSCH-MAN, one who lives in the woods; otherwise *Boschjeman*, or *Bushman*.

BOUNCER, a person who steals whilst bargaining with a tradesman; a lie.

all women as strumpets who dared to let the hair depart from a straight line upon their cheeks. The French prettily term them *accroche-cœurs*, whilst in the United States they are plainly and unpleasantly called SPIT-CURLS. Bartlett says:—"SPIT-CURL, a detached lock of hair curled upon the temple; probably from having been at first plastered into shape by the saliva. It is now understood that the mucilage of quince seed is used by the ladies for this purpose."

> "You may prate of your lips, and your teeth of pearl,
> And your eyes so brightly flashing;
> My song shall be of that SALIVA CURL
> Which threatens my heart to smash in."
> —*Boston Transcript*, October 30, 1858.

When men twist the hair on each side of their faces into ropes they are sometimes called BELL ROPES, as being wherewith to *draw the belles*. Whether BELL-ROPES or BOW-CATCHERS, it is singular they should form part of the prisoner's paraphernalia, and that a jaunty little kiss-me-quick curl should, of all things in the world, ornament a jail dock; yet such was formerly the case. Hunt, "the accomplice after the fact and king's evidence against" the murderer of Weare, on his trial, we are informed by the *Athenæum*, appeared at the bar with a highly pomatumed love-lock sticking tight to his forehead. Young ladies, think of this!

BOWL OUT, to put out of the game, to remove out of one's way, to detect.—*Cricketing term*.

BOWLAS, round tarts made of sugar, apple, and bread, sold in the streets.

BOWLES, shoes.

BOX-HARRY, a term with bagmen or commercial travellers, implying dinner and tea at one meal; also dining with "Duke Humphrey," *i.e.*, going without.—*Lincolnshire*.

BOX-OF-MINUTES, a watch, or watchmaker's shop.

"BOX THE COMPASS," to repeat the thirty-two points of the compass either in succession or irregularly. The method used at sea to learn boys the points of the mariner's compass.—*Sea*.

BRADS, money. Properly a small kind of nails used by cobblers.—*Compare* HORSE NAILS.

BRAIN-PAN, the skull.

BRAIN-CANISTER, the head.—*Pugilistic*.

BRAMBLE-GELDER, a derisive appellation for an agriculturist.—*Suffolk*.

BRACE UP, to pawn stolen goods.

BRACELETS, handcuffs.

BRAD-FAKING, playing at cards. Probably from BROADS.

BRAGGADOCIO, three months' imprisonment as a reputed thief or old offender,—sometimes termed a DOSE, or a DOLLOP.—*Household Words*, vol. i., p. 579.

BRANDY PAWNEE, brandy and water.—*Anglo-Indian.*

BRAN-NEW quite new. Properly, *Brent*, BRAND, or *Fire-new, i.e.*, fresh from the anvil.

BRASS, money.

BRASS, impudence. In 1803 some artillery-men stationed at Norwich were directed to prove some brass ordnance belonging to the city. To the report delivered to the corporation was appended this note:— "*N.B.*—It is customary for the corporal to have the old metal when any of the pieces burst." *Answer.*—"The corporation is of opinion that the corporal does not want BRASS."

BRAZEN-FACED, impudent, shameless. *See* BRASS. Such a person is said "to have rubbed his face with a brass candlestick."

BRAZIL, a hard red wood; "HARD AS BRAZIL," a common expression. *Quarles* in his *Emblems* says:—

"Thou know'st my brittle temper's prone to break.
Are my bones BRAZIL or my flesh of oak?"

BREAD-BAGS, a nickname given in the army and navy to any one connected with the victualling department, as a purser, or purveyor in the Commissariat.

BREAD-BASKET, DUMPLING-DEPOT, VICTUALLING-OFFICE, &c., are terms given by the "*Fancy*" to the digestive organ.

BREAK-DOWN, a noisy dance, and violent enough to break the floor down; a jovial, social gathering, a FLARE UP; in Ireland, a wedding—(*Qy*. American?)

"BREAK ONE'S BACK," a figurative expression, implying bankruptcy, or the crippling of a person's means.

"A story is current of a fashionable author answering a late and rather violent knock at his door one evening. A coal-heaver wanted to know if the gentleman would like a cheap ton of coals; he was sorry for troubling him so late, but 'the party as had a-ordered the two ton and a-half couldn't be found,' although he had driven his 'waggon for six blessed hours up and down the neighbourhood. Five-and-twenty is the price, but yer shall have them for 20s.' Our author was not to be tempted, he had heard of the trick before; so bidding the man go away from his house, he shut the door. The man, however, lingered there, expatiating on the quality of his coals—'Acterly givin 'em away, and the gent won't have 'em,' said he, addressing the neighbourhood in a loud voice; and the last that was heard of him was his anything but sweet voice whistling through the key-hole, ' Will eighteen bob BREAK YER BACK?'"

BREAK SHINS, to borrow money.

BREAK UP, the conclusion of a performance of any kind—originally a school term.

BREAKY-LEG, a shilling.

BREAKY-LEG, strong drink; "he's been to Bungay fair, and BROKE BOTH HIS LEGS," *i.e.*, got drunk. In the ancient Egyptian language the determinative character in the hieroglyphic verb "to be drunk," has the significant form of the leg of a man being amputated.

BREECHED, OR TO HAVE THE BAGS OFF, to have plenty of money; "to be well BREECHED," to be in good circumstances.

BREECHES, "to wear the BREECHES," said of a wife who usurps the husband's prerogative.

BREEF, probably identical with BRIEF, q. v., a plan of cheating at cards; thus described in an old book of games of about 1720:—

"Take a pack of cards and open them, then take out all the honours . . . and cut a little from the edges of the rest all alike, so as to make the honours broader than the rest, so that when your adversary cuts to you, you are certain of an honour. When you cut to your adversary cut at the ends, and then it is a chance if you cut him an honour, because the cards at the ends are all of a length. Thus you may make breefs end-ways, as well as sideways."

BREEKS, breeches.—*Scotch*, now common.

BRICK, a "jolly good fellow;" "a regular BRICK," a staunch fellow.

"I bonneted Whewell when we gave the Rads their gruel,
And taught them to eschew all their addresses to the Queen.
If again they try it on, why to floor them I'll make one,
Spite of Peeler or of Don, like a BRICK and a *Bean*."
—*The Jolly Bachelors*, Cambridge, 1840.

Said to be derived from an expression of Aristotle's—τετράγωνος ἀνήρ. A recently current story informs us that Lillywhite, the cricketer, was originally a brickmaker, and that from him a "stumping bowl" acquired the name of a "regular BRICK."

BRIDGE, a cheating trick at cards, by which any particular card is cut by previously curving it by the pressure of the hand. Used in France as well as in England, and termed in the *Parisian Argot* FAIRE LE PONT.

BRIEF, a pawnbroker's duplicate. Derived from the following:—

BRIEFS, cards constructed on a cheating principle. *See* BRIDGE, CONCAVES and CONVEXES, LONGS and SHORTS, REFLECTORS, &c. From the *German*, BRIEFE, which Baron Heinecken says was the name given to the cards manufactured at Ulm. BRIEF is also the synonyme for a card in the German *Rothwalsch* dialect, and BRIEFEN to play at cards. "Item—beware of the Joners, (gamblers,) who practise Beseflery with the BRIEF, (cheating at cards,) who deal falsely and cut one for the other, cheat with Boglein and spies, pick one BRIEF from the ground, and another from a cupboard," &c.—*Liber Vagatorum*, ed. by Martin Luther, in 1529. English translation, by J. C. Hotten, 1860, p. 47. *See* BREEF.

BRIM, a violent irascible woman, as inflammable and unpleasant as brimstone, from which the word is contracted.

BRINEY, the sea.

BRITT, the street shortening for the Britannia Theatre.

BRISKET-BEATER, a Roman Catholic.

BROAD-COOPER, a person employed by brewers to negotiate with publicans.

BROADS, cards. BROADSMAN, a card-sharper.

"BROAD AND SHALLOW," an epithet applied to the so-called "Broad Church," in contradistinction to the "High" and "Low" Churches. *See* HIGH AND DRY.

BROAD-FENCER, card-seller at races.

BROSIER, a bankrupt.—*Cheshire.* BROSIER-MY-DAME, school term, implying a clearing of the housekeeper's larder of provisions, in revenge for stinginess.—*Eton.*

BROTHER-CHIP, fellow carpenter. Also, BROTHER-WHIP, a fellow coachman; and BROTHER-BLADE, of the same occupation or calling—originally a fellow-soldier.

BROWN, a halfpenny.—*See* BLUNT.

BROWN, "to do BROWN," to do well or completely, (in allusion to roasting;) "doing it BROWN," prolonging the frolic, or exceeding sober bounds; "DONE BROWN," taken in, deceived, or surprised.

BROWN BESS, the old Government regulation musket; a musket with a browned barrel; also BLACK BESS. A suggestion has been made that BESS may be from the *German* BUSCHE, or BOSCHE, a barrel.

BROWN SALVE! an exclamation of surprise at what is heard, and at the same time means, "I understand you."

BROWN-STUDY, a reverie. Very common even in educated society, but hardly admissible in writing, and therefore considered a vulgarism. It is derived, by a writer in *Notes and Queries*, from BROW STUDY, and he cites the old German BRAUN, or AUG-BRAUN, an eye-brow.—*Ben Jonson.*

BROWN TALK, conversation of an exceedingly proper character, Quakerish. Compare BLUE.

BROWN-TO, to understand, to comprehend.—*American.*

BRUISER, a fighting man, a pugilist.—*Pugilistic. Shakspeare* uses the word BRUISING in a similar sense.

BRUSH, a fox's tail, a house-painter.

BRUSH, or BRUSH-OFF, to run away, or move on.—*Old Cant.*

BUB, drink of any kind.—*See* GRUB. *Middleton,* the dramatist, mentions BUBBER, a great drinker.

BUB, a teat, woman's breast, plural BUBBIES; no doubt from BIBE. Also the preceding.

BUBBLE, to over-reach, deceive.—*Old.* (*Acta Regia,* ii. 248, 1726.)

BUBBLE-AND-SQUEAK, a dish composed of pieces of cold boiled meat and greens, and afterwards fried, which have thus first BUBBLED in the *pot*, and then SQUEAKED or hissed in the *pan*.

BUBBLE-COMPANY, a swindling association.

BROWN PAPERMEN, low gamblers.

BRUM, a counterfeit coin. *Nearly obsolete.* Corruption of *Brummagem*, (Bromwicham,) the ancient name of *Birmingham*, the great emporium for plated goods and imitation jewellery.

BUCK, a gay or smart man; also an unlicensed cabman.

BUCKHORSE, a smart blow or box on the ear; derived from the name of a celebrated "bruiser" of that name.

BUCKLE, to bend; "I can't BUCKLE to that," I don't understand it; to yield or give in to a person. *Shakspeare* uses the word in the latter sense, *Henry IV.*, i. 1; and *Halliwell* says that "the commentators do not supply another example." How strange that in our own streets the term should be used every day! Stop the first costermonger, and he will soon inform you of the various meanings of BUCKLE.—*See Notes and Queries*, vols. vii., viii., ix.

BUCKLE-BEGGAR, a COUPLE-BEGGAR, which *see*.

BUCKLEY, "Who struck BUCKLEY?" a common phrase used to irritate Irishmen.

BUCKLE-TO, to bend to one's work, to begin at once, and with great energy—from buckling on one's armour before a combat.

BUCKRA, a white man.—*West Indian Negro*.

BUCKSHISH, a present of money. Over all India, and the East generally, the natives lose no opportunity of asking for BUCKSHISH. The usage is such a complete nuisance, that the word is sometimes answered with a blow; this is termed BAMBOO BUCKSHISH.

BUDGE, to move, to inform, to SPLIT, or tell tales.

BUFF, the bare skin; "stripped to the BUFF."

BUFF, to swear to, or accuse; to SPLIT, or peach upon.—*Old* word for boasting, 1582.

BUFFER, a navy term for a boatswain's mate, part of whose duties is to administer the "cat."

BUFFER, a familiar expression for a jolly acquaintance, probably from the *French* BOUFFARD, a fool or clown; a "jolly old BUFFER," said of a good-humoured or liberal old man. In 1737, a BUFFER was a "rogue that killed good sound horses for the sake of their skins, by running a long wire into them."—*Bacchus and Venus*. The term was once applied to those who took false oaths for a consideration.

BUFFLE-HEAD, a stupid or obtuse person.—*Miege*. German, BUFFEL-HAUPT, buffalo-headed. Occurs in *Plautus' Comedies made English*, 1694.

BUFFS, the third regiment of foot in the British army.

BUFFY, intoxicated.—*Household Words*, No. 183.

BUGGY, a gig, or light chaise. Common term in America and in India.

BUG-WALK, a coarse term for a bed.

BUBBLEY-JOCK, a turkey, or silly boasting fellow; a prig.—*Scottish*. In the north of England the bird is called a BOBBLE-COCK. Both names no doubt from its cry.

BUDGE, strong drink; BUDGY, drunk; BUDGING-KEN, a public-house; "cove of the BUDGING-KEN," the landlord. Probably a corruption of BOOZE.—*North*.

BUILD, applied in fashionable Slang to the make or style of dress, &c.; "it's a tidy BUILD, who made it?"

BULGER, large; synonymous with BUSTER.

BULL, one who agrees to purchase stock at a future day, at a stated price, but who does not possess money to pay for it, trusting to a rise in public securities to render the transaction a profitable one. Should stocks fall, the BULL is then called upon to pay the difference. See BEAR, who is the opposite of a BULL, the former selling, the latter purchasing—the one operating for a *fall* or a *pull down*, whilst the other operates for a *rise* or *toss up*.

BULL, a crown-piece, formerly BULL'S EYE. See "WORK THE BULLS."

BULL-BEEF, a term of contempt; "as ugly as BULL-BEEF," "go to the billy-fencer and sell yourself for BULL-BEEF."

"BULL THE CASK," to pour hot water into an empty rum puncheon, and let it stand until it extracts the spirit from the wood. The result is drunk by sailors in default of something stronger.—*Sea*.

BULLFINCH, a hunting term for a large, thick, quickset hedge, difficult alike to "top" or burst through. *Query*, corruption of BOLEFENCE?

BULLY, a braggart; but in the language of the streets, a man of the most degraded morals, who protects fallen females, and lives off their miserable earnings.—Shakspeare, *Midsummer Night's Dream*, iii. 1 : iv. 2. This epithet is often applied in a commendable sense among the vulgar; thus—a good fellow or a good horse will be termed "a BULLY fellow," "a BULLY horse;" and "a BULLY woman" signifies a right, good, motherly old soul.

BULLYRAG, to abuse or scold vehemently; to swindle one out of money by intimidation and sheer abuse, as alleged in a late cab case, (*Evans v. Robinson*.)

BUM, the part on which we sit.—*Shakspeare*. BUMBAGS, trousers; *Gael.* and *Fr.*, BUN, a base or bottom; *Welsh*, BON, the lowest or worst part of anything.

BUM-BAILIFF, a sheriff's-officer,—a term, some say, derived from the proximity which this gentleman generally maintains to his victims. *Blackstone* says it is a corruption of "bound bailiff."

BUMBLE, to muffle. BUMBLE-FOOTED, club-footed.

BUMBLES, coverings for the eyes of horses apt to shy in harness.

BUMBLE, a beadle. Adopted from *Dickens's* character in *Oliver Twist*. This and "BUMBLEDOM" are now common.

BUFFER, a dog. Their skins were formerly in great request—hence the term BUFF meaning in old English *to skin*. It is still used in the ring, BUFFED meaning stripped to the skin. In Irish Cant, BUFFER is a *boxer*. The BUFFER of a railway carriage doubtless received its very appropriate name from the old pugilistic application of this term.

BUG-HUNTER, a low wretch who plunders drunken men.

BULL, term amongst prisoners for the meat served to them in jail.

BULKY, a constable.—*North*.

BUMBLE-PUPPY, a game played in public-houses on a large stone, placed in a slanting direction, on the lower end of which holes are excavated, and numbered like the holes in a bagatelle-table. The player rolls a stone ball from the higher end, and according to the number of the hole it falls into the game is counted. It is undoubtedly the very ancient game of *Troule-in-madame.*

BUM-BOAT, a shore boat which supplies ships with provisions, and serves as means of communication between the sailors and the shore.

BUM-CURTAIN, an old name for an academical gown when they were worn scant and short, especially those of the students of St John's College. —*Camb. Univ.*

BUMMAREE. This term is given to a class of speculating salesmen at Billingsgate market, not recognised as such by the trade, but who get a living by buying large quantities of fish from the salesmen and re-selling them to smaller buyers. The word has been used in the statutes and bye-laws of the market for upwards of 200 years. It has been variously derived. Some persons think it may be from the *French* BONNE MAREE, good fresh fish! "Marée signifie toute sorte de poisson de mer que n'est pas sale; bonne marée—*marée fraiche,* vendeur de marée."—*Dict. de l'Acad. Franc.* The BUMMAREES are accused of many trade tricks. One of them is to blow up cod-fish with a pipe until they look double their actual size. Of course when the fish come to table they are flabby, sunken, and half dwindled away. In Norwich, to BUMMAREE ONE is to run up a score at a public-house just open, and is equivalent to "running into debt with one." One of the advertisements issued by Hy. Robinson's "OFFICE," over against Threadneedle Street, was this:—

"Touching Advice from the OFFICE, you are desired to give and take notice as followeth :—

"OF Monies to be taken up, or delivered on *Botto-maria,* commonly called *Bomarie.*

"OF money to be put out or taken upon interest," &c.

—*The Publick Intelligencer,* numb. 17, 25th June 1660.

BUMPER, according to Johnson from "bump," but probably from *French* BON-PERE, the fixed toast in monastic life of old, now used for "full measure." A match at quoits, bowls, &c., may end in a "BUMPER game," if the play and score be all on one side.

BUMPTIOUS, arrogant, self-sufficient.

BUNCH-OF-FIVES, the hand, or fist.

BUNDLE, "to BUNDLE a person off," *i.e.,* to pack him off, send him flying.

BUNDLING, a custom in Wales, and now frequently in America, of men and women sleeping, where the divisions of the house will not permit of better or more decent accommodation, with all their clothes on.

BUNG, the landlord of a public-house.

BUNG, to give, pass, hand over, drink, or indeed to perform any action. BUNG UP, to close up.—*Pugilistic.* "BUNG over the rag," hand over the money.—*Old,* used by *Beaumont and Fletcher,* and *Shakspeare.* Also, to deceive one by a lie, to CRAM, which *see.*

BUNKER, beer.

BUNKUM, American importation, denoting false sentiments in speaking, pretended enthusiasm, &c. The expression arose from a speech made by a North Carolina Senator.

BUNTS, costermongers' perquisites; the money obtained by giving light weight, &c.; costermongers' goods sold by boys on commission. Probably a corruption of *bonus*, BONE, being the Slang for good. BUNCE, *Grose* gives as the Cant word for money.

BURDON'S HOTEL, Whitecross Street Prison, of which the Governor is or was a Mr Burdon. Every prison has a nickname of this kind, either from the name of the Governor, or from some local circumstance. The Queen's Bench has also an immense number of names—SPIKE PARK, &c.; and every Chief-Justice stands godfather to it.

BURKE, to kill, to murder, secretly and without noise, by means of strangulation. From Burke, the notorious Edinburgh murderer, who, with an accomplice named Hare, used to decoy people into the den he inhabited, kill them, and sell their bodies for dissection. The wretches having been apprehended and tried, Burke was executed, while Hare, having turned king's evidence, was released. Bishop was their London imitator. The term BURKE is now usually applied to any project that is quietly stopped or stifled—as "the question has been BURKED." A book suppressed before publication is said to be BURKED.

BURRAH, great; as BURRA SAIB, a great man; BURRA KHANAH, a great dinner.—*Anglo-Indian*.

BUS or BUSS, abbrevation of "omnibus," a public carriage. Also, a kiss, abbrev. of *Fr.* BAISER. A Mr Shillibeer started the first BUS in London. Why is Temple Bar like a lady's veil? Because it wants to be removed to make way for the BUSSES.

BUS, business (of which it is a contraction) or action, on the stage.—*Theatrical*.

BUST, or BURST, to tell tales, to SPLIT, to inform. BUSTING, informing against accomplices when in custody.

BUSTER, (BURSTER,) a small new loaf; "twopenny BUSTER," a twopenny loaf. "A pennorth o' BEES-WAX (cheese) and a penny BUSTER," a common snack at beershops.

BUSTER, an extra size; "what a BUSTER," *i.e.*, what a large one; "in for a BUSTER," determined on an extensive frolic or spree. *Scotch*, BUSTUOUS; *Icelandic*, BOSTRA.

BUSY-SACK, a carpet-bag.

BUTCHA, a Hindoo word in use among Englishmen for the young of any

---

BUNK, to decamp. "BUNK it!" *i.e.*, be off.

BURERK, a lady, a showily-dressed woman.

"BURY A MOLL," to run away from a mistress.

BUSKER, a man who sings or performs in a public-house.—*Scotch*.

BUSK, (or BUSKING,) to sell obscene songs and books at the bars and in the tap-rooms of public-houses. Sometimes implies selling any articles.

BUSTLE, (money;) "to draw the BUSTLE."

animal. In England we ask after the children; in India the health of the BUTCHAS is tenderly inquired for.

BUTCHER, the king in playing-cards.

BUTCHER'S MOURNING, a white hat with a black mourning hat-band. This meaning is given on the authority of Mr George Cruikshank.

BUTTER, or BATTER, praise or flattery. To BUTTER, to flatter, cajole. *Punch* defines flattery as " the milk of human kindness churned into BUTTER."

BUTTER-FINGERED, apt to let things fall.

BUTTON, a decoy, sham purchaser, &c. At any mock or sham auction seedy specimens may be seen. Probably from the connexion of *buttons* with *Brummagem*, which is often used as a synonyme for a sham. —See BONNET.

BUTTONER, a man who entices another to play. See BONNETER.

BUTTONS, a page,—from the rows of gilt buttons which adorn his jacket.

BUTTONS, " not to have all one's BUTTONS;" to be deficient in intellect.

BUTTY, a word used in the mining districts to denote a kind of overseer. (2.) Also used by the Royal Marines in the sense of comrade; a policeman's assistant, one of the staff in a *mêlée*.

BUZ, to share equally the last of a bottle of wine, when there is not enough for a full glass to each of the party.

BUZ, a well-known flash game, played as follows :—The chairman commences saying " one," the next on the left hand " two," the next " three," and so on to *seven*, when " BUZ " must be said. Every seven and multiple of 7, as 14, 17, 21, 27, 28, &c., must not be mentioned, but " BUZ " instead. Whoever breaks the rule pays a fine, which is thrown on the table, and the accumulation expended in drink for the company. See " SNOOKS and WALKER " for more complicated varieties of a similar game.

BY GEORGE, an exclamation similar to BY JOVE. The term is older than is frequently imagined—vide *Bacchus and Venus*, (p. 117,) 1737. " 'Fore (or by) GEORGE, I'd knock him down." A street compliment to Saint

BUZ, to pick pockets; BUZ-FAKING, robbing.

BUZ-MAN, an informer.

BUZZER, a pickpocket. *Grose* gives BUZ-COVE and BUZ-GLOAK; the latter is very ancient Cant.

BUZ-BLOAK, a pickpocket, who principally confines his attention to purses and loose cash. *Grose* gives BUZ-GLOAK, (or CLOAK?) an ancient Cant word. BUZ-NAPPER, a young pickpocket.

BUZ-NAPPER'S ACADEMY, a school in which young thieves are trained. Figures are dressed up, and experienced tutors stand in various difficult attitudes for the boys to practise upon. When clever enough they are sent on the streets. It is reported that a house of this nature is situated in a court near Hatton Garden. The system is well explained in *Dickens's Oliver Twist.* Also BUZ-KNACKER.

George, the patron Saint of England, or possibly to the House of Hanover.

BY GOLLY, an ejaculation, or oath; a compromise for "by God." BY GUM, is another oblique oath. In the United States, small boys are permitted by their guardians to say GOL DARN anything, but they are on no account allowed to commit the profanity of G—d d——g anything. An effective ejaculation and moral waste-pipe for interior passion or wrath is seen in the exclamation—BY THE EVER-LIVING JUMPING-MOSES—a harmless phrase, that from its length expends a considerable quantity of fiery anger.

CAB, in statutory language, "a hackney carriage drawn by one horse." Abbreviated from CABRIOLET, *French;* originally meaning "a light, low chaise." The wags of Paris playing upon the word (quasi *cabri au lait*) used to call a superior turn-out of the kind a *cabri au crême*. Our abbreviation, which certainly smacks of Slang, has been stamped with the authority of "GEORGE, *Ranger.*" *See* the notices affixed to the carriage entrances of St James's Park.

CAB, to stick together, to muck, or tumble up.—*Devonshire.*

CABBAGE, pieces of cloth said to be purloined by tailors.

CABBAGE, to pilfer or purloin. Termed by *Johnson* a "Cant word," but adopted by later lexicographers as a respectable term. Said to have been first used in the above sense by *Arbuthnot.*

CABBAGE-HEAD, a soft-headed person.

CABOBBLE, to confuse.—*Suffolk.*

CABBY, the driver of a cab.

CACKLING-COVE, an actor. Also called a MUMMERY-COVE. *Theat.*

CACKLE-TUB, a pulpit.

CAD, or CADGER, (from which it is shortened,) a mean or vulgar fellow; a beggar; one who would rather live on other people than work for himself; a man who tries to worm something out of another, either money or information. *Johnson* uses the word, and gives *huckster* as the meaning, but I never heard it used in this sense. Apparently from CAGER, or GAGER, the *old Cant* term for a man. The exclusives at the English Universities apply the term CAD to all non-members.

CAD, an omnibus conductor.

CADGE, to beg in an artful wheedling manner.—*North.* In Scotland to CADGE is to wander, to go astray. *See* under CODGER.

CADGING, begging with an eye to pilfering when an opportunity occurs.

CAG, to irritate, affront, anger.

CAG-MAG, bad food, scraps, odds and ends; or that which no one could relish. *Grose* gives CAGG MAGGS, old and tough Lincolnshire geese, sent to London to feast the poor cockneys. *Gael., French,* and *Welsh,* CAG, and MAGN. A correspondent at Trinity College, Dublin, considers this as originally a University Slang term for a *bad cook,* κακὸς μάγειρος. There is also a *Latin* word used by Pliny, MAGMA, denoting dregs or dross.

CAGE, a minor kind of prison.—*Shakspeare*, Part ii. *Henry IV.*, iv. 4.

CAKE, a "flat;" a soft or doughy person, a fool.

"CALL A GO," in street "patter," is to remove to another spot, or address the public in different vein. Also to give in, yield, at any game or business.

CALEB QUOTEM, a parish clerk; a jack of all trades.

CAL., an abbreviation for "Calcraft," the common hangman.

CALABOOSE, a prison.—*Sea* Slang, from the Spanish.

CALIFORNIA, money. Derivation very obvious.

CAMERONIANS, THE, the Twenty-sixth Regiment of Foot in the British Army.

CAMESA, shirt or chemise.—*Span.* See its abbreviated form, MISH, from the *ancient Cant*, COMMISSION. Probably reintroduced by the remains of De Lacy Evans's Spanish Legion on their return. See Somerville's account of the Span. Leg., for the curious facility with which the lower classes in England adopt foreign words as Slang and Cant terms. *Italian*, CAMICIA.

CAMISTER, a preacher, clergyman, or master.

CANARY, a sovereign. This is stated by a correspondent to be a Norwich term, that city being famous for its breed of those birds.

CANISTER, the head.—*Pugilistic.*

CANISTER-CAP, a hat.—*Pugilistic.*

CANNIBALS, the training boats for the Cambridge freshmen, *i.e.*, "CAN-NOT-PULLS." The term is applied both to boats and rowers.—*See* SLOGGERS.

CANNIKEN, a small can, similar to PANNIKIN.—*Shakspeare.*

CANT, a blow or toss; "a CANT over the kisser," a blow on the mouth.— *Kentish.*

CANTAB, a student at Cambridge.

"CANT OF TOGS," a gift of clothes.

CANTANKEROUS, litigious, bad-tempered. An American corruption probably of contentious. A reviewer, however, of this book in the *Bookseller* of May 26 derives it from the *Anglo-Norman* CONTEK,* litigation or strife. Another correspondent suggests "cankerous" as the origin.

CANVASSEENS, sailors' canvas trousers.

CAP, a false cover to a tossing coin.—*See* COVER-DOWN.

CAPER-MERCHANT, a dancing-master.

CAPERS, dancing, frolicking; "to cut CAPER-SAUCE," *i.e.*, to dance upon nothing—be hanged, very coarse.

CAPPER-CLAWING, female encounter, where caps are torn, and nails freely used. Sometimes it is pronounced CLAPPER-CLAW. The word occurs in *Shakspeare.*—*Troilus and Cressida*, v., 4.

* Bailey has CONTEKE, contention, as a Spenserian word, and the O.E., CONTEKORS, quarrelsome persons.

CAKEY-PANNUM-FENCER, a man who sells street pastry.

CARAVAN, a railway train.

CARAVANSERA, a railway station. A "TIP" for the late pugilistic contest between King and Heenan was given in these words:—"The SCRATCH must be TOED at sharp five. The CARAVAN starting at that hour from the CARAVANSERA," *i.e.*, London Bridge.

CARBOY, a general term in most parts of the world for a very large glass or earthenware bottle.

CARD, a character. "A queer CARD," *i.e.*, an odd fish.

CARDINAL, a lady's cloak. This, I am assured, is the *Seven Dials* Cant term for a lady's garment; but, curiously enough, the same name is given to the most fashionable patterns of the article by Regent Street drapers. A cloak with this name was in fashion in the year 1760. It received its title from its similarity in shape to one of the vestments of a cardinal.

CARPET, "upon the CARPET," any subject or matter that is uppermost for discussion or conversation. Frequently quoted as *sur le tapis*, but it does not seem to be a correct Parisian phrase. Also *servants' Slang*. When a domestic is summoned by the master or mistress to receive a warning or reprimand, he or she is said to be CARPETED. The corresponding term in commercial establishments is a WIGGING, which *see*.

CARNEY, *s.*, soft hypocritical language. Also, *v.*, to flatter, wheedle, or insinuate one's-self.—*Prov.*

CARNISH, meat, from the *Ital.* CARNE, flesh; a *Lingua Franca* importation; CARNISH-KEN, a thieves' eating-house; "cove of the CARNISH-KEN," the keeper thereof.—*North Country Cant.*

CAROON, five shillings. French, COURONNE; Gipsy COURNA; Spanish COURNA, half-a-crown.

CARROT. "Take a CARROT!" a vulgar insulting phrase.

CARROTS, the coarse and satirical term for red hair. An epigram gives an illustration of the use of this term:—

> "Why scorn red hair? The Greeks, we know,
> (I note it here in charity)
> Had taste in beauty, and with them
> The graces were all Χάριται!"

CARRIER-PIGEON, a swindler, one who formerly used to cheat lottery office keepers. *Nearly obsolete.*

"CARRY ME OUT!" a pretended exclamation of astonishment on hearing news too good to be true, or a story too marvellous to be believed. Sometimes varied by "Let me die," *i.e.*, I can't survive that. Profanely derived from the *Nunc dimittis*, (Luke xi. 29.) The Irish say, "CARRY ME OUT, and bury me decently."

CARRY-ON, to joke a person to excess, to "carry on" a "spree" too far; "how we CARRIED ON, to be sure!" *i.e.*, what fun we had. *Nautical term*—from carrying on sail.

CARRIWITCHET, a hoaxing, puzzling question, not admitting of a satisfactory answer, as—"How far is it from the first of July to London

Bridge?" "If a bushel of apples cost ten shillings, how long will it take for an oyster to eat its way through a barrel of soap?"

CART, a race-course. *Query*, if a corruption of, or connected with, the well-known "correct card" of Dorling, and other clerks of the racing course?

CARTS, a pair of shoes. In Norfolk the carapace of a crab is called a *crab cart;* hence CARTS would be synonymous with CRAB SHELLS, which *see.*

CART-WHEEL, a five-shilling piece.

CA-SA, a writ of CAPIAS AD SATISFACIENDAM.—*Legal Slang.*

CASA, or CASE, a house, respectable or otherwise. Probably from the Italian CASA.—*Old Cant.* The *Dutch* use the word KAST in a vulgar sense for a house, *i.e.*, MOTTEKAST, a brothel. CASE sometimes means a water-closet.

CASCADE, to vomit.

CASE. A few years ago the term CASE was applied generally to persons or things; "what a CASE he is," *i.e.*, what a curious person; "a rum CASE that," or, "you are a CASE," both synonymous with the phrase "odd fish," common half-a-century ago. This would seem to have been originally a "case" for the police-court; drunkenness, &c. Among young ladies at boarding-schools a CASE means a love affair.

CASK, fashionable Slang for a brougham, or other private carriage.—*Household Words*, No. 183.

CASSAM, cheese—not CAFFAN, which Egan, in his edition of *Grose*, has ridiculously inserted.—*Ancient Cant.* Latin, CASEUS. Gael. and *Irish* CAISE.

"CAST UP ONE'S ACCOUNTS," to vomit.—*Old.*

CASTOR, a hat. CASTOR was once the ancient word for the animal commonly known as the BEAVER; and, strange to add, BEAVER was the Slang for CASTOR, or hat, thirty years ago, before gossamer came into fashion.

CAT, to vomit like a cat. Perhaps from CATARACT; but *see* SHOOT THE CAT.

CAT—CAT O' NINE TAILS, a whip with that number of lashes used to punish refractory sailors.—*Sea.*

CAT-FACED, a vulgar and very common expression of contempt in the North of England.

CATAMARAN, a disagreeable old woman.—*Thackeray.*

CATARACT, a black satin scarf arranged for the display of jewellery, much in vogue among "commercial gents."

CATCH-'EM-ALIVE, a trap; also a small-tooth comb.

CASE, a bad crown-piece. HALF-A-CASE, a counterfeit half-crown. There are two sources, either of which may have contributed this Slang term. CASER is the Hebrew word for a crown; and silver coin is frequently counterfeited by coating or CASING pewter or iron imitations with silver.

CAT, a lady's muff; "to free a CAT," *i.e.*, steal a muff.

CATCHY, (similar formation to *touchy*,) inclined to take an undue advantage.

CATERWAULING, applied derisively to inharmonious singing; also love-making, from the noise of cats similarly engaged—in both cases.

CATEVER, a queer, or singular affair; anything poor, or very bad. From the *Lingua Franca*, and *Italian*, CATTIVO, bad. Variously spelled by the lower orders.—*See* KERTEVER.

CATGUT-SCRAPER, a fiddler.

CAT-LAP, a contemptuous expression for weak drink.

CAT'S-MEAT, a coarse term for the lungs—the "lights" or lungs of animals being usually sold to feed cats.

CAT'S-WATER, " old Tom," or Gin.

CATCH-PENNY, any temporary contrivance to obtain money from the public; penny shows, or cheap exhibitions.

CAT - IN - THE - PAN, a traitor, a turn-coat—derived by some from the *Greek*, καταπαν, altogether; or from *cake in pan*, a pan-cake, which is frequently turned from side to side.

CAUCUS, a private meeting held for the purpose of concerting measures, agreeing upon candidates for office before an election, &c. This is an American term, and a corruption of CAULKER'S MEETING, being derived from an association of the shipping interest at Boston, previous to the War of Independence, who were very active in getting up opposition to England.—*See Pickering's Vocabulary.*

CAULK, to take a surreptitious nap, sleep generally from the ordinary meaning of the term; stopping leaks, repairing damages, so as to come out as good as new.—*Sea term.*

CAULKER, a dram.—*Noctes Ambrosianæ.*

CAULKER, a too marvellous story, a lie. CHOKER has the same sense.

CAVAULTING, a vulgar phrase equivalent to "*horsing.*" The *Italian* CAVALLINO, signifies a rake or debauchee.—*Lingua Franca*, CAVOLTA.

CAVE, or CAVE IN, to submit, shut up.—*American.* Metaphor taken from the sinking of an abandoned mining shaft.

CA-VE! *Latin*, beware! used by school-boys to give warning of the approach of the master.—*See* NIX.

CAVE-OF-HARMONY, the cider cellars, or Evans's singing saloon.—*Thackeray.*

CHAFF, to gammon, joke, quiz, or praise ironically. CHAFF-bone, the jaw-bone.—*Yorkshire.* CHAFF, jesting. In *Anglo-Saxon*, CEAF is chaff; and CEAFL, bill, beak, or jaw. In the *Ancren Riwle*, A.D. 1221, CEAFLE is used in the sense of idle discourse.

CHAFFER, the mouth; " moisten your CHAFFER," *i.e.*, take something to drink.

" CAT AND KITTEN SNEAKING," stealing pint and quart pots from public-houses.

CHALK OUT, or CHALK DOWN, to mark out a line of conduct or action; to make a rule or order. Phrase derived from the *Workshop*.

CHALK UP, to credit, make entry in account books of indebtedness; "I can't pay you now, but you can CHALK IT UP," *i.e.*, charge me with the article in your day-book. From the old practice of chalking one's score for drink behind the bar doors of public-houses.

CHALKS, "to walk one's CHALKS," to move off, or run away. An ordeal for drunkenness used on board ship, to see whether the suspected person can walk on a chalked line without overstepping it on either side.—*See* the following.

CHALKS, degrees, marks; so called from being made by a piece of chalk; "to beat by long CHALKS," *i.e*, to be superior by many degrees.

CHANCERY, "to get a man's head into CHANCERY," *i.e.*, to get an opponent's head firmly under one's arm, where it can be pummelled with immense power, and without any possibility of immediate extrication.—*Pugilistic term.*

CHANGE, small money. The overplus returned after paying for a thing in a round sum. Hence a Slang expression used when a person receives a "settler" in the shape either of a repartee or a blow—"Take your CHANGE out of that!"

CHAP, a fellow, a boy; "a low CHAP," a low fellow—abbreviation of CHAPMAN, a huckster. Used by *Byron* in his *Critical Remarks*.

CHAPEL, a printer's assembly, held for the purpose of discussing differences between employer and workmen, trade regulations, &c. The term is scarcely Slang, but some COMPOS. ask its insertion in this work.

CHAPEL-OF-EASE. *French*, CABINET D'AISANCE, a house of office.

CHARLEY, a watchman, a beadle.

CHATTER-BASKET, common term for a prattling child amongst nurses.

CHATTER-BOX, an incessant talker or chatterer.

CHATTS, lice, or body vermin. *Prov.*, any small things of the same kind.

CHATTY, a filthy person, one whose clothes are not free from vermin; CHATTY DOSS, a lousy bed.

CHAUNTER-CULLS, a singular body of men who used to haunt certain well-known public-houses, and write satirical or libellous ballads on any person, or body of persons, for a consideration. 7s. 6d. was the usual fee, and in three hours the ballad might be heard in St Paul's Churchyard, or other public spot. As strange as it may appear, there are actually two men in London at the present day who gain their living in this way. Very recently they were singing before the establishment of a fashionable tailor in Regent Street; and not long since they were bawling their doggerel rhymes outside the mansion of a Norfolk M.P. in Belgravia.

CHARIOT-BUZZING, picking pockets in an omnibus.

CHARLEY-PITCHER, a low, cheating gambler.

CHATTRY-FEEDER, a spoon.—*Millbank Prison.*

CHATTS, dice,—formerly the gallows; a bunch of seals.

CHAUNTERS, those street sellers of ballads, last copies of verses, and other broadsheets, who sing or bawl the contents of their papers. They often term themselves PAPER WORKERS.—*See* HORSE-CHAUNTERS.

CHAUNT, to sing the contents of any paper in the streets. CANT, as applied to vulgar language, was, in all probability, derived from CHAUNT.—*See Introduction* for origin of the term.

CHAW, to chew; CHAW UP, to get the better of one, finish him up; CHAWED UP, utterly done for.

CHAW OVER, to repeat one's words with a view to ridicule; CHAW-BACON a rustic.

CHEAP, "doing it on the CHEAP," living economically, or keeping up a showy appearance with very little means.

CHEAP JACKS, or JOHNS, oratorical hucksters and patterers of hardware, &c., at fairs and races. They put an article up at a high price, and then cheapen it by degrees, indulging all the time in vollies of coarse wit, until it becomes to all appearance a bargain, and as such it is bought by one of the crowd. The popular idea is that the inverse method of auctioneering saves them paying for the auction licence.—*See* DUTCH AUCTION.

CHEE-CHEE, this word is used in a rather offensive manner to denote Eurasians, or children by an English father and native mother. It takes its origin in a very common expression of these half-caste females, "CHEE-CHEE," equivalent to our Oh, fie!—Nonsense!—For shame!—*Anglo-Indian*.

CHEEK, share or portion; "where's my CHEEK?" where is my allowance?

CHEEK, impudence, assurance; CHEEKY, saucy or forward.

CHEEK, to irritate by impudence, to accuse.—*Lincolnshire*.

"CHEEK BY JOWL," side by side—said often of persons in such close confabulation as almost to have their faces touch.

CHEEKS! a jeering and insulting exclamation, believed to be of *Scotch* origin.

CHEESE, anything good, first-rate in quality, genuine, pleasant, or advantageous, is termed the CHEESE. *Mayhew* thinks CHEESE, in this sense, is from the *Saxon* CEOSAN, to choose, and quotes *Chaucer*, who uses CHESE in the sense of choice. The *London Guide*, 1818, says it was from some young fellows translating "c'est une autre CHOSE" into "that is another CHEESE." But the expression CHEESE may be found in the *Gipsy* vocabulary, and in the *Hindostanee* and *Persian* languages. In the last CHIZ means a thing.—*See* under STILTON; also p. 7 *Introd*.

CHEESE, or CHEESE IT, (evidently a corruption of *cease*,) leave off, or have done; "CHEESE your barrikin," hold your noise.

CHEESY, fine or showy.

CHAUNT, "to CHAUNT the play," to explain the tricks and manœuvres of thieves.

CHERRY-BUMS, or CHERUBIMS, a nickname given to the 11th Hussars, (Prince Albert's Own,) from their crimson overalls.

CHERRY-COLOUR, a term used in a cheating trick at cards. When the cards are being dealt, a knowing one offers to bet that he will tell the colour of the turn-up card. "Done!" says Mr Green. The sum being named, Mr Sharp affirms that it will be CHERRY-COLOUR; and as cherries are either black or red, he wins, leaving his victim a wiser man, it is to be hoped, and not a *better* for the future.

CHERRY-MERRY, a present of money. CHERRY-MERRY-BAMBOO, a beating.—*Anglo-Indian.*

CHERUBS, or CHERUBIMS, the chorister boys who chaunt in the services at the abbeys.

CHESHIRE CAT, "to grin like a CHESHIRE CAT," to display the teeth and gums when laughing. Formerly the phrase was "to grin like a CHESHIRE CAT *eating* CHEESE." A *hardly satisfactory* explanation has been given of this phrase—that Cheshire is a county palatine, and the cats, when they think of it, are so tickled with the notion that they can't help grinning.

CHICKEN, a term applied to anything young, small, or insignificant; CHICKEN STAKES; "she's no CHICKEN," said of an old maid.

CHICKEN-HEARTED, cowardly, fearful.

CHI-IKE, a hurrah; a good word, or hearty praise; term used by the *Costermongers*, who assist the sale of each other's goods by a little friendly although noisy commendation.

CHILDREN'S SHOES, to make, to be made naught of.—*See* SHOES.

CHIMNEY-SWEEPER, the aperient mixture commonly called a *black dose.*

CHINCHIN, a salutation, a compliment.—*Anglo-Chinese.*

CHINK, money.—*Ancient.*—*See* FLORIO.

CHINKERS, money.

CHIN-WAG, officious impertinence.

"CHIP OF THE OLD BLOCK," a child who resembles its father. BROTHER CHIP, one of the same trade or profession.

CHIPS, money; also a nickname for a carpenter.—*Sea.*

CHIRP, to give information, "peach."

CHISEL, to cheat, to take a slice off anything.

CHIT, a letter; corruption of a *Hindoo* word.—*Anglo-Indian.*

CHITTERLINGS, the shirt frills worn still by ancient beaux; properly the *entrails of a pig*, to which they are supposed to bear some resemblance. *Belgian*, SCHYTERLINGH.

CHIVE, or CHIVEY, a shout, a halloo, or cheer; loud tongued. From CHEVY-CHASE, a boy's game, in which the word CHEVY is bawled aloud; or from the *Gipsy ?—See Introduction.*

CHIVE-FENCER, a street hawker of cutlery.

CHIVEY, to chase round, or hunt about. Apparently from CHIVEY-CHASE.

CHOAKEE, the black hole.—*Military—Anglo-Indian.*

CHOCK-FULL, full till the scale comes down with a shock.—*French,* CHOC. A correspondent suggests CHOKED-FULL.

CHOKE OFF, to get rid of. Bull-dogs can only be made to loose their hold by choking them.

CHOKER, a cravat, a neckerchief. WHITE-CHOKER, the white neckerchief worn by mutes at a funeral, and waiters at a tavern. Clergymen are frequently termed WHITE-CHOKERS.

CHOKER, or WIND-STOPPER, a garotter.

CHONKEYS, a kind of mince-meat baked in a crust, and sold in the streets.

CHOOPS, a corruption of CHOOPRAO, keep silence.—*Anglo-Indian.*

CHOOTAH, small, insignificant.—*Anglo-Indian.*

CHOP, in the Canton jargon of *Anglo-Chinese,* this word has several significations. It means an official seal, a permit, a boat-load of teas. FIRST CHOP signifies first quality; and CHOP-CHOP, to make haste.

CHOP, to exchange, to "swop."—*Old.*

CHOPS, properly CHAPS, the mouth, or cheeks; "down in the CHOPS," or "down in the mouth," *i.e.,* sad or melancholy.

CHOUSE, to cheat out of one's share or portion. Hackluyt, CHAUS; Massinger, CHIAUS. From the *Turkish,* in which language it signifies an interpreter. *Gifford* gives a curious story as to its origin:—

> "In the year 1609 there was attached to the Turkish embassy in England an interpreter, or CHIAOUS, who, by cunning, aided by his official position, managed to cheat the Turkish and Persian merchants, then in London, out of the large sum of £4000, then deemed an enormous amount. From the notoriety which attended the fraud, and the magnitude of the swindle, any one who cheated or defrauded was said to *chiaous,* or *chause,* or CHOUSE; to do, that is, as this *Chiaous* had done."—*See Trench, Eng. Past and Present,* p. 87.

CHIAUS, according to *Sandys,* (*Travels,* p. 48,) is "one who goes on embassies, executes commandments," &c. The particular Chiaus in question is alluded to in *Ben Jonson's Alchymist,* 1610.

> "*D.* What do you think of me?
>   That I am a CHIAUS?
> *Face.*   What 's that?
> *D.* The Turk [who] was here.
>   As one would say, do you think I am a Turk?"

CHOUT, an entertainment.—*East end of London.*

CHOVEY, a shop.—*Costermonger.*

CHOW-CHOW, a mixture, food of any kind.—*Anglo-Chinese.*

CHUBBY, round-faced, plump.

CHIVALRY, coition. Probably a corruption from the *Lingua Franca.*

CHIVE, a knife; a sharp tool of any kind.—*Old Cant.* This term is especially applied to the tin knives used in gaols.

CHIVE, to cut, saw, or file.—*Prison.*

CHRISTENING, erasing the name of the maker from a stolen watch, and inserting a fictitious one in its place.

SLANG, CANT, AND VULGAR WORDS.

CHUCK, a schoolboy's treat.—*Westminster School.* Food, provision for an entertainment.—*Norwich.*

CHUCK, to throw or pitch.

CHUCK IN, to challenge—from the pugilistic custom of throwing a hat into the ring; a modern version of "throwing down the gauntlet."

"CHUCKING A JOLLY," when a costermonger praises the inferior article his mate or partner is trying to sell. *See* CHI-IKE.

CHUCKLE-HEAD, much the same as "buffle-head," "cabbage-head," "chowder-head," "cods-head,"—all signifying that large abnormal form of skull always supposed to accompany stupidity and weakness of intellect; as the Scotch proverb, "muckle head and little wit."—*Devonshire.*

CHUCK UP, to surrender, give in—from the custom of throwing up the sponge at a prize fight in token of yielding.

CHUCKS! Schoolboy's signal on the master's approach.

CHUFF IT, *i.e.*, be off, or take it away, in answer to a street seller who is importuning you to purchase. *Halliwell* mentions CHUFF as a "term of reproach," surly, &c.

CHULL, make haste. An abbreviation of the *Hindostanee* CHULLO, signifying "go along." CHULL is very commonly used to accelerate the motions of a servant, driver, or palanquin-bearer.

CHUM, an acquaintance. A recognised term, but in such frequent use with the lower orders that it demanded a place in this glossary. Stated to be from the *Gael.* CAOMH, a friend.

CHUM, to occupy a joint lodging with another person. *Latin,* CUM.

CHUMMING-UP, an old custom amongst prisoners when a fresh culprit is admitted to their number, consisting of a noisy welcome—rough music made with pokers, tongs, sticks, and saucepans. For this ovation the initiated prisoner has to pay, or FORK OVER, half a crown—or submit to a loss of coat and waistcoat. The practice is ancient.

CHUMMY, a chimney-sweep—probably connected with *chimney;* also a low-crowned felt hat.

CHUMP, the head or face.

CHUNK, a thick or dumpy piece of any substance.—*Kentish.*

CHURCHWARDEN, a long pipe, "A YARD OF CLAY;" probably so called from the long pipes which are usually placed before those functionaries as marks of respect when they honour the parlours of public-houses with their company.

CINDER, any liquor used in connexion with soda water, as to "take a soda with a CINDER in it." The cinder may be sherry, brandy, or any other liquor.

"CHUCK A STALL," where one rogue walks in front of a person while another picks his pockets.

"CHURCH A YACK," (or watch,) to take the works of a watch from its original case and put them into another one, to avoid detection.—*See* CHRISTEN.

CIRCUMBENDIBUS, a round-about way, or story.

CLACK-BOX, a garrulous person, so called from the rattle formerly used by vagrants to make a rattling noise and attract attention.—*Norfolk.*

⁎⁎ A common proverb in this county is, "your tongue goes like A BAKER'S CLAP-DISH," which is evidently a modern corruption of beggars' CLAP or CLACK DISH mentioned in *Shakspeare's Measure for Measure,* iii. 2. It was a wooden dish with a movable cover.

CLAGGUM, boiled treacle in a hardened state, *Hardbake.*—*See* CLIGGY.

CLAP, to place; "do you think you can CLAP your hand on him?" *i.e.,* find him out.

CLAPPER, the tongue.

CLAP-TRAP, high-sounding nonsense. An ancient *Theatrical term* for a "TRAP to catch a CLAP by way of applause from the spectators at a play."—*Bailey's Dictionary.*

CLARET, blood.—*Pugilistic.* Said to have originated at Badminton.

CLASHY, a low fellow, a labourer.—*Anglo-Indian.*

CLEAN, quite, or entirely; "CLEAN gone," entirely out of sight, or away.—*Old, see Cotgrave.*—*Shakespeare.* CLEAN CONTRARY, quite different, opposite.

CLEAN OUT, to thrash, or beat; to ruin, or bankrupt any one; to take all they have got, by purchase or force. *De Quincey,* in his article on *Richard Bentley,* speaking of the lawsuit between that great scholar and Dr Colbatch, remarks that the latter "must have been pretty well CLEANED OUT."

CLICK, a knock, or blow. CLICK-HANDED, left-handed.—*Cornish.*

CLICK, to snatch, to pull away something that belongs to another.

CLICKER, a female touter at the bonnet shops in Cranbourn Alley. In Northamptonshire, the cutter out in a shoemaking establishment.*

CLIGGY, or CLIDGY, sticky.—*Anglo-Saxon,* CLÆG, clay.—*See* CLAGGUM.

CLINCHER, that which rivets or confirms an argument, an incontrovertible position. Also a lie which cannot be surpassed, a stopper-up, said to be derived as follows:—Two notorious liars were backed to outlie each other. "I drove a nail through the moon once," said the first. "Right," said the other; "I recollect the circumstance well, for I went round to the back part of the moon and *clinched* it"—hence CLINCHER.

CLIPPING, excellent, very good. CLIPPER, anything showy or first-rate.

* In the *Dictionary of the Terms, Ancient and Modern, of the Canting Crew,* Lond. n. d. (but prior to 1700,) the CLICKER is described as "the shoemaker's journeyman or servant, that cuts out all the work, and stands at or walks before the door, and saies—'What d'ye lack, sir? what d'ye buy, madam?'"

CLIFT, to steal.

CLINCH, to get the, to be locked up in jail.

CLING-RIG, stealing tankards from public-houses, &c.

CLOCK. "to know what's o'CLOCK," a definition of knowingness in general.—*See* TIME O' DAY.

CLOD-HOPPER, a country clown.

"CLOUD, TO BE UNDER A," to be in disgrace, or disrepute.

CLOUD, TO BLOW A, to smoke a pipe.

CLOUT, or RAG, a cotton pocket-handkerchief.—*Old Cant.*

CLOUT, a blow, or intentional strike.—*Ancient.*

CLOVER, happiness, luck, a delightful position—from the supposed happiness which attends cattle when they suddenly find their quarters changed from a barren field to a meadow of clover.

CLUMP, to strike, to beat.—*Prov.*

CLY, a pocket.—*Old Cant* for to steal. A correspondent derives this word from the *Old English* CLEYES, claws; *Anglo-Saxon* CLEA. This pronunciation is still retained in Norfolk; thus, to CLY would mean to pounce upon, snatch.—*See* FRISK. *Gael.* CLIAH, (pronounced CLEE,) a basket.

COACH, a Cambridge term for a private tutor, termed a RURAL COACH when he is not connected with a college.

COACH-WHEEL, or TUSHEROON, a crown-piece, or five shillings.

COALS, "to haul (or pull) over the COALS," to take to task, to scold. Supposed by *Jamieson* to refer to the *ordeal by fire.*

COAL, money; "post the COAL," put down the money. The phrase was used by Mr Buckstone at the Theatrical Fund Dinner of 1863. From this is derived the theatrical term COALING, profitable, very good, which an actor will use if his part is full of good and telling speeches—thus, "my part is full of COALING lines."

COBBING, a punishment inflicted by sailors and soldiers among themselves. See *Grose*, and *Captain Marryat's* novels. A hand-saw is the general instrument of punishment.

COCK, a familiar term of address; "jolly old COCK," a jovial fellow, "how are you, old cock?" Frequently rendered now-a-days, COCK-E-E, a vulgar street salutation—corruption of COCK-EYE. The latter is frequently heard as a shout or street cry after a man or boy.

COCK, a smoking term; "COCKING a Brosely," *i.e.*, smoking a pipe. Broseley in Staffordshire is famous for "churchwardens."

COCK-A-HOP, in high spirits.

COCK-A-WAX, an amplification of the simple term COCK, sometimes "Lad of WAX" in S. S.

"COCK AND A BULL STORY," a long, rambling anecdote.—*See Notes and Queries*, vol. iv., p. 313.

COCK-AND-HEN-CLUB, a free and easy gathering, where females are admitted as well as men.

CLY-FAKER, a pickpocket.

COCK-AND-PINCH, the old-fashioned beaver hat, affected by "swells" and "sporting gents" forty years ago—COCKED back and front, and PINCHED up at the sides.

COCKER, "it is all right, according to Cocker," meaning that everything has been done *en règle*. The phrase refers to the celebrated writing-master of Charles II.'s time, whose Arithmetic, Dictionary, &c., were long the standard authorities. The Arithmetic, probably the work referred to, was first published in 1677-8, and though it reached more than sixty editions, is considered a very scarce book.* A curious fact may here be mentioned in connexion with this saying. It has been stated, and very well proved, that many words popular in Shakspeare's time, and now obsolete in this country, are still in every-day use in the older English settlements of North America. The editor of this work was surprised, when travelling through Western Canada, to find that instead of the renowned Cocker the people appealed to another and more learned authority. "According to GUNTER," is a phrase in continual Transatlantic use. This scientific worthy invented the sector in 1606; and in 1623, about the time of the great Puritan exodus to North America, he brought out his famous *Rule of Proportion*. This was popularly known as Gunter's Proportion, or "*Gunter's Line*," and the term soon became a vulgar standard of appeal in cases of doubt or dispute.

COCK-EYE, one that squints.

COCKED-HAT-CLUB, the principal clique amongst the members of the Society of Antiquaries, who virtually decide whether any person proposed shall be admitted or not. The term comes from the "cocked-hat" placed before the president at the sittings.

COCKLES, "to rejoice the COCKLES of one's heart," a vulgar phrase implying great pleasure.—*See* PLUCK.

COCKNEY, a native of London. Originally, a spoilt or effeminate boy, derived from COCKERING, or foolishly petting a person, rendering them of soft or luxurious manners. *Halliwell* states, in his admirable essay upon the word, that "some writers trace the word with much probability to the imaginary land of COCKAYGNE, the lubber land of the olden times." Grose gives Minsheu's absurd but comical derivation:—A citizen of London being in the country, and hearing a horse neigh, exclaimed, "*Lord! how that horse laughs!*" A bystander informed him that that noise was called neighing. The next morning, when the cock crowed, the citizen, to shew that he had not forgotten what was told him, cried out, "*do you hear how the* COCK NEIGHS?"

* COCKER. *Professor de Morgan* (*Notes and Queries*, Jan. 27, 1855) says that the main goodness of Cocker's Tutor consists in his adopting the abbreviated system of division; and suggests that it became a proverbial representative of arithmetic from Murphy's farce of *The Apprentice*, 1756, in which the strong point of the old merchant, Wingate, is his extreme reverence for Cocker and his arithmetic.

COCKCHAFER, the treadmill.

"COCK OF THE WALK," a master spirit, head of a party. Places where poultry are fed are called WALKS, and the barn-door cocks invariably fight for the supremacy till one has obtained it.

COCKS, fictitious narratives, in verse or prose, of murders, fires, and terrible accidents, sold in the streets as true accounts. The man who hawks them, a patterer, often changes the scene of the awful event to suit the taste of the neighbourhood he is trying to delude. Possibly a corruption of *cook*, a cooked statement, or, as a correspondent suggests, the COCK LANE ghost may have given rise to the term. This had a great run, and was a rich harvest to the running stationers.

"COCK ONE'S TOES," to die.

COCK-ROBIN SHOP, a small printer's office, where low wages are paid to journeymen who have never served a regular apprenticeship.

COCKSHY, a game at fairs and races, where trinkets are set upon sticks, and for one penny three throws at them are accorded, the thrower keeping whatever he knocks off. From the ancient game of throwing or "shying" at live cocks.

COCKSURE, certain.

COCKY, pert, saucy.

COCKYOLY BIRD, a little bird, frequently called "a dickey bird."—*Kingsley's Two Years Ago.*

COCK, "to COCK your eye," to shut or wink one eye.

COCUM, advantage, luck, resources; "Jack's got COCUM, he's safe to get on, he is,"—viz., he starts under favourable circumstances. *See* the following.

COCUM, cunning, sly, "to fight COCUM," to be wily and cautious. Allied perhaps to the Scottish KEEK. *German*, GUCKEN, to peep or pry into.

COD, to hoax, take a "*rise*" out of one.

CODDS, the "poor brethren" of the Charter House. At p. 133 of the *Newcomes*, Mr Thackeray writes, "The Cistercian lads call these old gentlemen CODDS, I know not wherefore." An abbreviation of CODGER.

CODDAM, a low public-house game, much affected by medical students and cabmen, three on each side. The game is "simplicity itself," but requires a great amount of low cunning, and peculiar mental ingenuity.

CODGER, or COGER, an old man; "a rum old CODGER," a curious old fellow. CODGER is sometimes used as synonymous with CADGER, and then signifies a person who gets his living in a questionable manner. "COGERS," the name of a debating society, formerly held in Bride Court, Fleet Street, and still in existence. The term is probably a corruption of COGITATORS.

COFFEE-SHOP, a water-closet, or house of office.

COG, to cheat at dice.—*Shakspeare.* Also, to agree with, as one cog-wheel does with another.

COLD BLOOD, a house licensed for the sale of beer "NOT to be drunk on the premises."

COLD COFFEE, misfortune; sometimes varied to COLD GRUEL.—*Sea.*

COLD COFFEE, an *Oxford* synonyme for a "Sell," which see.

COLD COOK, an undertaker.

COLD MEAT, a corpse. COLD MEAT BOX, a coffin.

COLD SHOULDER, "to shew or give any one the COLD SHOULDER," to assume a distant manner towards them, to evince a desire to cease acquaintanceship. Sometimes it is termed "COLD SHOULDER of *mutton.*"

COLFABIAS, a *Latinised Irish* phrase signifying the closet of decency, applied as a Slang term to a place of resort in Trinity College, Dublin.

COLLAR, "out of COLLAR," *i.e.*, out of place, no work. Probably a variation of the metaphorical expressions "in, or out of harness," *i.e.*, in or out of work—the horse being in collar when harnessed for his work.

COLLAR, to seize, to lay hold of. *Thieves'* Slang, *i.e.*, to steal.

"COLLAR AND ELBOW," a term for a peculiar throw in wrestling.

COLLOGUE, to conspire, talk mysteriously together in low tones, plot mischief. More connected with "*colloquy*" than "*colleague.*"—*East coast.*

COLLY-WOBBLES, the stomach ache, a person's bowels,—supposed by many of the lower orders to be the seat of feeling and nutrition; an idea either borrowed from, or transmitted by, the ancients.—*Devonshire.*

COLOUR, complexion, tint; "I've not seen the COLOUR of his money," *i.e.*, he has never paid me any. In fortune-telling by cards, a *diamond colour* is the fairest; *heart-colour*, fair, but not so fair as the last; *club colour*, rather swarthy; *spade colour*, an extremely dark complexion.

COLT, a murderous weapon, formed by slinging a small shot to the end of a rather stiff piece of rope. It is the original of the mis-named "life-preserver."

COLT, a person who sits as juryman for the first time.

COLT, to fine a new juryman a sum to be spent in drink, by way of "wetting" his office.

COLT, to make a person free of a new place, which is done by his standing treat, and submitting to be struck on the sole of the foot with a piece of board.—*Prov.*

COLT'S TOOTH, elderly persons of juvenile tastes are said to have a COLT'S TOOTH, *i.e.*, a desire to shed their teeth once more, to see life over again.

COMB-CUT, mortified, disgraced, "down on one's luck."—*See* OUT.

COME, a Slang verb used in many phrases; "an't he COMING IT?" *i.e.*, is he not proceeding at a great rate? "Don't COME TRICKS here," "don't COME THE OLD SOLDIER over me," *i.e.*, we are aware of your practices, and "twig" your manœuvre. COMING IT STRONG, exaggerating, going a-head, the opposite of "*drawing it mild.*" COMING IT also means informing or disclosing.

COME DOWN, to pay down.

COMMISSION, a shirt.—*Ancient Cant.* *Italian*, CAMICIA

> "As from our beds, we doe oft cast our eyes,
> Cleane linnen yeelds a shirt before we rise,
> Which is a garment *shifting* in condition;
> And in the *canting tongue,* is a COMMISSION.
> In weale or woe, in joy or dangerous drifts,
> A *shirt* will put a man unto his *shifts.*"
> —*Taylor's Works,* 1630.

COMMISTER, a chaplain or clergyman.—Originally *Old Cant.*

COMMON SEWER, a DRAIN,—vulgar equivalent for a drink.

COMMONS, rations, because eaten *in common.*—*University.* SHORT COMMONS, (derived from the University Slang term,) a scanty meal, a scarcity.

COMPRADOR, a purveyor.—*Anglo-Chinese.*

CONCAVES AND CONVEXES, a pack of cards contrived for cheating, by cutting all the cards from the two to the seven concave, and all from the eight to the king convex. Then by cutting the pack breadth-wise a convex card is cut, and by cutting it length-wise a concave is secured.—*See Longs and Shorts.*

CONJEE, a kind of gruel made of rice.—*Anglo-Indian.*

CONK, a nose. Possibly, from the *Latin* CONCHA, a shell. *Greek*, κόγχη—hence anything hollow. Somewhat of a parallel may be found in the *Latin* TESTA, an earthenware pot, a shell, (Cicero,) and in later *Latin*, a *scull*, (Anson;) from whence the *French* TESTE, or TETE, head. CONKY, having a projecting or remarkable nose. The Duke of Wellington was frequently termed "Old CONKY" in satirical papers and caricatures.

CONNAUGHT RANGERS, the Eighty-eighth Regiment of Foot in the British Army.

CONSHUN'S PRICE, fair terms, without extortion.—*Anglo-Chinese.*

CONSUMAH, a butler.—*Anglo-Indian.*

CONSTABLE, "to overrun the CONSTABLE," to exceed one's income, get deep in debt.

CONTANGO, among stock-brokers and jobbers, is a certain sum paid for accommodating a buyer or seller, by carrying the engagement to pay money or deliver shares over to the next account day.

COOEY, the Australian bush-call, now not unfrequently heard in the streets of London.

COOK, a term well known in the Bankruptcy Courts, referring to accounts that have been meddled with, or COOKED, by the bankrupt; also the forming a balance-sheet from general trade inferences; stated by a correspondent to have been first used in reference to the celebrated alteration of the accounts of the Eastern Counties Railway, by George Hudson, the Railway King.

CONVEY, to steal; "CONVEY, the wise it call."

CONVEYANCER, a pickpocket. *Shakspeare* uses the Cant expression CONVEYER, a thief. The same term is also *French Slang*.

"COOK ONE'S GOOSE," to kill or ruin a person.—*North.*

COOLER, a glass of porter as a wind up, after drinking spirits and water.

COOLIE, a soldier, in allusion to the *Hindoo* COOLIES, or day labourers.

COON, abbreviation of racoon.—*American.* A GONE COON—*ditto*, one in an awful fix, past praying for. This expression is said to have originated in the American war with a spy, who dressed himself in a racoon skin, and ensconced himself in a tree. An English rifleman taking him for a veritable coon, levelled his piece at him, upon which he exclaimed, "Don't shoot, I'll come down of myself, I know I'm a GONE COON." The Yankees say the Britisher was so flummuxed, that he flung down his rifle and "made tracks" for home. The phrase is pretty usual in England.

COOPER, stout "HALF-AND-HALF," *i.e.*, half stout and half porter. Derived from the coopers at breweries being allowed so much stout and so much porter a day, which they have mixed sooner than drink the porter after the stout.

COOPER, to destroy, spoil, settle or finish. COOPERED, spoilt, "done up," synonymous with the Americanism CAVED IN, fallen in, ruined. The vagabonds' hieroglyphic ▽, chalked by them on gate posts and houses, signifies that the place has been spoilt by too many tramps calling there.

COOTER, "a sovereign."—*See* COUTER. *Gipsy*, CUTA.

COP, to seize or lay hold of anything unpleasant; used in a similar sense to *catch* in the phrase "to COP (or catch) a beating," "to get COPT," &c.

COP, beware, take care. A contraction of COPRADOR.—*Anglo-Indian.*

COPER, properly HORSE-COUPER, a Scotch horse-dealer,—used to denote a dishonest one.

COPPER, a policeman, *i.e.*, one who COPS, which *see.*

COPPER, a halfpenny. COPPERS, mixed pence.

COPUS, a Cambridge drink, consisting of ale combined with spices, and varied by spirits, wines, &c. Corruption of HIPPOCRAS.

CORINTHIANISM, a term derived from the classics, much in vogue some years ago, implying pugilism, high life, "sprees," roistering, &c.—*Shakspeare*, 1 *Hen. IV.*, ii. 4. The immorality of *Corinth* was proverbial in Greece. Κορινθίαζεσθαι, to *Corinthianise*, indulge in the company of courtesans, was a *Greek* Slang expression. Hence the proverb—

<blockquote>Οὐ παντὸς ἀνδρὸς εἰς Κόρινθον ἔσθ' ὁ πλοῦς:</blockquote>

and *Horace*, Epist. lib. 1, xvii. 36—

<blockquote>"Non cuivis homini contingit adire Corinthum,"</blockquote>

in allusion to the spoliation practised by the "hetæræ" on those who visited them.

CORK, "to draw a CORK," to give a bloody nose—*Pugilistic.*

CORKED, said of wine which tastes of cork, from being badly decanted.

COOPER. to forge, or imitate in writing; "COOPER a moneker," to forge a signature.

CORKER, "that's a CORKER," *i.e.*, that settles the question, or closes the discussion.

CORKS, a butler.

CORKS, money; "how are you off for corks?" a soldier's term of a very expressive kind, denoting the means of "keeping afloat." CORK is also used in connexion with money when persons at a hotel provide their own wine—sixpence being charged for each "cork" drawn.

CORNED, drunk or intoxicated. Possibly from soaking or pickling one's-self like CORNED beef.

CORNER, "the CORNER," Tattersall's famous horse repository and betting rooms, so called from the fact of its situation, which is at Hyde-Park Corner.

CORNERED, hemmed in a corner, placed in a position from which there is no escape.—*American*.

CORNER-MAN, the end singer of a corps of Ethiopian or nigger minstrels. In a theatrical advertisement in the *Era* there was, "Wanted a good CORNER-MAN Tambo, who can dance." A particularly clever man is required for the corner station, and in this case he was required to play on the tambourine as well. We insert it as a specimen of *Theat. Slang*.

CORPORATION, the protuberant front of an obese person.

CORPSE, to confuse, or put out the actors by making a mistake.—*Theat.*

COSSACK, a policeman.

COSTERMONGER, a street seller of fish, fruit, vegetables, poultry, &c. The London costermongers number more than 30,000. They form a distinct class, occupying whole neighbourhoods, and are cut off from the rest of metropolitan society by their low habits, general improvidence, pugnacity, love of gambling, total want of education, disregard for lawful marriage ceremonies, *and their use of a Cant* (or so-called *back Slang*) *language*. COSTERMONGER *aliter* COSTARDMONGER, *i.e.*, an apple-seller. In *Nares's Glossary* (Ed. H. & W.) they are said to have been frequently Irish. So, Ben Jonson—

"Her father was an Irish COSTAR-MONGER."
—*Alchym.*, iv. 1.

"In England, Sir, troth I ever laugh when I think on't.
—— Why, sir, there all the COSTER-MONGERS are Irish."
—2 *P. Hen. IV.*, O. Pt. iii. 375.

Their noisy manners are alluded to in *Beaumont and Fletcher's Scornful Lady*, iv. 1.

"And then he'll rail like a rude COSTER-MONGER
That school-boys had couzened of his apples,
As loud and senseless."

COSTER, the short and Slang rendering of "costermonger," or "costardmonger," who was originally an apple-seller. COSTERING, *i.e.*, costermongering, acting as a costermonger would.

COTTON, to like, adhere to, or agree with any person; "to COTTON on to a man," to attach yourself to him, or fancy him. literally, to stick to him as cotton would. *Vide Bartlett*, who claims it as an Americanism, and *Halliwell*, who terms it an Archaism; also *Bacchus and Venus*, 1737.

> "Her heart's as hard as taxes, and as bad;
> She does not even COTTON to her dad."
> —*Halliday and Lawrance, Kenilworth Burlesque.*

COTTON LORD, a Manchester manufacturer.

COUNCIL-OF-TEN, the toes of a man who turns his feet inward.

COUNTER, to hit back, exchange blows.—*Pugilistic term.*

COUNTER-JUMPER, a shopman, a draper's assistant.

COUNTRY-SHIP, a ship belonging to the East Indies, and trading from port to port in that country.

COUNTRY-CAPTAIN, a spatch-cocked fowl, sprinkled with curry-powder. A favourite breakfast dish with the captains of COUNTRY-SHIPS.

COUPLE-BEGGAR, a degraded person, who officiated as a clergyman in performing marriages in the Fleet Prison.

COUTER, a sovereign. HALF-A-COUTER, half-a-sovereign. From the *Danubian-gipsy* word CUTA, a gold coin.

COVE, or COVEY, a boy or man of any age or station. A term generally preceded by an expressive adjective, thus a "flash COVE," a "rum COVE," a "downy COVE," &c. The feminine, COVESS, was once popular, but it has fallen into disuse. *Ancient Cant*, originally (temp. *Henry VII.*) COFE, or CUFFIN, altered in *Decker's* time to COVE. *See Witts' Recreations*, 1654; "there's a *gentry*-COVE here," *i.e.*, a gentleman. Probably connected with CUIF, which, in the North of England, signifies a lout or awkward fellow. Amongst *Negroes*, CUFFEE.

COVENTRY, "to send a man to COVENTRY," not to speak to or notice him. Coventry was one of those towns in which the privilege of practising most trades was anciently confined to certain privileged persons, as the freemen, &c. Hence a stranger stood little chance of custom, or countenance, and "to send a man to COVENTRY" came to be equivalent to putting him out of the pale of society.

COVER-DOWN, a tossing coin with a false cover, enabling either head or tail to be shown, according as the cover is left on or taken off. The cover is more generally called a CAP.

COW-COW, to be very angry, to scold or reprimand violently.—*Anglo-Chinese.*

COWAN, a sneak, an inquisitive or prying person. *Greek*, κύων, a dog. Term given by Freemasons to all uninitiated persons. Used in *Anderson's Constitutions*, edit. 1769, p. 97. If derived from κύων, its use was probably suggested by such passages in the N. T. as Matt. vii. 6, and Phil. iii. 2. The Moslems apply dog in a similar manner. It is probably Oriental. Other authorities say it is from COWAN, or KIRWAN, a *Scottish* word signifying a man who builds rough stone walls without mortar—a man who, though he builds, is not a practical mason.

COUNTY-CROP, (*i.e.*, COUNTY-PRISON CROP,) hair cut close and round, as if guided by a basin—an indication of having been in prison.

COW'S GREASE, butter.

COW-LICK, the term given to the lock of hair which costermongers and tramps usually twist forward from the ear; a large greasy curl upon the cheek, seemingly licked into shape. The opposite of NEWGATE-KNOCKER, which see.

COXY-LOXY, good-tempered, drunk.—*Norfolk.*

CRAB, or GRAB, a disagreeable old person. *Name of a wild and sour fruit.*

CRAB, "to catch a CRAB," to fall backwards by missing a stroke in rowing. An allusion, of course, to fishing for crabs.

CRAB, to offend, or insult; to expose or defeat a robbery, to inform against. CRAB, in the sense of "to offend," is *Old English.*

"If I think one thing and speak another,
I will both CRAB Christ and our Ladie His mother."
—*Packman's Paternoster.*

CRABSHELLS, or TROTTING CASES, shoes.—*See* CARTS.

CRACK, the favourite horse in a race.

CRACK, first-rate, excellent; "a CRACK HAND," an adept; a "CRACK article," a good one.—*Old.*

CRACK, dry firewood.—*Modern Gipsy.*

CRACK, "in a CRACK (of the finger and thumb)," in a moment.

"CRACK A BOTTLE," to drink. *Shakspeare* uses CRUSH in the same Slang sense.

CRACK UP, to boast or praise.—*Ancient English.*

CRACKED-UP, penniless, or ruined.

CRACKLE, the scored rind on a roast leg of pork; hence applied to the velvet bars on the gowns of the students at St John's College, Cambridge, long called "Hogs," and the covered bridge which connects one of the courts with the grounds, Isthmus of Suez, (SUIS, *Lat.* sus, a swine.)

CRAM, to lie or deceive, implying to fill up or CRAM a person with false stories; to impart or acquire learning quickly, to "*grind*" or prepare for an examination.

CRAMMER, one skilled in rapidly preparing others for an examination.

CRAMMER, a lie; or a person who commits a falsehood.

CRANKY, foolish, idiotic, rickety, capricious, not confined to persons. *Ancient Cant,* CRANKE, simulated sickness. *German,* KRANK, sickly.

CRAPPING CASE, or KEN, the closet of decency.

CRAWLY-MAWLY, in an ailing, weakly, or sickly state.

CRAW-THUMPER, a Roman Catholic. Compare BRISKET-BEATER.

CRACK, to break into a house; "CRACK A CRIB," to commit burglary.

CRACK-FENCER, a man who sells nuts.

CRACKSMAN, a burglar.

CRAPPED, hanged.

"CREAM OF THE VALLEY," gin.

CRIB, house, public or otherwise; lodgings, apartments; a situation. Very general in the latter sense.

CRIB, to steal or purloin; to appropriate small things.

CRIB, a literal translation of a classic author.—*University.*

CRIB-BITER, an inveterate grumbler; properly said of a horse which has this habit, a sign of its bad digestion.

CRIBBAGE-FACED, marked with the small-pox, full of holes like a cribbage board.

CRIKEY, profane exclamation of astonishment; "Oh, CRIKEY, you don't say so!" corruption of "*O Christ.*"

CRIPPLE, a bent sixpence.

CROAK, to die—from the gurgling sound a person makes when the breath of life is departing.—*Oxon.*

CROAKER, one who takes a desponding view of everything; an alarmist. *From the croaking of a raven.*—Ben Jonson.

CROAKER, a beggar.

CROAKER, a dying person beyond hope; a corpse.

CROAKS, last dying speeches, and murderers' confessions.

CROCODILES' TEARS, the tears of a hypocrite. An ancient phrase, introduced into this country by Mandeville, or other early English traveller.—*Othello,* iv., 1.

CRONY, a termagant or malicious old woman; an intimate friend. *Johnson* calls it *Cant.*

CROOKY, to hang on to, to lead, to walk arm-in-arm; to court or pay addresses to a girl.

CROPPER, "to go a CROPPER," *i.e.,* fail or fall.

CROSS, a deception—two persons pretending hostility or indifference to each other, being all the while in concert for the purpose of deceiving a third.

CROSS-BUTTOCK, an unexpected fling down or repulse; from a peculiar throw practised by wrestlers.

CROCUS, or CROAKUS, a quack or travelling doctor; CROCUS-CHOVEY, a chemist's shop.

CROOKED, a term used among dog-stealers, and the "fancy" generally, to denote anything stolen.

CROPPIE, a person who has had his hair cut, or CROPPED, in prison.

CROPPED, hanged.

CROSS, a general term amongst thieves expressive of their plundering profession, the opposite of SQUARE. "To get anything on the CROSS" is to obtain it surreptitiously. "CROSS-FANNING in a crowd," robbing persons of their scarf-pins. CROSSMAN, a thief, or one who lives by dishonest practices.

CROSSED, prohibited from taking food from the "Buttery."—*University.*

CROW, or COCK-CROW, to exult over another's abasement, as a fighting-cock does over his vanquished adversary.

CROW, "a regular CROW," a success, a stroke of luck,—equivalent to a FLUKE.

CROW, "I have a CROW to pick with you," *i.e.*, an explanation to demand, a disagreeable matter to settle.

CRUG, food.—*Household Words*, No. 183. Peculiar to the Christ's Hospital boys, who apply it only to *bread*.

CRUMBS, "to pick up one's CRUMBS," to begin to have an appetite after an illness; to improve in health, circumstances, &c., after a loss thereof.

CRUMMY, fat, plump.—*North.*

CRUMMY-DOSS, a lousy or filthy bed.

CRUNCH, to crush. *Corruption;* or, perhaps from the sound of teeth grinding against each other.

CRUSH, to run, decamp rapidly. CRUSH DOWN SIDES, run to a place of safety, or the appointed rendezvous.—*North Country Cant.*

CRUSHER, a policeman.

CRUSHING, excellent, first-rate.

CRUSTY, ill-tempered, petulant, morose.—*Old,* said to be a corruption of the *Anglo-Norman* CORUSEUX.

CUB, a mannerless, uncouth lout.—*See* UNLICKED.

CUBITOPOLIS, an appellation given by Londoners to the Warwick and Eccleston Square districts. Another name for it is MESOPOTAMIA.

CUE, properly the last word spoken by one actor, it being the CUE for the other to reply.

CULL, a man or boy.—*Old Cant.* RUM CULL, the manager of a theatre.

CULLET, broken glass. *French,* CUEILLETTE, a gathering or collection.

CULLY GORGER, a companion, a brother actor. *Theatrical.* *See* GORGER.

CULVER-HEADED, weak and stupid.

CUMSHAW, a present or bribe.—*Anglo-Chinese.*

CUPBOARD HEADED, an expressive designation of one whose head is both wooden and hollow.—*Norfolk.*

CUPBOARD-LOVE, affection arising from interested motives.

"A CUPBOARD LOVE is seldom true;
A love sincere is found in few."—*Poor Robin.*

CROSS COVE AND MOLLISHER, a man and woman who live by thieving.

CROSS-CRIB, a house frequented by thieves.

CROW, one who watches whilst another commits a theft, a confederate in a robbery. The CROW looks to see that the way is clear, whilst the SNEAK, his partner, commits the depredation.

CULE, thieves' term. Abbreviation of *Reticule.*

CULLING, or CULING, stealing from the carriages on race-courses.

CUP-TOSSER, a person who professes to tell fortunes by examining the grounds in tea or coffee cups. A cup or goblet, however, is the old mystic symbol of a juggler. *French*, JOUEUR DE GOBELET.

CURE, an odd person; a contemptuous term, abridged from CURIOSITY, which was formerly the favourite expression.—*Compare* STIPE. A correspondent objects to this definition as insufficient and erroneous. A CURE, according to him, is an exceedingly cunning, clever chaffer, who does not vulgarly insult like the old chaffers, but keeps the person he is chaffing in an alternate state of anger and complaisance. The CURE is impertinent, but by his submissive manners, and the turns he gives the conversation, CURES the wounds as soon as he inflicts them.

CURIOS, a corruption of "curiosities;" any articles of virtu brought from abroad. Used by naval and military travellers and others.—*See* CURE.

CURRENCY, a person born in Australia is there termed CURRENCY, while natives of England are termed STERLING. The allusion is to the difference between colonial and imperial money.

CURSE, anything worthless. Corruption of the *Old English* word KERSE, a small sour wild cherry; *French*, CERISE; *German*, KIRSCH. *Vision of Piers Ploughman:*—

> "Wisdom and witt nowe is *not worth a* KERSE,
> But if it be carded with cootis as clothers
> Kembe their woole."

The expression "not worth a CURSE," used frequently now-a-days, is therefore not properly profane, though it is frequently intensified by a still more profane expletive. *Horne Tooke* says from KERSE, or CRESS.

CURSE-OF-SCOTLAND, the Nine of Diamonds. Various hypotheses have been set up as to this appellation—that it was the card on which the "Butcher Duke" wrote a cruel order with respect to the rebels after the battle of Culloden;[*] that the diamonds are the nine lozenges in the arms of Dalrymple, Earl of Stair, detested for his share in the Massacre of Glencoe; that it is a corruption of *Cross of Scotland*, the nine diamonds being arranged somewhat after the fashion of a St Andrew's Cross; but the most probable explanation is, that in the game of Pope Joan the nine of diamonds is the POPE, of whom the Scotch have an especial horror.

CURTAIL, to cut off. Originally a Cant word—*vide Hudibras*, and *Bacchus and Venus*, 1737.

CUSHION, to hide or conceal.

CUSHION-SMITER, polite rendering of TUB-THUMPER, a clergyman, a preacher.

---

[*] The first supposition is evidently erroneous, for in *Dr Houstoun's Memoirs of his own Lifetime*, 1747, p. 92, the Jacobite ladies are stated to have nicknamed the Nine of Diamonds "the Justice-Clerk," after the rebellion of 1715, in allusion to the Lord Justice-Clerk Ormistone, who, for his severity in suppressing it, was called the Curse of Scotland. Gules a cross of lozenges are also the arms of Colonel Packer, who attended Charles I. on the scaffold, and commanded in Scotland afterwards with great severity.—*See Chatto on the Origin and History of Playing Cards*, p. 267.

CUSHMAWAUNEE, never mind. Sailors and soldiers who have been in India frequently say—

> "CUSHMAWAUNEE,
> If we cannot get arrack,
> We must drink pawnee."
>
> —*Anglo-Indian.*

CUSTOMER, synonymous with CHAP, a fellow; "a rum CUSTOMER," *i.e.*, a man likely to turn the tables on any one who attacked him, and therefore better be let alone, or very warily proceeded with; an "odd fish," or curious person.—*Shakspeare.*

CUSTOMHOUSE-OFFICER, an aperient pill.

CUT, to run away, move off quickly; to cease doing anything; CUT AND RUN, to quit work, or occupation, and start off at once—*Sea* phrase, "CUT the cable, and RUN before the wind;" to CUT DIDOES, synonymous with to CUT CAPERS; CUT A DASH, make a show; CUT A CAPER, to dance or shew off in a strange manner; CUT A FIGURE, to make either a good or bad appearance; CUT IT, desist, be quiet, go away, leave what you are doing and run; CUT IT SHORT, cease being prolix, "make short work" of what you have in hand; CUT OUT, to excel, thus in affairs of gallantry one Adonis is said to "CUT *the other out*" in the affections of the wished-for lady—*Sea* phrase, from CUTTING out a ship from the enemy's port. CUT THAT! be quiet, or stop; CUT OUT OF, done out of; CUT OF ONE'S JIB, the expression or cast of his countenance, [see JIB;] TO CUT ONE'S COMB, to take down a conceited person, from the practice of cutting the combs of capons, [see COMB-CUT;] CUT AND COME AGAIN, plenty, if one cut does not suffice, plenty remains to "come again;" CUT UP, to mortify, to criticise severely, or expose; CUT UP SHINES, to play tricks; CUT ONE'S STICK, to be off quickly, *i.e.*, to be in readiness for a journey, further elaborated into AMPUTATE YOUR MAHOGANY, [see STICK;] CUT IT FAT, to exaggerate or shew off in an extensive manner; to CUT UP FAT, to die, leaving a large property; CUT UNDER, to undersell; CUT YOUR LUCKY, to run off; CUT ONE'S CART, to expose their tricks; CUT AN ACQUAINTANCE, to cease friendly intercourse with them; "CUT UP ROUGH," to become obstreperous and dangerous; TO HAVE CUT ONE'S EYE-TEETH, *i.e.*, to be wide awake, knowing; TO DRAW CUTS, to cast lots with papers of unequal lengths—*See Comedy of Errors*, act v. scene 1.—*Cambridge. Old;* CUTTE, to say.

CUT, in theatrical language, means to strike out portions of a dramatic piece, so as to render it shorter for representation. A late treasurer of one of the so-called *Patent Theatres*, when asked his opinion of a new play, always gave utterance to the brief, but safe piece of criticism, "*wants* CUTTING."

CUT, tipsy.—*Household Words*, No. 183.

CUT, to compete in business; "a CUTTING trade," one conducted on competitive principles, where the profits are very closely shaved.

CUT-THROAT, a butcher, a cattle-slaughterer; a ruffian.

CUTE, sharp, cunning. Abbreviation of ACUTE.

CUTTER, a ruffian, a cut-purse. Of *Robin Hood* it was said—

> "So being outlaw'd, (as 'tis told,)
> He with a crew went forth
> Of lusty CUTTERS, bold and strong,
> And robbed in the north."

CUTTER, a swashbuckler—*balaffreux, taillebras fendeur de naseaux.—Cotgrave.*

> "He's out of cash, and thou know'st by CUTTER'S LAW,
> We are bound to relieve one another."
> (N. H. W.) —*Match at Midn. O. Pl.,* vii. 553.

This ancient Cant word now survives in the phrase, "to swear like a CUTTER."

CUTTING-SHOP, a place where cheap rough goods are sold.

CUTTY PIPE, a short clay pipe. *Scotch,* CUTTY, short.

CUTTY-SARK, a short chemise.—*Scotch.* A scantily-draped lady is so called by *Burns.*

DAB, or DABSTER, an expert person. Most probably derived from the Latin *adeptas.*

DAB, a bed. Probably *Back-Slang.*

DAB, street term for a flat fish of any kind.—*Old.*

DACHA-SALTEE, tenpence. Probably from the *Lingua Franca.* Modern Greek, δεκα; *Italian,* DIECI SOLDI, tenpence; Gipsy, DIK, ten. So also DACHA-ONE, *i.e., dieci uno,* elevenpence.—*See* SALTEE.

DADDLE, the hand; "tip us your DADDLE," *i.e.,* shake hands.

DADDY, the stage manager.—*Theatrical.* Also the person who gives away the bride at a wedding.

DAFFY, gin. A term with monthly nurses, who are always extolling the virtues of *Daffy's Elixir,* and who occasionally comfort themselves with a stronger medicine under Daffy's name.

DAGS, feat or performance; "I'll do your DAGS," *i.e.,* I will do something that you cannot do.

DAISY-CUTTER, a horse that trots or gallops without lifting its feet much from the ground.

DAISY-KICKER, the name hostlers at large inns used to give each other, now nearly obsolete. DAISY-KICKER, or GROGHAM, was likewise the Cant term for a horse.

The DAISY-KICKERS were sad rogues in the old posting days; frequently the landlords rented the stables to them, as the only plan to make them return a profit.

DAMAGE, in the sense of recompense; "what's the DAMAGE?" *i.e.,* what is to pay?

DADDY; at mock raffles, lotteries, &c., the DADDY is an accomplice, most commonly the getter up of the swindle, and in all cases the person that has been previously arranged to win the prize.

DAMPER, a shop till; to DRAW A DAMPER, *i.e.,* rob a till.

"DANCE UPON NOTHING," to be hanged.

DANDO, a great eater, who cheats hotels, eating shops, oyster-cellars, &c.; from a person of that name.

DANDER, passion, or temper; "to get one's DANDER up," to rouse his passion.—*Old*.

DANDY, a fop, or fashionable nondescript. This word, in the sense of a fop, is of modern origin. *Egan* says it was first used in 1820, and *Bee* in 1816. Johnson does not mention it, although it is to be found in all late dictionaries. DANDIES wore stays, studied feminity, and tried to undo their manhood. Lord Petersham headed them. At the present day dandies of this stamp are fast disappearing. The feminine of DANDY was DANDIZETTE, but the term only lived for a short season.

DANDY, a small glass of whisky.—*Irish*. "Dimidium, cyathi vero apud Metropolitanos Hibernicos dicitur DANDY."—*Father Tom and the Pope, Blackwood's Magazine for May* 1838.

DANDY, a boatman.—*Anglo-Indian*.

DANDYPRAT, a funny little fellow, a mannikin; originally a half-farthing.

DANNA, human ordure; DANNA DRAG, a nightman's or dustman's cart; hence DUNNY-KEN, which *see*.

DARBLE, the devil.—*French*, DIABLE.

DARK, "keep it DARK," *i.e.*, secret. DARK HORSE, in racing phraseology, a horse whose chance of success is unknown, and whose capabilities have not been made the subject of comment.

DARKEY, twilight; also a negro. DARKMANS, the night.

DARN, vulgar corruption of d——n.—*American*.

DASHING, showy, fast.

DAUB, in low language, an artist.

DAVID'S SOW, "as drunk as DAVID'S SOW," *i.e.*, beastly drunk.—*See* origin of the phrase in *Grose's Dictionary*.

DAVY, "on my DAVY," on my affi*davit*, of which it is a vulgar corruption. Latterly DAVY has become synonymous in street language with the name of the Deity; "so help me DAVY," Slang rendering of the conclusion of the oath usually exacted of witnesses.

DANCERS, stairs.—*Old Cant.*

DANCER, or DANCING-MASTER, a thief who prowls about the roofs of houses, and effects an entrance by attic windows, &c. Called also a *Garreter*.

DARBIES, handcuffs.—*Old Cant.*—*See* JOHNY DARBIES. Sir Walter Scott mentions these, in the sense of fetters, in his *Peveril of the Peak*—

"'Hark ye! Jem Clink will fetch you the DARBIES.' 'Derby!' interrupted Julian, 'has the Earl or Countess'"——

Had Sir Walter known of any connexion between them and this family he would undoubtedly have mentioned it. The mistake of the speaker is corrected in the next paragraph.

DAVY'S LOCKER, or DAVY JONES'-LOCKER, the sea, the common receptacle for all things thrown overboard;—a nautical phrase for death, the other world.—*See* DUFFY.

DAWDLE, to loiter, or fritter away time.

DAWK, the post.—*Anglo-Indian.*

DAYLIGHTS, eyes; "to darken his DAYLIGHTS," to give a person black eyes. Also the spaces left in glasses between the liquor and the brim,—not allowed when bumpers are drunk. The toast-master in such cases cries, "no DAYLIGHTS or HEELTAPS!"

DAZE, to confound or bewilder; an ancient form of dazzle used by *Spenser, Drayton,* &c.

DEAD-ALIVE, stupid, dull.

DEAD-AMISS, said of a horse that from illness is utterly unable to win a race.

DEAD-BEAT, utterly exhausted.

DEAD-HEAT, when two horses run in so exactly equal that the judge cannot place one before the other; consequently a DEAD-HEAT has to be run over again.—*See* NECK AND NECK.

DEAD HORSE, "to draw the DEAD HORSE;" DEAD-HORSE work—working for wages already paid; also any thankless or unassisted service.

DEAD-LETTER, an action of no value or weight; an article, owing to some mistake in its production, rendered utterly valueless,—often applied to any instrument in writing which, by some apparently trivial omission, becomes useless. Term derived from the Post-Office.

DEAD-MAN, a baker. Properly speaking, it is an extra loaf smuggled into the basket by the man who carries it out, to the loss of the master. Sometimes the DEAD MAN is charged to a customer, but never delivered.

DEAD-MEN, the term for wine bottles after they are emptied of their contents.—*Old.*—*See* MARINES.

DEAD-MEN'S SHOES, expectation of property after decease. "To wait for a pair of DEAD MAN'S SHOES," is considered a wearisome affair. It is used by Fletcher:—

"And 'tis a general shrift, that most men use,
But yet 'tis tedious waiting DEAD MEN'S SHOES."
—*Fletcher's Poems,* p. 256.

DEAD-SET, a pointed attack on a person.

DEANER, a shilling. *Provincial Gipsy,* DEANEE, a pound. Probably another form of DINARLY, or it may be the *Turkish* word introduced by the Wallachian Gipsies.

DEATH, "to dress to DEATH," *i.e.*, to the very extreme of fashion, perhaps so as to be KILLING.

DEATH-HUNTER, a running patterer, who vends last dying speeches and confessions.

DEAD-LURK, entering a dwelling-house during divine service.

DECK,* a pack of cards.—*Old.* Used by Bulwer as a Cant term. General in the *United States.*

DECOMPOSITION ROW, Rotten Row, the equestrian promenade in Hyde Park.—*West-end Slang.*—*Lit. Gaz.* April 12, 1862.

DEMIREP, (or RIP,) a courtesan. Contraction of DEMIREPUTATION.—*Grose.*

DERRICK, an apparatus for raising sunken ships, &c. The term is curiously derived from a hangman of that name frequently mentioned in Old Plays, as in the *Bellman of London,* 1616.

> "He rides circuit with the devil, and *Derrick* must be his host, and Tyborne the inn at which he will light."

DESPATCHERS, false "dice with two sides, double four, double five, and double six."—*Times,* 27th November 1856.

DEUCE, the devil.—*Old.* Stated by *Junius* and others to be from DEUS.

DEUCE, twopence; DEUCE at cards or dice, one with two pips or holes.

DEVIL, a printer's youngest apprentice, an errand-boy.

DEVIL-DODGER, a clergyman; also a person who goes sometimes to church and sometimes to meeting.

DEVIL'S-BED-POST, the four of clubs.—*See Capt. Chamier's* novel of *The Arethusa.*

DEVIL'S BOOKS, a pack of playing-cards; a phrase of Presbyterian origin, used in contradistinction to KINGS' BOOKS.—*See* FOUR KINGS.

DEVIL'S DUNG, the fetid drug, asafœtida.

DEVIL'S DUST, a term used in the manufacturing districts of Yorkshire to denote shreds of old cloth torn up to re-manufacture;† also called SHODDY.

DEVIL'S LIVERY, black and yellow.

DEVIL-MAY-CARE, reckless, rash.

DEVIL-SCOLDER, a clergyman.

DEVIL'S TEETH, dice.

DEVOTIONAL HABITS, horses weak in the knees and apt to stumble and fall are said to have these.—*Stable.*

DEW-BEATERS, feet; "hold out your DEW-BEATERS till I take off the darbies."—*Peveril of the Peak.* Forby says the word is used in *Norfolk* for heavy shoes to resist wet.

DEW-DRINK, a morning draught, such as is served out to labourers in harvest-time before commencing work.

DEWSKITCH, a good thrashing, perhaps from catching one's due.

---

* Used by *Shakspeare,* 3 *K. Hen. VI.* v. 1.

† Mr Ferrand, in his speech in the House, March 4, 1842, produced a piece of cloth made chiefly from DEVIL'S DUST, and tore it into shreds to prove its worthlessness.—*See Hansard's Parliamentary Debates,* third series, vol. lxi. p. 140.

DEE, a pocket-book, term used by tramps.—*Gipsy.*

DELICATE, a false subscription book carried by a LURKER.

DIBBS, money; so called from the huckle bones of sheep, which have been used from the earliest times for gambling purposes, being thrown up five at a time and caught on the back of the hand like halfpence.

DICKEY, bad, sorry, or foolish; food or lodging is pronounced DICKEY when of a poor description; "it's all DICKEY with him," *i.e.*, all over with him.

DICKEY, formerly the Cant for a worn-out shirt, but means, now-a-days, a front or half-shirt. DICKEY was originally TOMMY, (from the Greek, τομη, a section,) a name which I understand was formerly used in Trinity College, Dublin. The students are said to have invented the term, and the GYPS changed it to DICKEY, in which dress it is supposed to have been imported into England.

DICKEY, a donkey.—*Norfolk.*

DICKEY SAM, a native of Liverpool.

DICK, a riding whip; gold-headed DICK, one so ornamented.

DICK, abbreviation of "Dictionary," but often euphemistically rendered "Richard,"—fine language, long words.—*School.*

DICKENS, synonymous with devil; "what the DICKENS are you after?" what the d——l are you doing? Used by *Shakspeare* in the *Merry Wives of Windsor.*

DIDOES, pranks or capers; "to cut up DIDOES," to make pranks

DIG, a hard blow.

DIGGERS, spurs; also the spades on cards.

DIGGINGS, lodgings, apartments, residence; an expression probably imported from California, or Australia, with reference to *the gold diggings.*

DILLY DALLY, to trifle.

DIMBER, neat or pretty.—*Worcestershire,* but old Cant.

DIMBER DAMBER, very pretty; a clever rogue who excels his fellows; chief of a gang. *Old Cant* in the latter sense.—*English Rogue.*

DIMMOCK, money; "how are you off for DIMMOCK?" diminutive of DIME, a small foreign silver coin, in the United States 10 cents.

DINARLY, money; "NANTEE DINARLY," I have no money, corrupted from the *Lingua Franca,* "NIENTE DINARO," not a penny. *Turkish,* DINARI; *Spanish,* DINERO; *Latin,* DENARIUS.

DICK; "look! the bulky is DICKING," *i.e.,* the constable has his eye on you. —*North Country Cant.*

DIDDLE, old Cant word for geneva, or gin.

DIDDLE, to cheat, or defraud.—*Old.* In *German,* DUDELN is to play on the bagpipe; and the ideas of piping and cheating seem to have been much connected. "Do you think I am easier played on than a pipe?" occurs in *Hamlet.*

DIDDLER, or JEREMY DIDDLER, an artful swindler.

DIES, last dying speeches, and criminal trials.

DING, to strike; to throw away, or get rid of anything; to pass to a confederate. *Old*, used in old plays.

> "The butcher's axe (like great Alcides' bat)
> *Dings* deadly downe ten thousand thousand flat."
> —*Taylor's Works*, 1630.

DINGY, a small boat.—*Anglo-Indian*.

DIPPED, mortgaged.—*Household Words*, No. 183.

DIRT, TO EAT, an expression derived from the East, nearly equivalent "to eat humble (*Umble*) pie," to put up with a mortification or insult.

DIRTY-SHIRT CLUB, the "PARTHENON," in Regent Street, so called from the great unwashed who congregate there.

DISGUISED, intoxicated.—*Household Words*, No. 183.

> "Some say drinking does DISGUISE men."
> —*Old Song*.

> "The saylers and the shipmen all,
> Through foule excesse of wine,
> Were so DISGUISED that at the sea
> They shew'd themselves like swine."
> —*Thos. Deloney's Strange Histories*, p. 14.

DISH, to stop, to do away with, to suppress; DISHED, done for, floored, beaten, or silenced. A correspondent suggests that meat is usually DONE BROWN before being DISHED, and conceives that the latter term may have arisen as the natural sequence of the former.

DISHABBILLY, the ridiculous corruption of the *French* DÉSHABILLÉ, amongst fashionably affected, but ignorant "stuck-up" people.

DITHERS, nervous or cold shiverings; "it gave me the DITHERS."

DITTOES, A SUIT OF, coat, waistcoat, and trousers of the same material. —*Tailor's term*.

DITTY-BAG, the bug or huswife in which sailors keep needles, thread, buttons, &c., for mending their clothes.

DO, this useful and industrious verb has for many years done service as a Slang term. To DO a person is to cheat him. Sometimes another tense is employed, such as "I DONE him," meaning I cheated or "paid him out;" DONE BROWN, cheated thoroughly, befooled; DONE OVER, upset, cheated, knocked down, ruined; DONE UP, used up, finished, or quieted. DONE also means convicted, or sentenced; so does DONE-FOR. To DO a person in pugilism is to excel him in fisticuffs. Humphreys, who fought Mendoza, a Jew, wrote this laconic note to his supporter —"Sir,—I have DONE the Jew, and am in good health. Rich. Humphreys." Tourists use the expression, "I have DONE France and Italy," meaning I have completely explored those countries.

DOBIE, an Indian washerman; and though women wash clothes in this country, Anglo-Indians speak of a washerwoman as a DOBIE.—*Anglo-Indian*.

DIVE, to pick pockets.

DIVER, a pickpocket. Also applied to fingers, no doubt from a similar reason.

DOCTOR, to adulterate or drug liquor; to poison, to hocus; also to falsify accounts. On board ship the cook is always termed "the DOCTOR."—*See* COOK.

DODDY, a term applied in Norfolk to any person of low stature. Sometimes HODMANDOD and "HODDY-DODDY, all head and no body." DODMAN in the same dialect denotes a garden snail.

DODGE, a cunning trick. "DODGE, that homely but expressive phrase."—*Sir Hugh Cairns on the Reform Bill*, 2d March 1859. *Anglo-Saxon* DEOGIAN, to colour, to conceal. The TIDY DODGE, as it is called by street-folk, consists in dressing up a family clean and *tidy*, and parading the streets to excite compassion and obtain alms. A correspondent suggests that the verb DODGE may have been formed (like *wench* from *wink*) from DOG, *i.e.*, to double quickly and unexpectedly, as in coursing.

DOGBERRY, a foolish constable.

DOG-IN-A-BLANKET, a kind of pudding, made of preserved fruit spread on thin dough, and then rolled up and boiled.

DOGGERY, nonsense, transparent attempts to cheat.

DOGS, TO GO TO THE, to be commercially or socially ruined. Originally a stable term applied to old or worthless horses, sold to feed hounds.

DOG'S-BODY, a kind of pease pudding.—*Sea*.

DODGER, a tricky person, or one who, to use the popular phrase, "knows too much."—*See* DEVIL-DODGER.

DODGER, a dram. In *Kent*, a DODGER signifies a nightcap; which name is often given to the last dram at night.

DOG, to follow in one's footsteps on the sly, to track.

DOG-CHEAP, or DOG-FOOLISH, very or singularly cheap, or foolish. Latham, in his *English Language*, says:—"This has nothing to do with dogs. The first syllable is god = *good* transposed, and the second, the ch—p, is chapman, *merchant:* compare EASTCHEAP."—*Old term*.

DOG-LATIN, barbarous Latin, such as was formerly used by lawyers in their pleadings.

"DOG ON IT," a form of mild swearing used by boys.—*Back-Slang*.

DOGSNOSE, gin and beer, so called from the mixture being *cold*, like a dog's nose.

DOLDRUMS, difficulties, low spirits, dumps.—*Sea*.

DOLLOP, a lump or portion.—*Norfolk*. *Anglo-Saxon* DALE, *dole*.

DOLLOP, to *dole up*, give up a share.—*Ibid*.

DOLLYMOP, a tawdrily-dressed maid-servant, a street-walker.

DOLLY SHOP, an illegal pawnshop,—where goods, or stolen property, not good enough for the pawnbroker, are received, and charged at so much per day. If not redeemed the third day the goods are forfeited. *Anglo-Saxon*, DAEL, a part,—to dole?—*See* NIX. A correspondent thinks it may have been derived from the *black doll*, the usual sign of a rag shop.

DOMINE, a parson.

DOMINO, a common ejaculation of soldiers and sailors when they receive the last lash of a flogging. The allusion may be understood from the game of domino.

DOMINOS, the teeth.

DON, a clever fellow, the opposite of a muff; a person of distinction in his line or walk. At the English Universities, the Masters and Fellows are the DONS. DON is also used as an adjective, "a DON hand at a knife and fork," *i.e.*, a first-rate feeder at a dinner table.—*Spanish.*

DON PEDRO, a low game at cards. It is a compound of All Fours, and the Irish game variously termed All Fives, Five and Ten, Fifteen, Forty-five, &c. It was, no doubt, invented by the mixed English and Irish rabble who fought in Portugal in 1832-3.

DONE! the expression used when a bet is accepted.—*See* also DO.

DONE UP, an equivalent expression to "dead beat."

DONKEY, "three more and up goes the DONKEY," a vulgar street phrase for extracting as much money as possible before performing any task. The phrase had its origin with a travelling showman, the *finale* of whose performance was the hoisting of a DONKEY on a pole or ladder; but this consummation was never arrived at unless the required number of "browns" was first paid up, and "three more" was generally the unfortunate deficit.

DONKEY. I am unable to explain the phrase, but any one wearing a white hat, whether in town or country, is shouted after invariably by the street urchins, "Who stole the DONKEY?" to which another in the gang replies, "The man in the white hat," and they then disperse.

DONNA and FEELES, a woman and children. *Italian* or *Lingua Franca*, DONNE E FIGLIE.

DOOKIN, fortune-telling. *Gipsy*, DUKKERIN.

DOSS, a bed.—*North.* Probably from DOZE. *Mayhew* thinks it is from the Norman, DOSSEL, a hanging or bed canopy.

DOSS, to sleep, formerly spelt DORSE. Perhaps from the phrase to lie on one's *dorsum*, back. *Gael.* DOSAL, slumber.

DOSS-KEN, a lodging house.

DOUBLE, "to tip (or give) the DOUBLE," to run away from any person; to double back, turn short round upon one's pursuers, and so escape as a hare does.—*Sporting.*

DOUBLE-UP, to pair off, or "chum" with another man; to beat severely.

DOUBLE-SHUFFLE, a low, shuffling, noisy dance, common amongst costermongers.—*See* FLIP-FLAPS.

DOUGHEY, a sufficiently obvious nickname for a baker.

DOUSE, to put out; "DOUSE that glim," put out that candle. In Norfolk

---

" DONE FOR A RAMP,' convicted for thieving.

DOSE, three months' imprisonment as a known thief.—*See* BRAGGADOCIO.

this expression is DOUT, which is clearly for DO OUT—variations probably of the same word.—*Sea.* Also to knock down.

DOVER COURT, a noisy assemblage; "all talkers and no hearers, like DOVER COURT." At Dover Court in Essex, a court is annually held; and as the members principally consist of rude fishermen, the irregularity noticed in the proverbial saying frequently prevails. *Bramston* in his *Art of Politics* says :—

> " Those who would captivate the well-bred throng
> Should not too often speak, nor speak too long ;
> Church, nor church matters, ever turn to sport,
> Nor make St Stephen's Chapel DOVER COURT."

DOWD, a woman's nightcap.—*Devonshire;* also an *American* term; possibly from DOWDY, a slatternly woman.

DOWLAS, a linen-draper.

DOWN, to be aware of, or awake to, any move—in this meaning, synonymous with UP; "DOWN upon one's luck," unfortunate; "DOWN in the mouth," disconsolate; "to be DOWN on one," to treat him harshly or suspiciously, to pounce upon him, or detect his tricks.

DOWNER, a sixpence; apparently the *Gipsy* word TAWNO, "little one," in course of metamorphosis into the more usual "*tanner.*"

DOWNY, knowing or cunning; "a DOWNY COVE," a knowing or experienced sharper. In Norfolk, however, it means low-spirited.

" DOWN THE DOLLY," a favourite gambling contrivance, often seen in the tap-rooms of public-houses, at race courses, and fairs, consisting of a round board and the figure of an old man or "DOLL," down which is a spiral hole. A marble is dropped "DOWN THE DOLLY," and stops in one of the small holes or pits (numbered) on the board. The bet is decided according as the marble stops on a high or low figure.

DOWN-THE-ROAD, stylish, showy, after the fashion.

DOWRY, a lot, a great deal; "DOWRY of parny," lot of rain or water.—*See* PARNY. Probably from the *Gipsy.*

DOXY, the female companion of a tramp or beggar. In the West of England, the women frequently call their little girls DOXIES, in a familiar or endearing sense. A learned divine once described *orthodoxy* as being a man's own DOXY, and *heterodoxy* another man's DOXY.— *Ancient Cant.*

DRAB, a vulgar, or low woman.—*Shakspeare.*

DRAG, a cart of any kind, a coach; gentlemen drive to the races in DRAGS.

DRAG, a street, or road; BACK-DRAG, back street.

DRAGGING-TIME, the evening of a country fair day, when the young fellows begin pulling the wenches about.

DOWNS, Tothill Fields' Prison.

DRAG, or THREE MOON, three months in prison.

DRAGGING, robbing carts, &c.

DRAGSMEN, fellows who cut trunks from the backs of carriages. They sometimes have a light cart, and "drop" behind the plundered vehicle,

DRAIN, a drink; "to do a DRAIN," to take a friendly drink—"do a wet;" sometimes called a COMMON SEWER.

DRAW, used in several senses:—1, of a theatre, new piece or exhibition, when it attracts the public and succeeds; 2, to induce—as "DRAW him on;" 3, of pocket-picking—as "DRAW his wipe," "DRAW his ticker." In sporting parlance it is used with an ellipsis of "*trigger*," "I DREW on it as it rose before me." "Come, DRAW it mild!" *i.e.*, don't exaggerate; opposite of "come it strong," from the phraseology of the bar (of a PUBLIC,) where customers desire the beer to be DRAWN mild.

DRAW-BOY, a cunning device used by puffing tradesmen. A really good article is advertised or ticketed and exposed for sale in the shop window at a very low price, with a view of drawing in customers to purchase other and inferior articles at high prices.

DRAWERS, formerly the ancient Cant name for very long stockings, now a hosier's term.

DRAWING TEETH, wrenching off knockers.—*Medical Student* Slang.

DRAWLATCH, a loiterer.

DRAW-OFF, to throw back the body to give impetus to a blow; "he DREW off, and delivered on the left drum."—*Pugilistic*. A sailor would say, "he HAULED off and SLIPPED in."

DRIPPING, a cook.

DRIVE, a term used by tradesmen in speaking of business; "he's DRIVING a *roaring* trade," *i.e.*, a very good one; hence, to succeed in a bargain, "I DROVE a good bargain," *i.e.*, got the best end of it. TO LET DRIVE at one, to strike out.

DRIVE AT, to aim at; "what is he DRIVING AT?" "what does he intend to imply?" a phrase often used when a circuitous line of argument is adopted by a barrister, or a strange set of questions asked, the purpose of which is not very evident.

DRIZ, lace. In a low lodging house this singular autograph inscription

and then drive off in an opposite direction with the booty.—*Old Cant.* The Slang meaning is the drivers of DRAGS.

DRESS A HAT, to—a system of robbery very difficult of detection. It is managed by two or more servants or shopmen of different employers, exchanging their master's goods—as, for instance, a shoemaker's shopman receives shirts or other articles from a hosier's, in return for a pair of boots. Another very ingenious method may be witnessed about eleven o'clock in the forenoon in any of the suburban districts of London. A butcher's boy, with a bit of steak filched from his master's shop, or from a customer, falls in with a neighbouring baker's man, who has a loaf obtained in a similar manner. Their mutual friend, the pot-boy, in full expectation of their visit, has the tap-room fire bright and clear, and not only cooks the steak but "STANDS A SHANT OF GATTER" as his share. So a capital luncheon is improvised for the three, without the necessity of paying for it; and this practical communistic operation is styled DRESSING A HAT.

appeared over the mantelpiece, "Scotch Mary, with DRIZ, (lace,) bound to Dover and back, please God."

DRIZ FENCER, a person who sells lace.

DROP, to quit, go off, or turn aside; "DROP the main Toby," go off the main road.

DROP, "to DROP a man," to knock him down; "to DROP INTO a person," to give him a thrashing. *See* SLIP and WALK. "To DROP ON to a man," to accuse or rebuke him suddenly.

DRUM, a house, a lodging, a street; HAZARD-DRUM, a gambling-house; FLASH-DRUM, a house of ill-fame.

DRUM, the ear.—*Pugilistic.* An example of Slang synecdoche.

DRUM, as applied to the road, is doubtless from the *Wallachian Gipsy* word "DRUMRI," derived from the *Greek*, δρόμος.—*See* note on this source of words, p. 11.

DRUMSTICKS, legs; DRUMSTICK CASES, trousers.

DRYASDUST, an antiquary.

DRY-NURSE, when an inferior officer on board ship carries on the duty, on account of the captain's ignorance of seamanship, the junior officer is said to DRY-NURSE his captain. Majors and adjutants in the army also not unfrequently DRY-NURSE the colonels of their regiments in a similar manner.

DUB, to pay or give; "DUB UP," pay up.

DUBASH, a general agent.—*Anglo-Indian.*

DUBBER, the mouth; "mum your DUBBER," hold your tongue.

DUBLIN PACKET, to turn a corner; to "take the DUBLIN PACKET," viz., run round the corner,—probably a pun on *doubling a corner.*

DUCATS, money.—*Theatrical Slang.*

DUCK, a bundle of bits of the "stickings" of beef sold for food to the London poor.—*See* FAGOT.

DUCKS, trousers.—*Sea* term. The expression most in use on land is "white DUCKS," *i.e.*, white pantaloons or trousers.

"DUCKS AND DRAKES, "to make DUCKS AND DRAKES of one's money," to throw it away childishly,—derived from children "shying" flat stones on the surface of a pool, which they call DUCKS AND DRAKES, according to the number of skips they make.

DUDDER, or DUDSMAN, a person who formerly travelled the country as a pedlar, selling gown-pieces, silk waistcoats, &c., to countrymen. In selling a waistcoat-piece for thirty shillings or two pounds, which cost him perhaps five shillings, he would shew great fear of the revenue officer, and beg of the purchasing clodhopper *to kneel down in a puddle*

DRUMMER, a robber who first makes his victims insensible by drugs or violence, and then plunders them.

DUBS, a bunch of keys. *Nearly obsolete.*

DUBSMAN, or SCREW, a turnkey.

of water, crook his arm, and swear that it might never become straight if he told an exciseman, or even his own wife. The term and practice are nearly obsolete. In Liverpool, however, and at the east end of London, men dressed up as sailors, with pretended silk handkerchiefs and cigars "only just smuggled from the Indies," are still to be plentifully found.

DUDDS, clothes, or personal property. *Gaelic*, DUD; *Ancient Cant;* also *Dutch.*

DUFF, pudding; vulgar pronunciation of DOUGH.—*Sea.*

DUFFER, a hawker of "Brummagem" or sham jewellery; a sham of any kind; a fool, a worthless person. So Arthur Smith, in his *Summer Idyll:*—

"But Robinson, a thorough DUFFER he,
Troll'd out some feeble song about King Cole."

DUFFER was formerly synonymous with DUDDER, and was a general term given to pedlars. It is mentioned in the *Frauds of London* (1760) as a word in frequent use in the last century to express cheats of all kinds. From the *German*, DURFEN, to want?

DUFFING, false, counterfeit, worthless.

DUFFY, a term for a ghost or spirit among the West India negroes. In all probability the DAVY JONES of sailors.

DUKE, gin, a term amongst livery servants.—*Household Words*, No. 183.

DUMBFOUND, to perplex, to beat soundly till not able to speak. Originally a Cant word. Johnson cites the *Spectator* for the earliest use. *Scotch*, DUMFOUNDER.

DUMMACKER, a knowing or acute person.

DUMMIES, empty bottles, and drawers in an apothecary's shop, labelled so as to give the idea of an extensive stock.

DUMMY, in three-handed whist the person who holds two hands plays DUMMY.

DUMPY, short and stout.

DUMPISH, sullen, or glummy.

DUN, to solicit payment.—*Old Cant*, from the French DONNEZ, give; or from JOE DIN, the famous bailiff of Lincoln; or simply a corruption of DIN, from the *Anglo-Saxon* DUNAN, to clamour?

DUNDERHEAD, a blockhead.

DUNDREARY, an empty swell.

DUNG, an operative who works for an employer who does not give full or "society" wages.

DUMMY, a pocket-book. In this word, as in the two preceding, (*see* DUMMY and DUMMIES,) the idea is connected with DUMB, *i.e.*, that which gives no sign. As a thieves' term for a pocket-book, it is peculiarly applicable, for the contents of pocket-books, bank-notes, and papers make no noise, while the money in a purse betrays its presence by chinking.

DUMP-FENCER, a man who sells buttons.

DUNAKER, a stealer of cows or calves. *Nearly obsolete.*

DUNGAREE, low, common, vulgar.—*Anglo-Indian*. DUNGAREE is the name of a disreputable suburb of Bombay, and also of a coarse, blue cloth, worn by sailors.

> "As smart a young fellow as ever you'd see,
> In jacket and trousers of blue DUNGAREE."

DUNKHORNED, sneaking, shabby. DUNKHORN in *Norfolk* is the short, blunt horn of a beast, and the adjective is applied to a cuckold who has not spirit to resist his disgrace.

DUNNAGE, baggage, clothes. Also, a *Sea term* for wood or loose fagots laid at the bottom of ships, upon which is placed the cargo.

DUNNY-KEN, a water-closet.—From DANNA and KEN, which *see*.

DUST, money; "down with the DUST," put down the money.—*Ancient*. Dean Swift once took for his text, "He who giveth to the poor lendeth to the Lord." His sermon was short. "Now, my brethren," said he, "if you are satisfied with the security, down with the DUST."

DUST, a disturbance, or noise, "to raise a dust," to make a row.

DUST, to beat; "DUST one's jacket," *i.e.*, give him a beating.

DUSTY, a phrase used in answering a question where one expects approbation. "What do you think of this?" "Well, it's not so DUSTY," *i.e.*, not so bad; sometimes varied to "none so DUSTY."

DUST-HOLE, Sidney Sussex College at Cambridge.—*Univ. Slang*.

DUST-HOLE, the Queen's Theatre, Tottenham Court Road.—*Theat. Slang*.

DUSTOORIE, commission, doceur, bribe.—*Anglo-Indian*.

DUTCH AUCTION, a method of selling goods, adopted by "CHEAP JOHNS," to evade the penalties for selling without a licence. The article is offered all round at a high price, which is then dropped till it is taken.

DUTCH CONSOLATION, "thank God it is no worse."

DUTCH CONCERT, where each performer plays a different tune.

DUTCH COURAGE, false courage, generally excited by drink,—*pot-valour*.

DUTCH FEAST, where the host gets drunk before his guest.

DUTCH UNCLE, a personage often introduced in conversation, but exceedingly difficult to describe; "I'll talk to him like a DUTCH UNCLE!" conveys the notion of anything but a desirable relation.—*Americanism*.

DUTCH, or DOUBLE DUTCH, gibberish, or any foreign tongue.

EARL-OF-CORK, the ace of diamonds.—*Hibernicism*.

> "'What do you mean by the Earl of Cork?' asked Mr Squander. 'The ace of diamonds, your honour. It's the worst ace, and the poorest card in the pack, and is called the EARL OF CORK, because he's the poorest nobleman in Ireland.'"—*Carleton's Traits and Stories of the Irish Peasantry*.

EARWIG, a clergyman, also one who prompts another maliciously.

EARWIGGING, a rebuke in private; a WIGGING is more public.

DURRYNACKING, offering lace or any other article as an introduction to fortune-telling; generally pursued by women.

EAVES-DROPPER, a listener. The name is derived from the punishment which, according to *Oliver*, was directed in the Lectures, at the revival of Masonry in 1717, to be inflicted on a detected Cowan, [g. v.,] and which was

"To be placed under the eaves of the house in rainy weather, till the water runs in at his shoulders and out at his heels."
—*Mackey's Lexicon of Freemasonry.*

EFF, the vulgar abbreviation of EFFINGHAM SALOON, a favourite music hall at the east end of London.

EGG, or EGG on, to excite, stimulate, or provoke one person to quarrel with another, &c. *Corruption of edge, or edge on.*—*Ancient.*

ELBOW, "to shake one's ELBOW," to play at cards.

ELBOW GREASE, labour, or industry.—*See* PALM OIL.

ELEGANT EXTRACTS, a Cambridge University title for those students who, having unfortunately failed only slightly in some one subject, and being "plucked" accordingly, were allowed their degrees. This applied to the "Poll" List, as the "Gulf" did to the "Honours."

ELEPHANT, "to have SEEN THE ELEPHANT," to be "*up* to the latest move," or "*down* to the last new trick;" to be knowing, and not "green," &c. Possibly a metaphor taken from the travelling menageries, where the ELEPHANT is the *finale* of the exhibition.—Originally an *Americanism. Bartlett* gives conflicting examples. General now, however.

ENEMY, time, a'clock, the ruthless enemy and tell-tale of idleness; "what says the ENEMY?" *i.e.*, how goes the time?

ENTIRE ANIMAL.—*See* HOG.

ESSEX STILE, a ditch.

ESSEX LION, a calf.

EVAPORATE, to go, or run away.

EXES, expenses; written thus—E X S.

EXTENSIVE, frequently applied in a Slang sense to a person's appearance or talk; "rather EXTENSIVE that!" intimating that the person alluded to is shewing off, or "CUTTING IT FAT."

EXTRACTED, placed on the list of "ELEGANT EXTRACTS."—*Camb. Univ.*

EYE-WATER, gin.

FACE, credit at a public-house, impudence, confidence, brass; thus a BRAZEN FACE. "To *run one's* FACE," is to obtain credit in a bounceable manner.

EASE, to rob; "EASING a bloak," robbing a man.

EFTER, a thief who frequents theatres.

EVERLASTING STAIRCASE, the treadmill. Sometimes called "Colonel Chesterton's EVERLASTING STAIRCASE," from the gallant inventor or improver.

FACER, a tumbler of whisky-punch.

> "Cyathi dicti sunt faceres."
> —*Father Tom and the Pope.*

FACER, a blow on the face. In *Ireland*, a dram.

FAD, a hobby, a favourite pursuit.

FADGE, a farthing.

FADGE, a flat loaf.—*North.*

FADGE, to suit or fit; "it won't FADGE," it will not do. Used by *Shakspeare*, but now heard only in the streets.

FADGER, a glazier's frame.

FAG, a schoolboy who performs a servant's offices to a superior schoolmate. Probably from F. A. G., the fifth problem of Euclid. *Grose* thinks FAGGED OUT is derived from this.

FAG, to beat.

FAGGOT, a bundle of bits of the "stickings" (hence probably its name) sold for food to the London poor. It is sometimes called a DUCK. In appearance it resembles a Scotch "haggis." FAG-END of a thing, the inferior or remaining part, the refuse.

FAGOT, a term of opprobrium used by low people to children and women; "you little FAGOT, you!" FAGOT was originally a term of contempt for a dry, shrivelled old woman, whose bones were like a bundle of sticks, only fit to burn.—Compare the French expression for a heretic, *sentir le fagot.*

FAKE; "FAKE the rubber," *i.e.*, stand treat.

FAL-LALS, trumpery ornaments, gew-gaws. *Forby* suggests as a derivation the *Latin*, PHALERÆ, horse trappings.

FAMBLES, or FAMMS, the hands.—*Ancient Cant.* German, FANGEN.

FAN, a waistcoat.—*Houndsditch term.*

FANCY, the favourite sports, pets, or pastime of a person, *the ton of low life.* Pugilists are sometimes termed THE FANCY. *Shakspeare* uses the word in the sense of a favourite, or pet; and the paramour of a prostitute is still called her FANCY-MAN.

FANCY-BLOAK, a fancy or sporting man.

FAKE, to cheat, or swindle; to do anything; to go on, or continue; to make or construct; to steal, or rob,—a verb variously used. FAKED, done, or done for; "FAKE away, there's no down;" go on, there is nobody looking. *Mayhew* says it is from the *Latin*, FACIMENTUM. *Gaelic*, FAIGH, to get, acquire, reach.

FAKEMENT, a false begging petition, any act of robbery, swindling, or deception.

FAKEMENT CHARLEY, the owner's private mark.

FAKER, one who makes or FAKES anything.

"FAKE A CLY," to pick a pocket.

FAMILY MEN, or PEOPLE, thieves, or burglars.

FANNING, a beating.

FAN-QUI, a European; literally, foreign devil.—*Anglo-Chinese.*

FANTADLINS, pastry.

FAN-TAIL, a dustman's hat.

FARMER. In Suffolk this term is applied to the eldest son of the occupier of the farm. In London it is used derisively of a countryman, and denotes a farm-labourer, clodpole. Both senses are different from the general acceptation.

FAST, gay, spreeish, unsteady, thoughtless,—an *Americanism* that has of late ascended from the streets to the drawing-room. The word has certainly now a distinct meaning, which it had not thirty years ago. QUICK is the synonyme for FAST, but a QUICK MAN would not convey the meaning of a FAST MAN,—a person who, by late hours, gaiety, and continual rounds of pleasure, lives too fast, and wears himself out. In polite society a FAST young lady is one who affects mannish habits, or makes herself conspicuous by some unfeminine accomplishment,— talks Slang, drives about in London, smokes cigarettes, is knowing in dogs, horses, &c. An amusing anecdote is told of a FAST young lady, the daughter of a right reverend prelate, who was an adept in *horseflesh.* Being desirous of ascertaining the opinion of a candidate for ordination, who had the look of a bird of the same feather, as to the merits of some cattle just brought to her father's palace for her to select from, she was assured by him they were utterly unfit for a lady's use. With a knowing look at the horses' points, she gave her decision in these choice words, "Well, I agree with you; they *are* a rum lot, as the devil said of the ten commandments." *Charles Dickens,* in the Christmas number of *All the Year Round* for 1859, says that "FAST," when applied to a young man, is only another word for *loose,* as he understands the term; and the *Saturday Review* for July 28, 1860, defines a FAST GIRL as a woman who has lost her respect for men, and for whom men have lost their respect also.

FAST, embarrassed, wanting money, tied up. Synonymous with HARD UP. —*Yorkshire.*

FAT, a printer's term signifying the void spaces on a page, for which he is paid at the same rate as full or unbroken pages. This work afforded much FAT for the printers.

FAT, rich, abundant, &c.; "a FAT lot;" "to cut it FAT," to exaggerate, to show off in an extensive or grand manner, to assume undue importance; "cut up FAT," see under CUT. As a *Theatrical term,* a part with plenty of FAT in it is one which affords the actor an opportunity of effective display.

FAVOURITE, the horse that has the lowest odds laid against it in the betting list. When the FAVOURITE wins, the public generally are the gainers. When an OUTSIDER wins, the RING, that is to say, the persons who make a business of betting, are generally the gainers.

FATHER, or FENCE, a buyer of stolen property.

FAWNEY, a finger ring. *Irish,* FAINEE, a ring

FEATHERS, money, wealth; "in full FEATHER," rich.

FEED, a meal, generally a dinner.—*Stable Slang.*

FEEDER, a spoon.—*Old Cant.*

FEELE, a daughter, or child.—*Corrupted French.*

FELLOW-COMMONER, uncomplimentary epithet used at Cambridge for an empty bottle.

FELT, a hat.—*Old term, in use in the sixteenth century.*

FEN-NIGHTINGALES, toads and frogs, from their continued croaking at night.

FERINGEE, a European.—*Anglo-Indian.*

FERRICADOUZER, a knock-down blow, a good thrashing. Probably derived, through the *Lingua Franca*, from the *Italian*, FAR' CADER' MORTO, to knock down dead.

FEW, used in a Slang sense thus:—"Don't you call this considerably jolly?" "I believe you, my bo-ooy, A FEW." Another expression of the same kind is RATHER, which *see*.

FIB, to beat, or strike.—*Old Cant.*

FIBBING, a series of blows delivered quickly, and at a short distance.—*Pugilistic.*

FIDDLE, a whip.

FIDDLE, "to play second FIDDLE," to act subordinately, or succumb to another.

FIDDLE-FACE, a person with a wizened countenance.

FIDDLE-FADDLE, twaddle, or trifling discourse.—*Old Cant.*

FIDDLER, or FADGE, a farthing.

FAWNEY BOUNCING, selling rings for a wager. This practice is founded upon the old tale of a gentleman laying a wager that if he were to offer "real gold sovereigns" at a penny a-piece at the foot of London Bridge, the English public would be too incredulous to buy. The story states that the gentleman stationed himself with sovereigns on a tea tray, and sold only two within the hour,—winning the bet. This tale the FAWNEY BOUNCERS tell the public, only offering brass, double gilt-rings, instead of sovereigns.

FAWNEY, or FAWNEY RIG, ring-dropping. A few years ago, this practice, or RIG, was very common. A fellow purposely dropped a ring, or a pocket-book with some little articles of jewellery, &c., in it, and when he saw any person pick it up, ran to claim half. The ring found, the question of how the booty was to be divided had then to be decided. The FAWNEY says, "If you will give me eight or nine shillings for my share, the things are yours." This the FLAT thinks very fair. The ring of course is valueless, and the swallower of the bait discovers the trick too late.

FENCE, or FENCER, a purchaser or receiver of stolen goods; FENCE, the shop or warehouse of a FENCER.—*Old Cant.*

FENCE, to sell or pawn stolen property to a FENCER.

FIDDLER, a sixpence.—*Household Words*, No. 183.

FIDDLER, a sharper, a cheat; also one who dawdles over little matters, and neglects great ones.

FIDDLERS' GREEN, the place where sailors go to when they die. It is a place of fiddling, dancing, rum, and tobacco, and is undoubtedly the LAND OF COCAIGNE, mentioned in mediæval manuscripts.

FIDDLERS' MONEY, a lot of sixpences; 6d. was the remuneration to fiddlers from each of the company in old times.

FIDDLE STICKS! an exclamation signifying nonsense.

FIDDLING, doing any odd jobs in the streets, holding horses, carrying parcels, &c., for a living. Among the middle classes, FIDDLING means idling away time, or trifling; and amongst sharpers, it means gambling.

FID FAD, a game similar to chequers, or drafts, played in the West of England.

FIELD-LANE DUCK, a baked sheep's-head. *Field Lane* is a low London thoroughfare, leading from the foot of Holborn Hill to the purlieus of Clerkenwell. It was formerly the market for stolen pocket-handkerchiefs.

FIERA-FACIAS, a red-faced man is often jocularly said to have been served with a writ of FIERI-FACIAS.

FI-FA, a writ of *Fiera-Facias*.—*Legal*.

FI-FI, Mr Thackeray's term for Paul de Kock's novels, and similar modern French literature.

FIG, "in full FIG," *i.e.*, full-dress costume, "extensively got up." Possibly an allusion to the primeval dress of our first parents, or else an abbreviation of *figure*, in the references to plates in books of fashions.

FIG, "to FIG a horse," to play improper tricks with one in order to make him lively.

FIGARO, a barber.

FIGURE, "to cut a good or bad FIGURE," to make a good or indifferent appearance; "what's the FIGURE?" how much is to pay? FIGURE-HEAD, a person's face.—*Sea term*.

FILCH, to steal, or purloin. Originally a Cant word, derived from the FILCHES, or hooks, thieves used to carry, to hook clothes, or any portable articles from open windows.—*Vide Decker*. It was considered a Cant or Gipsy term up to the beginning of the last century. Harman has "FYLCHE, to robbe."

FILE, a deep or artful man, a jocose name for a cunning person. Originally a term for a pickpocket, when TO FILE was to cheat or rob. FILE, an artful man, was used in the thirteenth and fourteenth centuries.

FILLIBRUSH, to flatter, praise ironically.

FIMBLE-FAMBLE, a lame, prevaricating excuse.—*Scandinavian*.

FIDLUM BEN, thieves who take anything they can lay their hands upon.

FIN, a hand; "come, tip us your FIN," viz., let us shake hands.—*Sea*.

FINUF, a five-pound note. DOUBLE FINUF, a ten-pound note.—*German*, FUNF, five.

FIRE-EATER, a "swell" of any kind, a braggadocio or turbulent person who is always ready to fight.

FISH, a person; "a queer FISH," "a loose FISH," &c.

FISHY, doubtful, unsound, rotten—a term used to denote a suspicion of a "screw being loose," or "something rotten in the state of Denmark," in alluding to an unsafe speculation.

FIVES, "bunch of FIVES," the fist.

FIVE FINGERS, the five of trumps, at the game of Five-cards, or Don.

FIX, a predicament, dilemma; "an awful FIX," a terrible position; "to FIX one's flint for him," *i.e.*, to "settle his *hash*," "put a spoke in his wheel."

FIZ, champagne, wine.

FIZZING, first-rate, very good, excellent; synonymous with STUNNING.

FLABERGAST, or FLABBERGHAST, to astonish, or strike with wonder.—*Old*.

FLAG, a groat, or 4d.—*Ancient Cant*.

FLAG, an apron.

FLAG-OF-DISTRESS, poverty; when the end of a person's shirt protrudes through his trousers.—*Seven Dials wit*.

FLAM, nonsense, blarney, a lie.—*Kentish; Anglo-Saxon*.

FLAME, a sweetheart.

FLANNEL, or HOT FLANNEL, the old term for gin and beer, drunk hot, with nutmeg, sugar, &c. Also called FLIP. There is an anecdote told of Goldsmith helping to drink a quart of FLANNEL in a night house, in company with George Parker, Ned Shuter, and a demure, grave-looking gentleman, who continually introduced the words CRAP, STRETCH, SCRAG, and SWING. Upon the Doctor's asking who this strange person might be, and being told his profession, he rushed from the place in a frenzy, exclaiming, "Good God! and have I been sitting all this while with a hangman?"

FLARE UP, a jovial social gathering, a "break down," a "row."

FLASH, showy, smart, knowing; a word with various meanings. A person is said to be dressed FLASH when his garb is showy, and after a fashion, but without taste. A person is said to be FLASH when he apes the appearance or manners of his betters, or when he is trying to be superior to his friends and relations. FLASH also means "fast," roguish, and sometimes infers counterfeit or deceptive,—and this, perhaps, is its general signification. "FLASH, my young friend, or Slang, as others call it, is the classical language of the Holy Land; in other

---

FINDER, one who FINDS bacon and meat at the market before they are lost, *i.e.*, steals them.

FLAM, a ring.

words, St Giles's Greek."—*Tom and Jerry, by Moncreiff.* Vulgar language was first termed FLASH in the year 1718, by Hitchin, author of "*The Regulator of Thieves, &c., with account of* FLASH *words.*"

FLASH IT, show it—said when any bargain is offered.

FLASH-O'-LIGHTNING, the gold band on an officer's cap.—*Sea.*

FLAT, a fool, a silly or "soft" person, the opposite of SHARP. The terms appear to be shortenings for "sharp-witted" and "flat-witted." "Oh, Messrs Tyler, Donelson, and the rest, what FLATS you are!"—*Times*, 5th September 1847.

FLATS, playing cards. Also called BROADS.

FLATTY, a rustic, or uninitiated person.

FLAT-FEET, the battalion companies in the Foot Guards.

FLEMISH ACCOUNT.—*Old.* Still used by sailors for a tangled and unsatisfactory account or reckoning.

FLESH-AND-BLOOD, brandy and port in equal quantities.

FLESH-BAG, a shirt.

FLICK, or OLD FLICK, a comical old chap or fellow.

FLICK, or FLIG, to whip by striking, and drawing the lash back at the same time, which causes a stinging blow.

FLIES, trickery, nonsense. "There are no FLIES about me, sir." Connected with FLY, wide-awake, &c.

FLIM-FLAM, an idle story.—*Beaumont and Fletcher.*

FLIMSY, a bank-note. *See* the following.

FLIMSY, the thin prepared copying-paper used by newspaper reporters and "penny-a-liners" for making several copies at once, thus enabling them to supply different papers with the same article without loss of time.—*Printer's term.*

FLINT, an operative who works for a "society" master, *i.e.*, for full wages.

FLIP, corruption of FILLIP, a light blow.

FLIPPER, the hand; "give us your FLIPPER," give me your hand.—*Sea.* Metaphor taken from the flipper or paddle of a turtle.

FLOATER, a small suet dumpling put into soup.—*Whitechapel.*

FLOG, to whip. Cited both by *Grose* and the author of *Bacchus and Venus* as a Cant word. It would be curious to ascertain the earliest use; *Richardson* cites Lord Chesterfield.—*Latin.*

FLATTY-KEN, a public-house, the landlord of which is ignorant of the practices of the thieves and tramps who frequent it.

FLIMP, to hustle, or rob.

FLIP-FLAPS, a peculiar rollicking dance indulged in by costermongers when merry or excited—better described, perhaps, as the DOUBLE SHUFFLE, danced with an air of extreme *abandon*. Originally a kind of somersault, in which the performer throws himself over on his hands and feet alternately.—*Showman's Slang.*

FLOATING ACADEMY, the hulks.

FLOGGER, a whip.—*Almost obsolete.*

FLOOR, to knock down.—*Pugilistic.*

FLOORED, when a picture is hung on the lowest row at the Exhibition of the Royal Academy, it is in artistic Slang said to be FLOORED, in contra-distinction to SKYED, which *see.*

FLOORER, a blow sufficiently strong to knock a man down.

FLOP, plump; "to go FLOP down," to fall suddenly, and with violence and noise.

FLOWERY, lodging, or house entertainment; "square the omee for the FLOWERY," pay the master for the lodging.—*Lingua Franca.*

FLUE-FAKER, a chimney-sweep; also applied to low sporting characters, who are so termed from their chiefly betting on the *Great Sweeps.*

FLUFF IT, a term of disapprobation, implying "take it away, I don't want it."

FLUKE, at billiards, playing for one thing and getting another. Hence, generally what one gets accidentally, an unexpected advantage, "more by luck than wit."

FLUMMERY, flattery, gammon, genteel nonsense.

FLUMMUX, to perplex, hinder; FLUMMUXED, stopped, used up.

FLUNKEY, a footman, servant.—*Scotch.*

FLUSH, the opposite of HARD UP, in possession of money, not poverty-stricken.—*Shakspeare.*

FLUSH, to whip; "FLUSHED on the horse," to be privately whipped in jail.

FLY, knowing, wide-awake, fully understanding another's meaning.

FLY, to lift, toss, or raise; "FLY the *mags,*" *i.e.,* toss up the halfpence; "to FLY a window," *i.e.,* to lift one for the purpose of stealing.

"FLY THE KITE," or "RAISE THE WIND," to obtain money on bills, whether good or bad, alluding to tossing paper about as children do a kite.

"FLY THE KITE," to evacuate from a window,—term used in padding-kens, or low lodging-houses.

FLYING-MARE, a throw in wrestling.

FLYING-MESS, "to be in FLYING MESS" is a soldier's phrase for being hungry and having to mess where he can.—*Military.*

FLYING STATIONER, a paper-worker, hawker of penny ballads; "Printed for the Flying Stationers" is the *imprimatur* on hundreds of penny histories and sheet songs of the last and present centuries.

FLUMMUXED, done up, sure of a month in QUOD, or prison. In mendicant freemasonry, the sign chalked by rogues and tramps upon a gate-post or house corner, to express to succeeding vagabonds that it is unsafe for them to call there, is known as ⊙, or FLUMMUXED, which signifies that the only thing they would be likely to get upon applying for relief would be a "month in QUOD."—*See* QUOD.

FLYMY, knowing, cunning, roguish.—*Seven Dials* and *Low Life*.

FOALED, "thrown from a horse."—*Hunting term.*—*See* PURLED and SPILT.

FOGEY, or OLD FOGEY, a dullard, an old-fashioned or singular person. Grose says it is a nickname for an invalid soldier, from the *French*, FOURGEAUX, fierce or fiery, but it has lost this signification now. FOGGER, *old word* for a huckster or servant.

FOGGY, tipsy.

FOGLE, a silk handkerchief—not a CLOUT, which is of *cotton*. It has been hinted that this may have come from the *German*, VOGEL, a bird, from the *bird's-eye* spots on some handkerchiefs, [see BIRD'S-EYE-WIPE under BILLY,] but a more probable derivation is the Italian Slang (*Fourbesque*), FOGLIA, a pocket, or purse; or from the *French Argot*, FOUILLE, also a pocket.

FOGUS, tobacco.—*Ancient Cant.* FOGO, *old word for stench.*

FOONT, a sovereign, or 20s.

FOOTING, "to pay FOOTING."—*See* SHOE.

FORAKERS, the closet of decency, or house of office.—Term used by the boys at *Winchester school*.

FORK OUT, to bring out one's money, to pay the bill, to "stand for" or treat a friend; to hand over what does not belong to you.—Old Cant term for picking pockets, and very curious it is to trace its origin. In the early part of the last century, a little book was published on purloining, and of course it had to give the latest modes. FORKING was the newest mode, and it consisted in thrusting the fingers stiff and open into the pocket, and then quickly closing them and extracting any article thus caught.

FORKS, or GRAPPLING-IRONS, fingers.

FORTY-FOOT, a derisive appellation for a very short person.

FORTY-GUTS, vulgar term for a fat man.

FORTY-TWA, the common place of retirement on a well-known French plan at Edinburgh, so called from its accommodating that number of persons at once.

FORTY WINKS, a short sleep or nap.

FOU, slightly intoxicated.—*Scotch.*

FOUR-AND-NINE, or FOUR-AND-NINEPENNY GOSS, a cheap hat, so called from 4s. 9d., the price at which a noted advertising hat-maker sold his hats—

"Whene'er to slumber you incline,
Take a *short* NAP at 4 and 9."—1844.

"FOUR KINGS, HISTORY OF THE," an old name for a pack of playing cards. *See Sir Thomas Urquhart's Translation of Rabelais.* In *Argot*, LIVRE DES QUATRE ROIS.

FOUNTY, water,—from "fountain," probably.—*North.*

FOURTH, or FOURTH COURT, the court appropriated to the water-closets at Cambridge; from its really being No. 4 at Trinity College. A man leaving his room to go to this FOURTH COURT, writes on his door, in algebraic notation, GONE⁴, which expresses the Cambridge Slang phrase, "gone to the FOURTH."

FOX, to cheat or rob.—*Eton College.*

FOXED, a term used by print and book collectors to denote the brown spotted appearance produced by damp on paper.

FOXING, when one actor criticises another's performance.—*Theatrical.*

FOX'S SLEEP, or FOXING, purposely assumed indifference to what is going on. A fox is said to sleep with one eye open.

FOXY, rank, tainted, from the odour of the animal.—*Lincolnshire.*

FOXY, said also of a red-haired person.

FRAPPING, a beating. *French* FRAPPER.

FREE-AND-EASY, a club held at most public-houses, the members of which meet in the tap-room or parlour for the purpose of drinking, smoking, and hearing each other sing and "talk politics." The name indicates the character of the proceedings.

FREEMAN'S QUAY, "drinking at FREEMAN'S QUAY," *i.e.*, at another's cost. This quay was formerly a celebrated wharf near London Bridge, and the saying arose from the beer which was given gratis to porters and carmen who went there on business.

FRENCH CREAM, brandy.

FRENCH LEAVE, to leave or depart slyly, without saying anything.

FRESH, said of a person slightly intoxicated.

FRESHMAN, a University man during his first year. The official appellation for the students until they have passed the Previous or First University Examination, otherwise called the *Smalls* or *Little Go*, is *Junior Sophs* or *Sophisters*. After this they are *Senior Sophs* until their last term, when they are *Questionists*, or preparing "*ad respondendum quæstioni.*"

FRIZZLE, champagne.

FROG, a policeman.

FRONTISPIECE, the face.

FROW, a girl, or wife. *German*, FRAU; *Dutch*, VROUW.

FRUMMAGEMMED, annihilated, strangled, garroted, or spoilt.—*Old Cant.*

FRUMP, a slatternly woman, a gossip.—*Ancient.*

FRUMP, to mock or insult.—*Beaumont and Fletcher.*

F SHARPS, fleas. Compare B FLATS.

FUDGE, nonsense, stupidity. *Todd and Richardson* only trace the word to Goldsmith. *Disraeli*, however, gives the origin to a Captain Fudge,

---

Fox, to watch in the streets for any occurrence which may be turned to a profitable account.—*See* MOOCHING.

FREE, to steal—generally applied to horses.

FRISK, to search; FRISKED, searched by a constable or other officer.

"FRISK A CLY," to empty a pocket.

a great fibber, who told monstrous stories, which made his crew say in answer to any improbability, "you FUDGE it!"—*See Remarks on the Navy*, 1700. At page 87 of *A Collection of some papers of William Crouch*, (8vo, 1712,) the Quaker, we find a mention of this Captain. Degory Marshall informed Crouch that—

> "In the year 1664 we were sentenced for banishment to Jamaica by Judges Hyde and Twisden, and our number was 55. We were put on board the ship Black Eagle; the master's name was *Fudge*, by some called *Lying* FUDGE."

A correspondent asserts that, in his belief, the word comes from the *Gaelic*, FFUG, deception.

FUGGIES, hot rolls.—*School*.

FULLAMS, false dice, which always turn up high.—*Shakspeare*.

FULLY, "to be FULLIED," to be committed for trial. From the Slang of the penny-a-liner, "the prisoner was *fully* committed for trial."

FUNK, trepidation, nervousness, cowardice. To FUNK, to be afraid or nervous.

FUNK, to smoke out.—*North*.

"FUNKING THE COBBLER," a schoolboy's trick, performed with asafœtida and cotton stuffed into a hollow tube or cow's horn. The cotton being lighted, the smoke is blown in through the keyhole of a door, or the crannies of a cobbler's stall.

FUNNY-BONE, the extremity of the elbow—or rather, the muscle which passes round it between the two bones, a blow on which causes painful tingling in the fingers. Facetiously derived, from its being the extremity of the *humerus*, (humorous.)

FYE-BUCK, a sixpence.—*Nearly obsolete*.

GAB, GABBER, or GABBLE, talk; "gift of the GAB," loquacity, or natural talent for speech-making.—*Anglo-Norman*; GAB is also found in the *Danish* and *Old Norse*.

GAD, a trapesing, slatternly woman.—*Gipsy*. Anglo-Saxon, GÆDELING.

"GADDING THE HOOF," going without shoes. GADDING, roaming about, although used in an old translation of the Bible, is now only heard amongst the lower orders.

GAFF, a fair, or penny play-house.—*See* PENNY GAFF.

GAFFER, a master, or employer; term used by "navvies," and general in Lancashire and *North of England*. *Early English* for an old man. See "BLOW the GAFF."

GAFFING, tossing halfpence, or counters.—*North*, where it means tossing up three pennies.

GAG, language introduced by an actor into his part. In certain pieces this is allowed by custom, and these are called GAG-PIECES. *The Critic, or a Tragedy Rehearsed*, is one of these. Many actors, however, take French leave in this respect with most pieces.—*Theatrical Slang*.

> MR ROBSON AT BELFAST.—We (*Northern Whig*) suspected a little bit of what is professionally termed "GAG" in Mr Robson's *Daddy Hardacre* last night

He had occasion to say that one of the characters in the piece "understands me well enough," to which he added—"I wish some other people did the same," with an expressive glance at the pit; which we interpreted as having special reference to those appreciative persons in the audience whom we have already mentioned, who think it absolutely needful to roar with laughter at every sentence Mr Robson utters, without the least regard to whether it be humorous or pathetic—only because Mr Robson has fame as a comic actor.—*Jan.* 1863.

GAG, to hoax, "take a rise" out of one; to COD.

GAGE, a small quantity of anything; as "a GAGE of tobacco," meaning a pipeful; "a GAGE of gin," a glassful.

GALENY, old Cant term for a fowl of any kind; now a respectable word in the West of England, signifying a Guinea fowl.—*Vide Grose*. *Latin*, GALLINA.

GALLAVANT, to wait upon the ladies.—*Old*.

GALLIMAUFRY, a kind of stew made up of scraps of various kinds.

GALLIPOT, an apothecary.

GALLOWS, very, or exceedingly—a disgusting exclamation; "GALLOWS poor," very poor.

GALORE, abundance. *Irish*, GO LEOR, in plenty.

GAMB, a leg. Still used as a heraldic term, as well as by thieves, who probably get it from the *Lingua Franca*. *Italian*, GAMBA; *French*, JAMBE, a leg.

GAME, a term variously applied; "are you GAME?" have you courage enough? "what's your little GAME?" what are you going to do? "come, none of your GAMES," be quiet, don't annoy me; "on the GAME," out thieving.

GAME LEG, a lame or wounded leg.

GAMMON, deceit, humbug, a false and ridiculous story. *Anglo-Saxon*, GAMEN, game, sport.

GAMMON, to hoax, to deceive merrily, to laugh at a person, to tell an untrue but plausible story, to make game of, or, in the provincial dialect, to make GAME ON; "who's thou makin' thy GAM' ON?" *i.e.*, who are you making a fool of?—*Yorkshire*.

GAMMY, bad, unfavourable, poor tempered. Those householders who are known enemies to the street folk and tramps are pronounced by them to be GAMMY. GAMMY sometimes means forged, as "GAMMY-MONEKER," a forged signature; GAMMY STUFF, spurious medicine; GAMMY LOWR, counterfeit coin. *Hants*, GAMY, dirty. The hieroglyphic used by beggars and cadgers to intimate to those of the tribe coming after that things are not very favourable is known as ☐, or GAMMY. *Gaelic*, *Welsh*, and *Irish*, CAM, (GAM,) crooked, bad.

GANDER MONTH, the period when the monthly nurse is in the ascendant, and the husband has to shift for himself.

GAG, a lie; "a GAG he told to the beak."—*Thieves' Cant*.

GAMMY-VIAL, (Ville,) a town where the police will not let persons hawk.

GANGER, the person who superintends the work of a gang, or a number of navigators.

GAPE-SEED, something to look at; a lazy fellow, unmindful of his work, is said to be "looking for GAPE-SEED."

GAR, euphuistic rendering of the title of the Deity; "be GAR, you don't say so!"—*Franco-English.*

GARDEN, among tradesmen signifies Covent *Garden* Market; among theatrical performers, Covent *Garden* Theatre.

GARDENER, an awkward coachman; an insinuation that he is both coachman and gardener, and understands the latter branch of service better than the first; "get on, GARDENER," is a most insulting expression from a cabby to a real coachman.

GARGLE, medical-student Slang for drinkables.

GARNISH, the *douceur* or fee which, before the time of Howard the philanthropist, was exacted by the keepers of gaols from their unfortunate prisoners for extra comforts.

GARNISH, footing-money.—*Yorkshire.*

GARRET, the head.

GARROTING, a mode of cheating practised amongst card-sharpers, by concealing certain cards at the back of the neck.

GAS, "to give a person GAS," to scold him or give him a good beating. Synonymous with "to give him JESSIE."

GASSY, or GASEOUS, liable to "flare up" at any offence.

GATE, THE, Bilingsgate.

GATE-RACE, among pedestrians a mock race, got up not so much for the best runner to win, but for the money taken from spectators at the gate.

GATTER, beer; "shant of GATTER," a pot of beer. A curious Slang street melody, known in Seven Dials as *Bet, the Coaley's Daughter,* thus mentions the word in a favourite verse :—

> "But when I strove my flame to tell,
> Says she, ' Come, *stow that patter,*
> If you're a *cove* wot likes a gal,
> Vy don't you *stand* some GATTER?
> *In course* I instantly complied—
> Two brimming quarts of porter,
> With four *goes* of gin beside,
> Drain'd Bet the Coaley's daughter."

GAWF, a cheap red-skinned apple, a favourite fruit with costermongers, who rub them well with a piece of cloth, and find ready purchasers.

GAWKY, a lanky, or awkward person; a fool. *Saxon,* GEAC; *Scotch,* GOWK.

GAY, loose, dissipated; "GAY woman," a kept mistress or prostitute.

GARRETER, a thief who crawls over the tops of houses and enters garret-windows. Called also a DANCER, or DANCING-MASTER.

GARRET, the fob pocket.—*Prison term.*

GAY-TYKE-BOY, a dog-fancier.

GEE, to agree with, or be congenial to a person.

GEELOOT, a recruit, or awkward soldier.

GEN, a shilling. Also, GENT, silver. Abbreviation of the *French*, ARGENT.

GENT, a contraction of "gentleman,"—in more senses than one. A dressy, showy, foppish man, with a little mind, who vulgarises the prevailing fashion.

GENT, silver. From the *French*, ARGENT.

"GENTLEMAN OF FOUR OUTS;" in Ireland when a vulgar, blustering fellow asserts that he is a gentleman, the retort generally is, "Yes, a GENTLEMAN OF FOUR OUTS—that is, without wit, without money, without credit, and without manners."

"GENTLEMAN OF THREE INNS"—that is, in debt, in danger, and in poverty.

GEORDIE, general term in Northumberland and Durham for a pitman, or coal-miner. Origin not known; the term has been in use more than a century.

GERMAN DUCK, a sheep's-head stewed with onions; a favourite dish among the German sugar-bakers in the East End of London.

GERMAN DUCKS, bugs.—*Yorkshire*.

GET-UP, a person's appearance, or general arrangements. Probably derived from the decorations of a play.

> "There's so much GETTING UP to please the town,
> It takes a precious deal of coming down."
> —*Planché's Mr Buckstone's Ascent of Parnassus.*

GHOST, "the GHOST doesn't walk," *i.e.*, the manager is too poor to pay salaries as yet.—*Theatrical; Household Words*, No. 183.

GIB-FACE, properly the lower lip of a horse; "TO HANG ONE'S GIB," to pout the lower lip, be angry or sullen.

GIBBERISH, unmeaning jargon; the language of the Gipsies, synonymous with SLANG, another *Gipsy* word. Somner says, "*French*, GABBER; *Dutch*, GABBEREN; and our own GAB, GABBER; hence also, I take it, our GIBBERISH, a kind of canting language used by a sort of rogues we vulgarly call Gipsies, a *gibble gabble* understood only among themselves."—*Gipsy*. See Introduction. The GIBBERISH of schoolboys is formed by placing a consonant between each syllable of a word, and is called the GIBBERISH of the letter inserted. Thus, if F were the letter, it would be termed the F GIBBERISH; if L, the L GIBBERISH—as in the sentence, "How do you do?—*Howl dol youl dol*." A GIBBERISH is sometimes formed by adding *vis* to each word, in which the previous sentence would be—"*Howvisdovis youvis dovis?*" Schoolboys in France form a GIBBERISH, in a somewhat similar manner, by elongating their words two syllables, in the first of which an *r*, in the second a *g*, predominates. Thus the words *vous êtes un fou* are spoken, *vousdregue esdregue undregue foudregue*. Fast persons in Paris, of both sexes, frequently adopt terminations of this kind, from some popular song, actor, exhibition, or political event. In 1830, the favourite termination was *mar*, saying *epicemar* for epicier, *cafemar* for cafe. In 1823, when the diorama created a sensation in Paris, the people spoke in *rama* (*on parlait en rama*.) In *Balzac's* beautiful tale, *Le Pere Goriot*, the young painter at the boarding-house dinner-table mystifies the landlady by saying, "what a beautiful *soupeaurama !*" To which the old woman replies, to the great laughter of the company, "I beg your pardon, sir, it is *une soupe à choux*."

GIFFLE-GAFFLE, nonsense. *See* CHAFF. *Icelandic,* GAFLA.

GIG, a farthing. Formerly GRIG.

GIG, fun, frolic, a spree. *Old French*, GIGUE, a jig, a romp.

> "In search of *lark*, or some delicious GIG,
> The mind delights on, when 'tis in *prime twig*."
> —*Randall's Diary,* 1820.

> "No *heirs* have I," said mournful Matt;
> But Tom, still fond of GIG,
> Cried out, "No hairs? don't fret at that,
> When you can buy a wig."

GIGLAMPS, spectacles. In my first edition I stated this to be a *University term*. *Mr Cuthbert Bede*, however, in a communication to *Notes and Queries*, of which I have availed myself in the present edition, says—"If the compiler has taken this epithet from *Verdant Green*, I can only say that I consider the word not to be a 'University' word in general, but as only due to the inventive genius of Mr Bouncer in particular." The term, however, has been adopted, and is now in general use.

GILL, a homely woman; "Jack and GILL," &c.—*Ben Jonson.*

GILLS, the lower part of the face.—*Bacon.* "To grease one's GILLS," "to have a good feed," or make a hearty meal.

GILLS, a shirt collar.

GILT, money. *German,* GELD; *Dutch,* GELT.

GIMCRACK, a bijou, a slim piece of mechanism. *Old Slang* for "a spruce wench."—*New Bailey.*

"GIN-AND-GOSPEL GAZETTE," the *Morning Advertiser*, so called from its being the organ of the Dissenting party, and of the Licensed Victuallers' Association. Sometimes termed the TAP-TUB, or the 'TIZER.

GINGER, a showy, fast horse—as if he had been FIGGED with GINGER under his tail.

GINGERLY, to do anything with great care.—*Cotgrave.*

GINGER HACKLED, having flaxen light yellow hair.—*See* HACKLE.

GINGUMBOB, a bauble.

"GIRNIGO-GABY THE CAT'S COUSIN," a reproachful expression said to a crying child.

GIVE, to strike, to scold; "I'll GIVE it to you," *i.e.*, I will thrash you.

GLADSTONE, cheap claret, since that popular Chancellor of the Exchequer has reduced the duty on French wines.

GIFT, any article which has been stolen, and afterwards sold at a low price.

GLASGOW MAGISTRATE, a salt herring.—*Scotch.*
GLAZE, glass; generally applied to windows.
GLIB, a tongue; "slacken your GLIB," *i.e.*, "loosen your tongue."
GLIM, a light, a lamp; "dowse the GLIM," put out the candle.—*Sea and Old Cant.* GLIMS, spectacles. *Gaelic*, GLINN, light. *German*, (provincial,) GLIMM, a spark.
GLOAK, a man.—*Scotch.*
GLUM, sulky, stern; "to look GLUM," to appear annoyed or disconcerted.
GLUMP, to sulk.
GLUMPISH, of a stubborn, sulky temper.
GNOSTIC, a knowing one, or "sharper."—*Nearly obsolete in this vulgar sense.*
GO, a GO of gin, a quartern of that liquor. (This word, as applied to a measure of liquor, is stated by a correspondent to have arisen from the following circumstance :—Two well-known actors once met at the bar of a tavern to have a "wet" together. "One more glass and then we'll GO" was repeated so often on either hand, that in the end GO was out of the question with both of them, and so the word passed into a saying;) GO is also synonymous with circumstance or occurrence; "a rummy GO," and "a great GO," signify curious and remarkable occurrences; "no GO," no good; "here's a pretty GO !" here's a trouble ; GO, a term in the game of cribbage; "to GO the jump," to enter a house by the window; "all the GO," in fashion.—*See* LITTLE GO ; also CALL-A-GO.

> "Gemmen (says he,) you all well know
> The joy there is whene'er we meet ;
> It 's what I call the primest GO,
> And rightly named, 'tis—' quite a treat.'"
> —*Jack Randall's Diary*, 1820.

"GO DUE NORTH," to become bankrupt, to go to Whitecross Street.
GOB, the mouth; mucus, or saliva.—*North.* Sometimes used for GAB, talk—

> "There was a man called *Job*,
> Dwelt in the land of Uz ;
> He had a good gift of the GOB ;
> The same case happen us."
> ZACH. BOYD.

Gaelic—GAB and GOB, a mouth. *See* GAB.
GOB, a portion.
"GOD BLESS THE DUKE OF ARGYLE!" a Scottish insinuation made when one shrugs his shoulders, of its being caused by parasites or cutaneous affections.—*See* SCOTCH FIDDLE, SCOTCH GREYS. It is said to have been originally the thankful exclamation of the Glasgow folks, at finding a certain row of iron posts, erected by his grace in that city to mark the division of his property, very convenient to rub against.

GLIM LURK, a begging paper, giving a certified account of a dreadful fire —which never happened.
GO-ALONG, a thief.—*Household Words*, No. 183.

GODS, the people in the upper gallery of a theatre; "up amongst the GODS," a seat amongst the low persons in the gallery—so named from the high position of the gallery, and the blue sky generally painted on the ceiling of the theatre; termed by the *French*, PARADIS.

GODS, the quadrats used by printers in throwing on the imposing stone, similar to the movement in casting dice.—*Printer's term.*

GO IT, a term of encouragement, implying, "keep it up!" Sometimes amplified to GO IT, YE CRIPPLES; said to have been a facetious rendering of the last line of *Virgil's Eclogues*—

"Ite domum Saturæ, Venit Hesperus, *ite capellæ;*"

or, "GO IT, YE CRIPPLES, CRUTCHES ARE CHEAP."

GOLDFINCH, a sovereign.

GOLGOTHA, a hat, "place of a skull." Hence the "Don's gallery," at St Mary's, Cambridge.—*Vide* SKULL.

GOL-MOL, noise, commotion.—*Anglo-Indian.*

GOLOPSHUS, splendid, delicious, luscious.—*Norwich.*

GONNOF, or GUN, a fool, a bungler, an amateur pickpocket. A correspondent thinks this may be a corruption of *gone off*, on the analogy of GO-ALONG; but the term is really as old as *Chaucer's* time. During Kett's rebellion in Norfolk, in the reign of Edward VI., a song was sung by the insurgents in which the term occurs:—

"The country GNOFFES, Hob, Dick, and Hick,
With clubbes and clouted shoon,
Shall fill up Dussyn dale
With slaughter'd bodies soone."

GOOD-WOMAN, a not uncommon public-house sign, representing a woman without a head,—the ungallant allusion is that she cannot scold. The HONEST LAWYER, another sign, is depicted in the same manner.

GOOSE, a tailor's pressing iron.—Originally a Slang term, but now in most dictionaries.

GOOSE; "Paddy's GOOSE," *i.e.*, the white swan.

GOOSE, "to cook his GOOSE," to kill him; the same as "to give him his GRUEL," or "settle his HASH."

GOOSE, "to get the GOOSE," "to be goosed," signifies to be hissed while on t' stage. The BIG-BIRD, the terror of actors.—*See* BIG-BIRD.— *Theatrical.*

GOOSE, to ruin, or spoil; to hiss a play.—*Theatrical.*

GOOSEBERRY, to "play up old GOOSEBERRY" with any one, to defeat or silence a person in a quick or summary manner.

GOOSECAP, a booby, or noodle.—*Devonshire.*

GOOSER, a settler, or finishing blow.

GO-OVER, in clerical Slang, signifies to join the Church of Rome.

GORMED, a Norfolk corruption of a profane oath. So used by Mr Peggotty, one of Dickens's characters.

GORGER, a swell, a well-dressed, or *gorgeous* man—probably derived from

K

that word. Sometimes employed in the sense of an employer, or principal, as the manager of a theatre.

GOSPEL-GRINDER, a city missionary, or tract-distributor.

GOSS, a hat—from the gossamer silk with which modern hats are made.

GOSS, "to give a man GOSS," to requite for an injury, to beat, or kill him.

GOUROCK HAM, salt herrings. Gourock, on the Clyde, about twenty-five miles from Glasgow, was formerly a great fishing village.—*Scotch.*

GOVERNMENT SIGN-POST, the gallows.

GOVERNOR, a father, a master or superior person, an elder; "which way, GUV'NER, to Cheapside?"

GOWLER, a dog.—*North Country Cant.* Query, GROWLER.

GOWNSMAN, a student at one of the universities. A person of the town, not connected with the college, would be termed a SNOB.

"GOWN AND TOWN ROW," a fight between the students and townsmen at Cambridge.

GRAB, to clutch, or seize; GRABBED, caught, apprehended.

GRABBER, the hand.

GRACE-CARD, the six of hearts, so termed in Ireland. A Kilkenny gentleman, named Grace, being solicited, with promises of royal favour, to espouse the cause of William III., gave the following answer, written on the back of the six of hearts, to an emissary of Marshal Schomberg's, who had been commissioned to make the proposal to him:—"Tell your master I despise his offer; and that honour and conscience are dearer to a gentleman than all the wealth and titles a prince can bestow."

GRAFT, to work; "where are you GRAFTING?" *i.e.*, where do you live, or work?

GRANNY, importance, knowledge, pride; "take the GRANNY off them as has white hands," viz., remove their self-conceit.—*Mayhew*, vol. i., p. 364.

GRANNY, a knot which will not hold, from its being wrongly and clumsily tied.—*Sea.*

GRANNY, to know, or recognise; "do ye GRANNY the bloke?" do you know the man?

GRAPPLING IRONS, fingers.—*Sea.*

GRASS, "gone to GRASS," dead,—a coarse allusion to *burial;* absconded, or disappeared suddenly; "oh, go to GRASS," a common answer to a troublesome or inquisitive person,—possibly a corruption of "go to GRACE," meaning, of course, a directly opposite fate.

GRASS-COMBER, a country fellow, a haymaker.

GRASS-WIDOW, an unmarried mother; a deserted mistress. In the United States, during the gold fever in California, it was common for an adventurer to put both his wife (termed in his absence a GRASS-WIDOW) and his children to *school* during his absence.

GRAVEL, to confound, to bother; "I'm GRAVELLED," *i.e.*, perplexed or confused.—*Old.* Also, to prostrate, beat to the ground.

GRAVEL-RASH, a scratched face,—telling its tale of a drunken fall. A person subject to this is called a GRAVEL-GRINDER.

GRAVESEND SWEETMEATS, shrimps.

GRAY-COAT PARSON, a lay impropriator, or lessee of great tithes.

GRAYS, or SCOTCH GRAYS, lice.—*Scotch.*

GRAY, a halfpenny, with either two "heads" or two "tails"—both sides alike. *Low gamblers* use GRAYS. They cost from 2d. to 6d. each.

GREASE-SPOT, a minute remnant, the only distinguishable remains of an antagonist after a terrific contest.

GREASING a man is bribing; SOAPING is flattering him.

GREEKS, the low Irish. ST GILES'S GREEK, Slang or Cant language. *Cotgrave* gives MERRIE GREEK as a definition for a roistering fellow, a drunkard. The Greeks have always been regarded as a jolly, luxurious race; so much so, that the Latins employed the verb *Græcari* (lit. *to play the* GREEK) to designate fine living and free potations, a sense in which *Horace* frequently uses it; while *Shakspeare* often mentions the MERRY GREEKS; and "as merry as a GRIG" (or GREEK) was long a favourite allusion in old English authors.—*See* MEDICAL GREEK.

GREENWICH GOOSE, a pensioner of the Naval Hospital.

GREEN, ignorant, not wide-awake, inexperienced.—*Shakspeare.* "Do you see any GREEN in my eye?" ironical question in a dispute.

GREEN-HORN, a fresh, simple, or uninitiated person.

GREENLANDER, an inexperienced person, a spoon.

GRIDDLER, a person who sings in the streets without a printed copy of the words.—*Seven Dials.*

GRIDIRON, a County Court summons.

"GRIDIRON AND DOUGH-BOYS," the flag of the United States, in allusion to the stars and stripes.—*Sea.*

GRIEF, "to come to GRIEF," to meet with an accident, be ruined.

GRIFFIN, in India, a newly-arrived cadet; general for an inexperienced youngster. "Fast" young men in London frequently term an umbrella a GRIFFIN.

GRIND, "to take a GRIND," *i.e.*, a walk, or constitutional—*University.*

GRIND, to work up for an examination, to cram with a GRINDER, or private tutor.—*Medical*, but commencing to be general.

GRINDER, a tooth.

GRINDOFF, a miller.

GRIPES, the stomach-ache.—*See* TRIPES.

GROGGY, tipsy; when a prize-fighter becomes "weak on his pins," and nearly beaten, he is said to be GROGGY.—*Pugilistic.* The same term is applied to horses in a similar condition. *Old English,* AGGROGGYD weighed down, oppressed —*Prompt. Parvulorum.* Or it may only mean that unsteadiness of gait consequent on imbibing too much GROG.

GROG-BLOSSOMS, pimples on the face, caused by hard drinking. Of such a person it is often said, "He bears his blushing honours thick upon him."

GROG-FIGHT, a drinking party.—*Military.*

GRUB, meat or victuals of any kind,—GRUB signifying food, and BUB, drink.

GRUBBING-KEN, or SPINIKIN, a workhouse; a cook-shop.

GRUBBY, musty, or old-fashioned.—*Devonshire.*

GRUEL, "to give a person his GRUEL," to kill him. An expression in all probability derived from the report of a trial for poisoning. Compare "to settle his HASH," and "cook his GOOSE."

GULFED, a University term, denoting that a man is unable to enter for the classical examination from having failed in the mathematical.[*] Candidates for classical honours were compelled to go in for both examinations. From the alteration of the arrangements, the term is now obsolete.—*Cambridge.*

GULL, to cheat, deceive; also, one easily cheated.

GULPIN, a weak, credulous fellow, who will gulp down anything.

GUMMY, thick, fat—generally applied to a woman's ankles, or to a man whose flabby person betokens him a drunkard.

GUMPTION, or RUMGUMPTION, comprehension, capacity. From GAUM, to comprehend; "I canna GAUGE it, and I canna GAUM it," as a Yorkshire exciseman said of a hedgehog.

GUNNER'S DAUGHTER, a term facetiously applied to the method of punishing boys in the Royal Navy by tying them securely to the breech of a cannon, so as to present the proper part convenient for the cat, and flogging them. This is called "marrying" or "kissing the GUNNER'S DAUGHTER."

GUP, gossip.—*Anglo-Indian.*

GURRAWAUN, a coachman, a native Indian corruption of the English word coachman. For another curious corruption of a similar kind, *see* SIMKIN.—*Anglo-Indian.*

GUT-SCRAPER, a fiddler.

GUTTER BLOOD, a low or vulgar man.—*Scotch.*

GUTTER LANE, the throat.

GUY, a fright, a dowdy, an ill-dressed person. Derived from the effigy of Guy Fawkes carried about by boys on Nov. 5.

[*] These men's names appeared in the list of "DEGREES ALLOWED." The name "GULF" for this list is said to have arisen from the boast of a former "wooden spoon." "I would have you to know there is a great GULF between *me* and the captain of the poll."

GULLY-RAKERS, cattle thieves in Australia, the cattle being stolen out of almost inaccessible valleys, there termed GULLIES.

GURRELL, a fob.—*Westminster Slums.*

GYP, an undergraduate's valet at *Cambridge.* Corruption of GYPSY JOE, (*Saturday Review ;*) popularly derived by Cantabs from the *Greek,* GYPS, (γυψ,) a vulture, from their dishonest rapacity. At *Oxford* they are called SCOUTS.

HACKLE, "to show HACKLE," to be willing to fight. HACKLES are the long feathers on the back of a cock's neck, which he erects when angry,—hence the metaphor.

HACKSLAVER, to stammer in one's speech, like a dunce at his lesson.

HADDOCK, a purse.—*See* BEANS.

HAKIM, a medical man.—*Anglo-Indian.*

HALF-A-BEAN, half-a-sovereign.

HALF-A-BULL, two shillings and sixpence.

HALF-A-COUTER, half-a-sovereign.

HALF-A-HOG, sixpence; sometimes termed HALF-A-GRUNTER.

HALF-A-TUSHEROON, half-a-crown.

HALF-AND-HALF, a mixture of ale and porter, much affected by medical students; occasionally *Latinised* into DIMIDIUM DIMIDIUMQUE. —*See* COOPER.

HALF-BAKED, soft, doughy, half-witted, silly. HALF-ROCKED has a similar meaning.

HALF-FOOLISH, ridiculous; means often *wholly* foolish.

HALF-JACK.—*See* JACKS.

HALF-MOURNING, to have a black eye from a blow.

HALF-ROCKED, silly, half-witted.—Compare HALF-BAKED.

HALF-SEAS-OVER, reeling drunk.—*Sea.* Used by *Swift.*

HALL, the Leadenhall Market; the same as "THE GARDEN" refers to Covent Garden.

HAND, a workman, or helper, a person. "A COOL HAND," explained by Sir Thomas Overbury to be "one who accounts bashfulness the wickedest thing in the world, and therefore studies impudence."

HANDER, a second, or assistant, in a prize fight.

HANDICAP. HANDICAPPING, in racing affairs, now signifies the adjudgment of various weights to horses differing in age, power, and speed, to place them as much as possible on an equality, and thereby enable one or all to have a fair chance of winning the race.

The old game of HANDICAP (hand i' the cap) is a very different affair; and as it is now almost obsolete, being only played by gentlemen in Ireland, after hunting and racing dinners, when the wine has circulated pretty freely, merits a description here. It is played by three persons, in the following manner :—A wishes to obtain some article belonging to B, say a horse; and offers to "challenge" his watch against it. B agrees; and C is chosen as handicapper to "make the award"—that is, to name the sum of money that the owner of the article of lesser value shall give with it, in exchange for the more

---

HALF-A-STRETCH, six months in prison.

valuable one. The three parties, A, B, and C, put down a certain stake each, and then the handicapper makes his award. If A and B are both satisfied with the award, the exchange is made between the horse and watch, and the handicapper wins, and takes up the stakes. Or if neither be satisfied with the award, the handicapper takes the stakes; but if A be satisfied and B not, or *vice versa*, the party who declares himself satisfied gets the stakes. It is consequently the object of the handicapper to make such award as will cause the challenger and challenged to be of the same mind; and considerable ingenuity is required and exhibited on his part. The challenge having been made, as stated, between A's watch and B's horse, each party puts his HAND into a CAP or hat [or into his pocket] while C makes the award, which he purposely does in as rapid and complex a manner as possible. Thus, after humorously exaggerating the various excellences of the articles, he may say—"The owner of the superior gold lever watch shall give to the owner of the beautiful thoroughbred bay horse, called Flyaway, the watch and fifteen half-crowns, seven crowns, eighteen half-guineas, one hundred and forty groats, thirteen sovereigns, fifty-nine pence, seventeen shillings and sixty-three farthings. Draw, gentlemen!" A and B must instantly then draw out and open their hands. If money appears in both, they are agreed, and the award stands good; if money be in neither hand, they are also agreed, but the award is rejected. If money be only in one hand, they are not agreed, the award is off, and the stakes go as already stated. Very frequently, neither A nor B are sufficiently quick in their mental calculations to follow the handicapper, and not knowing on the instant the total of the various sums in the award, prefer being "off," and "draw" no money. As in this event the handicapper gets the stakes, the reason for the complex nature of his award is obvious.

When handicapping has once commenced in a convivial party, it is considered unsportsmanlike to refuse a challenge. So when the small hours draw on, and the fun becomes fast and furious, coats, boots, waistcoats, even shirts are challenged, handicapped, and exchanged, amidst an almost indescribable scene of good-humoured jovialty and stentorian laughter. This is the true HANDICAP. The application of the term to horse-racing has arisen from one or more persons being chosen to make the award between persons, who put down equal sums of money, on entering horses unequal in power and speed for the same race.

HANDLE, a nose; the title appended to a person's name; also a term in boxing, "to HANDLE one's fists," to use them against an adversary.

HANDLING, a method of concealing certain cards in the palm of the hand, one of the many modes of cheating practised by sharpers.

HAND-SAW, or "CHIVE-FENCER," a man who sells razors and knives in the streets.

HANDSELLER, or CHEAP JACK, a street or open-air seller, a man who carries goods to his customers, instead of waiting for his customers to visit him.

HANG OUT, to reside,—in allusion to the ancient custom of *hanging out signs*.

HANGMAN'S WAGES, thirteenpence halfpenny.—*Old.* 17*th century.*
> "'Sfoot, what a witty rogue was this to leave this fair thirteenpence halfpenny, and this old halter," intimating aptly—
> "Had the hangman met us there, by these presages
> Here had been his work, and here *his wages.*"
> —*Match at Midnight. Old Plays,* vii. 357.

HANNAH, "that's the man as married HANNAH," a Salopian phrase to express a matter begun.

HANSEL, or HANDSALE, the *lucky money*, or first money taken in the morning by a pedlar.—*Cocker's Dictionary,* 1724. "Legs of mutton (street term for sheep's trotters, or feet) two for a penny; who'll give me a HANSEL? who'll give me a HANSEL?"—*Cry at Cloth Fair at the present day.* Hence, earnest money, first fruits, &c. In Norfolk, HANSELLING a thing is using it for the first time, as wearing a new coat, taking seizin of it, as it were.—*Anglo-Saxon. Nich. Bailey.*

"**HA'PURTH O' COPPERS**," Habeas Corpus.—*Legal Slang.*

"**HA'PURTH O' LIVELINESS**," the music at a low concert, or theatre.

HARAMZADEH, a very general Indian term of contempt, signifying baseborn.—*Anglo-Indian.*

HARD LINES, hardship, difficulty.—*Soldier's term* for hard duty on the *lines* in front of the enemy. The editor of *Notes and Queries* proves *Lines* to have been formerly synonymous with *Lots,* from Ps. xvi. 6.—*Bible version*—"The LINES are fallen unto me in pleasant places;" *Prayer-Book do.*—"The LOT is fallen unto me in a fair ground."—Vol. xii., p. 287.

HARDY, a stone.—*North.*

HARD-UP, in distress, poverty stricken.—*Sea.*

HARD-UP, a cigar-end finder, who collects the refuse pieces of smoked cigars from the gutter, and having dried them, sells them as tobacco to the very poor.

HARRY, or OLD HARRY, (*i.e., Old Hairy?*) the Devil; "to play OLD HARRY with one," *i.e.,* ruin or annoy him.

HARRY-SOPH, (ἐρίσοφος, very wise indeed,) a student of law or physic at Cambridge, who being of the same standing as the students in arts in his year, is allowed to wear a full-sleeved gown when they assume their B.A. gowns, though he does not obtain his actual degree so soon. An undergraduate in his last *year* is a *Senior Soph,* in his last *term,* a *Questionist. Vide Cambridge University Calendar for* 1852, p. 38.—*Cambridge.*

HARUM-SCARUM, wild, dissipated, reckless; four horses driven in a line. This is also called SUICIDE. *See* TANDEM, RANDEM, UNICORN, &c.

HASH, a mess, confusion; "a pretty HASH he made of it;" to HASH UP, to jumble together without order or regularity. The term also occurs in the phrase "to settle his HASH," which is equivalent to "give him his GRUEL," or "cook his GOOSE," *i.e.,* kill him.

HATCHET, "to throw the HATCHET," to tell lies.

HATCHET, "to sling the HATCHET," to skulk.—*Sea*.
HAWBUCK, a vulgar, ignorant, country fellow.
HAWSE HOLES, the apertures in a ship's bows through which the cables pass; "he has crept in through the HAWSE-HOLES," said of an officer who has risen from the grade of an ordinary seaman.—*Navy*.
HAY BAG, a woman.
HAZE, to confuse and annoy a subordinate by contradictory, unnecessary, and perplexing orders.
HAZY, intoxicated.—*Household Words*, No. 183.
HEAD-BEETLER, the bully of the workshop, who lords it over his fellow-workmen by reason of superior strength, skill in fighting, &c. Sometimes applied to the foreman.
HEADER, a plunge head foremost into water, or a fall in the same posture from accident. Also a recently-adopted theatrical expression for the daring jump of the hero or heroine in sensational dramas. See newspaper reviews of the "Colleen Bawn."
"HEAD OR TAIL," "I can't make HEAD OR TAIL of it," *i.e.*, cannot make it out. Originally a betting phrase.
HEAD-RAILS, the teeth.—*Sea*.
HEAD-SERAG, a master; from SERANG, a boatswain.—*Bengalee*, and *Sea*.
HEAP, "a HEAP of people," a crowd; "struck all of a HEAP," suddenly astonished.
HEAT, a bout, or turn, in horse-racing; the gainer of two HEATS winning the race.
HEAVY DRAGOONS, bugs, in contradistinction to *fleas*, which are LIGHT INFANTRY.—*Oxford University*.
HEAVY WET, porter and beer,—because the more a man drinks of it, the heavier and more stupid he becomes.
HEDGE, to secure a doubtful bet by making others.—*Turf*. HEDGING, as a system of betting, is quite different from BOOKMAKING, and may be explained as follows :—The HEDGER, from information or good judgment, selects, say, three horses, A, B, and C, likely to advance in the betting, and takes 50 to 1—say £1000 to £20—against each of them. As the race-day approaches the horse A may fall out of the betting, from accident or other cause, and have to be written off as a dead loss of £20. But the other two horses, as anticipated, improve in public favour, and the HEDGER succeeds in laying 5 to 1—say £500 to £100 —against B, and 2 to 1—say £500 to £250—against C. The account then stands thus—A is a certain loss of £20; but if B wins, the HEDGER will receive £1000 and pay £500; balance in favour, £500. If B loses, the HEDGER will receive £100 and pay £20; balance in favour, £80. If C wins, the HEDGER will receive £1000 and pay £500; balance in favour, £500. If C loses, the HEDGER will receive £250 and pay £20; balance in favour, £230. Deducting, then, the loss of £20 on A, the HEDGER'S winnings will be considerable; and he cannot lose, providing his information or judgment lead to the required result, which, in two cases out of three, may be considered a certainty. But it

must never be forgotten that however well *Turf* speculations may look on paper, they are subject to the contingency of the bets being honourably paid on SETTLING-DAY. "The Druid" in *Post and Paddock* remarks:—

> "The term HEDGING has been quite superseded by "LAYING OFF;" and we had, in fact, quite forgotten it till we saw it stated in the papers lately, by a clergyman, who did not answer a question on doctrine as the Bishop of Exeter exactly liked, that his lordship addressed him to this effect: 'You are HEDGING, sir; you are HEDGING!'"

See BOOK and BOOKMAKING.

HEDGE-POPPING, shooting small birds about the hedges, as boys do; unsportsmanlike kind of shooting.

HEEL-TAP, the small quantity of wine or other beverage left in the bottom of a glass, considered as a sign that the liquor is not liked, and therefore unfriendly and unsocial to the host and the company. *See* DAY-LIGHT.

HEIGH-HO! a Cant term for stolen yarn, from the expression used to apprise the dishonest manufacturer that the speaker had stolen yarn to sell.—*Norwich Cant.*

HELL, a fashionable gambling-house. In printing-offices, the term is generally applied to the old tin box in which is thrown the broken or spoilt type, purchased by the founders for re-casting. *Nearly obsolete.*

"HELL AND TOMMY," utter destruction.

HEN-PECKED, said of one whose wife "wears the breeches."

HERRING-POND, the sea; "to be sent across the HERRING-POND," to be transported.

HIDING, a thrashing. *Webster* gives this word, but not its root, HIDE, to beat, flay by whipping.

HIGGLEDY-PIGGLEDY, all together,—as hogs and pigs lie.

HIGH CHURCH, in contradistinction to LOW CHURCH. *See* the following.

"HIGH AND DRY," an epithet applied to the *soi-disant* "orthodox" clergy of the last century, for whom, while ill-paid curates did the work, the *comforts* of the establishment were its greatest charms.

> "Wherein are various ranks, and due degrees,
> The Bench for honour, and the Stall for ease."

Though often confounded with, they are utterly dissimilar to, the modern High Church or Anglo-Catholic party. Their equally uninteresting opponents deserved the corresponding appellation of "LOW AND SLOW;" while the so-called "Broad Church" is defined with equal felicity as the "BROAD AND SHALLOW."

HIGH-FLY, "ON THE HIGH-FLY," on the begging or cadging system.

HIGH JINKS, "ON THE HIGH JINKS," taking up an arrogant position, assuming an undue superiority. *Scott* explains this game in his *Guy Mannering.*

"HEN AND CHICKENS," large and small pewter pots.

HIGH-FLYER, a genteel beggar or swindler.

HIGH-FLYER, a large swing, in frames, at fairs and races.

HIGH-LOWS, laced boots reaching a trifle higher than ankle-jacks.

HIGHFALUTEN, showy, affected, tinselled, affecting certain pompous or fashionable airs, stuck up; "come, none of yer HIGHFALUTEN games," *i.e.*, you must not show off or imitate the swell here.—*American* Slang, now common in Liverpool and the East End of London, from the *Dutch*, VERLOOTEN. Used recently by the *Times* in the sense of fustian, high-sounding, unmeaning eloquence, bombast.

HIGH-STRIKES, corruption of *Hysterics*.

HIP INSIDE, inside coat pocket.

HIP OUTSIDE, outside coat pocket.

HIPPED, piqued, offended, crossed, &c.

HITTITE, a facetious *Sporting* term for a prize-fighter.

HIVITE, a student of St Begh's College, Cumberland; pronounced ST BEE'S.—*University*.

HOAX, to deceive, or ridicule,—*Grose* says was originally a *University* Cant word. Corruption of HOCUS, to cheat.

HOBBLED, committed for trial; properly said of animals fed by the wayside, with their forelegs fastened together.

HOB COLLINGWOOD, according to *Brockett*, a North Country term for the four of hearts, considered an unlucky card.

HOBSON'S CHOICE, "this or none." Hobson was a carrier at Cambridge, and also a letter out of horses for hire, and is said to have always compelled his customers to take either the horse that stood in the stall next the stable door or none at all. He was a benefactor to the town, and *Hobson's Conduit* still stands as a memorial of him.

"HOB AND NOB," to act in concert with another; to "lay heads together;" to touch glasses in drinking; to fraternise in a convivial meeting or merry-making.

HOCKS, the feet; CURBY HOCKS, round or clumsy feet.

HOCK-DOCKIES, shoes.

HOCUS, to drug a person, and then rob him. The HOCUS generally consists of snuff and beer.

HOCUS POCUS, Gipsy words of magic, similar to the modern "presto fly." The Gipsies pronounce "*Habeas Corpus*," HAWCUS PACCUS, (see *Crabb's Gipsies' Advocate*, p. 18;) can this have anything to do with the origin of HOCUS POCUS? *Turner* gives OCHUS BOCHUS, an old demon. *Pegge*, however, states that it is a burlesque rendering of the words of the unreformed church service at the delivery of the host, HOC EST CORPUS, which the early Protestants considered as a species of conjuring, and ridiculed accordingly.

HODGE, a countryman or provincial clown. I don't know that it has been elsewhere remarked, but most country districts in England have one or more families of the name of HODGE; indeed, GILES and HODGE appear to be the favourite hobnail nomenclature. HODGE is said to be simply an abbreviation of Roger.

HOG, a shilling.—*Old Cant.*

HOG, "to go the whole HOG;" "the whole HOG or none," to do anything with a person's entire strength, not "by halves;" realised by the phrase "in for a penny in for a pound." *Bartlett* claims this to be a pure *American* phrase; whilst *Ker*, of course, gives it a *Dutch* origin.—*Old.* "TO GO THE WHOLE HOG" is frequently altered into going the ENTIRE ANIMAL, or THE COMPLETE SWINE!

HOGA, do. "That won't HOGA," *i.e.*, that won't do, is one of the very commonest of the Anglo-Indian Slang phrases.—*Anglo-Indian.*

HOLLOW, "to beat HOLLOW," to excel.

HOLY LAND, Seven Dials,—where the St Giles's Greek is spoken.

HOMO, a man. *Lingua Franca;* but *see* OMEE, the more usual Cockney pronunciation.

HONDEY, a Manchester name for an omnibus, and the abbreviation of HONDEYBUSH, the Lancashire pronunciation of the word.

HOOK, an expression at Oxford, implying doubt, either connected with Hookey Walker or with a note of interrogation (?) "Yes, with a HOOK at the end of it!" *i.e.*, with some reservation.

HOOK, to steal or rob.—*See* the following.

"HOOK OR BY CROOK," by fair means or foul—in allusion to the hook which footpads used to carry to steal from open windows, &c., and from which HOOK, to take or steal, has been derived. Mentioned in *Hudibras* as a Cant term.

HOOK IT, "get out of the way," or "be off about your business;" "TO HOOK IT," to run away, to decamp; "on one's own HOOK," dependant upon one's own exertions.—*See* the preceding for derivation.

HOOKS, "dropped off the HOOKS," said of a deceased person—derived from the ancient practice of suspending on hooks the quarters of a traitor or felon sentenced by the old law to be hung, drawn, and quartered, and which dropped off the hooks as they decayed.

HOOKEY WALKER! ejaculation of incredulity, usually shortened to WALKER!—which *see.* A correspondent thinks HOOKEY WALKER may have been a certain *Hugh K. Walker.*

"HOOK UM SNIVEY," (formerly "hook *and* snivey,") a low expression, meaning to cheat by feigning sickness or other means. Also a piece of thick iron wire crooked at one end, and fastened into a wooden handle, for the purpose of undoing from the outside the wooden bolt of a door.

HOP, a dance.—*Fashionable Slang.*

"HOP THE TWIG," to run away; also a flippant expression for to die. Many similar phrases are used by the thoughtless and jocose, as to "LAY DOWN ONE'S KNIFE AND FORK," "PIGGING OUT," "SNUFFING IT." —*Old.*

HOP-MERCHANT, a dancing-master.

HOISTING, shoplifting.

HOPPING GILES, a cripple. St Ægidius or Giles, himself similarly afflicted, was their patron saint. The ancient lazar houses were dedicated to him.

HOPPO, custom-house officer, or custom-house. Almost anything connected with custom-house business.—*Anglo-Chinese.*

HORRID HORN, term of reproach amongst the street Irish, meaning a fool, or half-witted fellow. From the *Erse*, OMADHAUN, a brainless fellow. A correspondent suggests HERRIDAN, a miserable old woman.

HORNSWOGGLE, nonsense, humbug. Believed to be of *American* origin.

HORRORS, the low spirits, or "blue devils," which follow intoxication.

HORSE, contraction of Horsemonger-Lane Gaol.

HORSE, a Slang term for a five-pound note.

HORSE-CHAUNTER, a dealer who takes worthless horses to country fairs and disposes of them by artifice. He is generally an unprincipled fellow, and will put in a glass eye, or perform other tricks.—*See* COPER.

HORSE-NAILS, money.—*Compare* BRADS.

HORSE-NAILS. At the game of cribbage, when a player finds it his policy to keep his antagonist back, rather than push himself forward, and plays accordingly, he is said "*to feed his opponent on* HORSE-NAILS."

HORSE MARINE, an awkward person. In ancient times the "JOLLIES," or Royal Marines, were the butts of the sailors, from their ignorance of seamanship. "Tell that to the MARINES, the blue jackets won't believe it!" was a common rejoinder to a "stiff yarn." Now-a-days they are deservedly appreciated as the finest regiment in the service. A HORSE MARINE (an impossibility) was used to denote one more awkward still.

HOT COPPERS, the feverish sensations experienced next morning by those who have been drunk over night.

HOT TIGER, an Oxford mixture of hot-spiced ale and sherry.

"HOUSE OF COMMONS," a humorous term for the closet of decency.

HOUSES; "safe as HOUSES," an expression to satisfy a doubting person; "Oh! it's as SAFE as HOUSES," *i.e.*, perfectly safe, apparently in allusion to the paying character of house property as an investment.

HOW MUCH? A facetious way of asking for an explanation of any pedantic expression. "Why don't you cook your potatoes in an anhydrohepsaterion?" A waggish listener might be excused for asking, An anhydro—HOW MUCH?

"HOW CAME YOU SO?" intoxicated.

HOXTER, an inside pocket.—*Old English,* OXTER.

HUBBLE-BUBBLE, the Indian pipe termed a *hookah* is thus designated by sailors.—*Sea.*

HUEY, a town or village.—*Tramps' term.*

HORSE'S NIGHTCAP, a halter; "to die in a HORSE'S NIGHTCAP," to be hanged.

HUFF, a dodge or trick; "don't try that HUFF on me," or "that HUFF won't do."—*Norwich.*

HUFF, to vex, or offend; a poor temper. HUFFY, easily offended.

HUGGER-MUGGER, underhand, sneaking.

HULK, to hang about in hopes of an invitation.—*See* MOOCH.

HULKY, extra-sized.—*Shropshire.*

HUM-BOX, a pulpit.

"HUM AND HAW," to hesitate, raise objections.—*Old English.*

HUMBLE PIE, to "eat HUMBLE PIE," to knock under, be submissive. The UMBLES, or entrails of a deer, were anciently made into a dish for servants, while their masters feasted off the haunch.

HUMBUG, an imposition, or a person who imposes upon others. A very expressive but Slang word, synonymous at one time with HUM AND HAW. Lexicographers have fought shy at adopting this term. *Richardson* uses it frequently to express the meaning of other words, but, strange to say, omits it in the alphabetical arrangement as unworthy of recognition! In the first edition of this work, 1785 was given as the earliest date at which the word could be found in a printed book. Since then I have traced HUMBUG half a century farther back, on the title-page of a singular old jest-book—"*The Universal Jester; or a pocket companion for the Wits: being a choice collection of merry conceits, facetious drolleries, &c., clenchers, closers, closures, bon-mots,* and HUMBUGS," by *Ferdinando Killigrew.* London, about 1735-40.

I have also ascertained that the famous Orator Henley was known to the mob as ORATOR HUMBUG. The fact may be learned from an illustration in that excedingly curious little collection of *Caricatures,* published in 1757, many of which were sketched by Lord Bolingbroke—Horace Walpole filling in the names and explanations. *Halliwell* describes HUMBUG as "a person who hums," and cites Dean Milles's MS., which was written about 1760. In the last century, the game now known as double-dummy was termed HUMBUG. Lookup, a notorious gambler, was struck down by apoplexy when playing at this game. On the circumstance being reported to *Foote,* the wit said—"Ah, I always thought he would be HUMBUGGED out of the world at last!" It has been stated that the word is a corruption of Hamburgh, from which town so many false bulletins and reports came during the war in the last century. "Oh, that is *Hamburgh* [or HUMBUG,"] was the answer to any fresh piece of news which smacked of improbability. *Grose* mentions it in his *Dictionary,* 1785; and in a little printed squib, published in 1808, entitled *Bath Characters,* by *T. Goosequill,* HUMBUG is thus mentioned in a comical couplet on the title-page:—

"Wee Thre Bath Deities bee,
HUMBUG, Follie, and Varietee."

Gradually from this time the word began to assume a place in periodical literature, and in novels not written by over-precise authors. In the preface to a flat, and, I fear, unprofitable poem, entitled, *The Reign* of HUMBUG, a *Satire*, 8vo., 1836, the author thus apologises for the use of the word—"I have used the term HUMBUG to designate this principle, [wretched sophistry of life generally,] considering that it is now adopted into our language as much as the words *dunce, jockey, cheat, swindler*, &c., which were formerly only colloquial terms." A correspondent, who in a late number of *Adersaria* ingeniously traced *bombast* to the inflated Doctor Paracelsus Bombast, considers that HUMBUG may, in like manner, be derived from *Homberg*, the distinguished chemist of the court of the Duke of Orleans, who, according to the following passage from *Bishop Berkeley's Siris*, was an ardent and successful seeker after the philosopher's stone !

"§ 194.—Of this there cannot be a better proof than the experiment of Monsieur Homberg, WHO MADE GOLD OF MERCURY BY INTRODUCING LIGHT INTO ITS PORES, but at such trouble and expense, that, I suppose, nobody will try the experiment for profit. By this injunction of light and mercury, both bodies became fixed, and produced a third different to either, to wit, real gold. For the truth of which FACT I refer to the memoirs of the French Academy of Sciences."—*Berkeley's Works*, vol. ii, p. 366, (Wright's edition.)

Another derivation suggested (see *The Bookseller* for May 26, 1860) is AMBAGE, a Latin word adopted into the English language *temp.* Charles I., (see *May's* translation of *Lucan's Pharsalia*,) and meaning conduct the reverse of straightforwardness. Again, in the (burlesque) *Loves of Hero and Leander*, (date 1642,) we find "MUM-BUG, quoth he, 'twas known of yore," a Cant expression, no doubt, commanding a person to "shut up," or hold his tongue, and evidently derived from the game of *mum-budget* or *silence*, upon which *Halliwell* (*Dict. Arch.*) has descanted.

AMBAGE is also used in the sense of "circumlocution." "Without any long studie or tedious AMBAGE."—*Puttenham. Art of Poesie.*

"Umh ! y' are full of AMBAGE"—*Decker's Whore of Babylon*, 1607.

"Thus from her cell Cumæan Sibyl sings
Ambiguous AMBACES, the cloyster rings
With the shrill sound thereof, in most dark strains."
—*Vicar's Virgil*, 1632.

De Quincey thus discourses upon the word :—

"The word HUMBUG, for instance, rests upon a rich and comprehensive basis ; it cannot be rendered adequately either by German or by Greek, the two richest of human languages ; and without this expressive word we should all be disarmed for one great case, continually recurrent, of social enormity. A vast mass of villany, that cannot otherwise be reached by legal penalties, or brought within the rhetoric of scorn, would go at large with absolute impunity were it not through the stern Rhadamanthean aid of this virtuous and inexorable word."—*Article on "Language."*

Since these notes were penned, I purchased the collection of essays known as the *Connoisseur*, from the late Mr Thackeray's library. At the end of vol. i. I found a memorandum in the great humorist's handwriting—"p. 108, 'HUMBUG,' a new-coined expression." On referring to that page, I note this paragraph :—

"The same conduct of keeping close to their ranks was observed at table, where the ladies seated themselves together. Their conversation was here also confined wholly to themselves, and seemed like the mysteries of the *Bona Dea*, in which men were forbidden to have any share. It was a continued laugh and whisper from the beginning to the end of dinner. A whole sentence was scarce ever spoken aloud. Single words, indeed, now and then broke forth; such as *odious, horrible, detestable,* shocking, HUMBUG. This last new-coined expression, which is only to be found in the nonsensical vocabulary, sounds absurd and disagreeable whenever it is pronounced; but from the mouth of a lady it is 'shocking,' 'detestable,' 'horrible,' and 'odious.'"—*From the third edition,* 1757.

The universal use of this term is remarkable; in California there is a town called *Humbug Flat*—a name which gives a significant hint of the acuteness of the first settler.

HUM-DRUM, tedious, tiresome, boring; "a society of gentlemen who used to meet near the Charter House, and at the King's Head, St John's Street, Clerkenwell. They were characterised by less mystery and more pleasantry than the Freemasons."—*Bacchus and Venus,* 1737. In the *West* the term applies to a low cart.

HUMP, to botch, or spoil.

HUMP UP, "to have one's HUMP UP," to be cross or ill-tempered—like a cat with its back set up.—*See* MONKEY.

HUMPTY-DUMPTY, short and thick.

HUNCH, to shove, or jostle.

HURKARU, a messenger.—*Anglo-Indian.*

HUNTER PITCHING, the game of cockshies—three throws a penny.— *See* COCKSHY.

"HUNT THE SQUIRREL," when hackney and stage coachmen try to upset each other's vehicles on the public roads.—*Nearly obsolete.*

HURDY-GURDY, a droning musical instrument shaped like a large fiddle, and turned by a crank, used by Savoyards and itinerant foreign musicians in England, now nearly superseded by the hand-organ. A correspondent suggests that the name is derived from being *girded* on the HURDIES, loins, or buttocks.—*Scotch; Tam o' Shanter.* In *Italy* the instrument is called VIOLA.

HUSH-MONEY, a sum given to quash a prosecution or evidence.

HUSH-SHOP, or CRIB, a shop where beer or spirits is sold "on the quiet" —no licence being paid.

HYPS, or HYPO, the blue devils. *From Hypochondriasis.*—SWIFT.

HY-YAW! an interjectional exclamation of astonishment.—*Anglo-Chinese.*

INFANTRY, children; LIGHT INFANTRY, fleas.

IN, "to be IN with a person," to be even with, or UP to him; also, to be on intimate terms with him.

"IN FOR IT," in trouble or difficulty of any kind.

NEXPRESSIBLES, UNUTTERABLES, UNWHISPERABLES, or SIT-UPONS, trousers, the nether garments.

IKEY, a Jew "fence." Corruption of Isaac, a common Hebrew name.

"IN FOR PATTER," waiting for trial, referring to the speeches of counsel, the statements of witnesses, the summing up of the judge, &c. The fuss of all which the prisoner sets down as "so much PATTER."

INNINGS, earnings, money coming in; "he's had long INNINGS," *i.e.*, a good run of luck, plenty of cash flowing in.

INSIDE LINING, dinner, &c.

INTERESTING, "to be in an INTERESTING situation," applied to females when *enceinte*.

INTO, "hold my hat, Jim, I'll be INTO him," *i.e.*, I will fight him. In this sense equivalent to PITCH INTO, or SLIP INTO.

INVITE, an invitation—a corruption used by stuck-up people of mushroom origin.

IPSAL DIXAL, Cockney corruption of *ipse dixit*—said of one's simple uncorroborated assertion.

IRISH APRICOTS, potatoes.

IRISH THEATRE, the temporary prison, guard-room, or lock-up in a barracks. The fond fancy of the soldier supplies it with other figurative appellations, as "the MILL," "the JIGGER," "the HOUSE THAT JACK BUILT." In Edinburgh Castle it is termed "the DRYROOM."

"ISTHMUS OF SUEZ," the covered bridge at St John's College, Cambridge, which connects the college with its grounds on the other side of the river.—*See* CRACKLE.

IVORIES, teeth; "a box" or "cage of IVORIES," a set of teeth, the mouth; "wash your IVORIES," *i.e.*, "drink." The word is also used to denote DICE.

JABBER, to talk, or chatter. A Cant word in *Swift's* time.

JACKED-UP, ruined, done for.

JACK KETCH, the public hangman.—*See* KETCH.

JACK NASTY-FACE, a sailor.—*Sea*.

JACK SPRAT, a diminutive boy or man.

JACK TAR, a sailor.

JACK-AT-A-PINCH, one whose assistance is only sought on an emergency; JACK IN-THE-WATER, an attendant at the waterman's stairs on the river and sea-port towns, who does not mind wetting his feet for a customer's convenience, in consideration of a douceur.

JACK, HALF JACK, a card counter, resembling in size and appearance a sovereign and a half-sovereign, for which it is occasionally passed to simple persons. In large gambling establishments the "heaps of gold" are frequently composed of JACKS.

JACK, the knave of trumps, at the game of all-fours.

JACKETING, a thrashing. Similar term to LEATHERING, COWHIDING, &c.

JACKEY, gin.—*Seven Dials* originally.

JACOB, a ladder. *Grose* says from Jacob's dream.—*Old Cant*.

"IT'S GOOD ON THE STAR," it's easy to open.

JACK-IN-A-BOX, a small but powerful kind of screw, used by burglars to break open safes.

JAGGER, a gentleman. German, JAGER, a sportsman.
JAIL-BIRD, a prisoner, one who has been in jail.
JAMES, a sovereign, or twenty shillings.
JANNOCK, sociable, fair dealing.—*Norfolk.*
JAPAN, to ordain.—*University.*
JARK, a "safe-conduct" pass.—*Oxford. Old Cant* for a seal.
JARVEY, the driver of a hackney-coach; JARVEY'S UPPER BENJAMIN, a coachman's over-coat.
JAW, speech, or talk; "hold your JAW," don't speak any more; "what are you JAWING about?" *i.e.*, what are you making a noise about?
JAWBONE, credit.

> "We have a few persons whose pockets are to let—men who have more complaints than dollars—individuals who, in digger's parlance, live on JAWBONE, (credit,) and are always to be found at saloons; a class of men who, when they are here, wish themselves yonder, and when yonder, wish themselves back "—*Times' Correspondent, San Francisco, Oct.* 21, 1862.

JAW-BREAKER, a hard or many-syllabled word.
JAZEY, a wig. A corruption of JERSEY, the name for flax prepared in a peculiar manner, and of which common wigs were formerly made; "the cove with the JAZEY," *i.e.*, the judge.
JEAMES, (a generic for "flunkeys,") the *Morning Post* newspaper—the organ of Belgravia and the "Haristocracy."
JEHU, old Slang term for a coachman, or one fond of driving.
JEMINY-O! a vulgar expression of surprise.
JEMMY, a sheep's-head.—*See* SANGUINARY JAMES.
JEMMY-DUCKS, the man whose business it is to look after the poultry on board a ship.—*Sea.*
JEMMY JESSAMY, a dandy.
JEMMY-JOHN, a jar for holding liquor; probably a corruption of demi-gallon.
JEREMIAD, a lament; derived, of course, from the Book of Lamentations, written by the prophet Jeremiah.
JEREMY DIDDLER, an adept at raising the wind.
JERRY, a beer-house.
JERRY, a chamber utensil; abbreviation of JEROBOAM.—*Swift.*
JERRY, a fog.
JERRY-GO-NIMBLE, the diarrhœa.
JERRY SNEAK, a hen-pecked husband,—a character in the *Mayor of Garret.*
JERUSALEM PONY, a donkey.
JESSIE, "to give a person JESSIE," to beat him soundly.—*See* GAS.

JEMMY, a crowbar.—*Prison term.*
JARK, a seal, or watch ornament.—*Ancient Cant.*

JEW'S EYE, a popular simile for anything valuable. Probably a corruption of the *Italian*, GIOJE; *French*, JOAILLE, a jewel. In ancient times, when a king was short of cash, he generally issued orders for many *Jew's eyes*, or equivalent sums of money. The Jews preferred paying the ransom, although often very heavy. This explanation has been given of the origin of JEW'S EYE. Used by *Shakspeare*.

JEW-FENCER, a Jew street salesman.

JEZEBEL, a showily-dressed woman of suspected respectability; derived, of course, from 2 Kings ix. 30, but applied in this sense from the time of the Puritans.

JIB, a first-year man.—*Dublin University*.

JIB, the face, or a person's expression; "the cut of his JIB," *i.e.*, his peculiar appearance. The sail of a ship, which in position and shape corresponds to the nose on a person's face.—*Sea*. A vessel is known by the *cut of the* JIB sail; hence the popular phrase, "to know a man by THE CUT OF HIS JIB."

JIB, or JIBBER, a horse that starts or shrinks. *Shakspeare* uses it in the sense of a worn-out horse.

JIBB, the tongue.—*Gipsy and Hindoo*. (Tramps' term.)

JIFFY, "in a JIFFY," in a moment.

JIGGER, a secret still, illicit spirits.—*Scotch*.

JIGGER, a door; "dub the JIGGER," shut the door. *Ancient Cant*, GYGER. In billiards, the *bridge* on the table is often termed the JIGGER. Also the curtain of a theatre.

JIGGER, "I'm JIGGERED if you will," a common form of mild swearing.— See SNIGGER.

JINGO, "by JINGO," a common form of oath, said to be a corruption of S Gingoulph.—*Vide Halliwell*.

JOB, a short piece of work, a prospect of employment. *Johnson* describes JOB as a low word, without etymology. It is, and was, however, Cant word, and a JOB, two centuries ago, was an arranged robbery. Even at the present day it is mainly confined to the streets, in the sense of employment for a short time. Amongst undertakers a JOB signifies a funeral; "to do a JOB," conduct any one's funeral; "by the JOB," *i.e.*, *piece*-work, as opposed to *time*-work. A JOB in political phraseology is a Government office or contract, obtained by secret influence or favouritism.

JOB, "a JOB *lot*," otherwise called a "*sporting lot*," any miscellaneous goods purchased at a cheap rate, or to be sold a bargain. Frequently used to conceal the fact of their being stolen, or otherwise dishonestly obtained.

JOB'S COMFORT, reproof instead of consolation.

JOB'S COMFORTER, one who brings news of additional misfortunes.

JIGGER-DUBBER, a term applied to a jailor or turnkey.
JILT, a crowbar or house-breaking implement.

JOB'S TURKEY, "as poor as JOB'S TURKEY," as thin and as badly fed as that ill-conditioned bird.

JOE, a too marvellous tale, a lie, or a stale joke. Abbreviated from "Joe Miller." The full name is occasionally used, as in the phrase "I don't see the JOE MILLER of it," *i.e.*, I don't perceive the wit you intend.

JOEY, a fourpenny piece. The term is derived (like BOBBY from Sir Robert Peel) from Joseph Hume, the late respected M.P. The explanation is thus given in *Hawkins's History of the Silver Coinage of England*:—

> "These pieces are said to have owed their existence to the pressing instance of Mr Hume, from whence they, for some time, bore the nickname of JOEYS. As they were very convenient to pay short cab fares, the Hon. M.P. was extremely unpopular with the drivers, who frequently received only a *groat* where otherwise they would have received a sixpence without any demand for change."

The term originated with the London cabmen, who have invented many others.

JOG-TROT, a slow but regular trot, or pace.

JOGUL, to play up, at cards or other game. *Spanish*, JUGAR.

JOHNNY, half-a-glass of whisky.—*Irish*.

JOHN-THOMAS, a generic for "flunkeys,"—more especially footmen with large calves and fine bushy whiskers.

JOHNNY-DARBIES, a nickname for policemen, an evident corruption of the *French* GENSDARMES. Also, a term applied to handcuffs.—*See* DARBIES.

JOHN ORDERLY, the signal to shorten the performance at a show. Whenever the master, who remains on the platform outside to take the money and regulate the performance, desires to refill the booth, he pokes his head inside and shouts, "Is JOHN ORDERLY there?" The actors instantly cut the piece short, the curtain falls, and the spectators are bundled out at the back, to make room for the fresh audience. According to tradition, John Orderly was a noted showman, who taught this move to the no less noted Richardson.

JOLLY, a word of praise, or favourable notice; "chuck Harry a JOLLY-Bill," *i.e.*, go and praise up his goods, or buy of him, and speak well of the article, that the crowd standing around his stall may think it a good opportunity to lay out their money. This is also called JOLLYING. "Chuck a JOLLY," lit. translated, is "throw a shout" or "good word."

JOLLY, a Royal Marine.—*See* HORSE MARINE.

JOMER, a sweetheart, or favourite girl.—*See* BLOWER.

JOSKIN, a countryman.

JOW, be off, be gone immediately. If the word JEHANUM be added, it forms a peremptory order to go to the place unmentionable to ears polite. Our word "Jericho," to go to, is probably derived from JEHANUM.—*Anglo-Indian*.

JUDAS, a deceitful person; JUDAS-HAIRED, red-haired, deceitful.

"JOE BLAKE THE BARTLEMY," to visit a low woman.

JUNIPER, gin.—*Household Words*, No. 183.
JUNK, salt beef.—*See* OLD HORSE.
JUWAUB, literally, in Hindostanee, an answer; but in Anglo-India Slang signifying a refusal. If an officer asks for leave and is refused, h is said to be JUWAUBED; if a gentleman unsuccessfully proposes fo the hand of a lady, he is said to have got the JUWAUB.—*Anglo-India*
KARIBAT, food, literally rice and curry; the staple dish of both native and Europeans in India.—*Anglo-Indian.*
KEEL-HAULING, a good thrashing or mauling, rough treatment,—from the old nautical custom of punishing offenders by throwing them ove board with a rope attached, and hauling them up from under th ship's keel.
"KEEP IT UP," to prolong a debauch, or the occasion of a rejoicing— metaphor drawn from the game of shuttle-cock.—*Grose.*
KELTER, coin, money,
KEN, a house.—*Ancient Cant.* KHAN, *Gipsy* and *Oriental.*
*** All Slang and Cant words which end in KEN, such as SPIELKE? SPINIKEN, or BOOZINGKEN, refer to *houses*, and are mainly of *Gips* origin.
KENNEDY, a poker, also to strike or kill with a poker. A St Giles's term so given from a man of that name being killed by a poker. Frequentl shortened to NEDDY.
KENT RAG, or CLOUT, a cotton handkerchief.
KERTEVER CARTZO, the disease known as the *morbo gallico.* Fro the *Lingua Franca*, CATTIVO, bad, and CAZZO.
KETCH, or JACK KETCH, the popular name for a public hangman; derive from a person of that name who officiated in the reign of Charles I —*See Macaulay's History of England,* p. 626.
KIBOSH, nonsense, stuff, humbug; "it's all KIBOSH," *i.e.*, palaver or no sense; "to put on the KIBOSH," to run down, slander, degrade, & —*See* BOSH. KIBOSH also means one shilling and sixpence.
KICK, a moment; "I'll be there in a KICK," *i.e.*, in a minute.
KICK, a sixpence; "two and a KICK," two shillings and sixpence.
KICK, a pocket; *Gaelic*, CUACH, a bowl, a nest; *Scotch*, QUAIGH.
KICKERABOO, dead. A West Indian negro's phrase.—*See* KICK TH BUCKET, of which phrase it is a corruption.
KICK THE BUCKET, to die.—*Norfolk.* According to *Forby*, a metaph taken from the descent of a well or mine, which is of course absur The *Rev. E. S. Taylor* supplies me with the following note from h MS. additions to the work of the East-Anglian lexicographer :—

JUG, a prison, or jail.
JUMP, to seize, or rob; "to JUMP a man," to pounce upon him, and eith rob or maltreat him; "to JUMP a house," to rob it.—*See* GO.
KEN-CRACKER, a housebreaker.

"The allusion is to the way in which a slaughtered pig is hung up,—viz., by passing the ends of a bent piece of wood behind the tendons of the hind legs, and so suspending it to a hook in a beam above. This piece of wood is locally termed a BUCKET, and so by a coarse metaphor the phrase came to signify to die. Compare the *Norfolk* phrase, 'as wrong as a BUCKET.'"

Another correspondent says the real signification of this phrase is to commit suicide by hanging, from a method planned and carried out by an ostler at an inn on the Great North Road. Standing on a bucket, he tied himself up to a beam in the stable; he then KICKED THE BUCKET away from under his feet, and in a few seconds was dead. The natives of the West Indies have converted the expression into KICKERABOO.

KICK UP, a noise or disturbance.

KICK UP, "to KICK UP a *row*," to create a tumult.

KICKSHAWS, trifles; made, or French dishes—not English, or substantial. Corruption of the *French*, QUELQUES CHOSES.

KICKSIES, trousers.

KICKSY, troublesome, disagreeable. *German*, KECK, bold.

KID, an infant, or child.

KID, to joke, to quiz, to hoax anybody.

KID-ON, to entice or incite a person to the perpetration of an act.

KIDDIER, a pork-butcher.

KIDDILY, fashionably or showily; "KIDDILY togg'd," showily dressed.

KIDDLEYWINK, a small shop where they retail the commodities of a village store. Also, a woman of unsteady habits.

KIDDY, a man or boy. Formerly a low thief.

KIDDYISH, frolicsome, jovial.

"Think on the KIDDYISH spree we had on such a day."
—*Randall's Diary*, 1820.

KIDNA, how much?—*Anglo-Indian*.

KIDNAPPER, one who steals children or adults. From KID, a child, and NAB, (corrupted to NAP,) to steal, or seize.

KIDNEY, "of that KIDNEY," of such a stamp: "strange KIDNEY," odd humour; "two of a KIDNEY," two persons of a sort, or as like as two peas, *i.e.*, resembling each other like two kidneys in a bunch.—*Old*. "Attempt to put their hair out of KIDNEY."—*Terræ Filius*, 1763.

KIDDEN, or KIDKEN, a low lodging-house for boys.

KID-RIG, cheating children in the streets sent on errands, or intrusted with packages.—*Nearly obsolete*.

KIDMENT, a pocket-handkerchief fastened to the pocket, and partially hung out, to entrap thieves; hence any inducement to dishonesty or crime. Also, a fictitious story or written statement got up to deceive the unwary. A begging letter; long rigmarole of any kind.

KIDSMAN, one who trains boys to thieve and pick pockets successfully.

KILKENNY CAT, a popular simile for a voracious or desperate animal or person, from the story of the two cats in that county, who are said to have fought and bitten each other until a small portion of the tail of one of them alone remained.

KILLING, bewitching, fascinating. The term is akin to the phrase "dressing to DEATH."

KIMBO, or A-KIMBO, holding the arms in a bent position from the body, and resting the hands upon the hips, in a bullying attitude. Said to be from A SCHEMBO, *Italian;* but more probably from KIMBAW, the old Cant for beating, or bullying.—*See Grose. Celtic*, CAM, crooked.

KINCHIN, a child.—*Old Cant.* From the *German* diminutive, KINDCHEN, a baby.

KINCOB, uniform, fine clothes, rich embroidered dresses.—*Anglo-Indian.*

KINGSMAN, the favourite coloured neckerchief of the costermongers. The women wear them thrown over their shoulders. With both sexes they are more valued than any other article of clothing. A coster's *caste*, or position, is at stake, he imagines, if his KINGSMAN is not of the most approved pattern. When he fights, his KINGSMAN is tied either around his waist as a belt, or as a garter around his leg. This very singular partiality for a peculiar-coloured neckcloth was doubtless derived from the Gipsies, and probably refers to an Oriental taste or custom long forgotten by these vagabonds. A strange similarity of taste for certain colours exists amongst the Hindoos, Gipsies, and London costermongers. Red and yellow (or orange) are the great favourites, and in these hues the Hindoo selects his turban and his robe; the Gipsy his breeches, and his wife her shawl or gown; and the costermonger, his plush waistcoat and favourite KINGSMAN. Among either class, when a fight takes place, the greatest regard is paid to the favourite coloured article of dress. The Hindoo lays aside his turban, the Gipsy folds up his scarlet breeches or coat, whilst the pugilistic costermonger of Covent Garden or Billingsgate, as we have just seen, removes his favourite neckerchief to a part of his body, by the rules of the "ring," comparatively out of danger. Amongst the various patterns of kerchiefs worn by the wandering tribes of London, red and yellow are the oldest and most in fashion. Blue, intermixed with spots, is a late importation, probably from the Navy, through sporting characters.

KING'S PICTURES, (now, of course, QUEEN'S PICTURES,) money.

KISKY, drunk, fuddled.

KISSER, the mouth.—*Pugilistic term.*

KISS-CURL, a small curl twisted on the temple.—*See* BOWCATCHER.

KISS-ME-QUICK, the name given to the very small bonnets worn by females since 1850.

KINCHIN COVE, a man who robs children; a little man.—*Ancient Cant.*

KIRK, a church or chapel; "crack a KIRK," *i.e.*, to break into a church.—*Prison Cant.*

KIT, a person's baggage. Also, a collection of anything, "the whole KIT of 'em," the entire lot. *Anglo-Saxon*, KYTH.—*North.*

KITE, *see* FLY THE KITE.

KITMEGUR, an under-butler, a footman.—*Anglo-Indian.*

KNACKER, an old horse; a horse-slaughterer.—*Gloucestershire.*

KNAP, to receive, to take; "oh, my! won't he just KNAP it when he can!" *i.e.*, won't he take anything if he gets a chance.

KNAP, *i.q.*, NAP, to break. — *Old English, but nearly obsolete.* See Ps. xlvi. 9, (*Prayer-book version*,) " He breaketh the bow, and KNAPPETH the spear in sunder;" probably sibilated into SNAP.

KNAPPING-JIGGER, a turnpike gate; "to dub at the KNAPPING-JIGGER," to pay money at the turnpike.

KNARK, a hard-hearted or savage person.

KNIFE, "to KNIFE a person," to stab; an un-English, but now-a-days a very common expression.

KNIFE IT, "cut it," cease, stop, don't proceed.

KNIFE-BOARD, the seat running along the roof of an omnibus.

> . . . . " On 'busses' KNIFEBOARDS stretch'd,
> The City clerks all tongue-protruded lay."
> —*A Summer Idyll, by Arthur Smith.*

KNIGHT, a common and ironical prefix to a man's calling,—thus " KNIGHT of the whip," a coachman; " KNIGHT of the thimble," a tailor.

"KNOCK ABOUT THE BUB," to hand or pass about the drink.

KNOCK-DOWN, or KNOCK-ME DOWN, strong ale.

KNOCK-'EM-DOWNS, a public-house game.

KNOCK OFF, to give over, or abandon. A saying used by workmen about dinner, or other meal times, for upwards of two centuries.

KNOCKED UP, tired, jaded, used up, done for. In the United States, amongst females, the phrase is equivalent to being *enceinte*, so that Englishmen often unconsciously commit themselves when amongst our Yankee cousins.

KNOCKER, "up to the KNOCKER," finely or showily dressed, the height of fashion; proficient, equal to the task.

KNOCK-IN, the game of *loo*.

KNOCK-OUTS, or KNOCK-INS, disreputable persons who visit auction rooms and unite to purchase the articles at their own prices. One of their number is instructed to buy for the rest, and after a few small bids as blinds to the auctioneer and bystanders, the lot is knocked down to the KNOCK-OUT bidders, at a nominal price—the competition to result from an auction being thus frustrated and set aside. At the conclusion of the sale the goods are paid for, and carried to a neighbouring public-house, where they are re-sold or KNOCKED-OUT, and the difference between the first purchase and the second—or tap-room KNOCK-OUT—is divided amongst the gang. As generally happens with

---

KNAP, to steal.—*Prison Cant.*

ill-gotten gains, the money soon finds its way to the landlord's pocket, and the KNOCK-OUT is rewarded with a red nose and a bloated face. Cunning tradesmen join the KNOCK-OUTS when an opportunity for money-making presents itself. The lowest description of KNOCK-OUTS, fellows with more tongue than capital, are termed BABES,—which *see*.

KNOWING, a Slang term for sharpness; "KNOWING codger," or "a KNOWING blade," one who can take you in, or cheat you, in any transaction you may have with him. It implies also deep cunning and foresight, and generally signifies dishonesty.

> "Who, on a spree with black-eyed Sal, his blowen,
> So swell, so prime, so nutty and so KNOWING."—*Don Juan*.

KNOW, in this sense, enters into several Slang phrases. "I KNOW a trick worth two of that," expresses that I am not to be taken in by such a shallow device. "He KNOWS a thing or two," *i.e.*, a cunning fellow.

KNOWLEDGE-BOX, the head.—*Pugilistic*.

KNUCKLE-DUSTER, an iron instrument contrived to cover the knuckles so as to protect them from injury when striking a blow, adding force to it at the same time, and with nobs or points projecting, so as to mutilate and disfigure the person struck. This brutal invention is American, but has been made too familiar here in the police cases between the officers and sailors of American vessels.

KNUCKLE TO, or KNUCKLE UNDER, to yield or submit.

KNULLER, old term for a chimney-sweep, who solicited jobs by ringing a bell. From the *Saxon*, CNYLLAN, to knell, or sound a bell.—*See* QUERIER.

KOOTEE, a house.—*Anglo-Indian*.

KOTOOING, misapplied flattery.—*Illustrated London News*, 7th January 1860. From a *Chinese* ceremony.

KUBBER, news.—*Anglo-Indian*.

KUDOS, praise; KUDIZED, praised. *Greek*, κυδος.—*University*.

KYPSEY, a basket.

LA! a euphuistic rendering of LORD, common amongst females and very precise persons; imagined by many to be a corruption of LOOK! but this is a mistake. Sometimes pronounced LAW, or LAWKS.

LAC, one hundred thousand.—*Anglo-Indian*.

LACING, a beating. From the phrase "I'll LACE your jacket."—*L'Estrange*. Perhaps to give a beating with a *lace* or *lash*.

LADDER, "can't see a hole in a LADDER," said of any one who is intoxicated.

LADDLE, a lady. Term with chimney-sweeps on the 1st of May. A correspondent suggests that the term may come from the brass *ladles* for collecting money, always carried by the sweeps' ladies.

KNUCKLE, to pick pockets after the most approved method.

KNUCKLER, a pickpocket.

LAG, a returned transport, or ticket-of-leave convict.

LAG, to void urine.—*Ancient Cant.*

LAGGER, a sailor.

LAMBASTING, a beating.—See LAMMING.

LAME DUCK, a stockjobber who speculates beyond his capital, and cannot pay his losses. Upon retiring from the Exchange he is said to "waddle out of the Alley."

LAMMING, a beating.—*Old English*, LAM; used by *Beaumont and Fletcher*. Not, as Sir W. Scott supposed, from one Dr Lamb, but the *Old Norse*, LAM, the hand; also, *Gaelic.*

LAMMY, a blanket.

LAND-LUBBER, sea term for "a landsman."—*See* LOAFER.

LAND-SHARK, a sailor's definition of a lawyer.

LANE, a familiar term for Drury Lane Theatre, just as *Covent Garden Theatre* is constantly spoken of as "the GARDEN."

LAP, liquor, drink.

"LAP THE GUTTER," to get drunk.

LARK, fun, a joke; "let 's have a jolly good LARK," let us have a piece of fun. *Mayhew* calls it "a convenient word covering much mischief."—*Anglo-Saxon*, LAC, sport; but more probably from the nautical term SKYLARKING, *i.e.*, mounting to the highest yards and sliding down the ropes for amusement, which is allowed on certain occasions.

LARRUP, to beat, or thrash.

LARRUPING, a good beating or hiding.—*Irish.*

LATCHPAN, the lower lip—properly a dripping-pan; "to hang one's LATCHPAN," to pout, be sulky.—*Norfolk.*

LAVENDER, "to be laid up in LAVENDER," in pawn; or, when a person is out of the way for an especial purpose.—*Old.*

LAW, "to give LAW to an animal" is a sporting term signifying to give the hare or stag a chance of escaping, by not setting on the hounds till it has run some distance. Also, figuratively used for giving any one a chance of succeeding in a difficult undertaking.

LAY, some, a piece. "Tip me a LAY of pannum," *i.e.*, give me a slice of bread.—*North.*

LAY, to watch; "on the LAY," on the look-out.—*Shakspeare.*

"LAY DOWN THE KNIFE AND FORK," to die.—*See* "PIGGING-OUT," and "HOPPING THE TWIG," for similar flippancies.

"LAY THEM DOWN," to play at cards.

LEAF, the drop on which executions take place, which are defined as the "FALL OF THE LEAF" by the ribald spectators.—*See* AUTUMN.

LAGGED, imprisoned, apprehended, or transported for a crime. From the *Old Norse*, LAGDA, "laid," laid by the leg.

LEARY, flash, or knowing.

LEARY, to look, or be watchful; shy.—*Old Cant.*

LEATHER, to beat or thrash. From the leather belt worn by soldiers and policemen, often used as a weapon in street rows.

LEATHERN-CONVENIENCY, a carriage. A Quaker being reprimanded by the Society of Friends for keeping a carriage, "contrary to the ancient testimonies," said, "it is not a carriage I keep, but merely a LEATHERN-CONVENIENCY."—*See* under SIMON PURE, in the Introduction.

LEAVING SHOP, an unlicensed house where goods are taken into pawn at exorbitant rates of interest.—*Daily Telegraph*, 1st August 1859.

LED CAPTAIN, a fashionable spunger, a "swell" who by artifice ingratiates himself into the good graces of the master of the house, and lives at his table.

LEEF, "I'd as LEEF do it as not," *i.e.*, I have no objection to do it.—Corruption of LIEF, or LEAVE. *Old English*, LIEF, inclined to.

LEER, empty.—*Oxfordshire*. Pure *German*, as is nearly so the next word.

LEER, print, newspaper. *German*, LEHREN, to instruct; hence *Old English*, LERE, "spelt in the LEER."—*See* SPELL.—*Old Cant*.

LEG, a part of a game. He who gains two LEGS, wins the game or rub.

LEG, or BLACKLEG, a disreputable sporting character, and racecourse *habitué*.

LEG-AND-LEG, the state of a game when each player has won a LEG. In Ireland a LEG is termed a HORSE, LEG-AND-LEG being there termed HORSE-AND-HORSE.

LEG IT, to run; "to give a LEG," to assist, as when one mounts a horse; "making a LEG," a countryman's bow,—projecting the leg from behind as a balance to the head bent forward.—*Shakspeare*.

LEG-OF-MUTTON, inflated street term for a sheep's trotter, or foot.

LENGTH, forty-two lines of a dramatic composition.—*Theatrical*.

LET DRIVE, to strike or attack with vigour.

LET IN, to cheat or victimise.

LET ON, to give an intimation of having some knowledge of a subject. *Ramsay* employs the phrase in the *Gentle Shepherd*. Common in Scotland.

LETTY, a bed. *Italian*, LETTO.—*Lingua Franca*.

LEVANTER, a card-sharper, or defaulting gambler. A correspondent states that it was formerly the custom to give out to the creditors, when a person was in pecuniary difficulties, and it was convenient for him to keep away, that he was gone to the *East*, or the LEVANT; hence, when one loses a bet, and decamps without settling, he is said to LEVANT.

LEVY, a shilling.—*Liverpool*.

LEARY BLOAK, a person who dresses showily.

LEG BAIL, (to give,) to escape from prison or arrest.

LEGGED, a prisoner in irons.

LENGTH, six months' imprisonment.—*See* STRETCH.

LICK, a blow; LICKING, a beating; "to put in big LICKS," a curious and common phrase meaning that great exertions are being made.—*Dryden; North.*

LICK, to excel, or overcome; "if you ain't sharp he 'll LICK you," *i.e.*, be finished first. Signifies, also, to whip, chastise, or conquer. *Ancient Cant.* LYCKE. *Welsh*, LLACHIO, to strike.

LICKSPITTLE, a coarse term for a parasite, who puts up with indignities for the sake of advantages.

LIG, a lie, a falsehood.—*Lancashire.* In old ballads the word "lie" is often spelt "LIG."

LIGHT, "to be able to get a LIGHT at a house" is to get credit.

LIGHTS, a worthless piece of meat, applied metaphorically to a fool, a soft or stupid person.

LIGHTS, the eyes. Also, the lungs; animals' lungs are always so called.

LIGHT BOB, a light infantry soldier.—*Military.*

LIGHT FEEDER, a silver spoon.

LIGHTNING, gin; "FLASH O' LIGHTNING," a glass of gin.

LIL, a book, a pocket-book.—*Gipsy.*

LILY-BENJAMIN, a white great-coat.—*See* BENJAMIN.

LIMBO, a prison, from LIMBUS or LIMBUS PATRUM, a mediæval theological term for purgatory.

LIMB-OF-THE-LAW, a lawyer, or clerk articled to that profession.

LINE, calling, trade, profession, "what LINE are you in?" "the building LINE."

LINGO, talk, or language. Slang is termed LINGO, amongst the lower orders. *Italian*, LINGUA.—*Lingua Franca.*

LINT-SCRAPER, a young surgeon. *Thackeray*, in *Lovel the Widower*, uses the phrase, and gives, also, the words *Æsculapius*, *Pestle-grinder*, and *Vaccinator*, for the same character.

LIONS, notabilities, either persons or sights worthy of inspection; an expression dating from the times when the royal lions at the Tower,[*] before the existence of Zoological Gardens and travelling menageries, were a London wonder, to visit which country cousins and strangers of eminence were constantly taken.

[*] The origin of the Tower collection was the three leopards sent by the Emperor Frederic to Henry III., as a living illustration of the royal arms of England. In the roll of John de Cravebeadell, constable of the Tower, B. M. Top. Collections, iii. p. 153, is a charge of 3d. per day "in support of the leopard of our lord the king." Edward III., when Prince of Wales, appears to have taken great interest in the animals; and

LIFER, a convict who is sentenced to transportation *for life*.

LIFT, to steal, pick pockets; "there's a clock been LIFTED," said when a watch has been stolen. The word is as old as the Border forays, and is used by *Shakspeare*. SHOPLIFTER is a recognised term. *Old Gothic*, LLIFAN, to steal; *Lower Rhenish*, LÖFTEN.

LIONISE, to conduct a stranger round the principal objects of attraction in a place; to act as cicerone.

LIP, bounce, impudence; "come, none o' yer LIP!"

LIP, to sing; "LIP us a chant," sing a song.

LIQUOR, or LIQUOR UP, to drink drams.—*Americanism.* IN LIQUOR, tipsy, or drunk.

LITTLE GO, the "Previous Examination," at Cambridge the first University examination for undergraduates in their second year of matriculation. At Oxford, the corresponding term is THE SMALLS.

LIVE-STOCK, vermin of the *insect* kind.

LIVERPUDLIN, a native of Liverpool.

LOAFER, a lazy vagabond. Generally considered an *Americanism*. LOPER, or LOAFER, however, was in general use as a Cant term in the early part of the last century. LANDLOPER was a vagabond who begged in the attire of a sailor; and the sea phrase, LAND-LUBBER was doubtless synonymous.—See *the Times,* 3d November 1859, for a reference to LOAFER.

LOAVER, money.—*See* LOUR.—*Lingua Franca.*

LOB, a till, or money-drawer.

LOBB, the head.—*Pugilistic.*

LOBLOLLY, gruel.—*Old;* used by *Markham* as a sea term for grit gruel, or hasty pudding.

LOBLOLLY BOY, a derisive term for a surgeon's mate in the navy.

"*Lob-lolly-boy* is a person, who on board of a man-of-war attends the surgeon and his mates, and one who knows just as much of the business of a seaman as the author of this poem."—*The Patent, a Poem,* 4to, 1776.

LOBS! schoolboys' signal on the master's approach. Compare CAVE! CHUCKS! Also, an assistant watcher, an under gamekeeper.

LOBS, words, talk.—*Gipsy.*

LOBSCOUSE, a dish made of potatoes, meat, and biscuits, boiled together.

LOBSTER, a soldier. A *policeman,* from the colour of his coat, is styled an *unboiled,* or *raw* LOBSTER.

LOBSTER-BOX, a barrack, or military station.

LOGGERHEADS, "to come to LOGGERHEADS," to come to blows.

LOGIE, theatrical jewellery, made mostly of zinc.

LOLLY, the head.—*See* LOBB.—*Pugilistic.*

after he became king, there was not only the old leopard, but "one lion, one lioness, and two cat-lions," says Stowe, "in the said Tower, committed to the custody of Robert, son of John Bowre." The menagerie was only abolished in 1834, and the practice was to allow any person to enter gratis who brought with him a little dog to be thrown to the lions!—*Dr Doran's Princes of Wales,* p. 120.

LITTLE SNAKES-MAN, a little thief, who is generally passed through a small aperture to open any door to let in the rest of the gang.

LONDON-ORDINARY, the beach at Brighton, where the "eight-hours-at-the-sea-side" excursionists dine in the open-air.

LONDRIX, London. Probably from the *French*, LONDRES.

LONG-BOW, " to draw," or "shoot with the LONG-BOW," to exaggerate.

LONG-GHOST, a tall, awkward person.

LONG-ODDS, in a bet this means staking the greater proportion against the smaller.—*See* ODDS.

LONG-TAILED-ONE, a bank-note or FLIMSY for a large amount.

LONGS-AND-SHORTS, cards made for cheating.

LONG-TAILS, among shooters, are pheasants; among coursers and dog-fanciers they are greyhounds.

LONG-SHORE BUTCHER, a coast-guardsman.—*Sea*.

LONG-TAILED BEGGAR, a cat. The tale that hangs thereby runs thus:—A boy, during his first, and a very short voyage, to sea, had become so entirely a seaman, that on his return he had forgotten the name of the cat, and was obliged, pointing to puss, to ask his mother "what she called that 'ere LONG-TAILED BEGGAR?" Accordingly, sailors, when they hear a freshwater tar discoursing too largely on nautical matters, are very apt to say, "But how, mate, about that 'ere LONG-TAILED BEGGAR?"

LOOF-FAKER, a chimney-sweep.—*See* FLUE-FAKER.

LOOKING-GLASS, a facetious synonyme for a *pot de chambre.—Grose*. See the story of *Father Tom and the Pope* in *Blackwood's Magazine*, by *Maga*, May 1843. In ancient times this utensil was the object of very frequent examination by the medical fraternity.

LOOSE.—*See* ON THE LOOSE.

LOOSE-BOX, a brougham or other vehicle kept for the use of a *dame de compagnie*. A more vulgar appellation for one is MOT-CART, the contemptuous sobriquet applied by the envious mob to a one-horse covered carriage.

LOOT, swag, or plunder.—*Hindoo*.

LOPE, this old form of *leap* is often heard in the streets.

LOP-SIDED, uneven, one side larger than the other.—*Old*.

LORD, "drunk as a LORD," a common saying, probably referring to the facilities a man of fortune has for such a gratification; perhaps a sly sarcasm at the supposed habits of the "haristocracy."

LORD, a hump-backed man.—*See* MY LORD.

LORD-MAYOR'S-FOOL, a personage who likes everything that is good, and plenty of it.

LORD-OF-THE-MANOR, a sixpence.

LOTHARIO, a gay deceiver.

LOUD, flashy, showy, as applied to dress or manner.—*See* BAGS.

LOUR, or LOWR, money; "gammy LOWR," bad money. From the *Wallachian Gipsy* word, LOWE, coined money.—*See* note, supra, p. 11.—*Old French*, LOWER, revenue, wages.—*Ancient Cant*, and *Gipsy*.

LOUSE-TRAP, a small-tooth comb.—*Old Cant.*—*See* CATCH-'EM-ALIVE.

LOVAGE, an old-fashioned cordial made from the carminative herb of that name, [*Ligusticum Scoticum,* LINN,] and sold in gin-shops.

LOVE, at billiards "five to none" would be "five LOVE,"—a LOVE being the same as when one player does not score at all. The term is also used at whist, "six LOVE," "four LOVE" when one of the parties has marked up six, four, or any other number, and the other none. A writer in the *Gentleman's Magazine,* for July 1780, derives it either from LUFF, an old *Scotch* word for the hand, or from the *Dutch,* LOEF, the LOOF, weather-gauge, (*Sewell's Dutch Dictionary,* 4to, 1754;) but it more probably, from the sense of the next word, denotes something done without reciprocity.—*Sea.*

LOVE, "*to do a thing* for LOVE," *i.e.,* for *nothing.* A man is said to marry for love when he gets nothing with his wife; and an Irishman, with the bitterest animosity against his antagonist, will fight him for LOVE, *i.e.,* for the mere satisfaction of beating him, and not for a stake.

LOVEAGE, tap droppings, a mixture of spirits, sweetened and sold to habitual dram-drinkers, principally females. Called also ALLS.

LOW CHURCHMAN. He has been defined by the *Times* as one "who loves a Jew and hates the Pope."

LOW-WATER, but little money in pocket, when the finances are at a low ebb

LUBBER, a clown, or fool.—*Ancient Cant,* LUBBARE.

LUBBER'S HOLE, an aperture in the maintop of a ship, by which a timid climber may avoid the difficulties of the "futtock shrouds;" hence, a sea term for any cowardly way of evading duty.

LUCK, "down on one's LUCK," wanting money, or in difficulty.

LUCKY, "to cut one's LUCKY," to go away quickly.—*See* STRIKE.

LUDLAM'S DOG, an indolent, inactive person is often said to be "as lazy as LUDLAM'S DOG, which leaned its head against the wall to bark." Sailors say as lazy as Joe the Marine, who laid down his musket to sneeze.

LUG, "my togs are in LUG," *i.e.,* in pawn.

LUG, the ear.—*Scotch.*

LUG, to pull, or slake thirst.—*Old.*

LUG CHOVEY, a pawnbroker's shop.

LUKE, nothing.—*North Country Cant.*

LUMBER, to pawn or pledge.—*Household Words,* No. 183.

LUMMY, jolly, first-rate.

LUMPER, a contractor. On the river, more especially a person who contracts to deliver a ship laden with timber.

LULLY PRIGGER, a rogue who steals wet clothes hung on lines to dry.

LULLY, a shirt.

LUMBERED, imprisoned.

LUMP IT, to dislike it; "if you don't like it you may LUMP IT;" sometimes varied to "if you don't like it you may do the other thing."

"LUMP THE LIGHTER," to be transported.

LUMP-WORK, work contracted for, or taken by the *lump*.

LUMPY, intoxicated.

LUNAN, a girl.—*Gipsy.*

LURCH, a term at the game of cribbage. A. is said to LURCH B. when the former attains the end, or sixty-first hole of the board before the latter has pegged his thirty-first hole; or, in more familiar words, before B. has turned the corner. A LURCH counts as a double game or rub.

LUSH, intoxicating drinks of all kinds, but generally used for beer. The *Globe*, 8th September 1859, says "LUSH and its derivatives claim *Lushington*, the brewer, as sponsor."

LUSH, to drink, or get drunk.

LUSH-CRIB, a public-house.

LUSHINGTON, a drunkard, or one who continually soaks himself with drams and pints of beer. Some years since there was a "LUSHINGTON Club" in Bow Street, Covent Garden.

LUSHY, intoxicated. *Johnson* says "opposite to pale," so red with drink.

LYLO, come hither.—*Anglo-Chinese.*

LYMPS, the Olympic Theatre.—*See* LANE.

MAB, a cab, or hackney-coach.

MAC TURK, a Scotch duellist, from a character in *St Ronan's Well*.

MADZA, half. *Italian*, MEZZA. This word enters into combination with various Cant phrases, mainly taken from the *Lingua Franca*, as MADZA CAROON, half-a-crown, two-and-sixpence; MADZA SALTEE, a halfpenny, [*see* SALTEE;] MADZA POONA, half-a-sovereign; MADZA ROUND THE BULL, half a pound of steak, &c.

MAG, a halfpenny.—*Ancient Cant*, MAKE. MEGS were formerly guineas.—*B. M. Carew*. MAKE, the old form, is still used by schoolboys in Scotland.

MAG, "not a blessed MAG!" would be the phrase of a cadger down on his luck to express his penniless state.

MAG, to talk. A variation of NAG.—*Old;* hence MAGPIE.

LUMPER, a low thief who haunts wharves and docks, and robs vessels; also a person who sells old goods for new.

LURK, a sham, swindle, or representation of feigned distress.

LURKER, an impostor who travels the country with false certificates of fires, shipwrecks, &c. Also, termed a SILVER BEGGAR, which *see*.

MACE, a dressy swindler who victimises tradesmen.

MACE, to spunge, swindle, or beg, in a polite way; "give it him (a shopkeeper) on the MACE," *i.e.*, obtain goods on credit and never pay for them; also termed "striking the MACE."

MAGGOTY, fanciful, fidgety. Whims and fancies were formerly termed MAGGOTS, from the popular belief that a maggot in the brain was the cause of any odd notion or caprice a person might exhibit.

MAHCHEEN, a merchant. Chinese pronunciation of the English word.—*Anglo-Chinese.*

MAHOGANY FLAT, a bug.

MAHOGANY; "to have one's feet under another man's MAHOGANY," to sit at his table, be supported on other than one's own resources; "amputate your MAHOGANY," *i.e.*, go away, or "cut your stick."

MAIL, to post a letter; "this screeve is MAILED by a sure hand."

MAKE-UP, personal appearance.—*Theatrical.*

MALAPROPISM, an ignorant, vulgar, misapplication of language, so named from Mrs Malaprop, a character in *Sheridan's* unrivalled comedy of the *Rivals*. Mrs Partington has lately succeeded to the mantle of Mrs Malaprop; but the phrase Partingtonism is as yet uncoined.

MALLEY, a gardener.—*Anglo-Indian.*

MANABLINS, broken victuals.

MANDOZY, a term of endearment; probably from the valiant fighter named Mendoza.

MANG, to talk.—*Scotch.*

MAN-HANDLE, to use a person roughly, as to take him prisoner, turn him out of a room, give him a beating.

MARBLES, furniture, movables; "money and MARBLES," cash and personal effects.

MARCHIONESS, a maid-of-all-work; a title now in regular use—but derived from the nickname of a character in *Charles Dickens's Old Curiosity Shop*.

MARE'S NEST, a Cockney discovery of marvels, which turn out no marvels at all. An old-preacher in Cornwall up to very lately employed a different version—viz., "a cow calving up in a tree."

MARINE, or MARINE RECRUIT, an empty bottle. This expression having once been used in the presence of an officer of marines, he was at first inclined to take it as an insult, until some one adroitly appeased his wrath by remarking that no offence could be meant, as all that it could possibly imply was, "one who had done his duty, and was ready to do it again."—*See* HORSE MARINE.—*Naval.*

MARPLOT, an officious bungler, who spoils everything he interferes with.

MAGSMAN, a street swindler, who watches for countrymen and "gullible" persons.

MAIN-TOBY, the highway, or the main road.

MAKE, a successful theft, or swindle.

MAKE, to steal.

MARINATED, transported; from the salt pickling fish undergo in Cornwall.—*Old Cant.*

MARRIAGE LINES, a marriage certificate.—*Provincial*.

MARROW, a mate, a fellow-workman, a pitman who works in a "shift" with another.—*Northumberland* and *Durham*.

MARROW-BONES, the knees; "I'll bring him down upon his MARROW-BONES," *i.e.*, I'll make him bend his knees as he does to the Virgin Mary.

MARROWSKYING.—*See* MEDICAL GREEK.

MARRY, a term of asseveration in common use, was originally (in Popish times) a mode of swearing by the Virgin Mary; *q.d.*, "BY MARY."

MARTINGALE, a gambling term. To double the stake every time you lose.

MARYGOLD, one million sterling.—*See* PLUM.

MASKEE, never mind, no consequence.—*Anglo-Chinese*.

"**MASSACRE OF THE INNOCENTS**," when the leader of the House of Commons goes through the doleful operation of devoting to extinction a number of useful measures at the end of the session, for want of time to pass them.—*Vide Times*, 20th July 1859: Mr C. Foster, on altering the time of the legislative sessions.—*Parliamentary Slang*.

"**MASTER OF THE ROLLS**," a baker.

"**MASTER OF THE MINT**," a gardener.

MATE, the term a coster or low person applies to a friend, partner, or companion; "me and my MATE did so and so," is a common phrase with a low Londoner.—Originally a *Sea term*.

MATEY, a labourer in one of her Majesty's dockyards.

MAULEY, a signature, from MAULEY, a fist; "put your FIST to it," is sometimes said by a low tradesman when desiring a fellow-trader to put his signature to a bill or note.

MAULEY, a fist, that with which one strikes as with a MALL.—*Pugilistic*.

MAUND, to beg; "MAUNDERING on the fly," begging of people in the streets.—*Old Cant*. MAUNG, to beg, is a term in use amongst the *Gipsies*, and may also be found in the *Hindoo* Vocabulary. MAUND, however, is pure *Anglo-Saxon*, from MAND, a basket. Compare "beg," which is derived from BAG, a curious parallel.

MAW, the mouth; "hold your MAW," cease talking.

MAWWORM, a hypocrite.

MAX, gin; MAX UPON TICK, gin obtained upon credit.

MAZARINE, the platform beneath the stage in large theatres. Probably corruption of *Italian*, MEZZANINO.

M. B. COAT, *i.e.*, *Mark of the Beast*, a name given to the long surtout worn by the clergy,—a modern Puritan form of abuse, said to have been accidentally disclosed to a Tractarian customer by a tailor's orders to his foreman.

MEALY-MOUTHED, plausible, deceitful.

MEASLEY, mean, miserable-looking. "seedy;" "what a MEASLEY-looking man!" *i.e.*, what a wretched, unhappy look he has.

M

MEDICAL GREEK, the Slang used by medical students at the hospitals. At the London University they have a way of disguising English, described by Albert Smith as the *Gower Street Dialect*, which consists in transposing the initials of words, e.g., "*poke a smipe*"—smoke a pipe; "*flutter-by*"—butterfly, &c. This disagreeable nonsense is often termed MARROWSKYING.—*See* GREEK, St Giles' GREEK, or the "*Ægidiac*" dialect, Language of ZIPH, &c.

MEISENSANG, a missionary, Chinese pronunciation of the English word.—*Anglo-Chinese.*

MENAGERY, the orchestra of a theatre.—*Theatrical.*

MENAVELINGS, odd money remaining after the daily accounts are made up at a railway booking-office,—usually divided among the clerks.—*See* OVERS and SHORTS.

"MERRY DUN OF DOVER," a large ship figuring in sailors' yarns. She was so large that when passing through the Straits of Dover her flying jib-boom knocked down Calais steeple; while, at the same time, the fly of her ensign swept a flock of sheep off Dover cliffs. She was so lofty that a boy who attempted to go to her mast-head found himself a gray old man when he reached the deck again. This yarn is founded on a story in the Scandinavian Mythology.

MESOPOTAMIA, a name given to a district in London.—*See* CUBITOPOLIS.—*Fashionable Slang.*

METAL, sweetmeats.—*Anglo-Indian.*

MIDDY, abbreviation of MIDSHIPMAN.—*Naval.*

MIDGE NET, a lady's veil.

MIKE, to loiter; or, as a costermonger defined it, to "lazy about." The term probably originated at St Giles's, which used to be thronged with Irish labourers, (Mike being so common a term with them as to become a generic appellation for Irishmen with the vulgar,) who used to loiter about the Pound, and lean against the public-houses in the "Dials" waiting for hire. A correspondent objects to this explanation, and says that the term is *Old English*, MICHE, to skulk, to loiter; *Old Norse*, MAK, leisure, idleness.

"Shall the blessed sun of heaven prove a MICHER?"
—*Shakspeare's Hen. IV.*, ii. 4.

MILD, second-rate, inferior.—*See* DRAW IT MILD. Also feeble, inefficient, as "a MILD attempt." Weak young men who keep bull-dogs, and dress in a "loud" stable style, from a belief that it is very becoming, are sometimes called MILD BLOATERS.

MILK, a term used in connexion with racing; when a horse is entered for a race which his owner does not intend him to win, and bets against him, the animal is said to "be MILKED."—*See* MILKING.

MILKING, a turf operation, described in the *Times* as "keeping a horse a favourite, at short odds, for a race in which he has no chance whatever, only to lay against him."

MILKY ONES, white linen rags.

MILL, a fight, or SET TO. *Ancient Cant*, MYLL, to rob.

MILL, to fight or beat.

MILL, the Insolvent Debtors' Court. *To go through the* MILL is equivalent to being *whitewashed*.

MILLER, to GIVE THE MILLER, is to engage a person in conversation of an apparently friendly character, when all at once the bystanders surround and pelt him with flour, grease, and filth of various kinds, flour predominating. This mode of punishing spies, informers, and other obnoxious individuals, is used by cabmen, omnibus conductors, *et hoc genus omne*.

MILLER, this word is frequently called out when a person relates a stale joke.—*See* JOE.

MILVADER, to beat.

MISH, a shirt, or chemise. From COMMISSION, the *Ancient Cant* for a shirt, afterwards shortened to K'MISH or SMISH, and then to MISH. French, CHEMISE; Italian, CAMICIA.

"With his snowy CAMESE and his shaggy capote."—*Byron.*

MITEY, a cheesemonger.

MITTEN, the fist.—*Pugilistic.*

MIZZLE, a frequentative form of "MIST" in both senses; as applied to weather, it is used by *John Gadbury* in his *Ephemeris* in 1695—"MISTY and MIZZLING"—to come down as mist; while the other sense may be expressed as to fade away like a mist, vanish into thin air, like the conclusion of the prayer of *Aruns* in the *Æneid*, lib. xi. 794:—

"Audiit, et voti Phœbus succedere partem
Mente dedit; partem volucres dispersit *in auras*."

MIZZLE, to run away, or decamp; to disappear as in a mist. From MIZZLE, a drizzling rain; a Scotch mist.

"And then one *mizzling* Michaelmas night,
The Count he MIZZLED too."—*Hood.*

MIZZLER, or RUM-MIZZLER, a person who is clever at effecting an escape, or getting out of a difficulty.

MOAB, a name applied to the turban-shaped hat fashionable among ladies, and ladylike swells of the other sex, in 1858-9. From the Scripture phrase, "Moab is my WASHPOT," (Ps. lx. 8,) which article the hat in question is supposed to resemble.—*University.*

MOB. *Swift* informs us, in his *Art of Polite Conversation*, that MOB was, in his time, the Slang abbreviation of *Mobility*, just as NOB is of *Nobility* at the present day.—*See* SCHOOL.

"It is perhaps this humour of speaking no more words than we needs must which has so miserably curtailed some of our words, that in familiar writings and conversation they often lose all but their first syllables, as in MOB., rep., pos., incog., and the like."—*Addison's Spectator.*

MILL, the tread-MILL, prison.

MILL-TOG, a shirt; most likely the prison garment.

MOBILITY, the populace; or, according to *Burke*, the "great unwashed." *Johnson* calls it a Cant term, although *Swift* notices it as a proper expression.

MODEST QUENCHER, a glass of gin and water.

"MOISTEN YOUR CHAFFER," a Slang phrase equivalent to "take something to drink."

MOKE, a donkey.—*Gipsy*.

MOKO, a name given by sportsmen to pheasants killed by mistake in partridge-shooting during September, before the pheasant-shooting comes in. They pull out their tails, and roundly assert that they are no pheasants at all, but MOKOS.

MOLL, a girl; nickname for Mary.—*Old Cant*.

MOLL'D, followed, or accompanied by a woman.

MOLLISHER, a low girl or woman; generally a female cohabiting with a man, who jointly get their living by thieving.

MOLLSACK, a reticule, or market basket.

"MOLL THOMSON'S MARK, that is, M. T.—empty; as "take away this bottle, it has MOLL THOMSON'S MARK on it."—*See* M. T.

MOLLYCODDLE, an effeminate man; one who caudles amongst the women, or does their work.

MOLLYGRUBS, or MULLIGRUBS, stomach-ache, or sorrow—which to the costermonger is much the same, as he believes, like the ancients, that the viscera is the seat of all feeling.

MOLROWING, "out on the *spree*," in company with so-called "gay women." In allusion to the amatory serenadings of the London cats.

MONK, a term of contempt; probably an abbreviation of MONKEY.

MONKEY, spirit, or ill temper; "to get one's MONKEY up," to rouse his passion. A man is said to have his MONKEY up, or the MONKEY on his back, when he is "*riled*," or out of temper; also to have his BACK or HUMP up.

MONKEY, the instrument which drives a rocket.—*Army*.

MONKEY, £500.—*Civic Slang*.

MONKEY-BOARD, the place or step attached to an omnibus, on which the conductor stands.

MONKEY-BOAT, a peculiar, long, narrow, canal boat.

"MONKEY WITH A LONG TAIL," a mortgage.—*Legal*.

MONKEY'S ALLOWANCE, to get blows instead of alms, more kicks than halfpence.

MONKERY, the country, or rural districts. Originally an *old* word for a quiet or monastic life.—*Hall*.

MOB, a companion; MOBSMAN, a dressy swindler.

MOLL-TOOLER, a female pickpocket.

MONEKEER, a person's name or signature.—*Tramps' Cant*.

MONKEY, a padlock.—*Prison Cant*.

MOOCH, to spunge; to obtrude one's-self upon friends just when they are about to sit down to dinner, or other lucky time—of course quite accidentally.—Compare BULK. To slink away, and allow your friend to pay for the entertainment. *In Wiltshire*, ON THE MOUTCH is to shuffle. —See the following.

MOOCHING, or ON THE MOOCH, on the look-out for any articles or circumstances which may be turned to a profitable account; watching in the streets for odd jobs, horses to hold, &c.; also, scraps of food, old clothes, &c.

MOOE, the mouth.—*Gipsy* and *Hindoo*. *Shakspeare* has MOE, to make mouths.

MOONEY, intoxicated.—*Household Words*, No. 183.

MOONLIGHT, or MOONSHINE, smuggled gin.

MOON-RAKER, a native of Wiltshire; because it is said that some men of that county, seeing the reflection of the moon in a pond, took it to be a cheese, and endeavoured to pull it out with a rake.

MOONSHEE, a learned man, professor, or teacher.—*Anglo-Indian*.

MOONSHINE, palaver, deception, humbug.

MOP, a hiring place (or fair) for servants. Steps are being taken to put down these assemblies, which have been proved to be greatly detrimental to the morality of the poor.

MOP UP, to drink, or empty a glass.—*Old Sea term*.

"MOPS AND BROOMS," intoxicated.—*Household Words*, No. 183.

MOPUSSES, money; "MOPUSSES ran taper," money ran short.

MORE-ISH, when there is scarcely enough of an eatable or drinkable it is said to taste MORE-ISH; as "this wine is very good, but it has a slight MORE-ISH flavour."

MORRIS, to decamp, be off. Probably from the ancient MORESCO, or MORRIS DANCE.

MORTAR-BOARD, the term given by the vulgar to the square college caps.

MORTGAGE-DEED, a pawnbroker's duplicate.

MOTT, a girl of indifferent character. Formerly *Mort*. *Dutch*, MOTT-KAST, a harlotry. MOTT-CART, *see* LOOSE-BOX.

MOUCHEY, a Jew.

MOULDY, gray-headed. Servants wearing hair-powder are usually termed MOULDY-PATES by street boys.

MOULDY-GRUBS, travelling showmen, mountebanks who perform in the open air without tent or covering. Doing this is called "MOULDY-GRUBBING."

MOON, a month—generally used to express the length of time a person has been sentenced by the magistrate; thus "ONE MOON" is one month. —See DRAG. It is a curious fact that the Indians of America and the roaming vagabonds of England should both calculate time by the MOON.

MOUNTAIN-DEW, whisky, advertised as from the Highlands.

MOUNTAIN-PECKER, a sheep's-head.—*See* JEMMY.

MOURNING, "a full suit of MOURNING," *two* black eyes; HALF-MOURNING, *one* black eye.

MOUSE, a black eye.

MOUTH, a common expression of contempt, equivalent to MUFF; "you are a MOUTH, and you will die a lip," is a vulgar form of abuse.

MOUTH-ALMIGHTY, a superlative form of the former expression, applied to a noisy, talkative person.

MOUTHPIECE, a lawyer, or counsel.

MOVE, a "dodge," or cunning trick; "up to a MOVE or two," acquainted with tricks. Probably derived from the game of chess.

M.P., member of the police, one of the Slang titles of the force.

MRS JONES, the house of office, a water-closet.

MRS HARRIS and MRS GAMP, nicknames of the *Morning Herald* and *Standard* newspapers, while united under the proprietorship of Mr Baldwin. MRS GAMP, a monthly nurse, was a character in *Mr Charles Dickens's* popular novel of *Martin Chuzzlewit*, who continually quoted an imaginary *Mrs Harris* in attestation of the superiority of her qualifications, and the infallibility of her opinions; and thus afforded a parallel to the two newspapers, which appealed to each other as independent authorities, being all the while the production of the same editorial staff.

M. T., railway Slang used by porters and pointsmen for *empties*, or empty carriages.—*See* MOLL THOMSON'S MARK.

"MUCH OF A MUCHNESS," alike, very much the same thing.

MUCK, to beat, or excel; "it's no use, luck's set in him; he'd MUCK a thousand."—*Mayhew*, vol. i., p. 18. TO RUN A MUCK, or GO A MUCKER, to rush headlong into certain ruin. From a certain religious phrenzy, which is common among the Malays, causing one of them, kreese in hand, to dash into a crowd and devote every one to death he meets with, until he is himself killed, or falls from exhaustion.—*Malay*, AMOK, slaughter.

MUCK-OUT, to clean out; often applied to one utterly ruining an adversary in gambling.

MUCK-SNIPE, one who has been "MUCKED OUT," or beggared, at gambling. —*See* MUCK.

MUCKENDER, or MUCKENGER, a pocket-handkerchief.—*Old*. Cf. SNOTTINGER. The original name of the "NECKINGER" in Bermondsey was the "devil's neck-handkerchief." *See* a review of this work in *The Bookseller*, May 26, 1860. This is the name of a locality. There is still a "NECKINGER road;" and Messrs Bevington & Sons' tannery in Bermondsey bears the name of the "NECKINGER mills."

MOUNTER, a false swearer. Derived from the borrowed clothes men used to MOUNT, or dress in, when going to swear for a consideration.

SLANG, CANT, AND VULGAR WORDS.

MUDFOG, "The British Association for the Promotion of Science."—*University.*

MUD-LARK, a man or woman who, with clothes tucked above knee, grovels through the mud on the banks of the Thames, when the tide is low, for silver spoons, old bottles, pieces of iron, coal, or any articles of the least value, deposited by the retiring tide, either from passing ships or the sewers. Occasionally applied to those men who cleanse the sewers, with great boots and sou' wester hats. Those who are employed in banks and counting-houses, in collecting and other outdoor duties, have also this appellation.

MUD-STUDENT, a farming pupil. The name given to the students at the Agricultural College, Cirencester.

MUFF, a silly, or weak-minded person; MUFF has been defined to be "a soft thing that holds a lady's hand without squeezing it."

MUFFIN-WORRY, an old ladies' tea party.

MUFTI, the civilian dress of a naval or military officer when off duty.—*Anglo-Indian.* From an Eastern word signifying a clergyman or priest.

MUG, the mouth, or face.—*Old.*

"'GOBLET AND MUG.'—Topers should bear in mind that what they quaff from the goblet afterwards appears in the MUG."

MUG, to strike in the face, or fight. Also, to rob by the garrote. *Gaelic,* MUIG, to suffocate, oppress; *Irish,* MUGAIM, to kill, destroy.

MUG, "to MUG one's-self," to get tipsy.

MUGGING, a thrashing,—synonymous with SLOGGING, both terms of the "ring," and frequently used by fighting men.

MUGGY, drunk.

MUG-UP, to paint one's face.—*Theatrical.* To "cram" for an examination.—*Army.*

MULL, "to make a MULL of it," to spoil anything, or make a fool of one's-self.—*Gipsy.*

MULLIGRUBS.—*Vide* MOLLYGRUBS.

MULLINGAR HEIFER, a girl with thick ankles.—*Irish.* The story goes that a traveller, passing through Mullingar, was so struck with this local peculiarity in the women, that he determined to accost the first he met next. "May I ask," said he, "if you wear hay in your shoes?" "Faith an' I do," said the girl, "and what then?" "Because," says the traveller, "that accounts for the calves of your legs coming down to feed on it."

MULTEE KERTEVER, very bad. *Italian,* MOLTO CATTIVO.—*Lingua Franca.*

MUMMER, a performer at a travelling theatre.—*Ancient.* Rustic performers at Christmas in the West of England.

MUMPER, a beggar.—*Gipsy.* Possibly a corruption of MUMMER.

MUNDUNGUS, trashy tobacco. *Spanish,* MONDONGO, black pudding.—*See* the *Gentleman's Magazine* for 1821, vol. xxv. p. 137.

MUNGARLY, bread, food. MUNG is an *old word* for mixed food, but

MUNGARLY is doubtless derived from the *Lingua Franca*, MANGIAR, to eat.—*See* the following.

MUNGARLY CASA, a baker's shop; evidently a corruption of some *Lingua Franca* phrase for an eating-house. The well-known "Nix mangiare" stairs at Malta derive their name from the endless beggars who lie there and shout NIX MANGIARE, *i.e.*, "nothing to eat," to excite the compassion of the English who land there,—an expression which exhibits remarkably the mongrel composition of the *Lingua Franca*, MANGIARE being *Italian*, and *Nix* an evident importation from Trieste, or other Austrian seaport.

MUNGING, or "MOUNGING," whining, begging, muttering.—*North.*

MUNS, the mouth. *German*, MUND.—*Old Cant.*

MURERK, the mistress of the house.—*See* BURERK.

MURKARKER, a monkey,—vulgar Cockney pronunciation of MACAUCO, a species of monkey. *Jackey Macauco* was the name of a famous fighting monkey, which used about thirty years ago to display his prowess at the Westminster pit, where, after having killed many dogs, he was at last "chawed up" by a bull terrier.

MURPHY, a potato. Probably from the Irish national liking for potatoes, MURPHY being a common surname amongst the Irish. *See* MIKE. MURPHIES (*edible*) are sometimes called DONOVANS.

MURPHY, "in the arms of MURPHY," *i.e.*, fast asleep. Corruption of MORPHEUS.

MUSH, an umbrella. Contraction of *mushroom*.

MUSH—(or MUSHROOM)—FAKER, an itinerant mender of umbrellas.

MUSHROOM, an inelegant round hat worn by demure ladies.

MUSLIN, a woman or girl; "he picked up a bit of MUSLIN."

MUSTA, or MUSTER, a pattern, one of a sort. *Anglo-Indian* term used in describing the make or pattern of anything, from the cut of a coat to the plan of a palace. A sample of any kind of merchandise. This word is very generally used in commercial transactions all over the world.

MUTTON, a contemptuous term for a woman of bad character, sometimes varied to LACED MUTTON. The expression was used as a Cant term for a "wild duck" in the reign of James I. As a Slang term it was employed by *Ben Jonson* in his masque of *Neptune's Triumph*, which was written for display at Court on Twelfth Night, 1623; "a fine LACED MUTTON or two," are the words applied to two wantons. *Shakspeare* has the term. In that class of English society which does not lay any claim to refinement, a fond lover is often spoken of as being "fond of his MUTTON."

MUTTON-CHOPS, a sheep's-head.

MUTTON-FIST, an uncomplimentary title for any one having a large coarse red hand.

MUTTON-WALK, the saloon at Drury Lane Theatre. A vulgar appellation applied to this place early in the last century, still in use in the neighbourhood of Covent Garden, which was formerly the great resort for the gay and giddy of both sexes.

MUZZLE, the mouth.

MUZZLE, to fight or thrash; to throttle or garrote.

MUZZY, intoxicated.—*Household Words*, No. 183.

MY AUNT, the closet of decency, or house of office.

MY LORD, a nickname given to a hunchback.

MY NABS, myself; in contradistinction to YOUR NIBS, which *see*.

MY TULIP, a term of endearment used by the lower orders to persons and animals; "kim up, MY TULIP," as the coster said to his donkey when thrashing him with an ash stick.

MY UNCLE, the pawnbroker,—generally used when any person questions the whereabouts of a domestic article. "Oh! only at MY UNCLE'S" is the reply. UP THE SPOUT has the same meaning. It is worthy of remark that the French call this useful relative MA TANTE, "my aunt."

NAB, to catch, to seize; "NAB the rust," to take offence.—*Ancient*, fourteenth century.—*See* NAP.

NABS, self; MY NABS, myself; HIS NABS, himself.—*North Country Cant*.

NAB THE RUST, to take offence.

NABOB, an Eastern prince, a retired Indian official,—hence a Slang term for a capitalist.

NAIL, to steal, or capture; "paid on the NAIL," *i.e.*, ready money; NAILED, taken up, or caught—probably in allusion to the practice of NAILING bad money to the counter. We say "as dead as a DOOR-NAIL;"—why? *Shakspeare* has the expression in *Henry IV*.—

"*Falstaff*. What! is the old king dead?
Pistol. As NAIL in door."

A correspondent thinks the expression is only alliterative humour, and compares as "flat as a flounder," "straight as a soldier," &c.

"NAIL IN ONE'S COFFIN," a dram, "a drop o' sumat' short," a jocular, but disrespectful phrase, used by the lower orders to each other at the moment of lifting a glass of spirits to their lips. "Well, good luck! here's another NAIL IN MY COFFIN." Another phrase with old topers is "SHEDDING A TEAR," also "WIPING AN EYE."

NAM, a policeman. Evidently *Back Slang*.

NAMBY PAMBY, particular, over-nice, effeminate. This, I think, was of Pope's invention, and first applied by him to the affected, short-lined verses addressed by Ambrose Phillips to Lord Carteret's infant children.—*See Johnson's Life of Pope*.

NAMUS, or NAMOUS, some one, *i.e.*, "be off, somebody is coming."—*Back Slang*, but general.—*See* VAMOS.

NANNY-SHOP, a disreputable house.

NANTEE, not any, or "I have none." Italian, NIENTE, nothing.—*See* DINARLY.—*Lingua Franca*.

NANTEE PALAVER, no conversation, *i.e.*, hold your tongue.—*Lingua Franca.*—See PALAVER.

NAP, or NAB, to take, steal, or receive; "you'll NAP it," *i.e.*, you will catch a beating.—*North;* also *Old Cant. Bulwer's Paul Clifford.*

NAP, to break, or rap with a hammer.—*See* KNAP.—*North.*

NAP, or NAPPER, a hat. From NAB, a hat, cap, or head.—*Old Cant.*

NAP NIX, a person who works at his trade, and occasionally goes on the stage to act minor parts without receiving any pay. The derivation is obvious.—*See* NAP and NIX, *i.e.*, NICHTS.

"NAP ONE'S BIB," to cry, shed tears, or carry one's point.

NATIONAL EXHIBITION, an execution at the Old Bailey; a term of the late Douglas Jerrold's, but now usual.

NARK, a person in the pay of the police; a common informer; one who gets his living by laying traps for publicans, &c.

NARK, to watch, or look after; "NARK the titter;" watch the girl.

NARP, a shirt.—*Scotch.*

NARY ONE, provincial for NE'ER A ONE, neither.

NASTY, ill-tempered, cross-grained.

NATION, very, or exceedingly. Corruption of DAMNATION.

NATTY, pretty, neat, tidy.—*Old.*

NATURAL, an idiot, a simpleton.

NAVVY, an excavator employed in making railways, canals, &c. Originally Slang, but now a recognised term.

N. C., "enough said," being the initials of NUF CED. A certain manager, it is said, spells in this style.—*Theatrical.*

NEARDY, a person in authority over another; master, parent, or foreman.—*North.*

"NECK AND CROP," entirely, completely; "he chuck'd him NECK AND CROP out of window."

NECKINGER, a cravat.—*See* MUCKENGER.

NEDDY, a considerable quantity, as "a NEDDY of fruit," "a NEDDY of fish," &c.—*Irish Slang.*

NECK, to swallow. NECK-OIL, drink of any kind.

"NECK AND NECK," horses run NECK AND NECK in a race when they are so perfectly equal that one cannot be said to be before the other.

"NECK OR NOTHING," desperate.—*Racing phrase.*

NEDDY, a life preserver.—Contraction of KENNEDY, the name of the first man, it is said, in St Giles's, who had his head broken by a poker.—*Vide Mornings at Bow Street.*

NEDDY, a donkey.

NED, a guinea. HALF-NED, half-a-guinea.

"NAP THE REGULARS," to divide the booty.

"NAP THE TEAZE," to be privately whipped in prison.

NED STOKES, the four of spades.—*North Hants.*—See *Gentleman's Magazine* for 1791, p. 141.

NEEDFUL, money, cash; the "one thing NEEDFUL," for the accomplishment of most pet designs.

"NEVER TRUST ME," an ordinary phrase with low Londoners, and common in Shakspeare's time, *vide Twelfth Night.* It is generally used instead of an oath, calling vengeance on the asseverator, if such and such does not come to pass.

NEWMARKET, in tossing halfpence, when the game is "two out of three," that is, he who gains the first two tosses wins. When the first toss is decisive, the game is termed SUDDEN DEATH.

NIB-COVE, a gentleman. NIBSOMEST CRIBS, best or gentlemen's houses. —*Beggar's Cant.*

NIB-LIKE, gentlemanly.

NIBS, the master, or chief person; a man with no means but high pretensions,—a "shabby genteel."

NICK, or OLD NICK, the evil spirit.—*Scandinavian*, KNICKAR, one of the names of Odin, as the destroying or evil principle.

NICK, to hit the mark; "he's NICKED it," *i.e.*, won his point.

NICK-KNACK, a trifle.—Originally *Cant.*

NIGGLING, trifling, or idling; taking short steps in walking.—*North.*

NIL, half; half profits, &c.

NILLY-WILLY, *i.e., Nill ye, will ye,* whether you will or no, a familiar version of the *Latin,* NOLENS VOLENS.

NIMMING, stealing. Immediately from the *German,* NEHMEN. *Motherwell,* the Scotch poet, thought the old word NIM (to snatch or pick up) was derived from *nam, nam,* the tiny words or cries of an infant, when eating anything which pleases its little palate. A negro proverb has the word:—

"Buckra man *nam* crab,
Crab *nam* buckra man."

Or, in the buckra man's language—

"White man eat [or steal] the crab,
And the crab eats the white man."

NEEDY, a nightly lodger, or tramp.

NEEDY MIZZLER, a shabby person; a tramp who runs away without paying for his lodging.

NEWGATE FRINGE, or FRILL, the collar of beard worn under the chin; so called from its occupying the position of the rope when Jack Ketch operates. Another name for it is a TYBURN COLLAR.

NEWGATE KNOCKER, the term given to the lock of hair which costermongers and thieves usually twist back towards the ear. The shape is supposed to resemble the knocker on the prisoners' door at Newgate —a resemblance that carries a rather unpleasant suggestion to the wearer. Sometimes termed a COBBLER'S KNOT, or COW-LICK, which *see*

NIBBLE, to take, or steal. NIBBLER, a petty thief.

NINCOMPOOP, a fool, a hen-pecked husband, a "Jerry Sneak."—Corruption of *non compos mentis*.

NINE CORNS, a pipeful of tobacco.

NINES, "dressed up to the NINES," in a showy or *recherché* manner.

NINEPENCE, "right as NINEPENCE," all right, right to a nicety. A correspondent says :—" This most undoubtedly should be NINE-PINS. For at the game of that name, in fairness to both parties, the nine pins must always be set up, with great accuracy, in this form ∴. There is no nicety in NINEPENCE!"

NINE SHILLINGS, cool audacity; most probably derived from the *French* NONCHALANCE.

NING-NANG, horse-coupers' term for a worthless thorough-bred.

NINNYHAMMER, a foolish ignorant person.—*Yorkshire*.

NIPPER, a small boy. *Old Cant* for a boy cut-purse.

NIX, nothing; "NIX my doll," synonymous with NIX. *German*, NICHTS, nothing.—*See* MUNGARLY.

NIX! the signal word of school-boys to each other that the master, or other person in authority, is approaching.

"NIX MY DOLLY," once a very popular Slang song, beginning—

"In the box of a stone jug I was born,
Of a hempen widow and a kid forlorn;
And my noble father, as I have heard say,
Was a famous merchant of capers gay;
NIX MY DOLLY, pals, fake away!"

NIZ-PRIZ, a writ of nisi-prius.—*Legal*.

NIZZIE, a fool, a coxcomb.—*Old Cant, vide Triumph of Wit*.

NOAH'S ARK, a long closely-buttoned overcoat, recently in fashion. So named by *Punch* from the similarity which it exhibits to the figure of Noah and his sons in children's toy arks.

NOB, the head—*Pugilistic;* "BOB A NOB," a shilling a head. *Ancient Cant*, NEB. NOB is an early English word, and is used in the romance of *Kynge Alisaunder* (thirteenth century) for a head; originally, no doubt, the same as *knob*.

NOB, a person of high position, a "swell," a *nobleman*,—of which word it may be an abbreviation.—*See* SNOB.

NOB, the knave of trumps, when turned up at the game of cribbage.

NOBBA, nine. *Italian*, NOVE; *Spanish*, NOVA,—the *b* and *v* being interchangeable, as Sebastópol and Sevastópol. Slang introduced by the "organ-grinders" from Italy.

NOBBA SALTEE, ninepence. *Lingua Franca*, NOVE SOLDI.

NOBBING, collecting money; "what NOBBINGS?" *i.e.*, how much have you got or collected from the crowd?

NOBBLE, to cheat, to overreach; to discover.

NOBBLER, a blow on the NOB, a finishing stroke; "that's a NOBBLER for him," *i.e.*, a settler.—*Pugilistic*.

NIP, to steal, take up quickly.—*See* NAP and NIB.

NOBBLER, a confederate of thimble-rigs, who plays earnestly as if a stranger to the "RIG," and thus draws unsuspecting persons into a game.—In NORTH OF ENGLAND, a low, cunning lawyer.

NOBBY, or NOBBISH, fine or showy; NOBBILY, showily.—*See* SNOB for derivation.

NOLI-ME-TANGERE, the Scotch fiddle, or other contagious disease.

NOMMUS, be off.—*See* NAMUS. Probably *Back Slang*.

NON-COM, a non-commissioned officer in the army.

NO ODDS, no matter, of no consequence.—*Latimer's Sermon before Edward VI.*

NORFOLK-HOWARDS, bugs; a person named Bug having lately adopted the more aristocratic appellation of NORFOLK HOWARD.

NORTH, cunning. The inhabitants of Yorkshire and the northern counties are supposed, like the canny Scots, to get the better of other people in dealing; hence the phrase "he's too far NORTH for me," *i.e.*, too cunning for me to deal with.

NORWICHER, more than one's share; said of a person who leaves less than half the contents of a tankard for his companion. In what way the term originated, or why Norwich was selected before any other city, I have not been able to discover.

NOSE, "to pay through the NOSE," to pay an extravagant price.

NOSE-BAG, a visitor at a watering-place, or house of refreshment, who carries his own victuals.—*Term applied by waiters.*

"NOSE OUT OF JOINT, TO PUT ONE'S"; to supplant, supersede, or mortify a person by excelling him.

NOSE EM, or FOGUS, tobacco.

NOSER, a bloody or contused nose.—*Pugilistic.*

NOT MEANT, said of a horse the owner of which, for interested reasons, does not intend that it shall win the race.

NOUSE, comprehension, perception.—*Old*, apparently from the *Greek*, νοῦς. *Gaelic* and *Irish*, NOS; knowledge, perception.

NO WHERE, the horses not placed in a race, that are neither first, second, nor third, are said to be NOWHERE.

NUB, a husband.

NUDDIKIN, the head.

"NUMBER OF HIS MESS," when a man dies in the army or navy, he is said to "lose the NUMBER OF HIS MESS."

FOR CANT NUMERALS, SEE UNDER SALTEE.

NURSE, a curious term lately applied to competition in omnibuses. Two omnibuses are placed on the road to NURSE, or oppose, each opposition "buss," one before, the other behind. Of course the central or

---

NOSE, a thief who turns informer, or Queen's evidence; a spy or watch; "on the NOSE," on the look-out.

NURSED buss has very little chance, unless it happens to be a favourite with the public. NURSE, to cheat, or swindle; trustees are said to NURSE property, *i.e.*, gradually eat it up themselves.

NUT, the head, in *Pugilistic Slang*. Used as an exclamation at a fight, it means strike him on the head. In tossing it is a direction to hide the head; to be "off one's NUT," to be in liquor, or "ALL MOPS AND BROOMS."

NUTS, to be NUTS upon anything or person is to be pleased with or fond of it; a self-satisfied man is said to be NUTS upon himself. NUTTED, taken in by a man who professed to be NUTS upon you.

NUT-CUT, roguish, mischievous. A good-natured term of reproach.—*Anglo-Indian.*

"OH, BE JOYFUL," a bottle of rum.—*Sea.*

OAK, the outer door of college rooms; to "sport one's OAK," to be "not at home" to visitors.—*See* SPORT.—*University.*

OAR, "to put in an OAR," to interfere.

"I put my OAR in no man's boat."
—*Thackeray.*

OAT-STEALER, an ostler.

OBFUSCATED, intoxicated.

OBSTROPOLOUS, Cockney corruption of *obstreperous.*

OCHRE, money, generally applied to *gold*, for a very obvious reason.

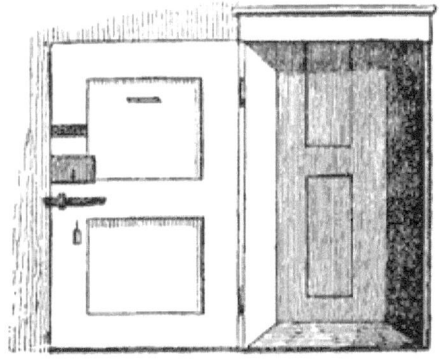

A "Sporting Door," or "Oak."

O'CLOCK, or A'CLOCK, "like ONE O'CLOCK," a favourite comparison with the lower orders, implying briskness; "to know what O'CLOCK it is," to be wide-awake, sharp, and experienced.

ODDS, a phrase used equivalent to "consequence;" "what's the ODDS," *i.e.*, what is the expected result? "It's no ODDS," *i.e.*, of no consequence. ODDS, in *sporting* phraseology, refers to the proportions or differences of a bet. Thus, a "bookmaker" will lay "six to one" against such a horse getting "a place," whilst another "turfite," more speculative, or in the receipt of a first-rate "tip," (information about the horse in question,) will lay "eight," or even "ten to one." This latter would be termed the "LONG ODDS."

ODD MAN, a street or public-house game at tossing. The number of players is three. Each tosses up a coin, and if two come down head, and one tail, or *vice versa*, the last is ODD MAN, and loses or wins, as may have been agreed upon. Frequently used to victimise a "flat." If all three be alike, then the toss goes for nothing, and the coppers are again "skied."

NUX, the "plant," or object in view; "stoll up to the NUX?" Do you fully comprehend what is wanted?—*North Country Cant.*

"OD DRAT IT," OD RABBIT, (*Colman's Broad Grins*,) OD'S BLOOD, and all other exclamations commencing with OD, are nothing but softened or suppressed oaths. OD is a corruption of GOD, and DRAT of ROT—*Shakspeare*.

"OFF AND ON," vacillating; "an OFF AND ON kind of a chap," one who is always undecided.

"OFF AT THE HEAD," crazy.—*Oxfordshire*.

"OFF ONE'S FEED," real or pretended want of appetite.—Originally *Stable Slang*.

OFFISH, distant, not familiar.

OFFICE, "to give the OFFICE," to give a hint dishonestly to a confederate, thereby enabling him to win a game or bet, the profits being shared.

OGLE, to look, or reconnoitre.

OGLES, eyes.—*Old Cant*. French, ŒIL.

"OIL OF PALMS," or PALM OIL, money.

OINTMENT, medical student Slang for butter.

O. K., a matter to be O. K., (OLL KORRECT, *i.e.*, all correct,) must be on the "square," and all things done in order.

OLDBUCK, an antiquary, from *Scott's* amusing novel.

OLD DOG, a knowing blade, an experienced person. *Butler* uses the phrase, *Hudibras*, part ii., canto iii., 208, where it was said of Sidrophel, "And was OLD DOG at physiology." The Irish proverb says, "OLD DOG for hard road," meaning that it requires an experienced person to execute a difficult undertaking.

OLD GENTLEMAN, the d—l. Also, a card almost imperceptibly longer than the rest of the pack, used by sharpers for the purpose of cheating.

OLD GOOSEBERRY (*see* GOOSEBERRY), OLD HARRY (query, *Old Hairey?*), OLD SCRATCH, all synonymes for the devil.

OLD GOWN, smuggled tea.

OLD HORSE, salt junk, or beef.—*Sea*.

OLD MAN, in American merchant ships signifies the master. The phrase is becoming common in English ships.

OLD SALT, a thorough sailor.

OLD TOM, gin; sometimes termed CAT'S WATER.

OLIVER, the moon; "OLIVER don't widdle," *i.e.*, the moon does not shine. Nearly obsolete.—*Bulwer's Paul Clifford*.

OLLAPOD, a country apothecary.

OMEE, a master or landlord; "the OMEE of the cassey's a nark on the pitch," the master of the house will not let us perform. *Italian*, UOMO, a man; "UOMO DELLA CASA," the master of the house. *Latin*, HOMO.—*Lingua Franca*.

ON, "to be ON," in public-house or vulgar parlance, is synonymous with getting "tight," or tipsy; "it's Saint Monday with him, I see he's ON again," *i.e.*, drunk as usual, or ON *the road* to it. "I'm ON" also expresses a person's acceptance of an offered bet. To GET ON a horse or a man is to make bets on him. "TRY IT ON," a defiant challenge to a person to dare to attempt anything.

"ON THE LOOSE," obtaining a living by prostitution, in reality on the streets. The term is applied to females only, excepting in the case of SPREES, when men carousing are sometimes said to be ON THE LOOSE.

> "Christmas Day is a very specific sort of festival. The man who does not spend it at home, or at the house of his nearest of kin, is in a very poor plight. He can hardly go ON THE LOOSE if he would: he seems to have no choice between innocent pleasure and the misery of hopeless solitude."—*Morning Star*, 29th March 1864.

"ON THE NOSE," on the watch or look-out.—*See* NOSE.

"ON THE TILES," out all night "on the spree," or carousing,—in allusion to the London cats on their amatory excursions.

"ONE IN TEN," a parson. In allusion to the tithing system.

ONE-ER, that which stands for ONE, a blow that requires no more. In *Dickens's* amusing work, the "Marchioness" tells Dick Swiveller that "her missus is a ONE-ER at cards."

ONION, a watch-seal.

"OPEN THE BALL," to lead off a race.—*Sporting*.

> "Romeo OPENED THE BALL by getting away in advance, Thomastown lying second, followed by Medora, Arbury," &c.—*Times*, Nov. 20, 1862.

ORACLE, "to work the ORACLE," to plan, manœuvre, to succeed by a wily stratagem.

O'TRIGGER, an Irish duellist, from a character in the *Rivals*.

OTTER, eightpence.—*Italian*, OTTO, eight.—*Lingua Franca*.

OTTOMY, a thin man, a skeleton, a dwarf. Vulgar pronunciation of "Anatomy." *Shakspeare* has 'ATOMY.

OUT, a dram glass. A *habitué* of a gin-shop, desirous of treating a brace of friends, calls for a quartern of gin and three OUTS, by which he means three glasses which will exactly contain the quartern.

OUT, in round games, where several play, and there can be but one loser, the winners in succession STAND OUT, while the others PLAY OFF.

"OUT AND OUT," prime, excellent, of the first quality. OUT-AND-OUTER, "one who is of an OUT-AND-OUT description," UP to anything. An ancient MS. has this couplet, which shews the antiquity of the phrase—

> "The Kyng was good alle aboute,
> And she was wycked OUTE AND OUTE."

OUTCRY, an auction.—*Anglo-Indian*.

"OUT OF COLLAR," out of place,—in allusion to servants. When in place, the term is COLLARED UP.—*Theatrical* and *general*.

"ON THE FLY," getting one's living by thieving or other illegitimate means; the phrase is applied to men the same as ON THE LOOSE is to women.

"ON THE SHELF," to be transported. With old maids it has another and very different meaning.

"OUT ON THE LOOSE," "on the spree," in search of adventures.—See ON THE LOOSE.

"OUT ON THE PICKAROON." PICARONE is *Spanish* for a thief, but this phrase does not necessarily mean anything dishonest, but ready for anything in the way of excitement to turn up; also, to be in search of anything profitable.

OUTSIDER, a person who does not habitually bet, or is not admitted to the "Ring." Also, a horse whose name does not appear among the "favourites."—*Sporting*.

OVER! or OVER THE LEFT, *i.e.*, the left shoulder—a common exclamation of disbelief in what is being narrated,—implying that the results of a proposed plan will be "OVER THE LEFT," *i.e.*, in the wrong direction, loss instead of gain.

OVER, generally used in connexion with COME, as "he CAME it rather strong OVER me," *i.e.*, tried to intimidate or compel me. The same phrase would also be used to imply that an excess of flattery or praise was being employed for a similar purpose, but that the adulation was being "laid on a little too thick" to be considered genuine. The term is also used in connexion with a proper noun, as "he CAME Tom Sayers OVER me," *i.e.*, pummelled me into submission or acquiescence.

"Is it in Nature," writes a visitor to Charlecote Hall, near Stratford-on-Avon, "to walk among open book-shelves covered with some of the rarest old works of the highest importance in art and English social history, and not feel inclined (not to steal, oh no !) to COME the Shakspeare OVER one or two of the dear books?"—*Morning Star*, April 28, 1864.

OVERS, the odd money remaining after the daily accounts are made up at a banking-house,—usually divided amongst the clerks.—See MENAVELINGS and SHORTS.

OWNED, a Slang expression used by the ultra-Evangelicals when a popular preacher makes many converts. The converts themselves are called his "SEALS."

P's AND Q's, particular points, precise behaviour; "mind your P'S AND Q'S," be very careful. Originating, according to some, from the similarity of p's and q's in the hornbook alphabet, and therefore the warning of an old dame to her pupils; or, according to others, of a French dancing master to his pupils, to mind their *pieds* (feet) and *queues* (wigs) when making a bow.

PACK, to go away; "now, then, PACK off there," *i.e.*, be off, don't stop here any longer. *Old*, "Make speede to flee, be PACKING and awaie."—*Baret's Alvearie*, 1580.

PACKETS, hoaxing lies. Sometimes used as an exclamation of incredulity.—*North.*

PAD, "to stand PAD," to beg with a small piece of paper pinned on the breast, inscribed, "I'm starving."

"PAD THE HOOF," to walk, not ride; "PADDING THE HOOF on the high toby," tramping or walking on the high road.

"Trudge, plod away o' the HOOF."—*Merry Wives*, i. 3.

PAD, the highway; a tramp.—*Lincolnshire.*

N

PADDING, the light articles in the monthly magazines, of which the serial stories are the main attraction.—*See* an article on this in the *Saturday Review*, Jan. 19, 1861.

PADDLE, to go or run away.—*Household Words*, No. 183.

PADDY, PAT, or PADDY WHACK, an Irishman.

> "I'm PADDY WHACK, from Ballyhack,
> Not long ago turn'd soldier ;
> In storm and sack, in front attack,
> None other can be boulder."
> *Irish Song.*

PADDY'S GOOSE, the sign of the White Swan, a noted flash public-house in the east of London.

PADDY'S LAND, "ould" Ireland.

PADRE, a clergyman.—*Anglo-Indian*.

PAL, a partner, acquaintance, friend, an accomplice. *Gipsy*, a brother.

PALAMPO, a quilt or bed-cover. Probably from PALANPORE, a town in India, renowned for its manufacture of chintz counterpanes.—*Anglo-Indian*.

PALAVER, to ask, or talk,—not deceitfully, as the term usually signifies; "PALAVER to the nibs for a shant of bivvy," ask the master for a quart of beer. In this sense used by *tramps.*—Derived from the *French*, PARLER.

PALL, to stop; "PALL that," spoken authoritatively, means cease what you are doing. From PALL, a small instrument which is used to stop the windlass or capstan at sea. When a man says "I am PALLED," he means he cannot or dare not say any more. A sailor, on receiving any extraordinary intelligence, will say, "you PALL me," *i.e.*, you confound me.

PALMER, a beggar who visits shops under the pretence of collecting *harp* halfpence. To induce shopkeepers to search for them, he offers thirteenpence for one shilling's-worth, when many persons are silly enough to empty a large quantity of copper on their counter. The PALMER is a proficient with his fingers, and generally contrives to conceal a certain number before he leaves the shop. Since the bronze pence and halfpence have been introduced, the PALMER has been unable to follow this branch of his profession.

PALM OIL, or PALM SOAP, money; also, a bribe.

PADDING-KEN, or CRIB, tramps' and boys' lodging-house.

PALL, to detect.

PALMING, robbing shops by pairs,—one thief bargaining with apparent intent to purchase, whilst the other watches his opportunity to steal. An amusing example of PALMING came off some time since. A man entered a "ready-made" boot and shoe shop and desired to be shewn a pair of boots,—his companion staying outside and amusing himself by looking in at the window. The one who required to be fresh shod was apparently of a humble and deferential turn, for he placed his hat on the floor directly he stepped into the shop. Boot after boot was

PAM, the knave of clubs at the game of loo; or, in street phraseology, Lord Palmerston.

PANNAM, food, bread.—*Lingua Franca*, PANNEN; *Latin*, PANIS; *Ancient Cant*, YANNAM.

PANNAM-BOUND, to stop the prison food or rations to a prisoner. PANNAM-STRUCK, very hungry.

PANNIKIN, a small pan.

PANTILE, a hat. The term PANTILE is properly applied to the mould into which the sugar is poured which is afterwards known as "loaf sugar." Thus, PANTILE, from whence comes the phrase, "a sugar-loaf hat," originally signified a tall, conical hat, in shape similar to that usually represented as the head gear of a bandit. From PANTILE, the more modern Slang term TILE has been derived. *Halliwell* gives PANTILE SHOP, a meeting-house. PANTILE also means a flat cake with jam on it, given to boys at boarding-schools instead of pudding.

PANTILER, a dissenting preacher. Probably from the practice of the Quakers, and many Dissenters, of not removing the hat in a place of worship. Another derivation is from the earthen tiles, technically PANTILES, (tiles hollowed in the middle, as distinguished from "pintiles," the older sort, which are flat, smaller, and pinned or nailed to the rafters,) with which meeting-houses of Dissenters are usually covered; hence the meeting-house came to be called a PANTILE, and its frequenters PANTILERS.

PAPER-MAKER, a rag-gatherer, or gutter-raker—similar to the chiffonnier of Paris. Also a man who tramps through the country, and collects rags on the pretence that he is an agent to a paper mill.

PAPER-WORKER, a wandering vendor of street literature; one who sells ballads, dying speeches, and confessions, sometimes termed a RUNNING STATIONER.

PARACHUTE, a parasol.

PARADISE, *French* Slang for the gallery of a theatre, "up amongst the GODS," which see.

PARISH LANTERN, the moon.

---

tried on until at last a fit was obtained,—when lo, forth came a man, snatched up the customer's hat left near the door, and down the street he ran as fast as his legs could carry him. Away went the customer after his hat, and Crispin, standing at the door, clapped his hands, and shouted, "go it, you'll catch him,"—little thinking that it was a concerted trick, and that neither his boots nor the customer would ever return. PALMING sometimes refers to secreting money or rings in the hand; also, bribing, bribery.

PANNY, a house—public or otherwise; "flash PANNY," a public-house used by thieves; PANNY-MEN, housebreakers. PANNY in thieves' Cant also signifies a burglary.

PARACHUTE, a thief's word for a parasol or umbrella.

PARISH PRIG, or PARISH BULL, a parson.—*Thieves' Cant.*

PARNEY, rain; "dowry of PARNEY," a quantity of rain. *Anglo-Indian* Slang from the *Hindoo*, PANI, water; *Gipsy*, PANE. Old Indian officers always call brandy-and-water "BRANDY PAWNEE."

PARSON TRULLIBER, a rude, vulgar country clergyman; the race is most probably now extinct.

PARSON'S NOSE, the hind part of a goose,—a savoury mouthful.

PART, to pay, restore, give up; "he's a right un, he is; I know'd he'd PART," *i.e.*, he is a liberal (or punctual) person, and pays his debts, or bestows gratuities. The term is in general use in *Sporting* circles, and is very commonly employed when speaking of the settlement of bets after a race or a "mill." It is probably derived from the very common colloquialism applied to stingy people as not "liking to PART with their money."

PARTER, a free, liberal person.

PARTY, a person,—a generic in very general use, similar in application to the *German* pronoun, Man, a person, people; "where's the PARTY as 'ad a' orter be lookin' arter this 'ere 'oss?" policeman's inquiry of the wrong cabman; "old PARTY," an elderly person. The term is said to have arisen in our old justice courts, where, to save "his worship" and the clerk of court any trouble in exercising their memories with the names of the different plaintiffs, defendants, and witnesses, the word PARTY was generally employed. *Dean Alford* remarks:—

"The word PARTY for a man is especially offensive. Strange to say, the use is not altogether modern. It occurs in the English version of the Apocryphal book of Tobit, vi. 7. 'If an evil spirit trouble any, one must make a smoke thereof before the man or the woman, and *the* PARTY shall be no more vexed.'"

In *Shakspeare* we find the term:—

"*Stephano.* How now shall this be compassed? Canst thou bring me to the PARTY?"—*Tempest*, iii. 2.

"I once heard," says the Dean just quoted, "a venerable dignitary pointed out by a railway porter as an OLD PARTY in a shovel." The last word is the vulgar term applied to the twisted hat worn by clerical dignitaries.

PASH, to strike; now corrupted to BASH, which *see*.—*Shakspeare.*

PASTEBOARD, a visiting card; "to PASTEBOARD a person," to drop a card at an absent person's house.

PASTE-HORN, the nose. Shoemakers nickname any shopmate with a large nose "old PASTE-HORN," from the horn in which they keep their paste.

PASTY, a bookbinder.

PATCH. This *Old English* term of reproach, long obsolete in polite language, may yet occasionally be heard in sentences like these:—"Why, he's not a PATCH upon him," *i.e.*, he is not to be compared with him; "one's not a PATCH to the other," &c. *Shakspeare* uses the word in the sense of a paltry fellow:—

"What a pied ninny's this? thou scurvy PATCH!"

PATENT COAT, a coat with the pockets inside the skirts,—termed PATENT from the difficulty of picking them.

PATTER, a speech or discourse, a pompous street oration, a judge's summing up, a trial. Ancient word for muttering. Probably from the Latin, PATER-NOSTER, or Lord's Prayer. This was said, before the Reformation, in a *low voice* by the priest, until he came to, "and lead us not into temptation," to which the choir responded, "but deliver us from evil." In our reformed Prayer-Book this was altered, and the Lord's Prayer directed to be said "with a *loud voice*." *Dr Pusey* takes this view of the derivation in his *Letter to the Bishop of London*, p. 78, 1851. *Scott* uses the word twice in *Ivanhoe* and the *Bride of Lammermoor*.

PATTER, to talk. PATTER FLASH, to speak the language of thieves, talk Cant.

PATTERER, a man who cries last dying speeches, &c., in the streets; applied also to those who help off their wares by long harangues in the public thoroughfares. These men, to use their own term, "are the haristocracy of the street sellers," and despise the costermongers for their ignorance, boasting that they live by their intellect. The public, they say, do not expect to receive from them an equivalent for their money—they pay to hear them talk.—*Mayhew*. PATTERERS were formerly termed "mountebanks."

PATTERN, a common vulgar phrase for "patent."

PAUL PRY, an inquisitive person. From the well-known comedy.

PAV., the Pavilion Theatre,—sometimes called the P. V., *i.e.*, pe-ve.

PAW, the hand. PAW-CASES, gloves.

PAY, to beat a person, or "serve him out." Originally a nautical term, meaning to stop the seams of a vessel with pitch, (*French*, POIX;) "here's the d——l to PAY, and no pitch hot," said when any catastrophe occurs which there is no means of averting; "to PAY over face and eyes, as the cat did the monkey;" "to PAY through the nose," to give a ridiculous price,—whence the origin? *Shakspeare* uses PAY in the sense of to beat, or thrash.

PAY, to deliver. "PAY that letter to Mr So-and-So" is a very common direction to a Chinese servant.—*Anglo-Chinese*.

PAY-AWAY, "go on with your story, or discourse." From the nautical phrase PAY-AWAY, meaning to allow a rope to run out of the vessel. When the hearer considers the story quite long enough, he, carrying out the same metaphor, exclaims HOLD ON.

PEACH, an informer against omnibus conductors and drivers, one especially hired by the proprietors to count passengers and stoppages. The term is in frequent use amongst omnibus-men.

PEACH, to inform against or betray. *Webster* states that *impeach* is now the modification mostly used, and that PEACH is confined principally to the conversation of thieves and the lower orders.

PATTER-CRIB, a flash house.

PEACOCK HORSE, amongst undertakers, is one with a showy tail and mane, and holds its head up well,—*che va favor-reggiando*, &c., *Italian*.

PEAKING, remnants of cloth. Term amongst drapers and cloth warehousemen.

PEC, a term used by the *Eton* boys for money, an abbreviation, of course, of the *Latin*, PECUNIA.

PECK, food; "PECK and booze," meat and drink.—*Lincolnshire*. Ancient Cant, PEK, meat.

PECK-ALLEY, the throat.

PECKER, "keep your PECKER up," *i.e.*, don't get down-hearted,—literally, keep your beak or head well up, "never say die!"

PECKHAM, a facetious meaning of the name of this district, implying a dinner; "all holiday at PECKHAM," *i.e., nothing to eat.*

PECKISH, hungry. *Old Cant*, PECKIDGE, meat.

PECKSNIFF, a hypocritical rascal. From *Dickens's Martin Chuzzlewit*.

PEEL, to strip, or disrobe.—*Pugilistic.*

PEELER, a policeman; so called from Sir Robert Peel, (*see* BOBBY;) properly applied to the Irish constabulary rather than the City police, the former force having been established by Sir Robert Peel.

PEEPERS, eyes; "painted PEEPERS," eyes bruised or blackened from a blow.—*Pugilistic.*

PEERY, suspicious, or inquisitive.

PEG, brandy-and-soda-water.

PEG, a shilling.—*Scotch.*

PEG, "to PEG away," to strike, run, or drive away; "PEG a hack," to drive a cab; "take down a PEG or two," to check an arrogant or conceited person,—derived from the use of PEG tankards.—*See* PIN.

PEG-TOPS, the loose trousers recently in fashion, small at the ankle and swelling upwards, in imitation of the Zouave costume.

PENANG-LAWYER, the long cane, now carried by footmen, though formerly by gentlemen.—*Anglo-Indian.*

PENNY GAFF, a shop turned into a temporary theatre, (admission one penny,) at which dancing and singing take place every night. Rude pictures of the performers are arranged outside to give the front a gaudy and attractive look, and at night-time coloured lamps and transparencies are displayed to draw an audience.

PENNY-A-LINER, a contributor of local news, accidents, fires, scandal, political and fashionable gossip, club jokes, and anecdotes, to a newspaper; not regularly "on the paper;" one who is popularly believed to be paid for each contribution at the rate of a *penny a line*, and whose interest is, therefore, that his article should be stuffed with fine words and long sentences.

PENNY STARVER, a penny roll.—*See* BUSTER.

PENINSULAR, or MOLL TOOLER, a female pickpocket.

PENSIONER, a man of the most degraded morals who lives off the miserable earnings of a prostitute.

PEPPER, to thrash, or strike.—*Pugilistic*, but used by *Shakspeare.*—*Eastern Counties*.

PEPPER-BOXES, the buildings of the Royal Academy and National Gallery in Trafalgar Square. The name was first given by a wag, in allusion to the cupolas erected by Wilkins, the architect, upon the roof, and which, from their form and awkward appearance, at a distance suggest to the stranger the fact of their being enlarged PEPPER-BOXES.—*See* BOILERS.

PERCH, or ROOST, a resting-place; "I'm off to PERCH," *i.e.*, I am going to bed.

> "Nor yet a single *perch*, for which my lucky stars to thank,
> Except the perch I've taken on this damp rheumatic bank."
> *The Lay of the Unsuccessful Angler*, by Arthur Smith.

PERKINS, beer. Dandy or affected shortening of the more widely-known Slang phrase, BARCLAY AND PERKINS.

PERSUADERS, spurs.

PESKY, an intensitive expression, implying annoyance; a PESKY, troublesome fellow. Corruption of PESTILENT; or, *Irish*, PEASGACH, rough, rugged.

PETER, a partridge.—*Poacher's term*.

PETER, a bundle, or valise.—*Bulwer's Paul Clifford*. Also, a cash-box.

PETER, to run short, or give out.

PETTICOAT, a woman.

PEWTER, money, like TIN, used generally to signify silver; also a pewter-pot. "Let me have my beer in the PEWTER," is a common request to waiters, made by "City" men, and others who affect habits of rude health.

PHILADELPHIA-LAWYER, this transatlantic limb of the law is considered to be the very acme of acuteness. Sailors relate many stories of his artful abilities, none, however, short enough to find a place here.

PHILISTINE, a policeman. The German students call all townspeople not of their body PHILISTER, as ours say CADS. The departing student says, mournfully, in one of the Burschenlieder—

> "Muss selber nun PHILISTER seyn!"

i.e., "I must now myself PHILISTINE be!"

PHYSOG, or PHIZ, the face. *Swift* uses the latter. Corruption of "physiognomy."

PETERER, or PETERMAN, one who follows hackney and stage coaches, and cuts off the portmanteaus and trunks from behind.—*Nearly obsolete*. Ancient term for a fisherman, still used at Gravesend.

PHILLIPER, a thief's accomplice, one who stands by and looks out for the police while the others commit the robbery.—*Times*, 5th September 1860.

PIC., the Piccadilly Saloon. The earlier abbreviation was DILLY. *Very* fast men were wont (it is now "used up") to call it "THE SANGUINARY DOUBLES, from the fact of its being situated at No. 222 in Piccadilly.

PICCADILLY BUTCHERS, a satirical name applied by the crowd to the regiment of Life Guards, known as the "Royal Blues," from their savage onslaught upon the crowd on the occasion of the arrest of Sir Francis Burdett at his house in Piccadilly, by order of the Speaker of the House of Commons.

PICK, "to PICK one's-self up," to recover after a beating or illness, sometimes varied to "PICK up one's crumbs;" "to PICK a man up," "to do," or cheat him.

PICKANINNY, a young child is thus styled by the West Indian negroes. The word is now completely naturalised among sailors and water-side people in England.

PICKERS, the hands.—*Shakspeare.*

PICKLE, a miserable or comical position; "he is in a sad PICKLE," said of any one who has fallen into the gutter, or got besmeared. "A PICKLE herring," a comical fellow, a merry-andrew.—*Old.* Also, a mischievous boy; "what a PICKLE he is to be sure!"

PICKLES! gammon; also a jeering and insulting exclamation.

PIDGEON, business, simply the Chinese pronunciation of the English word.—*Anglo-Chinese.*

PIECE, a contemptuous term for a woman; a strumpet.—*Shakspeare.*

PIG, or SOW'S BABY, a sixpence.

PIG, a mass of metal,—so called from its being poured in a fluid state from a sow, which *see.*—*Workmen's term.*

"PIG AND TINDER-BOX," the vulgar rendering of the well-known tavern sign, "*Elephant and Castle.*"

PIGEON, a gullible or soft person. The *French* Cant, or *Argot,* has the word PIGEON, dupe—"PECHON, PESCHON DE RUBY, apprenti gueux, enfant, (sans doute dérobé.)" The vagabonds and brigands of Spain also used the word in their *Germania,* or *Robbers' Language,* PALOMO, (pigeon,) ignorant, simple.

PIGEON'S MILK, boys are frequently sent, on the 1st of April, to "buy a pennyworth of PIGEON'S MILK."

PIG-HEADED, obstinate.

PIG'S EYE, the ace of diamonds in cards.

PIG'S WHISPER, a low or inaudible whisper; also a short space of time, synonymous with COCKSTRIDE, *i.e.,* cock's tread.

PIKE, a turnpike; "to bilk a PIKE," to cheat the keeper of the toll-gate.

"No PIKE I've seen, the only one was that unpleasant wicket,
Where threepence I was forced to pay, and now I have lost the ticket!"
The Lay of the Unsuccessful Angler, by Arthur Smith.

PIGEON, or BLUEY CRACKING, breaking into empty houses and stealing lead.

PIKE, to run, to be off with speed; "PIKE IT" is said as a hasty and contemptuous, if not angry dismissal; "if you don't like it, take a short stick and PIKE IT."

> "Joe quickly his sand had sold, sir,
> And Bess got a basket of rags;
> Then up to St Giles's they roll'd, sir;
> To every bunter Bess brags.
> Then unto the gin-shop they PIKE IT,
> And Bess was admitted, we hear;
> For none of the crew dare but like it,
> As Joey, her kiddy, was there."
> *The Sand-man's Wedding*, a Cantata.

"'Twas not our fault, dear Jack; we saw the watch going into the house the moment we came there, and we thought it proper to PIKE OFF."—*The Prison Breaker*, a Farce.

PILL, a doctor.—*Military*. PILL-DRIVER, a peddling apothecary.

PILL-BOX, a doctor's carriage.

PIN, "to put in the PIN," to refrain from drinking. From the ancient peg tankard, which was furnished with a row of PINS, or pegs, to regulate the amount which each person was to drink. A correspondent gives a different explanation. "When an Irishman makes a vow or promise to abstain from drinking for a time, he puts a PIN in the right-hand cuff of his coat. So that, in case he should ever forget his promise, he will see the pin, like an accusing angel, when lifting the glass to his mouth." A MERRY PIN, a roisterer.—*See* PEG.

PINCHBECK, inferior, deteriorated.

"Where, in these PINCHBECK days, can we hope to find the old agricultural virtue in all its purity?"—*Framley Parsonage*.

PINCHBECK was an inferior metal, compounded of copper and zinc, to resemble gold. It was very fashionable in the last century, and derived its name from a Mr PINCHBECK, a well-known London tradesman, who manufactured watches, buckles, and other articles out of it. PINCHBECK first obtained his notoriety by the invention of an ingenious candle-snuffers, which the author of *The Heroic Epistle to Sir William Chambers* made the vehicle of a facetious *Ode* that went through eight editions. The title of this *jeu d'esprit* ran thus:—

"*Ode to Mr Pinchbeck, upon his Newly-invented Candle-Snuffers*, by MALCOLM M'GREGOR, Esq., 1776.

> "Illustrious PINCHBECK! condescend,
> Thou well-beloved, and best king's friend,
> These lyric lines to view;
> Oh may they prompt thee, e'er too late,
> To snuff the candle of the State,
> That burns a little blue!"

PINCHBECK published a poetical reply, and the two pamphlets were for a long time the talk of town.

PINDARIC HEIGHTS, studying the odes of Pindar.—*Oxford*.

PINK, the *acme* of perfection.—*Shakspeare*.

PINK, to stab, or pierce.

PIN, to catch, apprehend. Also, to steal rapidly.

PINCH, to steal, or cheat; also, to catch, or apprehend.

PINNER-UP, a seller of old songs, pinned against a wall or framed canvass. Formerly many of these street salesmen carried on their little "paper trade" in London; now they are rarely seen.

PINS, legs.

PIPE, to follow or dog a person. Term used by *detectives*.

PIPE, to shed tears, or bewail; "PIPE one's eye."—*Sea term.*

"He first began to eye his pipe,
And then to PIPE HIS EYE."—*Old Song.*

Metaphor from the boatswain's pipe, which calls to duty.

PIPE, "to put one's PIPE out," to traverse his plans, "to take a rise" out of him.

PIPER, a person employed by an omnibus proprietor to act as a spy on the conductor.

PIPKIN, the stomach,—properly, an earthen round-bottomed pot.—*Norwich.*

PIT, a breast pocket.

PITCH, a fixed locality where a patterer can hold forth to a gaping multitude for at least some few minutes continuously; "to do a PITCH in the drag," to perform in the street.

PITCH INTO, to fight; "PITCH INTO him, Bill," *i.e.*, give him a thrashing.

"PITCH THE FORK," to tell a pitiful tale.

"PITCH THE NOB," PRICK THE GARTER, which *see*.

PLANT, a dodge, a preconcerted swindle; a position in the street to sell from. PLANT, a swindle, may be thus described: a coster will join a party of gambling costers that he never saw before, and commence tossing. When sufficient time has elapsed to remove all suspicions of companionship, his mate will come up and commence betting on each of his PAL'S throws with those standing around. By a curious quickness of hand, a coster can make the toss tell favourably for his wagering friend, who meets him in the evening after the play is over and shares the spoil.

PLANT, to mark a person out for plunder or robbery, to conceal, or place. —*Old Cant.* In the sense of conceal, there is a similar word in *Argot*, PLANQUER.

PLEBS, a term used to stigmatise a tradesman's son at Westminster School. Latin, PLEBS, the vulgar.

PLOUGHED, drunk.—*Household Words*, No. 183. Also a *University* term equivalent to PLUCKED.

PLUCK, the heart, liver, and lungs of an animal,—all that is PLUCKED away in connexion with the windpipe, from the chest of a sheep or hog; among low persons, courage, valour, and a stout heart.—*See* MOLLYGRUBS.

PLUCK'D-'UN, a stout or brave fellow; "he's a rare PLUCK'D-'UN," *i.e.*, dares face anything.

During the Crimean war, PLUCKY, signifying courageous, seemed likely to become a favourite term in May-Fair, even among the ladies.

An eminent critic, however, who had been bred a butcher, having informed the fashionable world that in his native town the *sheep's head* always went with the PLUCK, the term has been gradually falling into discredit at the West End.

It has been said that a brave soldier is PLUCKY in attack, and GAME when wounded. Women are more GAME than PLUCKY.

PLUCKED, turned back at an examination.—*University*. A correspondent says that "in ancient times it was the University practice of pulling (or PLUCKING) the sleeve—by the proctor, if I recollect aright—of those whose degrees were refused."

PLUM, £100,000, usually applied to the dowry of a rich heiress, or a legacy.—*Civic Slang*.

PLUM-CASH, prime cost.—*Anglo-Chinese*.

PLUMMY, round, sleek, jolly, or fat; excellent, very good, first rate.

PLUMPER, a single vote at an election, not a "split ticket."

PLUNDER, a common word in the horse trade to express profit. Also an *American* term for baggage, luggage.

PLUNGER, a cavalry-man.—*Military Slang*.

POCKET-PISTOL, a dram-flask.

PODGY, drunk; dumpy, short, and fat.

POGRAM, a Dissenter, a fanatic, formalist, or humbug. So called from a well-known dissenting minister of this name.

POKE, a bag, or sack; "to buy a pig in a POKE," to purchase anything without seeing it.—*Saxon*.

POKE, a Slang word for booty or plunder.—*Times*, Nov. 29, 1860.

POKE, "come, none of your POKING fun at me," *i.e.*, you must not laugh at me.

POKER, "by the holy POKER and the tumbling Tom!" an Irish oath.

POKERS, the Cambridge Slang term for the Esquire Bedels, who carry the silver maces (also called POKERS) before the Vice-Chancellor.

"Around, around, all, all around,
On seats with velvet lined,
Sat Heads of Houses in a row,
And Deans, and College Dons below,
With a POKER or two behind."

Rime of the New-Made Baccalere, 1841.

POKY, confined or cramped; "that corner is POKY and narrow."—*Times* article, 21st July 1859. Saxon, POKE, a sack.

POLE-AXE, vulgar rendering of the word "police."

POLICEMAN, a fly—more especially the earlier kind known as "blue bottles."

POLISH OFF, to finish off anything quickly—a dinner for instance; also to finish off an adversary.—*Pugilistic*.

POLL, or POLLING, one thief robbing another of part of the booty. In use in ancient times, *vide Hall's Union*, 1548.

POLL, the "ordinary degree" candidates for the B. A. Examination, who do not aspire to the "Honours" list. From the *Greek*, οἱ πολλοί, "the many." Some years ago, at Cambridge, Mr Hopkins being the most celebrated "honour coach," or private tutor for the wranglers, and Mr Potts the principal "crammer" of the non-honour men, the latter was facetiously termed the "POLLY HOPKINS" by the undergraduates.

POLL, a female of unsteady character; "POLLED UP," living with a woman in a state of unmarried impropriety.

POLONY, Cockney shortening and vulgar pronunciation of a *Bologna* sausage.

POMPADOURS, the Fifty-sixth Regiment of Foot in the British army.

POND, or HERRING-POND, the sea; so called by those who are sent across it at the national expense.

PONGE, or PONGELOW, beer, half-and-half; the term is also used as a verb, as in the Cockney phrase, "let's PONGELOW, shall we?"

PONY, twenty-five pounds.—*Sporting*.

POONA, a sovereign.—Corruption of "pound;" or from the *Lingua Franca*.

POP, to pawn or pledge; "to POP up the spout," to pledge at the pawnbroker's,—an allusion to the spout up which the brokers send the ticketed articles until such times as they shall be redeemed. The spout runs from the ground-floor to the wareroom at the top of the house.

POPE'S NOSE, the extremity of the rump of a roast fowl, devilled as a dainty for epicures.

POPS, pocket-pistols.

PORTRAIT, a sovereign, or twenty shillings.

POSA, a treasurer. A corruption of "purser," the name given to the treasurer in the large Anglo-Chinese mercantile establishments.—*Anglo-Chinese*.

POSH, a halfpenny, or trifling coin. Also a generic term for money.

POST, to pay down; "POST THE PONY" signifies to place the stakes played for on the table.

POST-HORN, the nose.—*See* PASTE-HORN.

POST-MORTEM, at Cambridge, the second examination which men who have been "plucked" have to undergo.—*University*.

POSTBOYS, THREE JOLLY, a method of tossing.

POSTERIORS, a correspondent insists that the vulgar sense of this word is undoubtedly Slang; (Swift, I believe, first applied it as such,) and remarks that it is curious the word *anterior* has not been so abused.

POSTED UP, well acquainted with the subject in question, "up to the mark,"—metaphor drawn from the counting-house.

POT, a sixpence, *i.e.*, the price of a pot or quart of half-and-half. A half-crown, in medical student Slang, is a FIVE-POT PIECE.

POT, "to GO TO POT," to die; from the classic custom of putting the ashes of the dead in an urn; also, to be ruined, or broken up,—often applied to tradesmen who fail in business. GO TO POT! *i.e.*, go and hang yourself, shut up and be quiet. *L'Estrange*, to PUT THE POT ON, to overcharge, or exaggerate. A correspondent, however, prefers looking to the refiner's shop for the origin of the expression, where refuse metal and worn-out plate are daily condemned "to go to POT."

POT, to finish; "don't POT me," term used at billiards, when a player holes his adversary's ball—generally considered shabby play. This word was much used by our soldiers in the Crimea, for firing at the enemy from a hole or ambush. These were called POT-SHOTS.

POT-HUNTER, a sportsman who shoots anything he comes across, having more regard to filling his bag than to the rules which regulate the sport.

POT LUCK, just as it comes; to take POT LUCK, *i.e.*, one's chance of a dinner,—a hearty term used to signify whatever the pot contains the visitor is welcome to.

POT-WALLOPER, an elector in certain boroughs before the passing of the Reform Bill, whose qualification consisted in being a housekeeper,— to establish which it was only necessary to boil a pot within the limits of the borough, by the aid of any temporary erection. This implied that he was able to provide for himself, and not necessitated to apply for parochial relief. Honiton, Tregoney, Ilchester, Old Sarum, &c., had this privilege before the passing of the Reform Bill.—*See Gentleman's Magazine* for June 1852. WALLOP, a word of *Anglo-Saxon* derivation, from the same root as *well*.

POTATO-TRAP, the mouth.—Originally a *Hibernicism*.

POTEEN, whisky made in an illicit still, once a favourite drink in *Ireland*, now almost unattainable.

POTTED, or POTTED OUT, cabined, confined; "the patriotic member of Parliament POTTED OUT in a dusty little lodging somewhere about Bury Street."—*Times* article, 21st July 1859. Also applied to burial, —a gardening allusion.

POTTY, indifferent, bad looking,—said of a rotten or unsound scheme.

POWER, a large quantity; "a POWER of money."—Especially *Irish*, but now general. *Deriv.* POER, *Old French* or *Norman*, large resources; also an army.

P. P., in Turf Slang a contraction of "PLAY OR PAY;" that is, the money must be paid whether the horse runs or not.

PRANCER, a horse.—*Ancient Cant.*

PRECIOUS, used in a Slang sense like very or exceeding; "a PRECIOUS little of that," *i.e.*, a very little indeed; a PRECIOUS humbug, rascal &c., *i.e.*, an eminent one.

PRAD, a horse.

PRAD-NAPPING, horse-stealing.

PRETTY HORSE-BREAKER, a phrase of recent adoption, applied to the ladies of the *demi-monde* by the *Times* and other newspapers. It is said that the livery stable-keepers of the West End find it to their advantage to provide horses and "traps" for these PRETTY HORSE-BREAKERS to display.

PRIAL, a corruption of PAIR-ROYAL, a term at the game of cribbage, meaning three cards of a similar description. Often used metaphorically for three persons or things of a kind. DOUBLE-PRIAL, a corruption of DOUBLE PAIR-ROYAL, means four persons or things of a similar description.

"PRICK THE GARTER," or "PITCH THE NOB," a gambling and cheating game common at fairs, and generally practised by thimble-riggers. It consists of a "garter" or a piece of list doubled, and then folded up tight. The bet is made upon your asserting that you can, with a pin, "prick" the point at which the garter is doubled. The garter is then unfolded, and nine times out of ten you will find that you have been deceived, and that one of the false folds has been pricked. The owner of the garter, I should state, holds the ends tightly with one hand. This was, doubtless, originally a Gipsy game, and we are informed by *Brand* that it was much practised by the Gipsies in the time of *Shakspeare*. In those days it was termed PRICKING AT THE BELT, or FAST AND LOOSE.

PRIG, a thief. Used by *Addison* in the sense of a coxcomb. *Ancient Cant*, probably from the *Saxon*, PRICC-AN, to filch, &c.—*Shakspeare*. PRIG, to steal, or rob. PRIGGING, thieving. In *Scotland* the term PRIG is used in a different sense from what it is in England. In Glasgow, or at Aberdeen, "to PRIG a salmon" would be to cheapen it, or seek for an abatement in the price. A story is told of two Scotchmen, visitors to London, who got into sad trouble a few years ago by announcing their intention of "PRIGGING a hat" which they had espied in a fashionable manufacturer's window, and which one of them thought he would like to possess.

PRIG, a conceited, stuck-up person, and contemptible withal; one who appropriates or adopts a manner or costume not suited to him.

PRIGGISH, conceited.

PRIMED, said of a person in that state of incipient intoxication that if he takes more drink it will become evident.

PRO, a professional.—*Theatrical*.

PROG, meat, food, &c. *Johnson* calls it "a low word."

PROP, a blow, the UPPER CUT.

PROPS, crutches.

PROPS, stage properties.—*Theatrical*.

PRIME PLANT, a good subject for plunder.—*See* PLANT.

PROP, a gold scarf pin.

PROP-NAILER, a man who steals, or rather snatches, pins from gentlemen's scarfs.

PROPER, very, exceedingly, sometimes ironically; "you are a PROPER nice fellow," meaning a great scamp.

PROS, a water-closet. Abbreviated form of πρὸς τινα τόπον.—*Oxford University.*

PROSS, to break in or instruct a stage-infatuated youth. Also, to "sponge" upon a comrade or stranger for drink.

PSALM-SMITER, a "Ranter," one who sings at a conventicle.—*See* BRISKET-BEATER.

PUB, or PUBLIC, a public-house; "what PUB do you use?" *i.e.*, which inn or public-house do you frequent?

PUCKER, poor temper, difficulty, *déshabillé*. PUCKER UP, to get in a poor temper.

PUCKERING, talking privately.

PUCKEROW, to seize, to take hold of. From the *Hindostanee,* PUCKERNA.—*Anglo-Indian.*

PUFF, to blow up, swell with praise; declared by a writer in the *Weekly Register*, as far back as 1732, to be illegitimate.

> "PUFF has become a Cant word, signifying the applause set forth by writers, &c., to increase the reputation and sale of a book, and is an excellent stratagem to excite the curiosity of gentle readers."

Lord Bacon, however, used the word in a similar sense a century before.

PUG, abbreviation of "pugilist." Sayers and Heenan would speak familiarly of themselves as "brother PUGS."

PULL, an advantage, or hold upon another; "I've the PULL over you," *i.e.*, you are in my power—perhaps an oblique allusion to the judicial sense.—*See the following.*

PULL, to have one apprehended; "to be PULLED up," to be taken before a magistrate.

PULL, to drink; "come, take a PULL at it," *i.e.*, drink up.

PULLET, a young girl.

PUMMEL, to thrash,—from POMMEL.

PUMP, to extract information by roundabout questioning.

PUNDIT, a person who assumes to be very grave and learned.—*Anglo-Indian.*

PUNKAH, a fan.—*Anglo-Indian.*

PUNT, to gamble; PUNTING-SHOP, a gambling-house. Common in ancient writers, but now disused. The word seems confined to playing for "chicken stakes."

PUBLIC PATTERERS, swell mobites who pretend to be dissenting preachers, and harangue in the open air to attract a crowd for their confederates to rob.

PUDDING-SNAMMER, one who robs a cook-shop.

PULLEY, a confederate thief,—generally a woman.

PUP AND RINGER, *i.e.,* the "Dog and Bell," the sign of a flash public-house.

PURDAH, a curtain.—*Anglo-Indian.*

PURL, hunting term for a fall, synonymous with FOALED, or SPILT; "he 'll get PURLED at the rails."

PURL, a mixture of hot ale and sugar, with wormwood infused in it, a favourite morning drink to produce an appetite; sometimes with gin and spice added :—

> "Two penn'orth o' PURL—
> Good 'early PURL,'
> 'Gin all the world
> To put your hair into a curl,
> When you feel yourself queer of a mornin'."

PUSH, a crowd.—*Old Cant.*

PUSSEY-CATS, corruption of *Puseyites,* a name constantly, but improperly, given to the "Tractarian" party in the Church, from the Oxford Regius Professor of Hebrew, who by no means approved of the Romanising tendencies of some of its leaders.

PUT, a game at cards.

"PUT THAT IN YOUR PIPE AND SMOKE IT," said of a blow or repartee, and equivalent to "take that and profit by it," *i.e.,* let it be a warning to you.

"PUT THE POT ON," to bet too much upon one horse.—*Sporting.*

PUT UP, to suggest, to incite, "he PUT me UP to it;" to have done with; PUT IT UP, is a vulgar answer often heard in the streets. PUT UP, to stop at a hotel or tavern for entertainment.

PUT UPON, cheated, victimised, oppressed.

PUTTUN, regiment.—*Anglo-Indian.*

PYAH, weak, useless, paltry. This word, much in use among sailors, is evidently derived from the *Indian* term PARIAH, signifying the lowest caste of Hindoos. Thus the Pariah dogs in India are termed PYAH dogs; and the Pariah descendants of the old Portuguese settlers are called PYAH PORTUGUESE. Sailors term the natives of St Helena,— a wretched-looking set of individuals,—PYAH ENGLISHMEN.

PYGOSTOLE, the least irreverent of names for the peculiar "M.-B." coats worn by Tractarian curates :—

> "It is true that the wicked make sport
> Of our PYGOSTOLES, as we go by ;
> And one gownsman, in Trinity Court,
> Went so far as to call me a 'Guy.'"

See M B.

PYJANDS, a kind of drawers or loose pantaloons.—*Anglo-Indian.*

QUAD. See QUOD.

QUAKER, an unlawful sir reverence.

QUALITY, gentry, high life.

PURE FINDERS, street-collectors of dogs' dung.

QUANDARY, described in the dictionaries as a "low word," may fittingly be given here. It illustrates, like HOCUS POCUS, and other compound colloquialisms, the singular origin of Slang expressions. QUANDARY, a dilemma, a doubt, a difficulty, is from the French, QU'EN DIRAI-JE?—*Skinner.*

QUARTEREEN, a farthing.—*Gibraltar term. Italian,* QUATTRINO.

QUAVER, a musician.

QUEEN BESS, the Queen of Clubs,—perhaps because that queen, history says, was of a swarthy complexion.—*North Hants.—See Gentleman's Magazine for* 1791, p. 141.

QUEER, an old Cant word, once in continual use as a prefix, signifying base, roguish, or worthless,—the opposite of RUM, which signified good and genuine. QUEER, in all probability, is immediately derived from the Cant language. It has been mooted that it came into use from a *quære* (?) being set before a man's name; but it is more than probable that it was brought into this country by the Gipsies from Germany, where QUER signifies "*cross*," or "*crooked*." At all events it is believed to have been first used in England as a Cant word.

QUEER, "to QUEER a flat," to puzzle or confound a "gull" or silly fellow.

"Who in a *row* like Tom could lead the van,
 Booze in the *ken*, or at the *spellken* hustle?
Who QUEER a flat," &c.
—*Don Juan,* canto xi. 19.

QUEER BAIL, worthless persons who for a consideration formerly stood bail for any one in court. Insolvent Jews generally performed this office, which gave rise to the term JEW-BAIL.—*See* MOUNTERS: both nearly obsolete.

QUEER STREET, "in QUEER STREET," in difficulty or in want.

QUEER CUFFEN, a justice of the peace, or magistrate—a very ancient term, mentioned in the earliest Slang dictionary.

QUERIER, a chimney-sweep who calls from house to house soliciting employment—formerly termed KNULLER, which *see.*

QUI-HI, an English resident at Calcutta.—*Anglo-Indian.*

QUICK STICKS, in a hurry, rapidly; "to cut QUICK STICKS," to start off hurriedly, or without more ado.—*See* CUT ONE'S STICK.

QUID, or THICK UN, a sovereign; "half a QUID," half a sovereign; QUIDS, money generally; "QUID for a QUOD," one good turn for another. The word is used by *Old French* writers:—

"Des testamens qu'on dit le maistre
De mon fait n'aura QUID ne QUOD."
—*Grand Testament de Villon.*

QUID, a small piece of tobacco—one mouthful. *Quid est hoc?* asked one, tapping the swelled cheek of another; *hoc est quid,* promptly replied

---

QUEAN, (not QUEEN,) a strumpet. *Saxon,* CWEAN, a barren old cow.

QUEER-BIT-MAKERS, coiners.

QUEER-SOFT, bad money.

the other, exhibiting at the same time "a chaw" of the weed. CUD is probably a corruption. Derivation, *O. F.*, or *Norman*, QUIDER, to ruminate.

QUID-NUNC, an inquisitive person, always seeking for news. The words translated simply signify "What now?"

QUIET, "on the QUIET," clandestinely, so as to avoid observation, "under the rose."

QUILL-DRIVER, a scrivener, a clerk,—satirical phrase similar to STEEL BAR-DRIVER, a tailor.

QUILLER, a parasite, a person who sucks neatly through a quill.—*See* SUCK UP.

QUILT, to thrash, or beat.

QUISBY, bankrupt, poverty-stricken.—*Household Words*, No. 183.

QUISI, roguish, low, obscene.—*Anglo-Chinese.*

QUI-TAM, a solicitor. It properly means "who so," and is the title given to an action in the nature of an information on a penal suit.

QUIZ, a prying person, an odd fellow. *Oxford Slang;* lately admitted into the dictionaries. Not noticed by *Johnson.*

QUIZ, to pry, or joke; to hoax.

QUIZZICAL, jocose, humorous.

QUIZZING-GLASS, an eye-glass.

QUOCKERWODGER, a wooden toy figure, which, when pulled by a string, jerks its limbs about. The term is used in a Slang sense to signify a pseudo-politician, one whose strings of action are pulled by somebody else.—*West.*

QUOD, a prison, or lock-up; QUODDED, put in prison. A Slang expression used by Mr Hughes, in *Tom Brown's Schooldays,* (*Macmillan's Magazine,* January 1860,) throws some light upon the origin of this now very common street term:—"Flogged or whipped in QUAD," says the delineator of student life, in allusion to chastisement inflicted within the *Quadrangle* of a college. Quadrangle is the term given to the prison enclosure within which culprits are allowed to walk, and where whippings were formerly inflicted. Quadrangle also represents a building of four sides; and to be "within FOUR WALLS," or prison, is the frequent Slang lamentation of unlucky vagabonds.

> "Breakfast was done, white tie put on,
> Wearily did we plod;
> Past Balliol, past Trinity,
> Into the *great-go* QUOD."
> —*The Rime of the New-Made Baccalere,* Oxford, 1841.

QUODGER, a contraction, or corruption rather, of the *Latin* law phrase, QUO JURE, by what law.—*Legal.*

RABBIT, when a person gets the worst of a bargain, he is said "to have bought the RABBIT."

RACKET, a dodge, manœuvre, exhibition; a disturbance.

RACKETY, wild or noisy.

RACKS, the bones of a dead horse. Term used by horse-slaughterers.

RACLAN, a married woman.—Originally *Gipsy*, but now a term with English tramps.

RAFE, or RALPH, a pawnbroker's duplicate.—*Norwich.*

RAG, to divide or share; "let's RAG IT," or "go RAGS," *i.e.*, share it equally between us.—*Norwich.*

RAGAMUFFIN, an ill-clad vagabond, a tatterdemalion.

RAG SPLAWGER, a rich man.

RAG, a bank-note.

RAG-SHOP, a bank.

RAIN NAPPER, an umbrella.

"RAISE THE WIND," to obtain credit, or money,—generally by pawning or selling property. Sometimes varied to "WHISTLE UP THE BREEZE."

RAMSHACKLE, to shatter as with a battering ram; RAMSHACKLED, knocked about, as standing corn is after a high wind. Corrupted from *ram-shatter*, or possibly from *ransack*.

RANCHO, originally a *Spanish-American* word, signifying a hunting-lodge, or cattle-station, in a wood or desert far from the haunts of men. A hunting or fishing station in the Highlands or elsewhere. In Washington, with their accustomed ingenuity in corrupting words and meanings, the Americans use the appellation for a place of evil report.

RANDALS-MAN.—*See* BILLY.

RANDAN, a boat impelled by three rowers, using four oars; the midship rower having two sculls, the bowman and strokesman one oar each.

RANDOM, three horses driven in line.—*See* TANDEM, SUDDEN DEATH, HARUM-SCARUM.

RANDY, rampant, violent, warm.—*North*, RANDY-BEGGAR, a Gipsy tinker.

RANK, to cheat.

RAN-TAN, " on the RAN-TAN," drunk.—*Household Words*, No. 183.

RANTIPOLL, a noisy rude girl, a "mad-cap."

RAP, a halfpenny; frequently used generically for money, thus :—I haven't a RAP," *i.e.*, I have no money whatever; "I don't care a RAP," &c. Originally a species of counterfeit coin used for small change in *Ireland*, against the use of which a proclamation was issued, 5th May 1737. Small copper or base metal coins are still called RAPPEN in the Swiss cantons. Irish robbers were formerly termed RAPPAREES.

RAP, to utter; "he RAPPED out a volley of oaths."

RAPPING, enormous; "a RAPPING big lie."

RAPSCALLION, a low tattered wretch—not worth a RAP.

RAMP, to thieve or rob with violence.

RAMPSMAN, a highway robber who uses violence when necessary.

RAT, a sneak, an informer, a turn-coat, one who changes his party for interest. The late Sir Robert Peel was called the RAT, or the TAMWORTH RATCATCHER, for altering his views on the Roman Catholic question. From rats deserting vessels about to sink. The term is often used amongst printers to denote one who works under price. *Old Cant* for a clergyman.

RAT, TO SMELL A, to suspect something, guess that there is something amiss.

RATHER! a ridiculous street exclamation synonymous with yes; "do you like fried chickens?" "RATHER!" "are you going out of town?" "RATHER!" Very often pronounced RAYTHER!

"**RATHER OF THE RATHEREST**," a phrase applied to anything slightly in excess or defect.

RATTLECAP, an unsteady, volatile person. Generally applied to girls.

RATTLER, a cab, coach, or cart.—*Old Cant.*

RATTLERS, a railway; "on the RATTLERS to the stretchers," *i.e.*, going to the races by railway.

RAW, a tender point, or foible; "to touch a man UPON THE RAW" is to irritate one by alluding to, or joking him on, anything on which he is peculiarly susceptible or "thin-skinned."—Originally *Stable Slang*.

"Liver and bacon, kidneys, ten pounds one!
He thinks me RAW. *I* think I'm rather DONE."
—*Phantom Barber.*

RAW, uninitiated; a novice.—*Old.* Frequently "JOHNNY RAW."

READY, or READY GILT, (properly GELT,) money. Used by *Arbuthnot*,—"Lord Strut was not very flush in READY."

READY-RECKONERS, the Highland regiments of the British army.

RECENT INCISION, the busy thoroughfare on the Surrey side of the Thames, known by sober people as the NEW CUT.

REDGE, gold.

RED HERRING, a soldier.

RED LANE, the throat.

RED LINER, an officer of the Mendicity Society.

RED RAG, the tongue.

RELIEVING OFFICER, a significant term for a father.—*University.*

RENAGE, to revoke, a word used in *Ireland* at the game of five-card.

RASPING-GANG, the mob of roughs and thieves who attend prize-fights.

READER, a pocket-book; "give it him for his READER," *i.e.*, rob him of his pocket-book.—*Old Cant.*

REAM, good or genuine. From the *Old Cant*, RUM.

REAM-BLOAK, a good man.

REDDING, a gold watch, probably RED 'UN.

REGULARS, a thief's share of the plunder. "They were quarrelling about the REGULARS."—*Times*, 8th January 1856.

RENCH, vulgar pronunciation of RINSE. "*Wrench* your mouth out," said a fashionable dentist one day.—*North.*

RE-RAW, "on the RE-RAW," tipsy or drunk.—*Household Words*, No. 183.

RESURRECTION PIE, a school phrase, to denote a Saturday dish, made of the scraps and leavings of meat that have appeared before.

RHINO, ready money.—*Old.*

> "Some as I know,
> Have parted with their READY RINO."
> —*The Seaman's Adieu*, Old Ballad, 1670.

> "Travelling forms a man; but it at the same time forms a very large hole in his finances. In Switzerland it is pleasant to run up hills, but the wanderer must simultaneously run up bills; and no Englishman can see the Rhine who does not possess the RHINO."—*Morning Star*, Aug. 21, 1863.

RHINOCERAL, rich, wealthy, abounding in RHINO.

RIB, a wife.—*North.*

RIBBON, gin, or other spirits.—*Servants' term.*—See SATIN.

RIBBONS, the reins.—*Middlesex.*

RIBROAST, to beat till the ribs are sore.—*Old;* but still in use:—

> "And he departs, not meanly boasting
> Of his magnificent RIBROASTING."—*Hudibras.*

RICH, spicy; also used in the sense of "too much of a good thing;" "a RICH idea," one too absurd or unreasonable to be adopted.

RICHARD, a dictionary.—*See* DICK.

RIDE, "to RIDE THE HIGH HORSE," or RIDE ROUGH-SHOD over one, to be overbearing or oppressive; to RIDE THE BLACK DONKEY, to be in an ill humour.

RIDER, in a University examination, a problem or question appended to another, as directly arising from or dependent on it;—beginning to be generally used for any corollary or position which naturally arises from any previous statement or evidence.

RIFF-RAFF, low, vulgar rabble.

RIG, or trick, "spree," or performance; "run a RIG," to play a trick.—*Gipsy.* "RIG the market," in reality to play tricks with it,—a mercantile Slang phrase often used in the newspapers.

RIGGED, "well RIGGED," well dressed.—*Old Slang*, in use 1736.—*See Bailey's Dictionary.*—*Sea.*

"RIGHT AS NINEPENCE," (corruption of NINE-PINS,) quite right, exactly right.—*See* NINEPENCE.

"RIGHT YOU ARE!" a phrase implying entire acquiescence in what has been said or done. The expression is singularly frequent and general amongst the lower and middle classes of the metropolis.

RIGHTS, "to have one TO RIGHTS," to be even with him, to serve him out.

RIGMAROLE, a prolix story.

RILE, to offend, to render very cross, irritated, or vexed. Properly, to render liquor turbid.—*Norfolk.*

RING, to change; "RINGING CASTORS," changing hats; "to RING the changes," in low life means to change bad money for good; in respectable society the phrase is sometimes employed to denote that the aggressor has been paid back in his own coin, as in practical joking, when the laugh is turned against the jester. The expression originally came from the belfry.

RING, a generic term given to horse-racing and pugilism,—the latter is sometimes termed the PRIZE-RING. From the practice of forming the crowd into a *ring* around the combatants, or outside the race course.

RING, "to go through the RING," to take advantage of the Insolvency Act, or be "whitewashed."

RIP, a rake: "an old RIP," an old libertine, or debauchee. Corruption of "Reprobate." A person reading the letters R. I. P. (*Requiescat in Pace*,) on the top of a tombstone as one word, said, soliloquising, "Rip! well, he *was* an old RIP, and no mistake."—*Cuthbert Bede*.

RIPPER, a first-rate man or article.—*Provincial*.

RIPPING, excellent, very good.

RISE, "to take a RISE out of a person." A metaphor from fly-fishing, the silly fish RISING to be caught by an artificial fly; to mortify, outwit, or cheat him, by superior cunning.

> "There is only one thing, unfortunately, of which Oxford men are economical, and that is their University experience. They not only think it fair that *Freshmen* should go through their ordeal unaided, but many have a sweet satisfaction in their distresses, and even busy themselves in obtaining elevations, or, as it is vulgarly termed, in getting RISES 'out of them.'"— *Hints to Freshmen*, Oxford, 1843.

RISE (or RAISE) A BARNEY, to collect a mob; term used by patterers, and "schwassle-box" (Punch and Judy) men.

ROARER, a broken-winded horse; or, in the more polite speech of the stable, "A HIGH BLOWER." ROARING, as applied to horses, is often termed "TALKING" by "turf-men."

ROARING TRADE, a very successful business.—*Shopkeepers' Slang*.

ROAST, to expose a person to a running fire of jokes at his expense from a whole company. QUIZZING is done by a single person only.

ROCK-A-LOW, an overcoat. Corruption of the *French* ROQUELAURE.

ROCKED, "he's only HALF-ROCKED," *i.e.*, half-witted.

ROGUE'S YARN, a thread of red or blue worsted, worked into the ropes manufactured in the Government dockyards, to identify them if stolen. Also a blue thread worked into canvas, for the same purpose.

ROMANY, a Gipsy, or the Gipsy language; the speech of the Roma or Zincali.—*Spanish Gipsy*. "Can you patter ROMANY?" *i.e.*, can you talk "black," or Gipsy lingo?

ROOK, a cheat, or tricky gambler; the opposite of PIGEON.—*Old*.

RING-DROPPING, *see* FAWNEY.

"ROLL OF SNOW," a piece of Irish linen.—*Prison term*.

ROOK, a clergyman, not only from his black attire, but also, perhaps, from the old nursery favourite, the *History of Cock Robin.*

> "I, says the ROOK,
> With my little book,
> I'll be the parson."

ROOKERY, a low neighbourhood inhabited by dirty Irish and thieves—as ST GILES'S ROOKERY.—*Old.* In *Military Slang* that part of the barracks occupied by subalterns, often by no means a pattern of good order.

ROOKY, rascally, rakish, scampish.

ROOST, synonymous with PERCH, which *see.*

ROOTER, anything good, or of a prime quality; "that *is* a ROOTER," *i.e.*, a first-rate one of the sort.

ROPER, MISTRESS, "to marry MRS ROPER" is to enlist in the Royal Marines.

ROPING, the act of pulling or restraining a horse, by its rider, to prevent it winning a race—a trick not unfrequently practised on the turf.

ROSE, an orange.

ROSE, "under the ROSE" (frequently used in its *Latin* form, *sub rosâ*,) *i.e.*, under the obligation of silence and secrecy, of which the rose was anciently an emblem, perhaps, as Sir Thomas Browne remarks, from the closeness with which its petals are enfolded in the bud. The Rose of Venus was given, says the classic legend, to Harpocrates, the God of Silence, by Cupid, as a bribe not to "peach" about the Goddess's amours. It was commonly sculptured on the ceilings of banqueting rooms, as a sign that what was said in free conversation there was not afterwards to be divulged; and about 1526 was placed over the Roman confessionals as an emblem of secrecy. The White Rose was also an emblem of the Pretender, whose health, as king, his secret adherents used to drink "under the ROSE."

ROSIN, beer or other drink given to musicians at a dancing party.

ROSIN-THE-BOW, a fiddler.

ROT, nonsense, anything bad, disagreeable, or useless.

ROT-GUT, bad small beer,—in *America*, cheap whisky.

ROUGH, bad; "ROUGH fish," bad or stinking fish.—*Billingsgate.*

ROUGH-IT, to put up with chance entertainment, to take pot luck, and what accommodation "turns up," without sighing for better. "ROUGHING IT *in the Bush*" is the title of an interesting work on Backwoods life.

ROUGHS, coarse, or vulgar men.

ROULEAU, a packet of sovereigns.—*Gaming.*

ROUND, to tell tales, to "SPLIT," which *see;* "to ROUND on a man," to swear to him as being the person, &c. Synonymous with "BUFF," which *see. Shakspeare* has ROUNDING, whispering.

ROUND, "ROUND dealing," honest trading; "ROUND sum," a large sum. Synonymous also in a *Slang* sense with SQUARE, which *see.*

ROUNDEM, a button.

ROUNDS, shirt collars—apparently a mere shortening of "All Rounds," or "All Rounders," names of fashionable collars.

ROUND, (in the language of the street,) the BEAT or usual walk of the costermonger to sell his stock. A term used by street folk generally.

> "Watchmen, sometimes they made their sallies,
> And walk'd their ROUNDS through streets and allies."
> —*Ned Ward's Vulgus Britannicus*, 1710.

ROUND ROBIN, a petition, or paper of remonstrance, with the signatures written in a circle,—to prevent the first signer, or ringleader, from being discovered.

ROUNDABOUT, a large swing with four compartments, each the size, and very much the shape, of the body of a cart, capable of seating six or eight boys and girls, erected in a high frame, and turned round by men at a windlass. Fairs and merry-makings generally abound with these swings. The frames take to pieces, and are carried in vans from fair to fair by miserable horses.

ROW, "the ROW," *i.e.*, Paternoster Row. The notorious Holywell Street is now called by its denizens "Bookseller's Row!"

ROW, a noisy disturbance, tumult, or trouble. Originally *Cambridge*, now universal. Seventy years ago it was written ROUE, which would indicate a *French* origin from *roué*, a profligate or disturber of the peace.—*Vide George Parker's Life's Painter*, 1789, p. 122.

ROWDY, money. In *America*, a ruffian, a brawler, a "rough."

ROWDY-DOW, low, vulgar; "not the CHEESE," or thing.

RUB, a quarrel or impediment; "there's the RUB," *i.e.*, that is the difficulty.—*Shakspeare and L'Estrange.*

RUBBED OUT, dead,—a melancholy expression, of late frequently used in fashionable novels.

RUBBER, a term at whist, &c., two games out of three.—*Old*, 1677.

RUCK, the undistinguished crowd; "to come in with the RUCK," to arrive at the winning-post among the non-winning horses.—*Racing term.*

RUGGY, fusty, frowsy.

RUM, like its opposite, QUEER, was formerly a much-used prefix, signifying fine, good, gallant, or valuable, perhaps in some way connected with ROME. Now-a-days it means indifferent, bad, or questionable, and we often hear even persons in polite society use such a phrase as "what a RUM fellow he is, to be sure," in speaking of a man of singular habits or appearance. The term, from its frequent use, long since claimed a place in our dictionaries; but, with the exception of *Johnson*, who says RUM, a Cant word for a clergyman (?), no lexicographer has deigned to notice it.

> "Thus RUMLY floor'd, the kind Acestes ran,
> And pitying, raised from earth the game old man."
> —*Virgil's Æneid*, book v., *Translation by Thomas Moore.*

RUMBOWLING, anything inferior or adulterated.—*Sea.*

RUMBUMPTIOUS, haughty, pugilistic.

RUMBUSTIOUS, or RUMBUSTICAL, pompous, haughty, boisterous, careless of the comfort of others.

RUMBLER, a four-wheeled cab. Not so common as BOUNDER.

RUM CULL, the manager of a theatre.—*Travelling Theatre.*

RUMGUMPTION, or GUMPTION, knowledge, capacity, capability,—hence, RUMGUMPTIOUS, knowing, wide-awake, forward, positive, pert, blunt.

RUM-MIZZLER, the *Seven Dials'* Cant for a person who is clever at making his escape, or getting out of a difficulty.

RUMPUS, a noise, disturbance, a "row."

RUM-SLIM, rum punch.

RUMY, a good woman, or girl.—*Gipsy Cant.* In the continental *Gipsy*, ROMI, a woman, a wife, is the feminine of RO, a man.

RUN, (good or bad,) the success of a performance.—*Theatrical.*

RUN, to comprehend, &c.; "I don't RUN to it," *i.e.*, I can't do it, I don't understand, or I have not money enough.—*North.*

RUN, "to get the RUN upon any person," to have the upper hand, or be able to laugh at them. RUN DOWN, to abuse or backbite any one; to "lord it," or "drive over" them. Originally *Stable Slang.*

RUNNING PATTERER, a street seller who runs or moves briskly along, calling aloud his wares.

RUNNING STATIONER, a hawker of books, ballads, dying speeches, and newspapers. Persons of this class formerly used to run with newspapers, blowing a horn, when they were sometimes termed FLYING STATIONERS. Now-a-days, in the event of any political or social disturbance, the miserable relics of these peripatetic newsmen bawl the heads of the telegram or information in quiet London thoroughfares, to the disturbance of the residents.

RUSH, "doing it on the RUSH," running away, or making off.

RUST, "to nab the RUST," to take offence. RUSTY, cross, ill-tempered, morose; one who cannot go through life like a person of easy and "polished" manners.

RUSTY GUTS, a blunt, rough, old fellow. Corruption of RUSTICUS.

SACK, to "get the SACK," to be discharged by an employer. Varied in the north of England to "get the BAG." In London it is sometimes spoken of as "getting the EMPTY."

SADDLE, an additional charge made by the manager to a performer upon his benefit night.—*Theatrical.*

SAD DOG, a merry fellow, a joker, a gay or "fast" man.

SAILS, the sail-maker on board ship.

SAINT MONDAY, a holiday most religiously observed by journeymen shoemakers, and other mechanics. An Irishman observed that this saint's anniversary happened every week.—*North*, where it is termed COBBLERS' MONDAY.

SAL, a salary.—*Theatrical.*

SALAAM, a compliment or salutation.—*Anglo-Indian.*

SALAMANDER, a street acrobat, and juggler who eats fire.

SALOOP, SALEP, or SALOP, a greasy-looking beverage, formerly sold on stalls at early morning, prepared from a powder made of the root of the *Orchis mascula,* or Red-handed Orchis. Within a few years coffee-stands have superseded SALOOP stalls; but Charles Lamb, in one of his papers, has left some account of this drinkable, which he says was of all preparations the most grateful to the stomachs of young chimney-sweeps.

SALT, "it's rather too SALT," said of an extravagant hotel bill. Also, a sort of black mail or tribute levied on visitors or travellers by the Eton boys, at their triennial festival called the "Montem," by ancient custom and privileges. It is now abolished. A periodical published at Eton many years ago for circulation amongst the boys was called "*The* SALT-*box.*" When a person about to sell a business connexion makes fictitious entries in the books of accounts, to simulate that a much more profitable trade is carried on than there really is, he is said to SALT the books—SALTING and COOKING being somewhat similar operations. At the gold diggings of Australia, miners sometimes SALT an unproductive hole by sprinkling a few grains of gold dust over it, and thus obtain a good price from a "green hand." Unpromising speculations are frequently thus SALTED to entrap the unwary, the wildest ideas being rendered palatable, *cum grano salis.* And though old birds are not readily caught by chaff, the efficacy of SALT in bird-catching is equally as proverbial.

SALTEE, a penny. Pence, &c., are thus reckoned:—

ONEY SALTEE, a penny, from the *Italian,*	UNO SOLDO.
DOOE SALTEE, twopence,	DUE SOLDI.
TRAY SALTEE, threepence,	TRE SOLDI.
QUARTERER SALTEE, fourpence,	QUATTRO SOLDI.
CHINKER SALTEE, fivepence,	CINQUE SOLDI.
SAY SALTEE, sixpence,	SEI SOLDI.
SAY ONEY SALTEE, or SETTER SALTEE, sevenpence,	SETTE SOLDI.
SAY DOOE SALTEE, or OTTER SALTEE, eightpence,	OTTO SOLDI.
SAY TRAY SALTEE, or NOBBA SALTEE, ninepence,	NOVE SOLDI.
SAY QUARTERER SALTEE, or DACHA SALTEE, tenpence,	DIECI SOLDI.
SAY CHINKER SALTEE, or DACHA ONE SALTEE, elevenpence	DIECI UNO SOLDI, &c.
ONEY BEONG, one shilling.	

A BEONG SAY SALTEE, one shilling and sixpence.
DOOE BEONG SAY SALTEE, or MADZA CAROON, half-a-crown, or two shillings and sixpence.

SALT-BOX, the condemned cell in Newgate.

∗ This curious list of numerals in use among the London street folk is, strange as it may seem, derived from the *Lingua Franca,* or bastard *Italian,* of the Mediterranean seaports, of which other examples may be found in the pages of this Dictionary. SALTEE, the Cant term used by the costermongers and others for a penny, is no other than the *Italian,* SOLDO, (plural, SOLDI,) and the numerals—as may be seen by the *Italian* equivalents—are a tolerably close imitation of the originals. After the number SIX, a curious variation occurs, which is peculiar to the London Cant, seven being reckoned as SAY ONEY, *six-one,* SAY DOOE, *six-two* = 8, and so on. DACHA, I may remark, is perhaps from the *Greek,* DEKA, (δέκα,) ten, which, in the Constantinopolitan *Lingua Franca,* is likely enough to have been substituted for the *Italian.* MADZA is clearly the *Italian* MEZZA. The origin of BEONG I have not been so fortunate as to discover, unless it be the *French,* BIEN, the application of which to a shilling is not so evident; but amongst costermongers and other street folk it is quite immaterial what foreign tongue contributes to their secret language. Providing the terms are unknown to the police and the public generally, they care not a rush whether the polite French, the gay Spaniards, or the cloudy Germans help to swell their vocabulary. The numbers of low foreigners, however, dragging out a miserable existence in our crowded neighbourhoods, organ grinders and image sellers, foreign seamen from the vessels in the river, and our own connexion with Malta and the Ionian Isles, may explain, to a certain extent, the phenomenon of these Southern phrases in the mouths of costers and tramps. Professor Ascoli, in his *Studj Critici,* absurdly enough derives these words from the ancient commercial importance of Italian settlers in England, when they gave a name to Lombard Street!!

SALT JUNK, navy salt beef.—*See* OLD HORSE.

SALVE, praise, flattery, chaff.

SAM, *i.e.,* DICKY-SAM, a native of Liverpool.

SAM, to "stand SAM," to pay for refreshment or drink, to stand paymaster for anything. An *Americanism,* originating in the letters U.S. on the knapsacks of the United States soldiers, which letters were jocularly said to be the initials of *Uncle Sam,* (the Government,) who pays for all. In use in this country as early as 1827.

SAMPAN, a small boat.—*Anglo-Chinese.*

SAMSHOO, a fiery, noxious spirit, distilled from rice. Spirits generally. —*Anglo-Chinese.*

SANDWICH, a human advertising medium, placed between two boards strapped over his shoulder. A "TOAD IN THE HOLE" is the term applied to the same individual when his person is confined by a four-sided box.

SANGUINARY JAMES, a raw sheep's-head.—*See* BLOODY JEMMY.

SANK WORK, making soldiers' clothes. *Mayhew* says from the *Norman,* SANC, blood,—in allusion either to the soldier's calling, or the colour of his coat.

SAP, or SAPSCULL, a poor green simpleton, with no heart for work.

SATIN, gin; "a yard of SATIN," a glass of gin. Term used by females on make-believe errands, when the real object of their departure from home is to replenish the private bottle. With servants the words TAPE and RIBBON are more common, the purchase of these feminine requirements being the general excuse for asking to "run out for a little while."—*See* WHITE SATIN.

SAUCEBOX, a pert young person. In low life it also signifies the mouth.

SAVELOY, a sausage of bread and chopped beef smoked, a minor kind of POLONY, which *see*.

SAVEY, to know; "do you SAVEY that?"—*French*, SAVEZ-VOUS CELA? In the nigger and *Anglo-Chinese patois*, this is SABBY, "me no SABBY." It is a general word among the lower classes all over the world. It also means acuteness or cleverness; as "that fellow has plenty of SAVEY."

SAW, a term at whist. A SAW is established when two partners alternately trump a suit, played to each other for the express purpose.

"SAW YOUR TIMBER," "be off!" equivalent to *cut your stick*. Occasionally varied with mock refinement, to AMPUTATE YOUR MAHOGANY. —*See* CUT.

SAWBONES, a surgeon.

SAWNEY, or SANDY, a Scotchman. Corruption of Alexander.

SAWNEY, a simpleton; a gaping, awkward lout.

SCAB, a worthless person.—*Old. Shakspeare* uses SCALD in a similar sense.

SCABBY-NECK, a native of Denmark.—*Sea*.

SCAB-RAISER, a drummer in the army, so called from one of the duties pertaining to that office, viz., inflicting corporal punishment on the soldiers.—*Military*.

SCABBY-SHEEP, epithet applied by the vulgar to a person who has been in questionable society, or under unholy influence, and become tainted.

SCALY, shabby, or mean. Perhaps anything which betokens the presence of the "*Old Serpent*," or it may be a variation on "FISHY." *Shakspeare* uses SCALD, an old word of reproach.

SCAMANDER, to wander about without a settled purpose;—possibly in allusion to the winding course of the Homeric river of that name.

SCAMMERED, drunk.

SCAMP, a graceless fellow, a rascal; formerly the Cant term for plundering and thieving. A ROYAL-SCAMP was a highwayman, whilst a FOOT-SCAMP was an ordinary thief with nothing but his legs to trust to in case of an attempt at capture. Some have derived SCAMP from *qui ex campo exit*, viz., one who leaves the field, a deserter.

SAWNEY, bacon. SAWNEY HUNTER, one who steals bacon.

SCALDRUM DODGE, burning the body with a mixture of acids and gunpowder, so as to suit the hues and complexions of the accident to be deplored.

SCAMP, to give short measure or quantity; applied to dishonest contractors. Probably the same as SKIMP and SCRIMP.

SCANDAL-WATER, tea; from old maids' tea-parties being generally a focus for scandal.

SCARAMOUCH, properly a tumbler, or SALTIMBANCO.

SCARCE, TO MAKE ONE'S-SELF; to be off; decamp.

SCARLET-TOWN, Reading, in Berkshire. As the name of this place is pronounced Redding, SCARLET-TOWN is probably a rude pun upon it.

SCARBOROUGH-WARNING, a warning too shortly given to be taken advantage of. When a person is driven over, and then told to keep out of the way, he receives SCARBOROUGH-WARNING. *Fuller* says the proverb alludes to an event, which happened at that place in 1557, when Thomas Stafford seized upon Scarborough castle before the townsmen had the least notice of his approach.

SCARPER, to run away.—*Spanish*, ESCAPAR, to escape, make off; *Italian*, SCAPPARE. "SCARPER with the feele of the donna of the cassey," to run away with the daughter of the landlady of the house; almost pure *Italian*, "SCAPPARE COLLA FIGLIA DELLA DONNA DELLA CASA."—*Seven Dials* and *Prison Cant*, from the *Lingua Franca*.

SCHISM-SHOP, a Dissenters' meeting-house.—*University*.

SCHROFF, a banker, treasurer, or confidential clerk.—*Anglo-Indian*.

SCHWASSLE BOX, the street performance of Punch and Judy.—*Household Words*, No. 183.—*See* SWATCHEL-COVE.

SCONCE, the head; judgment, sense.—*Dutch*.

SCORE, "to run up a SCORE at a public-house," to obtain credit there until pay-day, or a fixed time, when the debt must be WIPED OFF. From the old practice of scoring a tippler's indebtedness on the inside of a public-house door.

SCORF, to eat voraciously.

SCOT, a quantity of anything, a lot, a share.—*Anglo-Saxon*, SCEAT, pronounced SHOT.

SCOT, temper, or passion,—from the irascible temperament of that nation; "oh! what a SCOT he was in," *i.e.*, what temper he shewed,—especially if you allude to the following:—

SCOTCH-FIDDLE, the itch; "to play the SCOTCH FIDDLE," to work the index finger of the right hand like a fiddlestick between the index and middle finger of the left. This provokes a Scotchman in the highest degree, it implying that he is afflicted with the itch.

SCOTCH GRAYS, lice. Our northern neighbours are calumniously reported, from their living on oatmeal, to be peculiarly liable to cutaneous eruptions and parasites.

SCOTCH-COFFEE, biscuits toasted and boiled in water.—*Sea*.

SCHOFEL, bad money.—*See* SHOW-FULL.

SCHOOL, or MOB, two or more "patterers" working together in the streets.

SCHOOLING, a low gambling party.

SCOTCHES, the legs; also synonymous with NOTCHES.

SCOUT, a college valet, or waiter.—*Oxford.—See* GYP.

SCRAG, the neck.—*Old Cant. Scotch*, CRAIG. Still used by butchers. Hence, SCRAG, to hang by the neck, and SCRAGGING, an execution,—also *Old Cant*.

SCRAN, pieces of meat, broken victuals. Formerly the reckoning at a public-house. SCRANNING, or "out on the SCRAN," begging for broken victuals. Also, an *Irish* malediction of a mild sort, "Bad SCRAN to yer!"

SCRAN-BAG, a soldier's haversack.—*Military Slang*.

SCRAPE, a difficulty; SCRAPE, low wit for a shave.

SCRAPE, cheap butter; "bread and SCRAPE," the bread and butter issued to school-boys—so called from the butter being laid on, and then *scraped* off again, for economy's sake.

SCRAPING CASTLE, a water-closet.

SCRATCH, a fight, contest, point in dispute; "coming up to the SCRATCH," going or preparing to fight—in reality, approaching the line usually chalked on the ground to divide the ring. According to the rules of the prize ring, the toe must be placed at the SCRATCH, so the phrase often is TOEING.

SCRATCH, "no great SCRATCH," of little worth.

SCRATCH, to strike a horse's name out of the list of runners in a particular race. "Tomboy was SCRATCHED for the Derby, at 10 a.m., on Wednesday," from which period all bets made in reference to him (with one exception) are void.—*See* P.P.—*Turf*. One of *Boz's* characters asks whether horses are "really made more lively by being SCRATCHED."

SCRATCH-RACE, (on the *Turf*,) a race where any horse, aged, winner, or loser, can run with any weights; in fact, a race without restrictions. At *Cambridge* a boat-race, where the crews are drawn by lot.

SCREAMING, first-rate, splendid. Believed to have been first used in the *Adelphi* play-bills; "a SCREAMING farce," one calculated to make the audience scream with laughter. Now a general expression.

SCREEN, a bank-note; QUEER SCREEN, a forged bank-note.

SCREEVE, a letter, a begging petition.

SCREEVE, to write, or devise; "to SCREEVE a fakement," to concoct, or write, a begging letter, or other impostor's documents. From the *Dutch*, SCHRYVEN; *German*, SCHREIBEN; *French*, ECRIVANT, (old form,) to write.

SCREEVER, a man who draws with coloured chalks on the pavement figures of our Saviour crowned with thorns, specimens of elaborate writing, thunderstorms, ships on fire, &c. The men who attend these pavement chalkings, and receive halfpence and sixpences from the admirers of street art, are not always the draughtsmen. The artist or SCREEVER draws, perhaps, in half-a-dozen places in the course of the morning, and rents the spots out to as many cadaverous-looking men.

SCREW, an unsound, or broken-down horse, that requires both whip and spur to get him along.

SCREW, a mean or stingy person.

SCREW, salary or wages.

SCREW, "to put on the SCREW," to limit one's credit, to be more exact and precise; "to put under the SCREW;" to compel, to coerce, to influence by strong pressure.

SCREW LOOSE, when friends become cold and distant towards each other, it is said there is a SCREW LOOSE betwixt them; the same phrase is also used when anything goes wrong with a person's credit or reputation.

SCREW, a small packet of tobacco.—A "*twist*" of the "weed."

SCREWED, intoxicated or drunk.

SCRIMMAGE, or SCRUMMAGE, a disturbance or row.—*Ancient.* Corruption of *skirmish?*

SCRIMSHAW; anything made by sailors for themselves in their leisure hours at sea, is termed SCRIMSHAW-WORK.

SCROUGE, to crowd or squeeze.—*Wiltshire.*

SCRUFF, the back part of the neck seized by the adversary in an encounter.

SCRUMPTIOUS, nice, particular, beautiful.

SCUFTER, a policeman.—*North Country.*

SCULL, or SKULL, the head, or master of a college.—*University,* but nearly *obsolete;* the gallery, however, in St Mary's, (the University church,) where the "Heads of Houses" sit in solemn state, is still nicknamed the GOLGOTHA by the under-graduates.

SCURF, a mean fellow.

SEA-CONNIE, the steersman of an Indian ship. By the insurance laws he must be either a PYAH Portuguese, a European, or a Manilla man,—Lascars not being allowed to be helmsmen.

SEA-COOK, "son of a SEA-COOK," an opprobrious phrase used on board ship, equivalent to "SON OF A GUN," and other more vulgar expletives.

SEALS, a religious Slang term for converts.—*See* OWNED.

SEE. Like "GO" and "DO," this useful verb has long been supplemented with a Slang or unauthorised meaning. In street parlance, "to SEE" is to know or believe; "I don't SEE that," *i.e.,* "I don't put faith in what you offer, or I know what you say to be untrue."

SEEDY, worn-out, poverty-stricken, used-up, shabby. Metaphorical expression from the appearance of flowers when off bloom and running to *seed;* hence said of one who wears clothes until they crack and become shabby; "how SEEDY he looks," said of any man whose clothes are worn threadbare, with greasy facings, and hat brightened up by

---

SCREW, a key—skeleton, or otherwise.

SCREW, a turnkey.

SCROBY, "to get SCROBY," to be whipped in prison before the justices.

perspiration and continual polishing and wetting. When a man's coat begins to look worn-out and shabby he is said to look SEEDY and ready for *cutting*. This term has been "on the streets" for nearly two centuries, and latterly has found its way into most dictionaries. Formerly Slang, it is now a recognised word, and one of the most expressive in the English language. The French are always amused with it, they having no similar term.

> "Oh, let my hat be e'er sae brown,
> My coat be e'er sae SEEDY, O!
> My whole turn-out scarce worth a crown,
> Like gents well-bred, but needy, O!"
> —*Fisher's Garland for* 1835.

SELL, a deception, disappointment; also a lying joke.

SELL, to deceive, swindle, or play a practical joke upon a person. A sham is a SELL in street parlance. "SOLD again, and got the money," a costermonger cries after having successfully deceived somebody. *Shakspeare* uses SELLING in a similar sense, viz., blinding or deceiving.

SENSATION, a quartern of gin.

SERENE, all right; "it's all SERENE," a street phrase of very modern adoption, the burden of a song. SERENE, ALL SERENE! from the *Spanish* SERENO, equivalent to the *English* "ALL'S WELL," a countersign of sentinels, supposed to have been acquired by some filibusters who were imprisoned in Cuba, and liberated by the intercession of the British ambassador.

SERGEANT KITE, a recruiting sergeant. SERGEANT SNAP has a like meaning.

SERVE OUT, to punish, or be revenged on any one.

SETTER, sevenpence. *Italian*, SETTE.—*See* SALTEE.—*Lingua Franca*.

SETTER, a person employed by the vendor at an auction to run the biddings up; to bid against *bonâ-fide* bidders.

SETTLE, to kill, ruin, or effectually quiet a person.

SET TO, a sparring match, a fight; "a dead set," a determined stand, in argument or in movement.

SEWED-UP, done-up, used-up, intoxicated. *Dutch*, SEEUWT, sick.

SHACK, a "chevalier d'industrie." A scamp, a blackguard.—*Nottingham*.

SHACKLY, loose, rickety.—*Devonshire*.

SEVENDIBLE, a very curious word, used only in the north of Ireland, to denote something particularly severe, strong, or sound. It is no doubt derived from seven-double,—that is, seven-fold,—and is applied to linen cloth, a beating, a reprimand, &c.

SEVEN-SIDED-ANIMAL, a one-eyed man, as he has an inside, outside, left side, right side, foreside, backside, and a blind side.

SEVEN-UP, the game of All-fours, when played for seven chalks,—that is, when seven points or chalks have to be made to win the game.

SETTLED, transported; sometimes spoken of as WINDED-SETTLED.

SEVEN-PENNORTH, transportation for seven years.

SHACK-PER-SWAW, every one for himself,—a phrase in use amongst the lower orders at the east end of London, derived apparently from the *French*, CHACUN POUR SOI.

SHADY, an expression implying *decadence*. On "the SHADY side of forty" implies that a person is considerably older. SHADY also means inferiority in other senses. A SHADY TRICK is either a shabby one, mean or trumpery, or else it is one contemptible from the want of ability displayed.

SHAKE, a disreputable man or woman.—*North*.

SHAKE, or SHAKES, a bad bargain is said to be "no great SHAKES;" "pretty fair SHAKES" is anything good or favourable.—*Byron*. In *America*, a fair SHAKE is a fair trade or a good bargain.

SHAKE-DOWN, an impromptu bed.

SHAKER, a shirt.

SHAKES; "in a *brace of* SHAKES," *i.e.*, in an instant.

SHAKESTER, or SHICKSTER, a female. Amongst costermongers this term is invariably applied to *ladies*, or the wives of tradesmen and females, generally of the classes immediately above them.

"SHAKE THE ELBOW," to, a roundabout expression for dice-playing.

SHAKY, said of a person of questionable health, integrity, or solvency; at the *University*, of one not likely to pass his examination.

SHALER, a girl. Corrupt form of *Gaelic*, CAILLE, a young woman.

SHALLOW, a flat basket used by costers.

SHALLOW, a weak-minded country justice of the peace.

SHAM ABRAHAM, to feign sickness.—*See* ABRAHAM.

SHANDY-GAFF, ale and gingerbeer; perhaps SANG DE GOFF, the favourite mixture of one GOFF, a blacksmith.

SHANKS, legs.

SHANKS' NAG, "to ride SHANKS' NAG," to go on foot.

SHANT, a pot or quart; "SHANT of bivvy," a quart of beer.

SHAKE, to take away, to steal, or run off with anything; "what SHAKES, Bill?" "None," *i.e.*, no chance of committing a robbery.—*See under* SHAKE, above.

SHAKE-LURK, a false paper carried by an impostor, giving an account of a "dreadful shipwreck."

SHALLOWS, "to go on the SHALLOWS," to go half naked.

SHALLOW-COVE, a begging rascal who goes about the country half naked, with the most limited amount of rags upon his person, wearing neither shoes, stockings, nor hat.

SHALLOW-MOT, a ragged woman,—the frequent companion of the SHALLOW-COVE.

SHALLOW-SCREEVER, a man who sketches and draws on the pavement.—*See* SCREEVER.

P

SHANTY, a rude, temporary habitation. The word is principally employed to designate the huts inhabited by navigators, when constructing large lines of railway far distant from towns. It is derived from the *French*, CHANTIER, used by the Canadians for a log hut, and has travelled from thence, by way of the United States, to England.

SHAPES, "to cut up" or "shew SHAPES," to exhibit pranks, or flightiness.

SHARK, a sharper, a swindler. *Bow-Street* term in 1785, now in most dictionaries.—*Friesic* and *Danish*, SCHURK.—*See* LAND-SHARK.

SHARP, or SHARPER, a cunning cheat, a rogue,—the opposite of FLAT.

SHARP, a similar expression to "TWO PUN' TEN," (which *see*,) used by assistants in shops to signify that a customer of suspected honesty is amongst them. The shopman in this case would ask one of the assistants, in a voice loud enough to be generally heard, "has Mr SHARP come in yet?" "No," would probably be the reply; "but he is expected every minute." The signal is at once understood, and a general look-out kept upon the suspected party.

SHARP'S-ALLEY BLOOD-WORMS, beef sausages and black puddings. Sharp's Alley was very recently a noted slaughtering-place near Smithfield.

SHAVE, a false alarm, a hoax, a sell. This was much used in the Crimea during the Russian campaign.

SHAVE, a narrow escape. At Cambridge, "just SHAVING through," or "making a SHAVE," is just escaping a "pluck" by coming out at the bottom of the list.

> "My terms are anything but dear,
> Then read with me, and never fear;
> The examiners we're sure to queer,
> And get through, if you make a SHAVE on't."
> *The Private Tutor.*

SHAVE; "to SHAVE a customer," charge him more for an article than the marked price. Used in the drapery trade. When the master sees an opportunity of doing this, he strokes his chin, as a signal to his assistant who is serving the customer.

SHAVER, a sharp fellow; "a young" or "old SHAVER," a boy or man. —*Sea.*

"SHED A TEAR," to take a dram, or glass of neat spirits; jocular phrase used, with a sort of grim earnestness, by old topers to each other. "Now then, old fellow, come and SHED A TEAR!" an invitation to take "summat short." The origin may have been that ardent spirits, taken neat by younger persons, usually brings water to their eyes. With confirmed drinkers, however, the phrase is used with an air of mingled humour and regret at their own position. A still more pathetic phrase is—"putting a NAIL IN ONE'S COFFIN," which *see*.

SHEEBEEN, an unlicensed place where spirituous liquors are illegally sold.

SHEEN, bad money.—*Scotch.*

SHARPING-OMEE, a policeman. Partly *Lingua Franca.*

SHEEP'S EYES, "to make SHEEP'S EYES at a person," to cast amorous glances towards one on the sly.

> "But he, the beast, was casting SHEEP'S EYES at her
> Out of his bullock head."
> —*Colman, Broad Grins*, p. 57.

SHELF, "on the SHELF," not yet disposed of; young ladies are said to be so situated when they cannot meet with a husband. "On the SHELF" also means pawned, or laid by in trust.

SHELL OUT, to pay or count out money.

SHICE, nothing; "to do anything for SHICE," to get no payment. The term was first used by the Jews in the last century. *Grose* gives the phrase CHICE-AM-A-TRICE, which has a synonymous meaning. *Spanish*, CHICO, little; *Anglo-Saxon*, CHICHE, niggardly.

SHICER, a mean man, a humbug, a "duffer,"—a worthless person, one who will not work.

SHICKERY, shabby, bad.

SHICKSTER, a "gay" lady.—*See* SHAKESTER.

SHICKSTER-CRABS, ladies' shoes.—*Tramps' term.*

SHIGS, money, silver.—*East London.*

SHIKARI, a hunter, a sportsman.—*Anglo-India.* An English sportsman who has seen many ups and downs in the jungles of the East styles himself "the OLD SHEKARY."—*Anglo-Indian.*

SHILLY SHALLY, to trifle or fritter away time; irresolute. Corruption of "Shall I, shall I?"

SHINDY, a row, or noise.

SHINE, a row, or disturbance.

SHINE, "to take the SHINE out of a person," to surpass or excel him.

SHINER, a looking-glass.—*East London.*

SHINERS, sovereigns, or money.

SHINEY RAG, "to win the SHINEY RAG," to be ruined,—said in gambling, when any one continues betting after "luck has set in against him."

SHIN-PLASTER, a bank-note. Originally an *Americanism*.

SHINS, "to BREAK one's SHINS," figurative expression meaning to borrow money.

SHIP-SHAPE, proper, in good order; sometimes the phrase is varied to "SHIP-SHAPE and *Bristol* fashion."—*Sea.*

SHIRTY, ill-tempered, or cross. When one person makes another in an ill humour he is said to have "got his SHIRT out."

SHITTEN-SATURDAY, (corruption of SHUT-IN-SATURDAY,) the Saturday between Good Friday and Easter Sunday, when our Lord's body was enclosed in the tomb.—*School and Provincial.*

SHIVERING-JEMMY, the name given by street-folk to any cadger who exposes himself, half naked, on a cold day, to obtain alms. The "game" is unpleasant but exceedingly lucrative.

SHODDY, old cloth worked up into new; made from soldiers' and policemen's coats. The old cloth is pulled to pieces, the yarn unravelled and carded over again. This produces shoddy, which is very short in the fibre, and from it are produced, on again twisting and weaving, the finest of cloth fabrics, used for ladies' mantles, &c. Also, a term of derision applied to workmen in woollen factories.—*Yorkshire.*

SHOE, to free or initiate a person,—a practice common in most trades to a new-comer. The SHOEING consists in paying for beer, or other drink, which is drunk by the older hands. The cans emptied, and the bill paid, the stranger is considered properly SHOD.

SHOES, "to die in one's SHOES," to be hanged.

"SHOES, CHILDREN'S, TO MAKE," to suffer one's-self to be made sport of, or depreciated. Commonly used in Norfolk.—*Cf. Mrs Behn's* comedy, *The Roundheads.*

> *Hews.* "Who, pox! shall we stand MAKING CHILDREN'S SHOES all the year? No; let's begin to settle the nation, I say, and go through-stitch with our work."

SHOLL, to bonnet one, or crush a person's hat over his eyes.—*North.*

SHOOL, to saunter idly, become a vagabond, beg rather than work.—*Smollett's Roderick Random,* vol. i., p. 262.

SHOP, the House of Commons. The only instance we have met with of the use of this word in literature occurs in *Mr Trollope's Framley Parsonage:*—

> "'If we are merely to do as we are bid, and have no voice of our own, I don't see what's the good of our going to the SHOP at all,' said Mr Sowerby."

SHOP, to discharge a shopman. In *Military Slang,* to SHOP an officer, is to put him under arrest in the guard-room.

SHOP-WALKER, a person employed to walk up and down a shop, to hand seats to customers, and see that they are properly served. Contracted also to "WALKER."

SHOPPING, purchasing at shops. Termed by *Todd* a Slang word, but used by *Cowper* and *Byron.*

SHOPPY, to be full of nothing but one's own calling or profession; "to talk SHOP," to converse of nothing but professional subjects.

"SHOOT THE CAT," to vomit.

"SHOOT THE MOON," to remove furniture from a house in the night without paying the landlord.

"SHOOT WITH THE LONG BOW," to tell lies, to exaggerate. Synonymous with THROWING THE HATCHET.

SHORT, when spirit is drunk without any admixture of water, it is said to be taken "SHORT;" "summat SHORT," a dram. A similar phrase is used at the counters of banks; upon presenting a cheque, the clerk asks,

SHOE LEATHER! a thief's warning cry when he hears footsteps. This exclamation is used in the same spirit as Bruce's friend, who, when he suspected treachery towards him at King Edward's court, in 1306, sent him a purse and a pair of spurs, as a sign that he should use them in making his escape.

SHOP-BOUNCER, or SHOP-LIFTER, a person generally respectably attired, who, while being served with a small article at a shop, steals one of more value. *Shakspeare* has the word LIFTER, a thief.

SLANG, CANT, AND VULGAR WORDS.

"how will you take it?" *i.e.*, in gold, or in notes? Should it be desired to receive it in as small a compass as possible, the answer is, "SHORT."

SHORT, a conductor of an omnibus, or any other servant, is said to be SHORT, when he does not give all the money he receives to his master.

SHORT COMMONS, short allowance of food.—*See* COMMONS.

SHORTER, one who makes a dishonest profit by reducing the coin of the realm by clipping and filing. From a crown-piece a SHORTER could gain 5d. Another way was by chemical means: a guinea laid in aquafortis would, in twelve hours, precipitate 9d.-worth of sediment; in twenty-four, 1s. 6d.-worth.—*Rommany Rye*.

SHOT, from the modern sense of the word to SHOOT,—a guess, a random conjecture; "to make a bad SHOT," to expose one's ignorance by making a wrong guess, or random answer, without knowing whether it is right or wrong.

SHOT, from the once *English*, but now provincial word, to SHOOT, to subscribe, contribute in fair proportion;—a share, the same as SCOT, both being from the *Anglo-Saxon* word, SCEAT; "to pay one's SHOT," *i.e.*, share of the reckoning, &c.

> "Yet still while I have got
> Enough to pay the SHOT
> Of Boniface, both gruff and greedy O!"
> —*Fisher's Garland* for 1835.

SHOT, "I wish I may be SHOT, if," &c., a common form of mild swearing.

"SHOT IN THE LOCKER," money in pocket, or the having a resource of any kind in store.—*Navy*.

"SHOVE IN THE MOUTH," a glass of spirits.

SHOVEL, a term appled by the vulgar crowd to the inelegant twisted hats worn by the dignitaries of the Church. Dean Alford says, "I once heard a venerable dignitary pointed out by a railway porter as "an old party in a SHOVEL."—*Queen's English*, p. 228.

SHOWFULL, or SCHOFELL, a Hansom cab. This favourite carriage was the invention of a Mr Hansom, afterwards connected with the *Builder* newspaper. It has been asserted that the term SHOWFULL was derived from "shovel," the earliest Slang term applied to Hansoms by other cab-drivers, who conceived their shape to be after the fashion of a scoop or shovel.

SHOW-FULL, or SCHOFUL, bad money. *Mayhew* thinks this word is from the *Danish*, SKUFFE, to shove, to deceive, cheat; *Saxon*, SCUFAN,— whence the *English*, SHOVE. The term, however, is possibly one of the many street words from the *Hebrew*, (through the low Jews;) SHEPHEL, in that language, signifying a *low* or debased estate. *Chaldee*, SHAPHAL. —*See* Psalm cxxxvi. 23, "in our *low estate*." A correspondent suggests another very probable derivation, from the *German*, SCHOFEL, trash, rubbish,—the *German* adjective, SCHOFELIG, being the nearest possible translation of our *shabby*. Also, mock jewellery.

SHOULDER, when a servant embezzles his master's money, he is said to SHOULDER his employer.

SHOVE-HALFPENNY, a gambling pot-house game, played on a table.

SHOWFULL PULLET, a "gay" or unsteady woman.
SHRIMP, a diminutive person.—*Chaucer.*
SHUNT, to throw, or turn aside.—*Railway term.*
SHUT OF, or SHOT OF, *i.e.*, rid of. A very common expression amongst the London lower orders. One costermonger will say to another:— "Well, Ike, did yer get SHUT o' them there gawfs [apples]?" *i.e.*, did you sell them all?
SHUT UP! be quiet, don't make a noise; to stop short, to make cease in a summary manner, to silence effectually. "Only the other day we heard of a preacher who, speaking of the scene with the doctors in the Temple, remarked that the Divine disputant completely SHUT THEM UP!"—*Athen.* 30th July 1859. SHUT UP, utterly exhausted, done for.
SHY, a throw.—*See* the following :—
SHY, to fling; COCK-SHY, a game at fairs, consisting of throwing short sticks at trinkets set upon other sticks,—both name and practice derived from the old game of throwing or SHYING at live cocks.
SHY, "to fight SHY of a person," to avoid his society either from dislike, fear, or other reason. SHY has also the sense of flighty, unsteady, untrustworthy.
SICES, or SIZES, a throw of *sizes* at dice.
"SICK AS A HORSE," popular simile,—curious, because a horse never vomits.
SICKNER, or SICKENER, a dose too much of anything.
SIDE-BOARDS, or STICK-UPS, shirt collars. Name applied ten or fifteen years ago, before the "all-rounders" and "turn-downs" came into fashion.
SIGHT, "to take a SIGHT at a person," a vulgar action employed by street boys to denote incredulity, or contempt for authority, by placing the thumb against the nose and closing all the fingers except the little one, which is agitated in token of derision.—*See* WALKER.
SIM, one of a Methodistical turn in religion; a Low Churchman; originally a follower of the late Rev. Charles Simeon.—*Cambridge.*
SIMON, a sixpenny-piece.
SIMON, or SIMPLE SIMON, a credulous gullible person. A character in a song, but now common.

SHOWFULL-PITCHER, a passer of counterfeit money.
SHOWFULL-PITCHING, passing bad money.
SIDE, an affirmative expression in the Cant language of the northern towns. "Do you stoll the Gammy?" (Do you understand Cant?) Answer, SIDE, Cove, (yes, mate.)
SIFT, the same meaning as SHOULDER. The man having SIFTED the money and kept the larger pieces, that did not readily pass through the sieve!
SILVER BEGGAR, or LURKER, a vagabond who travels through the country with "briefs" containing false statements of losses by fire, shipwrecks, accidents, &c. Forged documents are exhibited with signatures of

SIMON PURE, "the real SIMON PURE," the genuine article. Those who have witnessed Mr C. Mathews's performance in *Mrs Centlivre's* admirable comedy of *A Bold Stroke for a Wife*, and the laughable coolness with which he, the *false* SIMON PURE, assuming the Quaker dress and character of the REAL ONE, elbowed that worthy out of his expected entertainment, will at once perceive the origin of this phrase. —*See* act v., scene i.

SIMPKIN, or SIMKIN, champagne.—*Anglo-Indian*. Derived from the manner in which native servants pronounce *champagne*.

SING OUT, to call aloud.—*Sea*.

SING SMALL, to lessen one's boasting, and turn arrogance into humility.

SING-SONG, a choral meeting at a pot-house, which then not unfrequently receives the name of "the *Cave of Harmony*."

SINKERS, bad money,—affording a man but little assistance in "keeping afloat."

SINKS, a throw of fives at dice. *French*, CINQS.

SI QUIS, a candidate for "orders." From the notification commencing SI QUIS—if any one.

SIR-HARRY, a close stool.

SIR-REVERENCE, a corruption of the old phrase SAVE YOUR REVERENCE, a sort of apology for alluding to anything likely to shock one's sense of decency. *Latin*, SALVÂ REVERENTIÂ. *Shakspeare's Romeo and Juliet* act i., scene iv., from this it came to mean the thing itself—human ordure generally, but sometimes other indecencies.

SISERARA, a hard blow.—*Suffolk*. *Moor* derives it from the story of Sisera in the Old Testament, but it is more probably a corruption of CERTIORARI, a Chancery writ reciting a complaint of hard usage.

SIT UNDER, a term employed in Dissenters' meeting-houses, to denote attendance on the ministry of any particular preacher.

SIT-UPON, to overcome or rebuke, to express contempt for a man in a marked manner.

SIT-UPONS, trousers.—*See* INEXPRESSIBLES.

SIVVY, "'pon my SIVVY," *i.e.*, upon my soul or honour. Corruption of *asseveration*, like DAVY, which is an abridgment of *affidavit*.

SIXES AND SEVENS, articles in confusion are said to be all SIXES AND SEVENS. The Deity is mentioned in the *Towneley Mysteries* as He that "sett all on seven," *i.e.*, set or appointed everything in seven days. A similar phrase at this early date implied confusion and disorder, and from these, *Halliwell* thinks, has been derived the phrase "to be at SIXES AND SEVENS." A Scotch correspondent, however, states that the phrase probably came from the workshop, and that amongst needle-makers, when the points and eyes are "heads and

magistrates and clergymen. Accompanying these are sham subscription-books. The former, in beggar parlance, is termed "a SHAM," whilst the latter is denominated "a DELICATE."

SITTING-PAD, sitting on the pavement in a begging position.

tails," ("heeds and thraws,") or in confusion, they are said to be SIXES AND SEVENS, because those numbers are the sizes most generally used, and in the course of manufacture have frequently to be distinguished.

SIXTY, "to go along like SIXTY," *i.e.*, at a good rate, briskly.

SIXTY-PER-CENT, a bill-discounter.

SIZE, to order extras over and above the usual commons at the dinner in college halls. Soup, pastry, &c., are SIZINGS, and are paid for at a certain specified rate *per* SIZE, or portion, to the college cook.—*Peculiar to Cambridge.* Minsheu says, "SIZE, a farthing which schollers in Cambridge have at the buttery, noted with the letter *s*."

SIZERS, or SIZARS, are certain poor scholars at Cambridge, annually elected, who get their dinners (including *sizings*) from what is left at the upper, or Fellows' table, free, or nearly so. They pay rent of rooms, and some other fees, on a lower scale than the "Pensioners" or ordinary students, and answer to the "battlers" and "servitors" at Oxford.

SIZINGS.—*See* SIZE.

SKEDADDLE. The American war has introduced a new and amusing word. A Northerner who retreats "retires upon his supports," but a Southerner is said to "SKEDADDLE." The *Times* remarked on the word, and Lord Hill wrote to prove that it was excellent Scotch. The Americans only misapply the word, which means, in Dumfries, "to spill"—milkmaids, for example, saying, you are "SKEDADDLING" all that milk. The *Times* and Lord Hill are both wrong, for the word is neither new nor in any way misapplied. The word is very fair Greek, the root being that of "SKEDANNUMI," to disperse, to "retire tumultuously," and it was probably set afloat by some professor at Harvard.

SKID, a sovereign. Fashionable Slang. Occasionally SKIV.

SKIE, or SKY, to throw upwards, to toss "coppers."—*See* ODD MAN.

SKILLIGOLEE, prison gruel. Also sailors' soup of many ingredients. The term is occasionally used in London workhouses.

SKIN, a purse.

SKIN, to abate, or lower the value of anything; "thin SKINNED," sensitive, touchy, liable to be RAW on certain subjects.

SKINFLINT, an old popular simile for a "close-fisted," stingy person. Sternberg, in his *Northamptonshire Glossary*, says the Eastern languages have the same expression. Abdul-Malek, one of the Ommeyade Khaliphs, noted for his extreme avarice, was surnamed RASCHAL-HEGIARAH, literally, "the skinner of a flint."

SKIN-THE-LAMB, a game at cards, a very expressive corruption of the term *lansquenet*, also a racing term. When a non-favourite wins a race,

SKATES-LURK, a begging impostor dressed as a sailor.

SKILLY, broth served on board the hulks to convicts.—*Lincolnshire*. Abbreviation of SKILLIGOLEE.

"bookmakers" are said to "SKIN the LAMB," under the supposition that they win all their bets, no person having backed the winner.

SKIPPER, the master of a vessel. *Dutch*, SCHIFFER, from *schiff*, a ship; sometimes used as synonymous with "governor."

SKIPPER, a barn.—*Ancient Cant*. From the *Welsh*, YSGUBOR, pronounced SCYBOR, or SCIBOR, the proper word in that language for a barn.

SKIPPER-BIRDS, or KEYHOLE-WHISTLERS, persons who sleep in barns or outhouses in preference to lodging-houses.

SKIPPER-IT, to sleep in the open air, or in a rough way.

SKIT, a joke, a squib.

SKITTLES, a game similar to Ten Pins, which, when interdicted by the Government, was altered to Nin Pins, or SKITTLES. They are set up in an alley, and are *thrown at* (not bowled) with a round piece of hard wood, shaped like a small flat cheese. The costers consider themselves the best players in London.

SKOW-BANKER, a fellow who loiters about the premises of any one willing to support him without the necessity of working for his living; a rogue, a rascal. Common at Melbourne, Australia.

SKROUGE, to push or squeeze.—*North*.

SKULL-THATCHER, a straw-bonnet-maker,—sometimes called "a bonnet-BUILDER."

SKY, a disagreeable person, an enemy.—*Westminster School*.

SKY, to toss up towards the sky. Term used in tossing with halfpence; "it's all right, Jim SKYED the browns," *i.e.*, threw them up.

SKY-BLUE, London milk much diluted with water, or from which the cream has been too closely skimmed.

"Hence, Suffolk dairy wives run mad for cream,
And leave their milk with nothing but the name;
Its name derision and reproach pursue,
And strangers tell of three times-skimm'd—SKY-BLUE."
—*Bloomfield's Farmer's Boy*.

SKY-BLUE formerly meant gin.

SKYED, artists say that a picture is SKYED when it is hung on the upper line at the Exhibition of the Royal Academy.—*See* FLOORED.

SKY-LARK.—*See under* LARK.

SKY-PARLOUR, the garret.

SKY-SCRAPER, a tall man; "are you cold up there, old SKY-SCRAPER?" Properly a sea term; the light sails, which some adventurous skippers set above the royals in calm latitudes, are termed SKY-SCRAPERS and MOON-RAKERS.

SKY-WANNOCKING, unsteady, frolicking.—*Norfolk*.

SLACK, "to hold on the SLACK," to skulk; a slack rope not requiring to be held.—*Sea*.

SLAM, a term at the game of whist. When two partners gain the whole thirteen tricks, they win a SLAM, which is considered equal to a rubber.

SLAMMOCK, a slattern or awkward person.—*West*, and *Norfolk*.

SLANG, low, vulgar, unwritten, or unauthorised language. *Gipsy*, SLANG, the secret language of the Gipsies, synonymous with GIBBERISH, another Gipsy word. The word is only to be found in the Dictionaries of *Webster* and *Ogilvie*. It is given, however, by *Grose*, in his *Dictionary of the Vulgar Tongue*, 1785. SLANG, since it has been adopted as an English word, generally implies vulgar language not known or recognised as CANT; and latterly, when applied to speech, has superseded the word FLASH. The earliest instance of the use of the word that we can find, is the following:—

> "Let proper Nurses be assigned to take care of these Babes of Grace, [young thieves,] . . . the Master who teaches them should be a man well versed in the Cant Language commonly called the SLANG *Patter*, in which they should by all means excel."—*Jonathan Wild's Advice to his Successor.* LONDON, *J. Scott*, 1758.

SLANG, a travelling show.

SLANG, to cheat, to abuse in foul language.

SLANG-WHANGER, a long-winded speaker.—*Parliamentary.*

SLANGY, flashy, vulgar; loud in dress, manner, and conversation.

SLANTINGDICULAR, oblique, awry,—as opposed to PERPENDICULAR. Originally an Americanism, now a part of the vocabulary of London "high life below stairs."

SLAP, paint for the face, rouge.

SLAP, exactly, precisely; "SLAP in the wind's eye," *i.e.*, exactly to windward.

SLAP-BANG, suddenly, violently. From the strike of a ball being felt before the report reaches the ear,—the SLAP first, the BANG afterwards.

SLAP-BANG-SHOPS, low eating-houses, where you have to pay down the ready money with a SLAP-BANG.—*Grose.*

SLAP-DASH, immediately, or quickly.—*See* SLAP-BANG.

SLAP-UP, first-rate, excellent, very good.

SLASH, a pocket in an overcoat.

SLASHER, a powerful roisterer, a pugilist; "the TIPTON SLASHER."

SLASHERS, the Twenty-eighth Regiment of Foot in the British army.

SLATE, "he has a SLATE loose," *i.e.*, he is slightly crazy.

SLATE, to pelt with abuse, to beat, to "LICK;" or, in the language of the reviewers, to "cut up."

SLATE, to knock the hat over one's eyes, to bonnet.—*North.*

SLAVEY, a maid-servant.

SLAWMINEYEUX, a Dutchman. Probably a corruption of the Dutch, *ja mynheer*; or German, *ja mein Herr.*—*Sea.*

SLANG, counterfeit or short weights and measures. A SLANG quart is a pint and a half. SLANG measures are lent out at 2d. per day to street salesmen. The term is used principally by costermongers.

SLANG, a watch-chain.—*Westminster.*

SLANG, "out on the SLANG," *i.e.*, to travel with a hawker's licence.

SLEEPLESS-HATS, those of a napless character, better known as WIDE-AWAKES.

SLENDER, a simple country gentleman.

SLEWED, drunk, or intoxicated.—*Sea term.* When a vessel changes the tack she, as it were, staggers, the sails flap, she gradually heels over, and the wind catching the waiting canvas, she glides off at another angle. The course pursued by an intoxicated, or SLEWED man, is supposed to be analogous to that of the ship.

SLICK, an *Americanism*, very prevalent in England since the publication of Judge Haliburton's facetious stories. As an *adjective*, SLICK means rapidly, effectually, utterly ; as a *verb*, it has the force of " to despatch rapidly," turn off, get done with a thing.

SLING, to pass from one person to another.

SLIP, "to give the SLIP," to run away, or elude pursuit. *Shakspeare* has "*you gave me the counterfeit*," in *Romeo and Juliet*. GIVING THE SLIP, however, is a *Sea phrase*, and refers to fastening an anchor and chain cable to a floating buoy, or water-cask, until such a time arrives that is convenient to return and take them on board. In fastening the cable, the home end is *slipped* through the hawse pipe. Weighing anchor is a noisy task, so that giving it the SLIP infers to leave it in quietness.

SLIP, or LET SLIP ; "to SLIP into a man," to give him a sound beating ; "to LET SLIP at a cove," to rush violently upon him, and assault with vigour.

SLIPPING, a trick of card-sharpers, in performance of which, by dexterous manipulation, they place the cut card on the top, instead of at the bottom of the pack. It is the *faire sauter la coupe* of the French.

SLOG, or SLOGGER, (its original form,) to beat, baste, or wallop. *German*, SCHLAGEN ; or, perhaps a vulgar corruption of SLAUGHTER. The pretended *Greek* derivation from σλογω, which *Punch* puts in the mouth of the schoolboy, in his impression of 4th May 1859, is of course only intended to mystify grandmamma, there being no such word in the language.

SLOGGERS, *i.e.*, SLOW-GOERS, the second division of race-boats at *Cambridge*. At *Oxford* they are called TORPIDS.—*University.* A hard hitter at cricket is termed a SLOGGER.

SLOGGING, a good beating.

SLOP, a policeman. Probably at first *back Slang*, but now general.

SLOP, cheap, or ready made, as applied to clothing, is generally supposed to be a modern appropriation ; but it was used in this sense in 1691, by *Maydman*, in his *Naval Speculations;* and by *Chaucer* two centuries before that. SLOPS properly signify sailors' working clothes, which are of a very cheap or unexpensive character.

SLOPE, to decamp, to run, or rather *slip* away. Originally from LOPE, to make off ; the *s* probably became affixed as a portion of the preceding

---

SLICK-A-DEE, a pocket-book.

word, as in the case of "let's lope," let us run.—*Americanism.* A correspondent says that Tennyson is decidedly partial to Slang, and instances amongst other proofs a passage from the laureate's famous *Locksley Hall:*—

> "Many a night, from yonder ivied casement, ere I went to rest,
> Did I look on great Orion SLOPING slowly to the west."

SLOPS, chests or packages of tea; "he shook a slum of SLOPS," *i.e.*, stole a chest of tea.

SLOUR'D buttoned up; SLOUR'D HOXTER, an inside pocket buttoned up.

SLUBBERDEGULLION, a paltry, dirty, sorry wretch.

> "Quoth she, although thou hast deserved,
> Base SLUBBERDEGULLION, to be served
> As thou didst vow to deal with me,
> If thou hadst got the victory."
> —*Hudibras.*

SLUICERY, a gin-shop or public-house.

"SLUICING ONE'S BOLT," drinking.

SLUM, a chest, or package.—*See* SLOPS.

SLUM, an insinuation, a discreditable inuendo.

SLUM, gammon, "UP TO SLUM," wide awake, knowing

> "And this, without more SLUM began,
> Over a flowing Pot-house can.
> To settle, without botheration,
> The rigs of this here tip-top nation.
> —*Jack Randall's Diary,* 1820.

SLUM, or BACK SLUM, a dark retreat, low neighbourhood; "the Westminster SLUMS," favourite haunts for thieves.

SLUM, to saunter about, with a suspicion, perhaps, of immoral pursuits —*Cambridge University Slang.*

"SLUM THE GORGER," to cheat on the sly, to be an eye-servant. SLUM in this sense is *Old Cant.*

SLUSH, the grease obtained from boiling the salt pork eaten by seamen, and generally the cook's perquisite.

SLUSHY, a ship's cook.

SLUTER, butter.—*North.*

SMACK SMOOTH, even, level with the surface, quickly.

SMALL-BEER; "he doesn't think SMALL-BEER of himself," *i.e.*, he has a great opinion of his own importance. SMALL COALS is also used in the same sense.

SMALL HOURS, the early hours after midnight.

SMALLS, a University term for the first general examination of the stu

---

SLOUR, to lock, or fasten.—*Prison Cant.*

SLOWED, to be locked up—in prison.

SLUM, a letter.—*Prison Cant.*

SLUMMING, passing bad money.

dents. It is used at Cambridge, but properly belongs to Oxford. The Cambridge term is LITTLE GO.

SMASH, to become bankrupt, or worthless; "to go all to SMASH," to break, "go to the dogs," to fall in pieces.

SMASH, to pass counterfeit money.

SMASHER, one who passes bad coin, or forged notes.

SMASHFEEDER, a Britannia-metal spoon,—the best imitation shillings are made from this metal.

SMASH-MAN-GEORDIE, a pitman's oath.—*Durham* and *Northumberland.*—See GEORDIE.

SMELLER, a blow on the nose, or "a NOSER."

SMIFF-BOX, the nose.—*Pugilistic term.*

SMISH, a shirt, or chemise. Corruption of the *Spanish* COMMISSION.—See MISH.

SMITHERS, or SMITHEREENS; "all to SMITHEREENS," all to smash. SMITHER, is a *Lincolnshire* word for a fragment.

SMOKE, London. Country-people when going to the metropolis frequently say, they are on their way to the SMOKE; and Londoners when leaving for the country say, they are going out of the SMOKE.

SMOKE, to detect, or penetrate an artifice. Common term with London detectives.

SMUDGE, to smear, obliterate, daub. Corruption of SMUTCH. *Times*, 10th August 1859.

SMUG, smuggling.—*Anglo-Chinese.*

SMUG, extremely neat, after the fashion, in order.

SMUG, to snatch another's property and run.

SMUGGINGS, snatchings, or purloinings,—shouted out by boys, when snatching the tops, or small play property, of other lads, and then running off at full speed.

"Tops are in; spin 'em agin.
Tops are out; SMUGGING about."

SMUT, a copper boiler. Also, the "blacks" from a furnace.

SMUTTY, obscene,—vulgar as applied to conversation.

SNACK, booty, or share. Also, a light repast.—*Old Cant and Gipsy term.*

SNAFFLE, conversation on professional or private subjects which the rest of the company cannot appreciate. In *East Anglia*, to SNAFFLE is to talk foolishly.

SNAGGLE TEETH, those that are uneven, and unpleasant looking.—*West.* SNAGS, (*Americanism*,) ends of sunken drift-wood sticking out of the water, on which river steamers are often wrecked.

SMIGGINS, soup served to convicts on board the hulks.

SNAFFLED, arrested, "pulled up,"—so termed from a kind of horse's bit, called a SNAFFLE.

SNAGGLING, angling after geese with a hook and line, the bait being a worm or snail. The goose swallows the bait, and is quietly landed and bagged.

SNAGGY, cross, crotchety, malicious.

SNAM, to snatch, or rob from the person.

SNAPPS, share, portion; any articles or circumstances out of which money may be made; "looking out for SNAPPS," waiting for windfalls, or odd jobs.—*Old. Scotch*, CHITS,—term also used for "coppers," or halfpence.

SNAPPS, Hollands gin.—*Dutch*, SCHNAPPS.

SNEEZER, a snuff-box; a pocket-handkerchief.

SNICK-A-SNEE, a knife.—*Sea*. *Thackeray* uses the term in his humourous ballad of the *Boy-Billie*.

SNICKER, a drinking-cup. A HORN-SNICKER, a drinking-horn.

SNID, a sixpence.—*Scotch*.

SNIGGER, "I'm SNIGGERED if you will," a mild form of swearing. Another form of this is JIGGERED.

SNIGGERING, laughing to one's-self.—*East*.

SNIP, a tailor,—apparently from SNIPES, a pair of scissors.

SNIPE, a long bill or account; also a term for attorneys,—a race remarkable for their propensity to long bills.

SNIPES, "a pair of SNIPES," a pair of scissors. They are occasionally made in the form of that bird.

SNOB, a low, vulgar, or affected person. Supposed to be from the nickname usually applied to Crispin, a maker of shoes; but believed by a writer in *Notes and Queries* to be a contraction of the *Latin*, SINE OBOLO. A more probable derivation, however, has just been forwarded by an ingenious correspondent. He supposes that NOBS, *i.e.*, *Nobiles*, was appended in lists to the names of persons of gentle birth, whilst those who had not that distinction were marked down as S. NOB., *i.e.*, SINE NOBILITATE, without marks of gentility,—thus reversing its meaning. Another "word-twister" remarks that, as at college sons of noblemen wrote after their names in the admission lists, *fil nob*., son of a lord, and hence all young noblemen were called NOBS, and what they did NOBBY, so those who imitated them would be called *quasi-nobs*, "like a nob," which by a process of contraction would be shortened to *si-nob*, and then SNOB, one who pretends to be what he is not, and apes his betters. The short and expressive terms which many think fitly represent the three great estates of the realm, NOB, SNOB, and MOB, were all originally Slang words. The last has safely passed through the vulgar ordeal of the streets, and found respectable quarters in the standard dictionaries.

SNEAKSMAN, a shoplifter; a petty, cowardly thief.

SNEEZE-LURKER, a thief who throws snuff in a person's face, and then robs him.

SNITCHERS, persons who turn Queen's evidence, or who tell tales. In *Scotland*, SNITCHERS signify handcuffs.

SNOBBISH, stuck up, proud, make believe.

SNOB-STICK, a workman who refuses to join in strikes, or trade unions. Query, properly NOB-STICK.

SNOOKS, an imaginary personage often brought forward as the answer to an idle question, or as the perpetrator of a senseless joke. Said to be simply a shortening or abbreviation of "Sevenoaks," the Kentish village.

SNOOKS-AND-WALKER, a game resembling BUZ, but more complicated. Every three and multiple of three must be termed SNOOKS, and every five and multiple of five, WALKER; thus—One, two, SNOOKS; four, WALKER-SNOOKS; seven, eight, SNOOKS-WALKER; eleven, SNOOKS-SNOOKS; fourteen, SNOOKS-WALKER, the last being a multiple of both three and five.—*See* BUZ.

SNOOZE, or SNOODGE, (vulgar pronunciation,) to sleep or doze.

SNOOZE-CASE, a pillow-slip.

SNOT, a term of reproach applied to persons by the vulgar when vexed or annoyed. In a Westminster school vocabulary for boys, published in the last century, the term is curiously applied. Its proper meaning is the glandular mucus discharged through the nose.

SNOT, a small bream, a slimy kind of flat fish.—*Norwich.*

SNOTTINGER, a coarse word for a pocket-handkerchief. The German *schnupftuch* is, however, nearly as plain. A handkerchief was also anciently called a MUCKINGER, or MUCKENDER.

SNOW, wet linen.—*Prison term and Old Cant.*

SNUFF, "up to SNUFF," knowing and sharp; "to take SNUFF," to be offended. *Shakspeare* uses SNUFF in the sense of anger, or passion.

SNUFF OUT, to die; a flippant expression, similar to "LAYING DOWN ONE'S KNIFE AND FORK," "HOPPING THE TWIG," &c.

SNUFFY, tipsy, drunk.

SNYDER, a tailor. *German,* SCHNEIDER.

SOAP, flattery.—*See* SOFT SOAP.

SOCIAL EVIL, a name beginning to be applied to street-walkers in consequence of the articles in the newspapers being so headed, which treat on the evils of prostitution. A good story is told in the *Saturday Review* for July 28, 1860. "A well-known divine and philanthropist was walking in a crowded street at night in order to distribute tracts to promising subjects. A young woman was walking up and down, and he accosted her. He pointed out to her the error of her ways, implored her to reform, and tendered her a tract with fervent entreaties to go home and read it. The girl stared at him for a moment or two in sheer bewilderment; at last it dawned on her what he meant, and for what he took her, and looking up with simple amazement in his face, she exclaimed, "Lor' bless you, sir, I ain't a SOCIAL EVIL; I'm waitin' for the 'bus!'"

SNOTTER, or WIPE-HAULER, a pickpocket who commits great depredations upon gentlemen's pocket-handkerchiefs.—*North.*

SNOW-GATHERER, or SNOW-DROPPER, a rogue who steals linen from hedges and drying-grounds.

SOCK, the Eton-College term for a treat, synonymous with CHUCK used at Westminster and other schools. Believed to be derived from the monkish word SOKE. An old writer speaks of a pious man "who did not SOKE for three days," meaning he fasted. A correspondent informs me that the word is still used by the boys of Heriot's Hospital School at Edinburgh, and signifies a sweetmeat; being derived from the same source as sugar, *suck*, SUCRE, &c.

"SOCK INTO HIM," *i.e.*, give him a good drubbing; "give him SOCK," *i.e.*, thrash him well.

SOCKET-MONEY, money extorted by threats of exposure.

SOFT, foolish, inexperienced. An old term for bank-notes.

SOFT-HORN, a simpleton, a donkey, whose ears, the substitutes of horns, are soft.

SOFT-SAWDER, flattery easily laid on, or received. Probably introduced by *Sam Slick*.

SOFT-SOAP, or SOFT-SAWDER, flattery, ironical praise.

SOFT-TACK, bread.—*Sea*.

SOFT-TOMMY, loaf-bread, in contradistinction to hard biscuit.

SOLD. "SOLD again! and the money taken," gulled, deceived.—*Vide* SELL.

SOLD UP, or OUT, broken down, bankrupt.

SOLDIER, a red herring. Common term in seaport towns.

SOMETHING DAMP, a dram, a drink.

"SON OF A GUN," a contemptuous title for a man. In the army it is sometimes applied to an artilleryman.

SOOR, an abusive term. *Hindostanee*, a pig.—*Anglo-Indian*.

SOOT-BAG, a reticule.

SOP, a soft or foolish man. Abbreviation of MILKSOP.

SOPH, (abbreviation of SOPHISTER,) a title peculiar to the University of *Cambridge*. Undergraduates are *junior* SOPHS before passing their "*Little Go*," or first University examination,—*senior* SOPHS after that.

SORT, used in a Slang sense thus—"*That's your sort*," as a term of approbation. Pitch it into him, that's your SORT, *i.e.*, that is the proper kind of plan to adopt.

SOUND, to pump, or draw information from a person in an artful manner.

SOW, the receptacle into which the liquid iron is poured in a gun-foundry. The melted metal poured from it is termed PIG.—*Workmen's terms*.

SOW'S BABY, a pig; sixpence.

SPANK, a smack, or hard slap.

SPANK, to move along quickly; hence a fast horse or vessel is said to be "a SPANKER to go."

SPANKING, large, fine, or strong; *e.g.*, a SPANKING pace, a SPANKING breeze, a SPANKING fellow.

SPECKS, damaged oranges.—*Costermonger's term*.

SPECIALTY, any one's peculiar *forte* or weakness. From the *French,* SPÉCIALITÉ.

SPELL, a turn of work, an interval of time. "Take a SPELL at the capstern."—*Sea.* "He took a long SPELL at that tankard." "After a long SPELL."

SPELL, "to SPELL for a thing," hanker after it, intimate a desire to possess it.

SPELL, to advertise, to put into print. "SPELT in the leer," *i.e.,* advertised in the newspaper.

SPELLKEN, or SPEELKEN, a playhouse. *German,* SPIELEN.—*See* KEN.—*Don Juan.*

SPICK AND SPAN, applied to anything that is quite new and fresh.—*Hudibras.*

SPIDIREEN, the name of an imaginary ship, sometimes mentioned by sailors. If a sailor be asked what ship he belongs to, and does not wish to tell, he will most probably reply—"The SPIDIREEN frigate, with nine decks, and ne'er a bottom."

SPIFFED, slightly intoxicated.—*Scotch Slang.*

SPIFFS, the per-centage allowed by drapers to their young men when they effect a sale of old-fashioned or undesirable stock.

SPIFFY, spruce, well-dressed, *tout à la mode.*

SPIFLICATE, to confound, silence, annihilate, or stifle. A corruption of the last word, or of "suffocate."

SPILL, to throw from a horse or chase.—*See* PURL.

SPIN, to reject from an examination.—*Army.*

SPINDLESHANKS, a nickname for any one who has thin legs.

SPIN-'EM ROUNDS, a street game consisting of a piece of brass, wood, or iron, balanced on a pin, and turned quickly round on a board, when the point, arrow-shaped, stops at a number, and decides the bet one way or the other. The contrivance very much resembles a sea compass, and was formerly the gambling accompaniment of London piemen. The apparatus then was erected on the tin lids of their pie-cans, and the bets were ostensibly for pies, but more frequently for "coppers," when no policemen frowned upon the scene, and when two or three apprentices or porters happened to meet.

SPINIKEN, St Giles's Workhouse. LUMP, Marylebone do. PAN, St Pancras.

SPIRT, or SPURT, "to put on a SPIRT," to make an increased exertion for

---

SPEEL, to run away, make off; "SPEEL the drum," to go off with stolen property.—*North.*

SPELL, contracted from SPELLKEN. "Precious rum squeeze at the SPELL," *i.e.,* a good evening's work at the theatre, would be the remark of a successful pickpocket!

SPIKE PARK, the Queen's-Bench prison.—*See* BURDON'S HOTEL.

a brief space, to attain one's end; a nervous effort. Abbreviation or shortening of SPIRIT.—*Old*.

> "So here for a man to run well for a SPURT, and then to give over, . . . is enough to annul all his former proceedings, and to make him in no better estate then if he had never set foot into the good waies of God."—*Gataker's Spirituall Watch*, 4to, 1619, p. 10.

SPITALFIELDS' BREAKFAST. At the East end of London this is understood as consisting of a tight necktie and a short pipe. Amongst workmen it is usual, I understand, to tighten the apron string when no dinner is at hand.

SPITFIRE, a passionate person.

SPLASH, complexion powder used by ladies to whiten their necks and faces. The finest rice flour, termed in France, *poudre de riz*, is generally employed.—*See* SLAP.

SPLENDIFEROUS, sumptuous, first-rate. SPLENDACIOUS, sometimes used with similar meanings.

SPLICE, to marry; "and the two shall become one flesh."—*Sea*. Also, a WIFE.

"SPLICE THE MAIN BRACE," to take a drink.—*Sea*.

SPLIT, to inform against one's companions, to tell tales. "To SPLIT with a person," to cease acquaintanceship, to quarrel.

SPLODGER, a lout, an awkward countryman.

SPOFFY, a bustling busybody is said to be SPOFFY.

SPONGE, "to throw up the SPONGE," to submit, give over the struggle,—from the practice of throwing up the SPONGE used to cleanse the combatants' faces at a prize fight, as a signal that the "mill" is concluded.

SPOON, synonymous with SPOONEY. A SPOON has been defined to be "a thing that touches a lady's lips without kissing them."

SPOONEY, a weak-minded and foolish person, effeminate or fond; "to be SPOONEY on a girl," to be foolishly attached to one.

SPOONS, "when I was SPOONS with you," *i.e.*, when young, and in our courting days before marriage.—*Charles Mathews*, in the farce of *Everybody's Friend*.

SPOONS, a method of designating large sums of money, disclosed at the Bankruptcy Court during the examination of the great leather failures of Streatfield & Laurence in 1860-61. The origin of the phrase was stated to be the reply of the bankrupt Laurence to an offer of accommodating him with £5000,—"Oh, you are feeding me with a TEA-SPOON." Hence £5000 came to be known in the firm, as a TEA-SPOON, £10,000, a DESSERT-SPOON; £15,000, a TABLE-SPOON; and £20,000, as a GRAVY-SPOON. The public were amused at this TEA-SPOON phraseology, but were disgusted that such levity should cover a gigantic swindle of the kind. It came out in evidence, however, that it was not the ordinary Slang of the discount world, but it may not improbably become so.

SPORT, to exhibit, to wear, &c.,—a word which is made to do duty in a variety of senses, especially at the University.—*See* the *Gradus ad Cantabrigiam*. "To SPORT a new tile;" "to SPORT an *Ægrotat*," (*i.e.*, a permission from the "Dons" to abstain from lectures &c., on account of illness;) "to SPORT ONE'S OAK," to shut the outer door and exclude the public, — especially *duns*, and boring acquaintances. Common also, in the Inns of Court.—See *Notes and Queries*, 2d series, vol. viii., p. 492, and *Gentleman's Magazine*, December 1794.

SPORTING DOOR, the outer door of chambers, also called the OAK.—*See* under SPORT.—*University.*

SPOUT, "up the SPOUT," at the pawnbroker's; SPOUTING, pawning.—*See* POP for origin.

SPOUT, to preach, or make speeches; SPOUTER, a preacher or lecturer.

SPRAT, sixpence.

SPREAD, butter. Term with workmen and schoolboys.

SPREAD, a lady's shawl. SPREAD, at the *East* end of London, a feast, or a TIGHTENER; at the *West* end a fashionable re-union, an entertainment, display of good things.

SPREE, a boisterous piece of merriment; "going on the SPREE," starting out with intent to have a frolic. *French,* ESPRIT. In the *Dutch* language, SPREEUW is a jester.

SPRINGER-UP, a tailor who sells low-priced ready-made clothing, and gives starvation wages to the poor men and women who "make up" for him. The clothes are said to be SPRUNG-UP, or "blown together."

SPRY, active, strong, manly.—*Originally an Americanism.*

SPUDDY, a seller of bad potatoes. In *Scotland,* a SPUD is a raw potato; and roasted SPUDS are those cooked in the cinders with their jackets on.

SPUN, when a man has failed in his examination at Woolwich, he is said to be SPUN; as at the Universities he is said to be PLUCKED.

SPUNGING-HOUSE, the sheriff's officer's house, where prisoners, when arrested for debt, are sometimes taken. As extortionate charges are made there for accommodation, the name is far from inappropriate.

SPUNK, spirit, *fire,* courage, mettle.

"In that snug room, where any man of SPUNK
Would find it a hard matter to get drunk."
—*Peter Pindar,* i. 245.

Common in *America.* For derivation see the following:—

SPUNKS, lucifer-matches.—*Herefordshire; Scotland.* SPUNK, says Urry, in his MS. notes to Ray, "is the excrescency of some tree, of which they make a sort of tinder to light their pipes with."

SPUNK-FENCER, a lucifer-match seller.

SPURT.—*Old.*—*See* SPIRT.

SQUABBY, flat, short and thick.

SQUARE, honest; "on the SQUARE," *i.e.,* fair and strictly honest; "to turn SQUARE," to reform, and get one's living in an honest manner,—the opposite of CROSS. The expression is, in all probability, derived from the well-known masonic emblem the "*square,*" the symbol of evenness and rectitude.

"You must keep within the compass, and act *upon the* SQUARE with all man-

SPOTTED, to be known or marked by the police.

kind; for your masonry is but a dead letter if you do not habitually perform its reiterated injunctions."—*Oliver's Lectures on Signs and Symbols,* p. 190.

SQUARE, "to be SQUARE with a man," to be *even* with him, or to be revenged; "to SQUARE up to a man," to offer to fight him. *Shakspeare* uses SQUARE in the sense of to quarrel.

SQUARE RIGGED, well dressed.—*Sea.*

SQUARUM, a cobbler's lapstone.

SQUASH, to crush; "to go SQUASH," to collapse.

SQUEAL, to inform, peach. A north country variation of *squeak; s. s.* SQUEALER, an informer, also an illegitimate baby.

SQUIB, a temporary *jeu d'esprit*, which, like the firework of that denomination, sparkles, bounces, stinks, and vanishes.—*Grose.*

SQUIBS, paint-brushes.

SQUINNY-EYED, said of one given to squinting.—*Shakspeare.*

SQUIRT, a doctor, or chemist.

"STAB YOURSELF AND PASS THE DAGGER," help yourself and pass the bottle.—*Theatrical Slang.*

STAB, "on the STAB," *i.e.*, on the *establishment*, of which word it is an abridgment.—*Printer's term.*

STAB-RAG, a regimental tailor.—*Military Slang.*

STAFF-NAKED, gin.

STAG, a shilling.

STAG, a term applied during the railway mania to a speculator without capital, who took "scrip" in "*Diddlesex Junction*," and other lines, *ejus et sui generis*, got the shares up to a premium, and then sold out. *Punch* represented the house of Hudson, "the Railway King," at Albert Gate, with a STAG on it, in allusion to this term.

STAG, to see, discover, or watch,—like a STAG at gaze; "STAG the push," look at the crowd. Also, to dun, or demand payment.

STAGE-WHISPER, one loud enough to be heard.

STAGGERING-BOB, an animal to whom the knife only just anticipates death from natural disease or accident,—said of meat on that account unfit for human food.

STALL, to lodge, or put up at a public house. Also, to act a part.—*Theatrical.*

SQUARE COVE, an honest man.

SQUARE MOLL, an honest woman.

"SQUARING HIS NIBS," giving a policeman money.

"SQUEAK ON A PERSON," to inform against, PEACH.

SQUEEZE, silk; also, by a very significant figure, a thief's term for *the neck.*

STAG, to demand money, to "cadge."

STAGGER, one who looks out, or watches.

STALL, or STALL OFF, a dodge, a blind, an excuse. STALL is *ancient Cant.*

"STALL YOUR MUG," go away; spoken sharply by any one who wishes to get rid of a troublesome or inconvenient person.

STALKING-HORSE, originally a horse covered with loose trappings, under which the mediæval sportsman concealed himself with his bow, so as to approach his game unobserved. Subsequently a canvas figure, made light, so as to be easily moved with one hand.

STAMPERS, shoes.—*Ancient Cant.*

STAND, "to STAND treat," to pay for a friend's entertainment; to bear expense; to put up with treatment, good or ill; "this house STOOD me in £1000," *i.e.*, cost that sum, (a correspondent queries the *Latin* CONSTAT, it cost me;) "to STAND PAD," to beg on the curb with a small piece of paper pinned on the breast, inscribed, "*I'm starving.*"

STAND IN, to make one of a party in a bet or other speculation; to take a side in a dispute.

STANDING, the position at a street corner, or on the curb of a market street, regularly occupied by a costermonger, or street seller.

STANDING PATTERERS, men who take a stand on the curb of a public thoroughfare, and deliver prepared speeches to effect a sale of any articles they have to vend.—*See* PATTERER.

STANGEY, a tailor; a person under petticoat government,—derived from the custom of "*riding the* STANG," mentioned in *Hudibras*:—

"It is a custom used of course
Where the gray mare is the better horse."

STAR, a common abbreviation of the name of the well-known "Star and Garter" Inn at Richmond.

STARCHY, stuck-up, high-notioned, showily dressed, stiff and unbending in demeanour.

STARK-NAKED, (originally STRIP-ME-NAKED, *vide Randall's Diary*, 1820,) raw gin.—*Bulwer's Paul Clifford.*

STAR IT, to perform as the centre of attraction, with inferior subordinates to set off one's abilities.—*Theatrical.*

START, "THE START," London,—the great starting point for beggars and tramps.

START, a proceeding of any kind; a "rum START," an odd circumstance; "to get the START of a person," to anticipate him, overreach him.

STARVE 'EM, ROB 'EM, and CHEAT 'EM, the adjoining towns of Stroud, Rochester, and Chatham are so designated by soldiers and sailors; probably not without reason.

STALL OFF, to blind, excuse, hide, to screen a robbery during the perpetration of it by an accomplice.

STALLSMAN, an accomplice.

"STAR THE GLAZE," to break the window or show-glass of a jeweller or other tradesman, and take any valuable articles, and run away. Sometimes the glass is cut with a diamond, and a strip of leather fastened to the piece of glass cut out to keep it from falling in and making a noise. Another plan is to cut the sash.

STASH, to cease doing anything, to refrain, be quiet, leave off; "STASH it, there, you sir!" *i.e.*, be quiet, sir; to give over a lewd or intemperate course of life is termed STASHING IT.

STEAM-ENGINE, potato-pie at Manchester is so termed.

STEEL-BAR DRIVERS, or FLINGERS, journeymen tailors.

STEMS, the legs.

STEP IT, to run away, or make off.

STICK, a derogatory expression for a person; "a rum" or "odd STICK," a curious man. More generally a "poor STICK."—*Provincial*.

STICK, "cut your STICK," be off, or go away; either simply equivalent to a recommendation to prepare a walking staff in readiness for a journey —in allusion to the Eastern custom of cutting a stick before setting out—or from the ancient mode of reckoning by notches or tallies on a stick. In Cornwall the peasantry tally sheaves of corn by cuts in a stick, reckoning by the score. CUT YOUR STICK in this sense may mean to make your mark and pass on—and so realise the meaning of the phrase "IN THE NICK (or notch) OF TIME." *Sir J. Emerson Tennent*, in *Notes and Queries*, (December 1859,) considers the phrase equivalent to "cutting the connexion," and suggests a possible origin in the prophet's breaking the staves of "Beauty" and "Bands,"—*vide* Zech. xi. 10, 14.

STICK, to cheat; "he got STUCK," he was taken in; I'M STUCK, a common phrase to express that the speaker has spent or lost all his money, and can neither play nor pay any longer; STICK, to forget one's part in a performance—*Theatrical*; STICK UP, to place in an account; "STICK IT UP TO ME," *i.e.*, give me credit for it; STICK ON, to overcharge or defraud; STICK UP FOR, to defend a person, especially when slandered in his absence; STICK UP TO, to persevere in courting or attacking, whether in fisty-cuffs or argument; "to STICK in one's gizzard," to rankle in one's heart; "to STICK TO a person," to adhere to one, be his friend through adverse circumstances,—to COTTON to him.

STICKS, furniture, or household chattels; "pick up your STICKS and cut!" summary advice to a person to take himself and furniture away.— *Cumberland*.

STICK-UPS, or GILLS, shirt collars.

STICKINGS, bruised or damaged meat sold to sausage-makers and penny pie shops.—*North*.

STICKY, wax.

STIFF, paper, a bill of acceptance, &c.; "how did you get it, STIFF or hard?" *i.e.*, did he pay you cash or give a bill? STIFF, "to do a bit of STIFF," to accept a bill.—*See* KITE.

STIFF-FENCER, a street-seller of writing paper.

STIFF 'UN, a corpse.—*Term used by undertakers*.

STEEL, the house of correction in London, formerly named the *Bastile*, but since shortened to STEEL.—*See* BASTILE.

STICKS, pistols.—*Nearly obsolete*.

STILLS, the undertaker's Slang term for STILL-BORN children. The fee paid by nurses and others is usually 2s. 6d. A separate coffin is never given; the STILLS are quietly introduced into one containing an adult about to be buried. STILLS are allowed to accumulate at the undertaker's until they sometimes number as many as a dozen.

STILTON, "that's the STILTON," or "it is not the STILTON," *i.e.*, that is quite the thing, or that is not quite the thing;—polite rendering of "that is not the CHEESE," which *see.*

STINGO, strong liquor.—*Yorkshire.*

STINK, a disagreeable exposure.

STINKOMALEE, a name given to the then New London University by Theodore Hook. Some question about *Trincomalee* was agitated at the same time. It is still applied by the students of the old Universities, who regard it with disfavour from its admitting all denominations.

STIPE, a stipendiary magistrate.—*Provincial.*

STIR-UP SUNDAY, the Sunday next before Advent, the collect for that day commencing with the words "Stir up." School-boys, growing excited at the prospect of the vacation, irreverently commemorate it by stirring up—pushing and poking each other. CRIB-CRUST MONDAY and TUG-BUTTON TUESDAY are distinguished by similar tricks; while on PAY-OFF WEDNESDAY they retaliate small grudges in a playful facetious way. Forby says good housewives in Norfolk consider themselves reminded by the name to mix the ingredients for their Christmas mince-pies.

STOCK; "to STOCK cards" is to arrange cards in a certain manner for cheating purposes.

STOCK, "to take STOCK of one," to scrutinise narrowly one whom you have reason to suspect; taken from the tradesmen's term for the annual examination and valuation of their stock of goods.

STOCKDOLAGER, a heavy blow, a "finisher." *Italian*, STOCCADO, a fencing term. Also (in a general sense) a disastrous event.—*Americanism.*

STODGE, to surfeit, gorge, or clog with food.

STOLL, to understand.—*North Country Cant.*

STORY, a falsehood,—the soft synonyme for a *lie*, allowed in family circles and boarding-schools. A Puritanism that came into fashion with the tirade against romances, all novels and stories being considered as dangerous and false.

STOT, a young bullock. In *Northumberland* the term STOT means to rebound.

STIR, a prison, a lock-up; "IN STIR," in jail. *Anglo-Saxon*, STYR, correction, punishment.

STONE-JUG, a prison.

STOOK, a pocket-handkerchief.

STOOK-HAULER, or BUZZER, a thief who takes pocket-handkerchiefs.

STOP, a detective policeman.

STOTOR, a heavy blow, a settler.—*Old Cant.*

STOW, to leave off, or have done; "STOW it, the gorger's leary," leave off, the person is looking.—*See* STASH, with which it is synonymous.—*Ancient Cant.*

STOW FAKING! leave off there, be quiet! FAKING implying anything that may be going on.

STRAP, a barber.

STRAW. Married ladies are said to be "IN THE STRAW" at their *accouchements.* The phrase is a coarse allusion to farm-yard animals in a similar condition.

STRAWING, *selling* straws in the streets, (generally for a penny,) and *giving* the purchaser a paper (indecent or political) or a gold (!) ring,—neither of which, the patterer states, he is allowed by Act of Parliament to sell.

STREAK, to decamp, run away.—*Saxon.* In America the phrase is "to make STREAKS," or "make TRACKS."

STREAKY, irritated, ill-tempered.

STREET-PITCHERS, negro minstrels, ballad singers, long-song men, men "working a board" on which have been painted various exciting scenes in some terrible drama, the details of which the STREET-PITCHER is bawling out, and selling in a little book or broadsheet (price one penny;) or any persons who make a stand in the streets, and sell articles for their living.

STRETCH, a walk.—*University.*

STRETCHER, a falsehood.

STRETCHER, a contrivance with handles, used by the police to carry off persons who are violent or drunk.

STRETCHER-FENCER, one who sells braces.

"STRIKE ME LUCKY!" an expression used by the lower orders when making a bargain, derived from the old custom of striking hands together, leaving in that of the seller a LUCK PENNY as an earnest that the bargain is concluded. In Ireland, at cattle markets, &c., a penny, or other small coin, is always given by the buyer to the seller to ratify the bargain.—*Hudibras.* Anciently this was called a GOD'S PENNY.

"With that he cast him a God's penny."—*Heir of Linne.*

The origin of the phrase being lost sight of, like that of many others, it is often corrupted now-a-days into STRIKE ME SILLY.

STRETCH, abbreviation of "STRETCH one's neck," to hang, be executed as a malefactor.—*Bulwer's Paul Clifford.*

STRETCH, twelve months,—generally used to intimate the time any one has been sentenced by the judge or magistrate. ONE STRETCH is to be imprisoned twelve months, TWO STRETCH is two years, THREE STRETCH is three years, and so on.

STRETCHING MATCH, an execution.—*See* STRETCH.

"STRIKE A JIGGER," to pick a lock, or break open a door.

STRILLS, cheating lies.—*North Country Cant.*

STROKE, a companion in a rowing boat who times his oar with yours.—*University.*

> "He [the man who rows] looks round at a wine-party to see if his 'STROKE' be present, and, descrying him not, cannot see how a few glasses of wine, and a plate or so of ice, can possibly interfere with his training."—*Hints to Freshmen,* 1847.

STROMMEL, straw.—*Ancient Cant.* Halliwell says that in Norfolk STROMMEL is a name for hair.

STRONG, "to come it STRONG."—*See* COME.

STUCK, moneyless.—*See* STICK.

STUCK-UP, "purse-proud"—a form of snobbishness very common in those who have risen in the world. Mr Albert Smith has written some amusing papers on the *Natural History of* STUCK-UP *People.*

STUFF, money.

STUFF, to make false but plausible statements, to praise ironically, to make game of a person,—literally, to STUFF or CRAM him with gammon or falsehood.

STUMP, to go on foot.

STUMPED, bowled out, done for, bankrupt, poverty-stricken.—*Cricketing term.*

STUMPS, legs, or feet.

STUMPY, money.

STUMP UP, to give one's share, to pay the reckoning, to bring forth the money reluctantly.

STUN, to astonish.

STUNNER, a first-rate person or article.

STUNNERS, feelings of great astonishment; "it put the STUNNERS on me," *i.e.,* it confounded me.

STUNNING, first-rate, very good. "STUNNING pears," shouts the coster, "only eight a penny."—*Vide Athenæum,* 26th March 1859. Sometimes amplified to STUNNING JOE BANKS! when the expression is supposed to be in its most intense form. JOE BANKS was a noted character in the last generation. He was the proprietor of a public-house in Dyott Street, Seven Dials, and afterwards, on the demolition of the Rookery, of another in Cranbourne Alley. His houses became well-known from their being the resort of the worst characters, at the same time that the strictest decorum was always maintained in them. JOE BANKS also acquired a remarkable notoriety by acting as a medium betwixt thieves and their victims. Upon the proper payment to Joe, a watch or a snuff-box would at any time be restored to its lawful owner—"no questions in any case being asked." The most daring depredators in London placed the fullest confidence in Joe, and it is believed (although the *Biographie Universelle* is quiet upon this point) that he never, in any instance, "sold" them. He was of the middle height, stout, and strongly made, and was always noted for a

---

STRIP-BUSH, a fellow who steals clothes put out to dry after washing.

showy pin, and a remarkably STUNNING *neck-tie*. It was this peculiarity in the costume of Mr Banks, coupled with those true and tried qualities as a friend, for which, as I have just remarked, he was famous, that led his customers to proclaim him as STUNNING JOE BANKS! The Marquis of Douro, Colonel Chatterley, and men of their stamp, were accustomed to resort to a private room at his house, when too late or too early to gain admittance to the clubs or more aristocratic establishments.

SUB, a subaltern officer in the army.

SUB, all.—*Anglo-Indian.*

SUBLIME RASCAL, a lawyer.

SUCK, a parasite, flatterer of the "nobs."—*University.*

SUCK, to pump, or draw information from a person.

SUCK-CASA, a public-house.—*Lingua Franca.*

"SUCK THE MONKEY," to rob a cask of liquor by inserting a straw through a gimlet hole, and sucking a portion of the contents. Captain Marryatt, however, describes this as rum inserted into cocoa nuts, in place of the milk, for the private use of the sailors.—*See* TAP-THE-ADMIRAL.

SUCK UP, "to SUCK UP to a person," to insinuate one's-self into his good graces.

SUDDEN DEATH, the first toss in a bet, to be decided by SKYING a copper.

SUFFERER, a tailor; the loser at any game.

SUGAR, money.

SUICIDE, four horses driven in a line.—*See* HARUM-SCARUM.

SUIT, a watch and seals.

SULKY, a one-horse chaise, having only room for one person.

SUMSY, an action of *assumpsit.*—*Legal Slang.*

"SUN IN THE EYES," to have too much drink.—*Dickens.*

SUP, abbreviation of "supernumerary."—*Theatrical.*

SURAT, an adulterated article of inferior quality. This word affords a remarkable instance of the manner in which Slang phrases are coined. In the report of an action for libel in the *Times*, May 8, 1863, it is stated "that, since the American civil war, it has been not unusual for manufacturers to mix American cotton with Surat, and, the latter being an inferior article, the people in Lancashire have begun to apply the term SURAT to any article of inferior or adulterated quality. The plaintiffs were brewers, and the action was brought to recover special damages resulting from the publication of an advertisement in these

---

"STUNNED ON SKILLY," to be sent to prison and compelled to eat SKILLY, or SKILLIGOLEE.

STURABAN, a prison. *Gipsy*, DISTARABIN.

SUPER, a watch; SUPER-SCREWING, stealing watches.

words:—'All in want of beerhouses must beware of Beaumont & White, the SURAT brewers.'"

SURF, an actor who frequently pursues another calling.—*Theatrical.*

SWAB, an epaulet.—*Sea.*

SWACK-UP, a falsehood.

SWADDLER, a Wesleyan Methodist; a name originally given to members of that body by the Irish mob; said to have originated with an ignorant Romanist, to whom the words of the English Bible were a novelty, and who, hearing one of John Wesley's preachers mention the swaddling clothes of the Holy Infant, in a sermon on Christmas-day at Dublin, shouted out in derision, "A SWADDLER! a SWADDLER!" as if the whole story were the preacher's invention.—*Southey's Life of Wesley,* vol. ii., p. 109.

SWADDY, or COOLIE, a soldier. The former was originally applied to a discharged soldier, and perhaps came from SHODDY, which is made from soldiers' and worn-out policemen's coats.—*See that term.*

SWAG, a lot or plenty of anything, a portion or division of property. In Australia the term is used for the luggage carried by diggers. Scotch, SWEG, or SWACK; German, SWEIG, a flock. *Old Cant* for a shop.

SWAG-SHOP, a warehouse where "Brummagem" and general wares are sold, fancy trinkets, plated goods, &c. Jews are the general proprietors, and the goods are very low-priced, trashy, and showy. SWAG-SHOPS were formerly plunder depôts.—*Old Cant.*

SWANKEY, cheap beer.—*West.*

SWAP, to exchange. *Grose* says it is *Irish* Cant, but the term is now included in most dictionaries as an allowed vulgarism.

SWATCHEL-COVE, the master of a Punch-and-Judy exhibition who "fakes the slum," and does the necessary squeak for the amusement of the bystanders.—*See* SCHWASSLE BOX. The orthography of many of these colloquial expressions differs. It was thought best to give the various renderings as collected.

SWEAT, to extract money from a person, to "bleed." Also, to squander riches.—*Bulwer.*

SWEATER, common term for a "cutting" or "grinding" employer,—one who SWEATS his work-people.

SWEEP, a contemptuous term for a low or shabby man.

SWEET, loving or fond; "how SWEET he was upon the moll," *i.e.*, what marked attention he paid the girl.

SWEETENER, a person who runs up the prices of articles at an auction. —*See* JOLLYING, BONNET, &c.

SWELL, a man of importance; a person with a showy, jaunty exterior; "a rank SWELL," a very "flashy" dressed person, a man who by excessive dress apes a higher position than he actually occupies.

SWAG, booty, or plundered property; "collar the SWAG," seize the booty.

SWAGSMAN, one who carries the booty after a burglary.

Anything is said to be SWELL or SWELLISH that looks showy, or is many coloured, or is of a desirable quality. Dickens and Wilkie Collins are termed great SWELLS in literature; so indeed are the first persons in the learned professions.

SWELL-FENCER, a street salesman of needles.

"SWELL HUNG IN CHAINS," said of a showy man in the habit of wearing much jewellery.

SWELL STREET, the West end of London.

SWIG, a hearty drink.

SWIG, to drink. *Saxon*, SWIGAN.

SWILL, to drink. SWILL, hog-wash.—*Norfolk*.

SWINDLER, although a recognised word in standard dictionaries, commenced service as a Slang term. It was used as such by the poor Londoners against the German Jews who set up in London about the year 1762, also by our soldiers in the German war about that time. SCHWINDEL, in *German*, signifies to cheat.

SWING, to be hanged; "if you don't accede to my desires, I'll SWING for you," *i.e.*, take your life—a common threat in low neighbourhoods.

SWINGING, large, huge.

SWIPES, sour or small beer. SWIPE, to drink.—*Sea*.

SWIPEY, (from SWIPES,) intoxicated.

SWISH, to flog, derived no doubt from the sound.

SWISHED, or SWITCHED, married.

SWIVEL-EYE, a squint.

SWIZZLE, small beer, drink.

SWOT, mathematics; also a mathematician; as a verb, to work hard for an examination, to be diligent in one's studies.—*Army*. This word originated at the great Slang manufactory for the army, the Royal Military College, Sandhurst, in the broad Scotch pronunciation of Dr Wallace, one of the Professors, of the word *sweat*.—*See Notes and Queries*, vol. i., p. 369.

SYCE, a groom.—*Anglo-Indian*.

T, "to suit to a T," to fit to a nicety.—*Old*. Perhaps from the T-square of carpenters, by which the accuracy of work is tested.

TABOOED, forbidden. This word, now very common, is derived from a custom of the South-Sea Islanders, first noticed in "Cook's Voyages."

TACK, a taste foreign to what was intended; a barrel may get a TACK upon it, either permanently mouldy, sour, or otherwise.

TACKLE, clothes.—*Sea*. Also to encounter a person in argument.

SWIM, "a good SWIM," a good run of luck, a long time out of the policeman's clutches.—*Thieves' term*. A correspondent says this is really a piscatorial term—"a good SWIM" is a *good pitch* for a part where fish are plentiful. Thus one who is in luck, or doing a good business, is said to be in a good SWIM.

TAFFY, (corruption of *David*,) a Welshman. Compare SAWNEY, (from *Alexander*,) a Scotchman.

TAG, an actor.

TAG-RAG-AND-BOBTAIL, a mixed crowd of low people, mobility.

TAIL-BLOCK, a watch.—*Sea*.

TAKE, to succeed, or be patronised; "do you think the new opera will TAKE?" "No, because the same company TOOK so badly under the old management;" "to TAKE ON," to grieve; *Shakspeare* uses the word TAKING in this sense. To "TAKE UP for any one," to protect or defend a person; "to TAKE OFF," to mimic; "to TAKE HEART," to have courage; "to TAKE down a peg or two," to humiliate, or tame; "to TAKE UP," to reprove; "to TAKE AFTER," to resemble; "to TAKE IN," to cheat or defraud, from the lodging-house-keepers' advertisements, "single men TAKEN IN AND DONE FOR,"—an engagement which is as frequently performed in a bad as a good sense; "to TAKE THE FIELD," when said of a General, to commence operations against the enemy; when a racing man TAKES THE FIELD he stakes his money against the favourite.

TAKE BEEF, to run away.

TAKE IN, a cheating or swindling transaction,—sometimes termed "a DEAD TAKE IN." *Shakspeare* has TAKE IN in the sense of conquering. TO BE HAD, or TO BE SPOKEN TO, were formerly synonymous phrases with TO BE TAKEN IN.

TALKING, a stable term, of a milder kind, applied to those horses which are addicted to ROARING.—*See the latter expression*.

TALL, extensive, exaggerated,—generally applied to conversation, as LOUD is to dress, or personal appearance; "TALL talk that," *i.e.*, conversation too boastful or high-flown to be true.

TALLY, five dozen bunches of turnips.—*Costermongers' term*.

TALLY, "to live TALLY," to live in a state of unmarried impropriety; "TALLY-WIFE," a woman who cohabits with a man to whom she is not married; a "TALLYMAN" is an accommodating salesman who takes payment by instalments to suit the convenience of the purchaser.

TAN, to beat or thrash; "I'll TAN your hide," *i.e.*, give you a good beating.

TAN, an order to pull.—*Anglo-Indian*.

TANNER, a sixpence. *Gipsy*, TAWNO, little, or *Latin*, TENER, slender?

TANNY, or TEENY, little. *Gipsy*, TAWNO, little.

TANTREMS, pranks, capers, frolicking; from the *Tarantula* dance.—*See account of the involuntary frenzy and motions caused by the bite of the tarantula in Italy.*—*Penny Cyclopædia*.

TAPE, gin,—term with female servants. Also, a military term used in barracks when no spirits are allowed.—*See* RIBBON.

TAPER, to give over gradually, to run short.

"TAP THE ADMIRAL," to suck liquor from a cask by means of a straw,

---

TAIL-BUZZER, a thief who picks coat pockets.

said to have been first done with the rum-cask in which Lord Nelson's body was brought to England, to such an extent as to leave the gallant Admiral high and dry.

TAP-TUB, the *Morning Advertiser*,—so called by vulgar people from the fact that this daily newspaper is the principal organ of the London brewers and publicans. Sometimes termed THE GIN AND GOSPEL GAZETTE.

TARADIDDLE, a falsehood.

TAR-BRUSH, a person, whose complexion indicates a mixture of Negro blood, is said to have had a lick of the TAR-BRUSH.

TAR OUT, to punish, to serve out.

TARPAULIN, a sailor.

TART. My old servant, "Jim the Patterer," (one of the collectors of Seven Dials' terms for the first edition of this work,) whose unfortunate habit for contracting small loans induced me at length to lend him a whole half-crown at once, in the hope that he might not pay, and thus not trouble me again, has recently sent me some words from Birmingham, where he says he is doing well with "a SCHWASSLE BOX, having learnt the squeak." Amongst them is the following, given in Mr Jim's own words:—

> "TART, a term of approval applied by the London lower orders to a young woman for whom some affection is felt. The expression is not generally employed by the young men, unless the female is in 'her best,' with a coloured gown, red or blue shawl, and plenty of ribbons in her bonnet—in fact, made pretty all over, like the jam tarts in the swell bakers' shops."*

TARTAR, a savage fellow, an "ugly customer." CATCHING A TARTAR.

TAT-BOX, a dice-box.

TATER, "s'elp my TATER," another street evasion of a profane oath, sometimes varied by "s'elp my GREENS."

TATS, dice.

TATS, old rags; MILKY TATS, white rags.

TATTING, gathering old rags.

TATTOO, a pony.—*Anglo-Indian.*

TAW, a large or principal marble; "I'll be one on your TAW," I will pay you out, or be even with you,—a simile taken from boys aiming always at winning the TAW when playing at marbles.

TEAGUELAND, Ireland.

TEA-FIGHT, an evening party, *alias* A MUFFIN-WORRY.

TEA-SPOON, five thousand pounds.—*See* SPOONS.

TEETH, "he has cut his *eye* TEETH," *i.e.*, is old and 'cute enough.

TEETH-DRAWING, wrenching off knockers.—*Medical Students'* term.

---

* The language used by Mr Jim is certainly far above his position in life. This evidence of education existing amongst certain persons of the tramping fraternity has been alluded to at page 23.

TATLER, a watch; "nimming a TATLER," stealing a watch.

TEETOTALLER, a total abstainer from alcoholic drinks.

TEETOTALLY, amplification of TOTALLY.

TE-HE, to titter, "Upon this I TE-HE'D;" *Madame d'Arblay.* As an interjection it is as old as *Chaucer.—See Miller's Tale*"—"TE-HE, quod she, and clapt the window to."

TELL ON, to tell about, to talk of.

TEN COMMANDMENTS, a virago's fingers, or nails. Often heard in a female street disturbance.

"TENPENCE TO THE SHILLING," a vulgar phrase denoting a deficiency in intellect.

TESTER, sixpence. From TESTONE, a shilling in the reign of Henry VIII., but a sixpence in the time of Queen Elizabeth.—*Shakspeare.* French, TESTE, or TÊTE, the head of the monarch on the coin.

TEVISS, a shilling.—*Costermonger* and *Tramps'* term.

THICK, intimate, familiar. Scotch, CHIEF; "the two are very CHIEF now," *i.e.,* friendly.

THICK; "to lay it on THICK," to flatter unduly, to surfeit with praise or adulation.

THICK-UN, a sovereign; a crown piece, or five shillings.

THIMBLE-RIG, a noted cheating game played at fairs and places of great public thronging, consisting of two or three thimbles rapidly and dexterously placed over a pea, when the THIMBLE-RIGGER, suddenly ceasing, asks you under which thimble the pea is to be found. If you are not a practised hand you will lose nine times out of ten any bet you may happen to make with him. The pea is sometimes concealed under his nail.

THINGUMY, THINGUMBOB, expressions used for the name of a thing which cannot be recollected at the instant.

THINSKINNED, over nice, petulant, apt to get a RAW.—*See* that term.

THREE-CORNERED-SCRAPER, a cocked hat.—*Sea.*

"THREE SHEETS IN THE WIND," unsteady from drink.—*Sea.*

THREE-UP, a gambling game played by costers. Three halfpennies are thrown up, and when they fall all "heads," or all "tails," it is a mark; and the man who gets the greatest number of marks out of a given amount—three, five, or more—wins. The costers are very quick and skilful at this game, and play fairly at it amongst themselves; but should a stranger join in they invariably unite to cheat him.

THRUMMER, a threepenny bit.

TENCH, the Penitentiary, of which it is a contraction.—*See* STEEL.

THEATRE, a police court; a place for acting, or assuming a part which is not natural to the performer.

THIMBLE, or YACK, a watch.—*Prison Cant.*

THIMBLE-TWISTERS, thieves who rob persons of their watches.

THRUMS, threepence.

THRUPS, threepence.—*See* the preceding.

THUMPING, large, fine, or strong.

THUNDERER, the *Times* newspaper, sometimes termed "the THUNDERER of Printing-House Square," from the locality where it is printed.

THUNDERING, large, extra sized.

TIB'S EVE, "neither before Christmas nor after," an indefinite period; like the Greek Kalends, TIB'S EVE has a future application; an indefinite period of *past* time is sometimes said to be "when Adam was an oakum-boy in Chatham dockyard."

TIBBING OUT, going out of bounds.—*Charterhouse*.

TICK, credit, trust. Johnson says it is a corruption of *ticket*,—tradesmen's bills being formerly written on tickets or cards. ON TICK, therefore, is equivalent to *on ticket*, or on trust. In use in 1668. Cuthbert Bede, in *Notes and Queries*, supplies me with an earlier date, from the *Gradus ad Cantabrigiam*.

> "No matter upon landing whether you have money or no—you may swim in twentie of their boats over the river UPON TICKET."—*Decker's Gulls' Hornbook*, 1609.

TICKER, a watch. Formerly Cant, now street Slang.

TICKET, "that's the TICKET," *i.e.*, what was wanted, or what is best. Corruption of "that is not *etiquette*," by adding, in vulgar pronunciation, *th* to the first *e* of "etiquette;" or, perhaps, from TICKET, a bill or invoice. This phrase is sometimes extended into "that's the TICKET FOR SOUP," in allusion to the card given to beggars for immediate relief at soup kitchens.—*See* TICK.

TIDY, tolerably, or pretty well; "how did you get on to-day?"—"Oh, TIDY."—*Saxon*.

TIDDLYWINK, slim, puny; sometimes TILLYWINK.

TIED UP, given over, finished; also married, in allusion to the hymeneal knot, unless a jocose allusion be intended to the *halter*, (altar.)

TIFF, a pet, a fit of ill humour.

TIFFIN, a breakfast, *déjeûner à la fourchette*.—*Anglo-Indian Slang*.

TIFFY, easily offended, apt to be annoyed.

TIGER, a parasite; also a term for a ferocious woman.

TIGER, a boy employed to wait on gentlemen; one who waits on ladies is a page.

TIGHT, close, stingy; hard up, short of cash; TIGHT, spruce, strong, active; "a TIGHT lad," a smart, active young fellow; TIGHT, drunk, or nearly so; "TIGHT-laced," puritanical, over-precise. Money is said to be TIGHT, when the public, from want of confidence in the aspect of affairs, are not inclined to speculate.

TIGHTNER, a dinner, or hearty meal.—*See* SPITALFIELDS' BREAKFAST.

TIKE, or BUFFER-LURKING, dog-stealing.—*See* GAY TIKEBOY.

TILE, a hat; a covering for the head.

> "I'm a gent, I'm a gent,
> In the Regent-Street style,—
> Examine my vest.
> And look at my TILE."—*Popular Song.*

Sometimes used in another sense, "having a TILE loose," *i.e.*, being slightly crazy.—*See* PANTILE.

TIMBER MERCHANT, or SPUNK FENCER, a lucifer-match seller.

TIME O' DAY, a dodge, the latest aspect of affairs; "that's your TIME O' DAY," *i.e., Euge,* well done; to PUT A PERSON UP TO THE TIME O' DAY, let him know what is o' clock,—to instruct him in the knowledge needful for him.

TIME, cabman's Slang for money. If they wish to express 9s. 9d. they say that "it is a quarter to ten;" if 3s. 6d., half-past three; if 11s. 9d., a quarter to twelve. Cab drivers exultingly say the police cannot comprehend the system.

TIN, money,—generally applied to silver.

TINGE, the per-centage allowed by drapers and clothiers to their assistants, upon the sale of old-fashioned articles.—*See* SPIFFS.

TIN-POT, "he plays a TIN-POT game," *i.e.*, a low or shabby one. In the *Contes d'Eutrapel*, a French officer at the siege of Chatillon is ridiculously spoken of as Captain TIN-POT—*Capitaine du Pot d'Etain.—Billiards.*

TIP, advice or information respecting a horse-race, so that the person TIPPED may know how to bet to the best advantage. Notice when and where a prize-fight is to come off. Private information of any kind — *See* TIPSTER.

TIP, a douceur; "a good TIP," a piece likely to be set in an Addiscombe or Sandhurst examination, hence, "that's the TIP," *i.e.*, that's the proper thing to do. "To miss one's TIP," to fail in a scheme.—*Old Cant.*

TIP, to give, lend, or hand over anything to another person; "come, TIP up the tin," *i.e.*, hand up the money; "TIP the wink," to inform by winking; "TIP us your fin," *i.e.*, give me your hand; "TIP one's boom off," to make off, depart.—*Sea.*

TIPPER, a kind of ale brewed at Brighton.

TIPSTER, a "tout," or "turf" agent who collects early information of the condition and racing capabilities of horses in the training districts, and posts the same to his subscribers to guide their betting.

> "The racing TIPSTERS have much less patronage than formerly, before "Geoffrey Greenhorn" laid a trap for them, and published the tips he received in *The Life.* Professor Ingledue, M.A., the mesmerist, is silent; and if their subscribers, 'for whose interests I have collected my old and able staff, with many additional ones, who are already at work in the training districts,' could only get a sight of the 'old and able staff,' they would find it consisting of a man and a boy, 'at work' in the back room of a London public-house, and sending different winners for every race to their subscribers."—*Post and Paddock,* by the *Druid.*

TILL-BOY, an apprentice or shopman who makes free with the cash in his master's till.

"TIP THE DOUBLE," to "bolt," or run away from a creditor or officer. Sometimes TIP THE DOUBLE TO SHERRY, *i.e.*, to the sheriff.

TIP-TOP, first-rate, of the best kind.

TIP-TOPPER, a "swell," or dressy man, a "*Gorger*."

TIT, a favourite name for a horse.

TIT FOR TAT, an equivalent.

TITIVATE, to put in order, or dress up.

TITLEY, drink, generally applied to intoxicating beverages.

TITTER, a girl; "nark the TITTER," *i.e.*, look at the girl.—*Tramps' term*.

'TIZER, the *Morning Advertiser*.—*See* TAP TUB.

TIZZY, a sixpence. Corruption of TESTER.

TOAD-IN-THE-HOLE, a kind of pudding, consisting of a piece of meat surrounded with batter, and baked. Also, a term applied to advertising mediums.—*See* SANDWICH.

TOASTING-FORK, a regulation sword, indicative of the general uselessness of that weapon.

TODDLE, to walk as a child.

TO-DO, (pronounced quickly, and as one word,) a disturbance, trouble; "here's a pretty TO-DO," here is an unpleasant difficulty. This exactly tallies with the *French* word AFFAIRE (*à faire*).—*See Forby's Vocabulary of East Anglia*.

TOFF, a dandy, a swell of rank. Corruption probably of TUFT.—*See* TOFT.

TOFFER, a well-dressed "gay" woman.

TOFFICKY, dressy, showy.

TOFT, a showy individual, a SWELL, a person who, in a Yorkshireman's vocabulary, would be termed UPPISH.—*See* TUFT.

TOG, a coat. *Latin*, TOGA.—*Ancient Cant*.

TOG, to dress, or equip with an outfit; "TOGGED out to the nines," dressed in the first style.

TOGGERY, clothes, harness, domestic paraphernalia of any kind.

TOGS, clothes; "Sunday TOGS," best clothes. One of the oldest Cant words—in use in the time of Henry VIII.—*See* CANT.

TOKE, dry bread.

TOL-LOL, or TOL-LOLLISH, tolerable, or tolerably.

TOLL-SHOP, a Yorkshire correspondent gives this word as denoting in that county a prison, and also the following verse of a song, popular at fairs in the East Riding:—

> "But if ivver he get out agean,
> And can but raise a frind,
> Oh! the divel may tak' TOLL SHOP,
> At Beverley town-end!"

TOBY CONSARN, a highway expedition. TOBY is Old Cant.

TOBY, a road; "high TOBY," the turnpike road. "High TOBY spice," robbery on horseback.—*Don Juan*, canto xi., 19.

TOM AND JERRY, a low drinking shop. Probably some allusion to Pierce Egan's famous characters in his *Life in London.*

TOMBSTONE, a pawnticket—" In memory of," &c., a well-known Slang expression with those Londoners who are in the habit of following " My Uncle."

TOM-FOOL'S COLOURS, scarlet and yellow, the ancient motley. Occasionally as a rhyme,

> " Red and yellow,
> TOM FOOL'S colour."

A proposition is said to be TOM FOOL when it is too ridiculous to be entertained or discussed.

TOMMY.—*See* DICKEY.

TOMMY, bread,—generally a penny roll. Sometimes applied by workmen to the supply of food which they carry in a handkerchief as their daily allowance.

TOMMY, a truck, barter, the exchange of labour for goods, not money. Both term and practice general among English operatives for half-a-century.

TOMMY DODD, in tossing when the odd man goes out. A phrase in frequent use at the London Music Halls. Origin not known.

TOMMY-MASTER, one who pays his workmen in goods, or gives them tickets upon tradesmen, with whom he shares the profit.

TOMMY-SHOP, where wages are generally paid to mechanics or others, who are expected to " take out " a portion of the money in goods.

TOM-TOM, a street instrument, a kind of small drum beaten with the fingers, somewhat like the ancient tabor; a performer on this instrument. It was imported, doubtless, with the *Nigger* melodies, TOM-TOMS being a favourite instrument with the " darkies."

TOM TOPPER, a waterman, from a popular song, entitled, " *Overboard he vent.*"

TOM TUG, a waterman.

TONGUE, " to TONGUE a person," *i.e.*, talk him down. TONGUED, talkative.

TONY LUMPKIN, a young, clownish country fellow.

TOOL, " a poor TOOL," a bad hand at anything.

TOOL, to drive a mail coach, or any other vehicle.

TOOTH, " he has cut his eye TOOTH," *i.e.*, he is sharp enough, or old enough, to do so; " up in the TOOTH," far advanced in age,—said often of old maids. *Stable term* for aged horses which have lost the distinguishing mark in their teeth.

TOOTSIES, feet, those of ladies and children in particular. In married

TOOL, to pick pockets.

TOOL, a very little boy employed by burglars to put in at small apertures, so as to open a door for the larger thieves outside.

TOOLER, a pickpocket. MOLL-TOOLER, a female pickpocket.

life it is said the husband uses this expression for the first six months, after that he terms them HOOFS.

TOOZLE, to romp.—*Scotch.*

TOP, the signal among tailors and seamstresses for snuffing the candle; one cries TOP, and all the others follow, he who last pronounces the word has to snuff the candle.

TOP-HEAVY, drunk.

TOPPER, anything or person above the ordinary.

TOPPER, a blow on the head; "give him a TOPPER and chance it," "let him have a TOPPER for luck."—*Pugilistic Slang.*

TOP-SAWYER, the principal of a party, or profession. "A TOP-SAWYER signifies a man that is a master genius in any profession. It is a piece of *Norfolk* Slang, and took its rise from Norfolk being a great timber county, where the *top* sawyers get double the wages of those beneath them."—*Randal's Diary*, 1820.

TOPSY-TURVY, the bottom upwards. *Grose* gives an ingenious etymology of this once Cant term, viz., "*top-side turf-ways,*"—turf being always laid the wrong side upwards.

TO-RIGHTS, excellent, very well, or good.

TORMENTORS, the large iron flesh-forks used by cooks at sea.—*Sea.*

TORPIDS, the second-class race-boats at Oxford, answering to the Cambridge SLOGGERS.

TOSS, a measure of sprats.—*Billingsgate and Costermonger.*

TOT, a small glass; a "TOT O' WHISKY" is the smallest quantity sold.

TOUCH, a slang expression in common use in phrases which express the extent to which a person is interested or affected as "a fourpenny TOUCH," *i.e.*, costing that amount.—See an example in Mr, afterwards Sir Erasmus, Philipp's Diary, at Oxford, in 1720. (*Notes and Queries,* 2d series, p. 365.)

Sept. 21. "At night went to the ball at the Angel, *A Guinea Touch.*" It is also used at Eton in the sense of a "tip," or present of money.

TOUCHED, slightly intoxicated; also said of a consumptive person.

TOUCHER, "as near as a TOUCHER," as near as possible without actually touching.—*Coaching term.* The old jarveys, to shew their skill, used to drive against things so close as absolutely to *touch,* yet without injury. This they called a TOUCHER, or, TOUCH AND GO, which was hence applied to anything which was within an ace of ruin.

TOUCHY, peevish, irritable. *Johnson* terms it a low word.

TOUT, in sporting phraseology a TOUT signifies an agent in the training districts, on the look-out for information as to the condition and capabilities of those horses entered for a coming race.—*See* TIPSTER.

TOUT, to look out, or watch.—*Old Cant.*

TOPPED, hanged, or executed.

TOPS, dying speeches and gallows' broadsides.

TOSHERS, men who steal copper from ships' bottoms in the Thames.

TOUTER, a looker out, one who watches for customers, a hotel runner. A term in general use, derived from the old Cant word.

TOWEL, to beat or whip. In *Warwickshire* an oaken stick is termed a TOWEL—whence, perhaps, the vulgar verb.

TOWELLING, a rubbing down with an *oaken* TOWEL, a beating.

TOWN-LOUT, a derogatory title at Rugby School for those pupils who reside with their parents in the town, in contradistinction to those who live in the boarding-houses.

TOW-POWS, grenadiers.

TRACKS, " to make TRACKS," to run away.—*See* STREAK.

TRANSLATOR, a man who deals in old shoes or clothes, and refits them for cheap wear.

TRANSLATORS, second-hand boots mended and polished, and sold at a low price. Monmouth Street, Seven Dials, is a great market for TRANSLATORS.

TRANSMOGRIPHY, to alter or change.

TRAP, a "fast" term for a carriage of any kind. TRAPS, goods and chattels of any kind, but especially luggage and personal effects; in Australia, SWAG.

TRAP, "up to TRAP," knowing, wide awake,—synonymous with "up to SNUFF."

TRAP, a sheriff's officer.

TRAPESING, gadding or gossiping about in a slatternly way.—*North*. Generally applied to girls and women in low neighbourhoods whose clothes are carelessly fastened, causing them to trail on the ground.

TREE, "up a TREE," in temporary difficulties,—out of the way. *American expression*, derived from RACCOON or BEAR-HUNTING. When Bruin is TREED, or is forced UP A TREE by the dogs, it means that then the tug of war begins.—*See* 'COON. Hence when an opponent is fairly run to bay, and can by no evasion get off, he is said to be TREED. These expressions originated with Colonel Crockett, of Backwoods' celebrity. In *Scotland* the phrase is "up a CLOSE," *i.e.*, a passage out of the usual track, or removed from observation.

TRIANGLES, a Slang term for *delirium tremens*, during a fit of which everything appears out of the SQUARE.

TRIMMINGS, the necessary adjuncts to a cooked leg of mutton, as turnips, bread, beer, salt, &c. Bets are frequently made for a leg of mutton and TRIMMINGS. Or one person will forfeit the mutton if another will "stand the TRIMMINGS." It is generally a supper feast, held in a public house, and the rule is for the landlord to charge as TRIMMINGS everything, except the mutton, placed on the table previous to the removal of the cloth.

TRAVELLER, name given by one tramp to another. "A TRAVELLER at her Majesty's expense," *i.e.*, a transported felon, a convict.

TRINE, to hang.—*Ancient Cant*.

TRIPES, the bowels.
> "Next morning Miss Dolly complained of her TRIPES, Drinking cold water had given her the gripes."

TROLLING, sauntering or idling, hence TROLL and TROLLOCKS, an idle slut, a MOLL, which see.

TROLLY, or TROLLY-CARTS, term given by costermongers to a species of narrow cart, which can either be drawn by a donkey, or driven by hand

TROT, to "run up," to oppose, to bid against at an auction. Private buyers at auctions know from experience how general is the opposition against them from dealers, "knock-outs," and other *habitués* of sales who regard the rooms as their own peculiar domain; "we TROTTED him up nicely, didn't we?" *i.e.*, we made him (the private buyer) pay dearly for what he bought.

TROTTER, a tailor's man who goes round for orders.—*University.*

TROTTER CASES, shoes.

TROTTERS, feet. Sheep's TROTTERS, boiled sheep's feet, a favourite street delicacy.

TRUCK, a hat—from the cap on the extremity of a mast.—*Sea.*

TRUCK, to exchange or barter.

TRUCK-GUTTED, pot-bellied, corpulent.—*Sea.*

TRUCKS, trousers.

TRUMP, a good fellow; "a regular TRUMP," a jolly or good-natured person,—in allusion to a TRUMP card; "TRUMPS may turn up," *i.e.*, fortune may yet favour me.

TRUNKS, trousers—*Theatrical.*

TUBS, a butterman.

TUB-THUMPING, preaching or speech-making, from the old Puritan fashion of "holding forth" from a tub, or beer barrel, as a mark of their contempt for decorated pulpits.

TUCK, a schoolboy's term for fruit, pastry, &c. TUCK IN, or TUCK OUT, a good meal.

TUFTS, fellow-commoners, *i.e.*, students at the University, generally the sons of noblemen, who pay higher fees, dine with the Dons, and are distinguished by golden TUFTS, or tassels, in their caps.

TUFT-HUNTER, a hanger on to persons of quality or wealth—one who seeks the society of wealthy students. Originally *University Slang,* but now general.—*See* preceding.

TUMBLE, to comprehend or understand. A coster was asked what he thought of *Macbeth,*—"the witches and the fighting was all very well, but the other moves I couldn't TUMBLE to exactly; few on us can TUMBLE to the jaw-breakers; they licks us, they do."

TRUFF, to steal.—*North Country Cant.*

TUCK-UP-FAIR, the gallows. The notion of tucking up in connexion with hanging is derived from tucking up the bedclothes before going to sleep—the last preparation.

"TUNE THE OLD COW DIED OF," an epithet for any ill-played or discordant piece of music. Originally the name of an old ballad, alluded to in the dramatists of Shakspeare's time.

TUP, a young bullock. *Smithfield*, and drovers' term.

TURF, horse-racing, and betting thereon; "on the TURF," one who occupies himself with race-course business; said also of a street-walker, nymph of the *pavé*.

TURKEY MERCHANTS, dealers in plundered or contraband silk. Poulterers are sometimes termed TURKEY MERCHANTS in remembrance of Horne Tooke's answer to the boys at Eton, who wished in an aristocratic way to know who *his* father was: a TURKEY MERCHANT, replied Tooke—his father was a poulterer. TURKEY MERCHANT, also, was formerly Slang for a driver of turkeys or geese to market.

TURNIP, an old-fashioned watch, so called from its thickness.

TURN OUT, personal show or appearance; a man with a showy carriage and horses is said to have a good TURN OUT.

TURN-OVER, an apprentice who finishes with a second master the indentures he commenced with the first.

TURNPIKE SAILORS, beggars who go about dressed as sailors.

TURN UP, a street fight; a sudden leaving, or making off.

TURN UP, to appear unexpectedly.

TURN UP, to quit, change, abscond, or abandon; "Ned has TURNED UP," *i.e.*, run away; "I intend TURNING IT UP," *i.e.*, leaving my present abode, or altering my course of life. Also to happen; "let's wait, and see what will TURN UP."

TUSHEROON, a crown piece, five shillings.

TUSSLE, a pull, struggle, fight, or argument. *Johnson* and *Webster* call it a vulgar word.

TUSSLE, to struggle, or argue.

TWELVER, a shilling.

TWICE-LAID, a dish made out of cold fish and potatoes.—*Sea*. Compare BUBBLE AND SQUEAK and RESURRECTION PIE.

TWIG, style, *à la mode;* "get your strummel faked in TWIG," *i.e.*, have your hair dressed in style; PRIME TWIG, in good order and high spirits.—*Pugilistic*.

TWIG, "to hop the TWIG," to decamp, "cut one's stick," to die.

TURNED UP, to be stopped and searched by the police.

TURNED OVER, remanded by the magistrate or judge for want of evidence.

TURNER OUT, a coiner of bad money.

TWELVE GODFATHERS, a jury, because they give a name to the crime the prisoner before them has been guilty of; whether murder or manslaughter, felony or misdemeanour. Consequently it is a vulgar taunt to say, "You will be christened by TWELVE GODFATHERS some day before long."

TWIG, to understand, detect, or observe.

TWIST, brandy and gin mixed.

TWIST, capacity for eating, appetite; "Will's got a capital TWIST."

TWITCHETY, nervous, fidgety.

TWITTER, "all in a TWITTER," in a fright or fidgety state.

TWO-FISTED, expert at fisticuffs.

TWO-HANDED, awkward, a singular reversing of meaning.

TWOPENNY, the head; "tuck in your TWOPENNY," bend down your head.

TWOPENNY-HALFPENNY, paltry, insignificant. A TWOPENNY-HALFPENNY fellow, a not uncommon expression of contempt.

TWOPENNY-HOPS, low dancing rooms, the price of admission to which was formerly—and not infrequently now—twopence. The clog hornpipe, the pipe dance, flash jigs, and hornpipes in fetters, à la Jack Sheppard, are the favourite movements, all entered into with great spirit and "joyous, laborious capering."—*Mayhew*.

"TWO UPON TEN," or "TWO PUN' TEN," an expression used by assistants to each other, in shops, when a customer of suspected honesty makes his appearance. The phrase refers to "two eyes upon ten fingers," shortened as a money term to "TWO PUN' TEN." When a supposed thief is present, one shopman asks the other if that TWO PUN' (pound) TEN matter was ever settled. The man knows at once what is meant, and keeps a careful watch upon the person being served. If it is not convenient to speak, a piece of paper is handed to the same assistant, bearing the to him very significant amount of

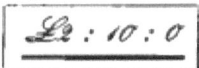

—*Compare* SHARP, JOHN ORDERLY.

TYBURNIA, the Portman and Grosvenor Square districts. It is facetiously divided by the Londoners into TYBURNIA FELIX, TYBURNIA DESERTA, and TYBURNIA SNOBBICA. The old gallows at Tyburn stood near the N.E. corner of Hyde Park, at the angle formed by the Edgware Road and the top of Oxford Street. In 1778 this was two miles out of London.

TYE, or TIE, a neckerchief. Proper hosier's term now, but Slang thirty years ago, and as early as 1718. Called also SQUEEZE.

TYKE, a clownish Yorkshireman.

TYPO, a printer.

UNBLEACHED AMERICAN, the new Yankee term for coloured natives of the United States, the word nigger being now voted low.

UNCLE, the pawnbroker.—*See* MY UNCLE.

TYBURN COLLAR, the fringe of beard worn under the chin.—*See* NEWGATE COLLAR.

UNBETTY, to unlock.—*See* BETTY.

"UNDER THE ROSE."—*See* ROSE.

UNICORN, a style of driving with two wheelers abreast and one leader—termed in the *United States* a SPIKE TEAM. TANDEM is one wheeler and one leader. RANDOM, three horses in line.—*See* HARUM-SCARUM.

UNLICKED, ill-trained, uncouth, rude, and rough; an UNLICKED CUB is a loutish youth who has never been taught manners; from the tradition that a bear's cub, when brought into the world, has no shape or symmetry until its dam licks it into form with her tongue.

UNUTTERABLES, or UNWHISPERABLES, trousers.—*See* INEXPRESSIBLES.

UP, "to be UP to a thing or two," to be knowing, or understanding; "to put a man UP to a move," to teach him a trick; "it's all UP with him," *i.e.*, it is all over with him, often pronounced U.P., naming the two letters separately; "UP a tree,"—*see* TREE; "UP TO TRAP," "UP TO SNUFF," wide awake, acquainted with the last new move; "UP to one's GOSSIP," to be a match for one who is trying to take you in; "UP TO SLUM," proficient in roguery, capable of committing a theft successfully; so also, "what's UP?" *i.e.*, what is the matter? what is the news?

U. P., United Presbyterian.—*Scotch clerical Slang.*

UPPER BENJAMIN, or BENJY, a great coat.

UPPER STORY, or UPPER LOFT, a person's head; "his UPPER STORY is unfurnished," *i.e.*, he does not know very much.

UPPISH, proud, arrogant.—*Yorkshire.*

USED UP, broken-hearted, bankrupt, fatigued, vanquished.

VAKEEL, a barrister.—*Anglo-Indian.*

VAMOS, VAMOUS, or VAMOOSH, to go, or be off. *Spanish*, VAMOS, "let us go!" Probably NAMUS, or NAMOUS, the costermonger's word, was from this, although it is generally considered back Slang.

VAMP, to spout, to leave in pawn.

VAMPS, old stockings. From VAMP, to piece.

VARDO, to look; "VARDO the cassey," look at the house. VARDO formerly was *Old Cant* for a waggon.

VARDY, verdict, vulgarly used as opinion, thus, "My VARDY on the matter is the same as yourn."

VARMENT, "you young VARMENT, you!" you bad, or naughty boy. Corruption of *vermin*.

VELVET, the tongue.

VERTICAL CARE-GRINDER, a Slang term for the treadmill.

VAMPERS, fellows who frequent public-houses and pick quarrels with the wearers of rings and watches, in hopes of getting up a fight, and so enabling their "pals" to steal the articles.

"UNDER THE SCREW," to be in prison.

UPTUCKER, the hangman, Jack Ketch.—*See* TUCK-UP.

VARNISHER, an utterer of false sovereigns.

VIC., the Victoria Theatre, London,—patronised principally by coster-mongers and low people; also the street abbreviation of the Christian name of her Majesty the Queen.

VILLAGE, or THE VILLAGE, *i.e.*, London.—*Sporting*. Also a Cambridge term for a disreputable suburb of that town, viz., Barnwell, generally styled "*the* VILLAGE."

VILLE, or VILE, a town or village—pronounced *phial*, or *vial*.—*French*.

VINNIED, mildewed, or sour.—*Devonshire*.

VOKER, to talk; "can you VOKER Romany?" can you speak the canting language?—*Latin*, VOCARE; *Spanish*, VOCEAR.

VOWEL, "to VOWEL a debt" is to pay with an I O U.

WABBLE, to move from side to side, to roll about. *Johnson* terms it a "low, barbarous word."—*See* the following.

WABLER, a foot soldier, a term of contempt used by a cavalryman.

WALKER, a letter-carrier or postman.

WALKER! or HOOKEY WALKER! an ejaculation of incredulity, said when a person is telling a story which you know to be all gammon, or false. The *Saturday Reviewer's* explanation of the phrase is this:—"Years ago there was a person named *Walker*, an aquiline-nosed Jew, who exhibited an orrery, which he called by the erudite name of *Eidouranion*. He was also a popular lecturer on astronomy, and often invited his pupils, telescope in hand, to *take a sight* at the moon and stars. The lecturer's phrase struck his school-boy auditory, who frequently 'took a sight' with that gesture of outstretched arm and adjustment to nose and eye which was the first garnish of the popular saying. The next step was to assume phrase and gesture as the outward and visible mode of knowingness in general." A correspondent, however, denies this, and states that HOOKEY WALKER was a magistrate of dreaded acuteness and incredulity, whose hooked nose gave the title of BEAK to all his successors; and, moreover, that the gesture of applying the thumb to the nose and agitating the little finger, as an expression of "Don't you wish you may get it?" is considerably older than the story in the *Saturday Review* would seem to indicate. There is a third explanation of HOOKEY WALKER in *Notes and Queries*, iv., 425.

"WALKING THE PEGS," a method of cheating at the game of cribbage, by a species of legerdemain, the sharper either moving his own pegs forward, or those of his antagonist backward, according to the state of the game.

WALK INTO, to overcome, to demolish; "I'll WALK INTO his affections," *i.e.*, I will scold or thrash him. The word DRIVE (which *see*) is used in an equally curious sense in Slang speech. WALK INTO also means to get into the debt of any one, as, "he WALKED INTO THE AFFECTIONS of all the tradesmen in the neighbourhood."

WALK OVER, a re-election without opposition.—*Parliamentary*, but derived from the *Turf*, where a horse which has no rivals entered WALKS OVER the course, and wins without exertion.

"WALK THE BARBER," to lead a girl astray.

"WALK YOUR CHALKS," be off, or run away,—spoken sharply by any one who wishes to get rid of a troublesome person.—*See* CHALKS.

WALL-FLOWER, a person who goes to a ball, and looks on without dancing, either from choice or not being able to obtain a partner.

WALL-FLOWERS, left-off and "regenerated" clothes exposed for sale on the bunks and shop-boards of Monmouth Street.

WALLOP, to beat, or thrash. Mr John Gough Nichols derives this word from an ancestor of the Earl of Portsmouth's, one Sir John Wallop, Knight of the Garter, who in King Henry VIII.'s time distinguished himself by WALLOPING the French; but it is more probably connected with WEAL, a livid swelling in the skin after a blow.—*See* POT-WALLOPER.

WALLOPING, a beating or thrashing; sometimes used in an adjective sense, as big, or very large.

WAPPING, or WHOPPING, of a large size, great.

WARM, rich, or well off.

WARM, to thrash, or beat; "I'll WARM your jacket." To WARM the wax of one's ear is to give a severe blow on the side of the head.

WARMING-PAN, a large old-fashioned watch. A person placed in an office to hold it for another.—*See* W. P.

WAR PAINT, military uniform.

WASH, "it won't WASH," *i.e.*, will not stand investigation, will not "bear the rub," is not genuine, can't be believed.

WATCH AND SEALS, a sheep's head and pluck.

WATER-BEWITCHED, very weak tea, the third brew, (or the first at some houses;) grog much diluted.

WATER-DOGS, Norfolk dumplings.

WATER OF LIFE, gin. Apparently from *eau de vie*.

WATERMAN, a light blue silk handkerchief. The Oxford and Cambridge boats' crews always wear these—light blue for Cambridge, and a darker shade for Oxford.

"WATER THE DRAGON," "WATER ONE'S NAG," hints for retiring.

WATTLES, ears.

WAXY, cross, ill-tempered.

WEATHER-HEADED, so written by *Sir Walter Scott* in his *Peveril of the Peak*, but it is more probably WETHER-HEADED, as applied to a person having a "sheepish" look.

WEAVING, a notorious card-sharping trick, done by keeping certain cards on the knee, or between the knee and the underside of the table, and using them when required by changing them for the cards held in the hand.

"WEAVING LEATHERN APRONS." When a knowing blade is asked what he has been doing lately, and does not choose to tell, his reply is, that he has been very busy WEAVING LEATHERN APRONS.—(*See* news-

---

WATCHMAKER, a pickpocket or stealer of watches.

paper reports of the trial for the gold robberies on the South-Western Railway.) Other similar replies, "I have been MAKING A TRUNDLE FOR A GOOSE'S EYE," or "A WHIM-WHAM TO BRIDLE A GOOSE."

WEDGE, silver.—*Old Cant.*

WEDGE-FEEDER, a silver spoon.

WEED, a cigar; *the* WEED, tobacco generally.

WEED, a hat-band.

WEJEE, a chimney-pot. Often applied to any clever invention, as "that' a regular WEJEE."

WELCHER, a person who makes a bet without the remotest chance of being able to pay, and, losing it, absconds, or "makes himself scarce." In the betting ring a WELCHER is often very severely handled upon his swindling practices being discovered. The Catterick "Clerk of the Course," once provided some stout labourers and a tar-barrel for the special benefit of the WELCHERS who might visit that neighbourhood The word is modern, but the practice is ancient.

> "One Moore, the unworthy incumbent of the 'Suffolk Curacy,' dedicated book to 'Duke Humphrey,' and was then entirely lost sight of by his old college friends, till one of them espied him slung up in 'the basket,' for not paying his bets at a cock-pit."—*Post and Paddock.*

WELL, to pocket, or place as in a well.

WEST CENTRAL, a water-closet, the initials being the same as those of the London Postal District. It is said that for this reason very delicate people refuse to obey Rowland Hill's instructions in this particular An old maid, who lived in this district, was particularly shocked at having w.c. marked on all her letters, and informed the letter-carrier that she could not think of submitting to such an indecent fashion On being informed that the letters would not be forwarded without the obnoxious initials, she remarked that she would have them left at the Post-Office. "Then, marm," said the fellow, with a grin, "they will put P.O. on them, which will be more 'ondacenter than the tother.'"

WET, a drink, a "drain."

WET, to drink. Low people generally ask an acquaintance to WET any recently-purchased article, *i.e.*, to stand treat on the occasion; "WET your whistle," *i.e.*, take a drink; "WET the other eye," *i.e.*, take another glass.—*See* SHED A TEAR.

WET QUAKER, a drunkard of that sect; a man who pretends to be religious, and is a dram-drinker on the sly.

WET 'UN, a diseased cow, unfit for human food, but nevertheless sold to make into sausages.—*Compare* STAGGERING-BOB.

WHACK, a share or lot; "give me my WHACK," give me my share.—*Scotch* SWEG, or SWACK.

WHACK, or WHACKING, a blow, or a thrashing.

WHACK, to beat.

WHACKING, large, fine, or strong.

WHALE, "very like a WHALE in a teacup," said of anything that is very improbable; taken from a speech of Polonius's in *Hamlet.*

"WHAT D'YE CALL 'EM, a similar expression to THINGUMY.

WHEEDLE, to entice by soft words. "This word cannot be found to derive itself from any other, and is therefore looked upon as wholly invented by the CANTERS."—*Triumph of Wit*, 1705.

WHERRET, or WORRIT, to scold, trouble, or annoy.—*Old English.*

WHID, a word.—*Old Gipsy Cant.*

WHID, a fib, a falsehood, a word too much.—*Modern Slang* from the *Ancient Cant.*

WHIDDLE, to enter into a parley, or hesitate with many words, &c.; to inform, or discover.—*See* WHEEDLE.

WHIM-WHAM, an alliterative term, synonymous with FIDDLE-FADDLE, RIFF-RAFF, &c., denoting nonsense, rubbish, &c.

WHIP, after the usual allowance of wine is drunk at mess, those who wish for more put a shilling each into a glass handed round to procure a further supply.—*Naval and Military.*

WHIP, to "WHIP anything up," to take it up quickly; from the method of hoisting heavy goods or horses on board ship by a WHIP, or running tackle, from the yard-arm. Generally used to express anything dishonestly taken.—*L'Estrange* and *Johnson.*

WHIP JACK, a sham shipwrecked sailor, called also a TURNPIKE SAILOR.

"WHIP THE CAT," when an operative works at a private house by the day. Term used amongst tailors and carpenters.

WHIPPER-IN, the member of the House of Commons whose duty it is to collect and keep together his party to vote at divisions. To give him greater influence, the ministerial WHIPPER-IN holds, or is supposed to hold, the minor patronage of the Treasury.—*See* WOODEN SPOON.

WHIPPER-SNAPPER, a waspish, diminutive person.

WHISKER. There is a curious Slang phrase connected with this word. When an improbable story is told, the remark is, "the mother of that was a WHISKER," meaning it is a lie.

WHISTLE, "as clean as a WHISTLE," neatly, or "SLICKLY done," as an American would say; "to WET ONE'S WHISTLE," to take a drink. This last is a very old expression. *Chaucer* says of the Miller of Trumpington's wife (*Canterbury Tales*, 4153)—

"So was hir joly WHISTAL well Y-WET;"

"to WHISTLE FOR ANYTHING," to stand small chance of getting it, from the nautical custom of WHISTLING for a wind in a calm, which of course comes none the sooner for it.

WHITECHAPEL, or WESTMINSTER BROUGHAM, a costermonger's donkey-barrow.

WHITECHAPEL, the "upper-cut," or strike.—*Pugilistic.*

WHITECHAPEL, in tossing, two out of three wins.—*See* SUDDEN DEATH.

WHITECHAPEL FORTUNE, a clean gown and a pair of pattens.

WHITE FEATHER, "to shew the WHITE FEATHER," to evince cowardice. In times when great attention was paid to the breeding of game-cocks, a white feather in the tail was considered a proof of cross-breeding.

WHITE LIE, a harmless lie, one told to reconcile people at variance; "mistress is not at home, sir," is a WHITE LIE often told by servants

WHITE-LIVERED, or LIVER-FACED, cowardly, much afraid, very mean.

WHITE PROP, a diamond pin.—*East London.*

WHITE SATIN, gin,—term amongst women.—*See* SATIN.

WHITE SERJEANT, a man's superior officer in the person of his better-half.

WHITE TAPE, gin,—term used principally by female servants.—*See* RIBBON.

WHITEWASH, when a person has taken the benefit of the Insolvent Act he is said to have been WHITEWASHED.

WHITEWASH, a glass of sherry as a finale, after drinking port and claret.

WHITE WINE, the fashionable term for gin.
"Jack Randall then impatient rose,
And said, 'Tom's speech were just as fine
If he would call that first of GO's
By that genteeler name—WHITE WINE."
Randall's Diary, 1820.

WHOP, to beat, or hide. Corruption of WHIP; sometimes spelled WAP.

WHOP-STRAW, Cant name for a countryman; *Johnny* WHOP-STRAW, in allusion to threshing

WHOPPER, a big one, a lie.

WIDDLE, to shine.—*See* OLIVER.

WIDE-AWAKE, a broad-brimmed felt, or stuff hat,—so called because it never had a *nap*, and never wants one.

WIDO, wide awake, no fool.

WIFFLE-WOFFLES, in the dumps, sorrow, stomach ache.

WIG, move off, go away.—*North Country Cant.*

WIGGING, a rebuke before comrades. If the head of a firm calls a clerk into the parlour, and rebukes him, it is an EARWIGGING; if done before the other clerks, it is a WIGGING.

WILD, a village.—*Tramps' term.*—*See* VILE.

WILD, vexed, cross, passionate,—said to be from WILLED (SELF-WILLED) in opposition to "tamed" or "subdued." In the United States the word *mad* is supplemented with a vulgar meaning similar to our Cockneyism WILD; and to make a man MAD on the other side of the Atlantic is to vex him, or "rile" his temper—not to render him a raving maniac, or a fit subject for Bedlam.

WILD OATS, youthful pranks.

WILLIAM, a bill. The derivation is obvious.

WIFE, a fetter fixed to one leg.—*Prison.*

WIND, "to raise the WIND," to procure money; "to slip one's WIND," coarse expression meaning to die.—*See* RAISE.

WIND, "I'll WIND your cotton," *i.e.*, I will give you some trouble. The Byzantine General, Narses, used the same kind of threat to the Greek Empress,—" I will spin such a thread that they shall not be able to unravel."

WINDOWS, the eyes, or "peepers."

WINEY, intoxicated.

WINKIN, "he went off like WINKIN," *i.e.*, very quickly. Probably connected with WINK, to shut the eye quickly.

WINKS, periwinkles.

WINN, a penny.—*Ancient Cant.*—*See ante*, page 20.

WIPE, a pocket-handkerchief.—*Old Cant.*

WIPE, a blow. Frequently sibilated to SWIPE, a cricket term.

WIPE, to strike; "he fetcht me a WIPE over the knuckles," he struck me on the knuckles; "to WIPE a person down," to flatter or pacify; to WIPE off a score, to pay one's debts, in allusion to the slate or chalk methods of account-keeping; "to WIPE a person's eye," to shoot game which he has missed—*Sporting term;* hence to obtain an advantage by superior activity. With old topers "WIPING ONE'S EYE," is equivalent to giving or taking another drink.

WIRE-IN, a London street phrase in general use at the present time, the meaning of which I have not been able to discover.

WOBBLE-SHOP, where beer is sold without a licence.

WOODEN SPOON, the last junior optime who takes a University degree; denoting one who is only fit to stay at home, and stir porridge.—*Cambridge.* The expression is also *Parliamentary Slang.*—*See* the following:—

> "WOODEN SPOON.—We have said that a rigorous account is kept of all the divisions, and that every vote of every member of the Government is posted. We will now tell our readers what is done with this list. Every year at the close of the session, as our readers know, the Ministers dine together at the Trafalgar. Well, after dinner, the chief whip produces his account and reads it aloud; and it is said that the man whose name appears in the division-list the smallest number of times has a WOODEN SPOON presented to him. When the Derbyites were in power last, Sir John Pakington, it is asserted, was the successful candidate for the SPOON, Mr Whiteside presenting it to the right honourable Baronet with infinite humour and fun. Why a wooden spoon is used we cannot tell. Perhaps in ancient times the poor man got that and nothing else. If any of our readers should be curious to know what is really symbolised by this ceremony, let them understand that we cannot help them. We refer them to the editor of *Notes and Queries*."—*Illustrated Times.*

WOODEN SURTOUT, a coffin, generally spoken of as a wooden surtout with nails for buttons.

WINDED-SETTLED, transported for life.

WIRE, a thief with long fingers, expert at picking ladies' pockets

WOODEN WEDGE, the last name in the classical honours list at Cambridge. The last in mathematical honours had long been known as the WOODEN SPOON; but when the classical Tripos was instituted, in 1824, it was debated among the undergraduates what *sobriquet* should be given to the last on the examination list. Curiously enough, the name that year which happened to be last was WEDGEWOOD (a distinguished Wrangler.) Hence the title.

The "Wedge" and the "Spoon.

WOOLBIRD, a lamb; "wing of a WOOLBIRD," a shoulder of lamb.

WOOL-GATHERING, said of any person's wits when they are wandering or in a reverie.—*Florio.*

WOOL-HOLE, the workhouse.

WOOLLY, out of temper.

WOOLLY, a blanket.

WORK, to plan, or lay down and execute any course of action, to perform anything; "to WORK the BULLS," *i.e.*, to get rid of false crown pieces "to WORK the ORACLE," to succeed by manœuvring, to concert a wily plan, to victimise,—a possible reference to the stratagems and bribes used to corrupt the *Delphic oracle*, and cause it to deliver a favourable response. "To WORK a street or neighbourhood," trying at each house to sell all one can, or so bawling that every housewife may know what you have to sell. The general plan is to drive a donkey barrow a short distance, and then stop and cry. The term implies thoroughness; to "WORK a street well" is a common saying with a coster.

WORM.—*See* PUMP.

WORM, the latest Slang term for a policeman.

WORMING, removing the beard of an oyster or muscle.

W. P., or WARMING-PAN, a clergyman who holds a living *pro tempore* under a bond of resignation, is styled a W. P., or WARMING-PAN rector because he keeps the place warm for his successor.—*Clerical Slang.*

WRINKLE, an idea, or fancy; an additional piece of knowledge which is supposed to be made by a WRINKLE *à posteriori.*

WRITE, "to WRITE ONE'S NAME on a joint," to have the first cut at anything; leaving sensible traces of one's presence on it.

WYLO, be off.—*Anglo-Chinese.*

WOOL, courage, pluck; "you are not half-WOOLED," term of reproach from one thief to another.

X, LETTER X, a method of arrest used by policemen with desperate ruffians —by getting a firm grasp on the collar, and drawing the captive's hand over the holding arm, and pressing the fingers down in a peculiar way —the captured person's arm in this way can be more easily broken than extricated

YAFFLE, to eat.—*Old English.*

YAM, to eat. This word is used by the lowest class all over the world; by the Wapping sailor, West India negro, or Chinese coolie. When the fort, called the Dutch Folly, near Canton, was in course of erection by the Hollanders, under the pretence of being intended for an hospital, the Chinese observed a box containing muskets among the alleged hospital stores. "Hy-aw!" exclaimed John Chinaman, "how can sick man YAM gun?" The Dutch were surprised and massacred the same night.

"YARD OF CLAY," a long, old-fashioned tobacco pipe, also called a CHURCH-WARDEN.

YARMOUTH CAPON, a bloater, or red herring.—*Old.*—*Ray's Proverbs.*

YARMOUTH MITTENS, bruised hands.—*Sea.*

YARN, a long story, or tale; "a tough YARN," a tale hard to be believed; "spin a YARN," tell a tale.—*Sea.*

YAY-NAY, "a poor YAY-NAY" fellow, one who has no conversational power, and can only answer *yea* or *nay* to a question.

YELLOW-BELLY, a native of the Fens of Lincolnshire, or the Isle of Ely,—in allusion to the frogs and a yellow-bellied eel caught there; they are also said to be *web-footed.*

YELLOW-BOY, a sovereign, or any gold coin.

YELLOW-GLOAK, a jealous man.

YELLOW-JACK, the yellow fever prevalent in the West Indies.

YELLOW-MAN, a yellow silk handkerchief.—*Pugilistic* and *Sporting.*

YOKEL, a countryman.—*West.*

YOKUFF, a chest, or large box.

YORKSHIRE, "to YORKSHIRE," or "come YORKSHIRE over any person," to cheat or BITE them.—*North.* The proverbial overreaching of the rustics of this county has given rise to this phrase, which is sometimes pronounced YORSHAR. "YORSHAR, to put YORKSHIRE to a man, is to trick or deceive him."—*Lancashire Dialect,* 1757.

YORKSHIRE COMPLIMENT, a gift of something of no manner of use to the giver.

YORKSHIRE ESTATES; "I will do it when I come into my YORKSHIRE ESTATES,"—meaning if I ever have the money or the means. The phrase is said to have originated with *Dr Johnson.*

YORKSHIRE, YORKSHIRE BECKONING, where every one pays his own.

YOUNKER, in street language, a lad or a boy. Term in general use amongst costermongers, cabmen, and old-fashioned people. *Barnefield's Affectionate Shepherd,* 1594, has the phrase, "a seemelie YOUNKER." *Danish* and *Friesic,* JONKER. In the *Navy,* a naval cadet is usually termed a YOUNKER.

YOUR NIBS, yourself.

YACK, a watch; to "church a YACK," to take it out of its case to avoid detection.

ZIPH, LANGUAGE OF, a way of disguising English in use among the students at *Winchester College.* Compare MEDICAL GREEK. *De Quincey*, in his *Autobiographic Sketches*, (Edin. 1853, p. 209,) says that he acquired this language as a boy, from a Dr Mapleton, who had three sons at Winchester who had imported it from thence as their sole accomplishment, and that after the lapse of fifty years he could, and did with Lord Westport, converse in it with ease and rapidity. It was communicated at Winchester to new-comers for a fixed fee of half a guinea. The secret is this,—repeat the vowel or diphthong of every syllable, prefixing to the vowel so repeated the letter G, and placing the accent on the intercalated syllable. Thus, for example, "Shall we go away in an hour?" "SHAGALL WEGE GOGO AGAWAGAY IGIN HOUGOUR?" "Three hours we have already staid," "THREEGEE HOUGOURS WEGE HAGAVE AGALREAGEADYGY STAGAID." Evidently any consonant will answer the purpose, F or L would be softer and so far better.—*See* GIBBERISH. A correspondent says this system is not confined to Winchester College, and has much the appearance of a bequest of ancient times. It is recorded and accurately described amongst many other modes of cryptical communication, oral and visual, spoken written, and symbolic, in an "*Essay towards a Real Character and a Philosophic Language,*" (founded on or suggested by a treatise published just before, by Geo. Dalgarne,) *by John Wilkins, Bishop of Chester*, published by order of the Royal Society, fol. 1668, and as the bishop does not speak of it as a recent invention, it may probably at that time have been regarded as an antique device for conducting a conversation in secrecy amongst bystanders.

ZOUNDS! a sudden exclamation—abbreviation of *God's wounds.*

YOXTER, a convict returned from transportation before his time.

ZIFF, a juvenile thief.

SOME ACCOUNT

OF

THE BACK SLANG,

THE SECRET LANGUAGE OF COSTERMONGERS.

The costermongers of London number between thirty and forty thousand. Like other low tribes, they boast a language, or secret tongue, in which they hide their earnings, movements, and other private affairs. This costers' speech offers no new fact, or approach to a fact, for philologists; it is not very remarkable for originality of construction; neither is it spiced with low humour, as other Cant. But the costermongers boast that it is known only to themselves; that it is far beyond the Irish, and puzzles the Jews.

The main principle of this language is spelling the words backwards,—or rather, pronouncing them rudely backwards. Sometimes, for the sake of harmony, an extra syllable is prefixed or annexed; and occasionally the word is given quite a different turn in rendering it backwards, to what an uninitiated person would have expected. One coster told Mayhew that he often gave the end of a word "a new turn, just as if he chorused it with a tol-de-rol." Besides, the coster has his own idea of the *proper* way of spelling words, and is not to be convinced but by an overwhelming show of learning,—and frequently not then, for he is a very headstrong fellow. By the time a coster has spelt an ordinary word of two or three syllables in the proper way, and then spelt it backwards, it has become a tangled knot that no etymologist could unravel. The word GENERALISE, for instance, is considered to be "shilling" spelt backwards. Sometimes Slang and Cant words are introduced, and even these, when imagined to be tolerably well known, are pronounced backwards. Other terms, such as GEN, a shilling, and FLATCH, a halfpenny, help to confuse the outsider.

After a time, this back language, or BACK SLANG, as it is called by the costermongers themselves, comes to be regarded by the rising generation of street-sellers as a distinct and regular mode of speech. They never refer words, by inverting them, to their originals; and the YENEPS, ESCLOPS, and NAMOWS, are looked upon as proper, but secret terms. "But it is a curious fact, that lads who become costermongers' boys, without previous association with the class, acquire a very ready command of the language, and this though they are not only unable to spell, but 'don't know a letter in a book.'"* They soon obtain a considerable stock vocabulary, so that they converse rather from the memory than the understanding. Amongst the senior costermongers, and those who pride themselves on their proficiency in BACK SLANG, a conversation is often sustained for a whole evening, especially if any "flatties" are present whom they wish to astonish or confuse. The women use it sparingly, but the girls are generally well acquainted with it.

The addition of an *s*, I should state, always forms the plural, so that this is another source of complication. For instance, *woman* in the BACK SLANG is NAMOW, and NAMUS, or NAMOWS, is *women*, not NEMOW. The explorer, then, in undoing the BACK SLANG, and turning the word NAMUS once more into English, would have *suman*,—a novel and very extraordinary rendering of *women*. Where a word is refractory in submitting to a back rendering, as in the case of *pound*, letters are made to change positions for the sake of harmony; thus, we have DUNOP, a pound, instead of *dnuop*, which nobody could pleasantly pronounce. This will remind the reader of the Jews' "*old clo'! old clo'!*" instead of *old*

* *Mayhew*, vol. i, p. 24.

clothes, old clothes, which would tire even the patience of a Jew to repeat all day.

This singular BACK tongue has been in vogue about twenty-five years. It is, as before stated, soon acquired, and is principally used by the costermongers (as the specimen Glossary will shew) for communicating the secrets of their street tradings, the cost and profit of the goods, and for keeping their natural enemies, the police, in the dark. COOL THE ESCLOP (look at the police) is often said among them, when one of the constabulary makes his appearance.

Perhaps on no subject is the costermonger so silent as on his money affairs. All costs and profits, he thinks, should be kept profoundly secret. The Back Slang, therefore, gives the various small amounts very minutely:—

FLATCH, halfpenny.
YENEP, penny.
OWT-YENEPS, twopence.
ERTH-YENEPS, threepence.
ROUF-YENEPS, fourpence.
EVIF, or EWIF-YENEPS, fivepence.
EXIS-YENEPS, sixpence.
NEVIS-YENEPS, sevenpence.
TEAICH, or THEG-YENEPS, eightpence.
ENIN-YENEPS, ninepence.
NET-YENEPS, tenpence.
NEVELÉ-YENEPS, elevenpence.
EVLÉNET-YENEPS, twelvepence.
GEN, or GENERALISE, one shilling, or twelvepence.
YENEP-FLATCH, three halfpence.
OWT-YENEP-FLATCH, twopence halfpenny.
&c. &c. &c.
GEN, or ENO-GEN, one shilling.
OWT-GENS, two shillings.
ERTH-GENS, three shillings.

The GENS continue in the same sequence as the YENEPS above, excepting THEG-GENS, 8s., which is usually rendered

THEG-GUY,—a deviation with ample precedents in all civilised tongues.

>YENORK, a crown piece, or five shillings.
>FLATCH-YENORK, half-a-crown.

Beyond this amount the costermonger reckons after an intricate and complicated mode. Fifteen shillings would be ERTH-EVIF-GENS, or, literally, three times 5s.; seventeen shillings would be ERTH-YENORK-FLATCH, or three crowns and a half; or, by another mode of reckoning, ERTH-EVIF-GENS FLATCH-YENORK, *i.e.*, three times 5s., and half-a-crown.

>DUNOP, a pound.

Further than which the costermonger seldom goes in money reckoning.

In the following Glossary only those words are given which costermongers continually use,—the terms connected with street traffic, the names of the different coins, vegetables, fruit, and fish, technicalities of police courts, &c.

The reader might naturally think that a system of speech so simple as the BACK SLANG would require no Glossary; but he will quickly perceive, from the specimens given, that a great many words in frequent use in a BACK sense, have become so twisted as to require a little glossarial explanation.

This kind of Slang, formed by reversing and transposing the letters of a word, is not peculiar to the London costermongers. Instances of an exactly similar secret dialect are found in the Spanish GERMANIA and French ARGOT. Thus:—

Spanish.	*Germania.*	*English.*
PLATO.	TAPLO.	PLATE.
DEMIA.	MEDIA.	STOCKINGS.

French.	*Argot.*	*English.*
F'OL.	LOFFE.	FOOLISH.
LORCEFE.	LA FORCE.	LA FORCE, the prison of that name.

INDIAN BACK SLANG.

The Bazeegars, a wandering tribe of jugglers in India, form a BACK SLANG, on the basis of the Hindustanee, in the following manner:—

Hindustanee.	Bazeegar.	English.
AG.	GA.	FIRE.
LAMBA.	BALUM.	LONG.
DUM.	MUDU.	BREATH.

GLOSSARY OF THE BACK SLANG.

BIRK, a "crib,"—house.

COOL, to look.

COOL HIM, look at him. A phrase frequently used when one costermonger warns another of the approach of a policeman.

DAB, bad. Also, a bed, pronounced "bad."

DABHENO, one bad, or a bad market.—*See* DOOGHENO.

DAB TROS, a bad sort.

DA-ERB, bread.

DEB, or DAB, a bed; "I'm on to the DEB," I'm going to bed.

DILLO NAMO, an old woman.

DLOG, gold.

DOOG, good.

DOOGHENO, literally "one good," or "good-one," but implying generally a good market.

DOOGHENO HIT, one good hit. A coster remarks to a "mate," "*Jack made a* DOOGHENO HIT *this morning,*" implying that he did well at market, or sold out with good profit.

DUNOP, a pound.

ERTH, three.

EARTH * GENS, three shillings.

EARTH SITH-NOMS, three months.

EARTH YANNOPS, or YENEPS, threepence.

EDGABAC, cabbage.

EDGENARO, an orange.

E-FINK, knife.

EKAME, a "make," or swindle.

EKOM, a "moke," or donkey.

ELRIG, a girl.

ENIF, fine.

ENIN GENS, nine shillings.

ENIN YENEP, ninepence.

ENIN YANNOPS, or YENEPS, ninepence.

ENO, one.

ERIF, fire.

ERTH GENS, three shillings.

* My informant preferred EARTH to ERTH,—for the reason, he said, "that it looked more sensible!"

ERTH-PU, three-up, a street game.

ERTH SITH-NOMS, three months,—a term of imprisonment unfortunately very familiar to the lower orders.

ERTH-YENEPS, threepence.

ESCLOP, the police.

ES-ROPH, or ES-ROCH, a horse.

EVIF-YENEPS, fivepence.

EVLENET-GENS, twelve shillings.

EVLENET SITH-NOMS, twelve months.

EWIF-GENS, a crown, or five shillings.

EWIF-YENEPS, fivepence.

EXIS GENS, six shillings.

EXIS-EWIF-GENS, six times five shillings, *i.e.*, 30s. All moneys may be reckoned in this manner, either with YENEPS or GENS.

EXIS-EVIF YENEPS, elevenpence,—literally, "sixpence and fivepence = elevenpence." This mode of reckoning, distinct from the preceding, is also common amongst those who use the Back Slang.

EXIS SITH-NOMS, sixth months.

EXIS-YENEPS, sixpence.

FI-HEATH, a thief.

FLATCH, a half, or halfpenny.

FLATCH KEN-NURD, half drunk.

FLATCH YENEP, a halfpenny.

FLATCH-YENORK, half-a-crown.

GEN, twelvepence, or one shilling. Possibly an abbreviation of ARGENT, Cant term for silver.—*See* following.

GENERALISE, a shilling, generally shortened to GEN.

GEN-NET, or NET GENS, ten shillings.

HEL-BAT, a table.

HELPA, an apple.

KENNETSEENO, stinking.

KENNURD, drunk.

KEW, a week.

KEWS, or SKEW, weeks.

KIRB, a brick.

KOOL, to look.

LAWT, tall.

LEVEN, in Back Slang, is sometimes allowed to stand for *eleven*, for the reason that it is a number which seldom occurs. An article is either 10d. or 1s.

LUR-AC-HAM, mackerel.

MOTTAB, bottom.
MUR, rum.
NALE, or NAEL, lean.
NAM, a man.
NAMESCLOP, a policeman.—*See* ESCLOP.
NAMOW, a woman; DILO NAMOW, an old woman.
NEERGS, greens.
NETENIN GENS, nineteen shillings.
NEETEWIF GENS, fifteen shillings.
NEETEXIS, or NETEXIS GENS, sixteen shillings.
NETNEVIS GENS, seventeen shillings.
NET-THEG GENS, eighteen shillings.
NEETRITH GENS, thirteen shillings.
NEETROUF GENS, fourteen shillings.
NET-GEN, ten shillings, or half a sovereign.
NET-YENEPS, tenpence.
NEVELE GENS, eleven shillings.
NEVELE YENEPS, elevenpence,—generally LEVEN YENEPS.
NEVIS GENS, seven shillings.
NEVIS STRETCH, seven years' transportation, or imprisonment.—*See* STRETCH, in the *Slang Dictionary*.
NEVIS YENEPS, sevenpence.
NIRE, rain.
NIG, gin.
NI-OG OT TAKRAM, going to market.
NITRAPH, a farthing.
NOL, long.
NOOM, the moon.
NOS-RAP, a parson.
OCCABOT, tobacco; "tib of OCCABOT," bit of tobacco.
ON, no.
ON DOOG, no good.
OWT GENS, two shillings.
OWT YENEPS, twopence.
PAC, a cap.
PINURT POTS, turnip tops.
POT, top.
RAPE, a pear.
REEB, beer.
REV-LIS, silver.

ROUF-EFIL, for life,—sentence of punishment.
ROUF-GENS, four shillings.
ROUF-YENEPS, fourpence.
RUTAT, or RATTAT, a "tatur," or potato.
SAY, yes.
SEE-O, shoes.
SELOPAS, apples.
SHIF, fish.
SIR-ETCH, cherries.
SITH-NOM, a month.
SLAOC, coals.
SLOP, a policeman.—*See* under this term in the *Dictionary of Slang and Cant Words*.
SNEERG, greens.
SOUSH, a house.
SPINSRAP, parsnips.
SRES-WORT, trousers.
STARPS, sprats.
STOOB, boots.
STORRAC, carrots.
STUN, nuts.
STUNLAWS, walnuts.
SWRET-SIO, oysters.
TACH, a hat.
TAF, or TAFFY, fat.
THEG, or TEAICH GENS, eight shillings.
TEAICH-GUY, eight shillings,—a slight deviation from the numerical arrangement of GENS.
TENIP, a pint.
THEG YENEPS, eightpence.
TIB, a bit, or piece.
TOAC, or TOG, a coat. TOG is the *Old Cant* term.—*See* the *Dictionary of Slang*, &c.
TOAC-TISAW, a waistcoat.
TOL, lot, stock, or share.
TOP O' REEB, a pot of beer.
TOP-YOB, a pot-boy.
TORRAC, a carrot.
TRACK, (or TRAG,) a quart.
TROSSENO, literally, "one sort," but the costermongers use it to imply anything that is bad.

WAR-RAB, a barrow.
WEDGE, a Jew.
YAD, a day; YADS, days.
YADNAB, brandy.
YENEP, a penny.
YENEP-A-TIME, penny each time,—term in betting.
YENEP-FLATCH, three halfpence,—all the halfpence and pennies continue in the same sequence.
YAP-POO, pay up.
YEKNOD, or JERK-NOD, a donkey.
YENORK, a crown.
YOB, a boy.
ZEB, best

SOME ACCOUNT

OF

THE RHYMING SLANG,

THE SECRET LANGUAGE OF CHAUNTERS AND PATTERERS.

THERE exists in London a singular tribe of men, known amongst the "fraternity of vagabonds" as chaunters and patterers. Both classes are great talkers. The first sing or chaunt through the public thoroughfares ballads—political and humorous—carols, dying speeches, and the various other kinds of gallows and street literature. The second deliver street orations on grease-removing compounds, plating powders, high-polishing blacking, and the thousand-and-one wonderful pennyworths that are retailed to gaping mobs from a London kerb-stone.

They are quite a distinct tribe from the costermongers; indeed, amongst tramps, they term themselves the "harristocrats of the streets," and boast that they live by their intellects. Like the costermongers, however, they have a secret tongue or Cant speech known only to each other. This Cant, which has nothing to do with that spoken by the costermongers, is known in Seven Dials and elsewhere as the RHYMING SLANG, *or the substitution of words and sentences which rhyme with other words intended to be kept secret*. The chaunter's Cant, therefore, partakes of his calling, and he transforms and uses up into a rough speech the various odds and ends of old songs, ballads, and street nick-names, which are found suitable to his purpose. Unlike nearly all other systems of Cant, the Rhyming Slang is not founded upon allegory; unless we except a few rude similes, thus—I'M AFLOAT is the Rhyming Cant for "boat," SORROWFUL TALE is equivalent to "three months in jail," ARTFUL DODGER signifies a "lodger," and a SNAKE IN THE GRASS stands for a "looking-glass"—a meaning that would delight a fat Chinaman, or a collector of Oriental proverbs. But, as in the case of the costers' speech and the old gipsy-vagabond Cant, the chaunters and patterers so interlard this "Rhyming Slang" with their general remarks, while their ordinary language is so smothered and subdued, that, unless when they are professionally engaged, and talking of their wares, they might almost pass for foreigners.

From the inquiries I have made of various patterers and "paper-workers," I learn that the Rhyming Slang was introduced about twelve or fifteen years ago.* Numbering this class of oratorical and bawling wanderers at twenty thousand, scattered over Great Britain, including London and the large provincial towns, we thus see the number of English vagabonds who converse in rhyme and talk poetry, although their habitations and mode of life constitute a very unpleasant Arcadia. These nomadic poets, like the other talkers of Cant or secret languages, are stamped with the vagabond's mark, and are continually on the move. The married men mostly have lodgings in London, and come and go as occasion may require. A few never quit London streets, but the greater number tramp to all the large provincial fairs, and prefer the MONKERY (country) to town life. Some transact their business in a systematic way, sending a post-office order to the Seven Dials printer, for a fresh supply of ballads or penny books, or to the SWAG SHOP, as the case may be, for trinkets and gewgaws, to be sent on by rail to a given town by the time they shall arrive there.

When any dreadful murder, colliery explosion, or frightful railway accident has happened in a country district, three or four chaunters are generally on the spot in a day or two after the

* This was written in 1858.

occurrence, vending and bawling "*A True and Faithful Account,*" &c., which "true and faithful account" was concocted purely in the imaginations of the successors of Catnach and Tommy Pitts,* behind the counters of their printing shops in Seven Dials. And but few fairs are held in any part of England without the patterer being punctually at his post, with his nostrums, or real gold rings, (with the story of the wager laid by the gentleman—see FAWNEY-BOUNCING, in the Dictionary,) or save-alls for candlesticks, or paste which, when applied to the strop, makes the dullest razor keen enough to hack broom handles and sticks, and after that to have quite enough sharpness left for splitting hairs, or shaving them off the back of one of the hands of a clodhopper, looking on in amazement. And CHEAP JOHN, too, with his coarse jokes, and no end of six-bladed knives, and pocket-books, containing information for everybody, with pockets to hold money, and a pencil to write with into the bargain, and a van stuffed with the cheap productions of Sheffield and "Brummagem,"—he, too, is a patterer of the highest order, and visits fairs, and can hold a conversation in the Rhyming Slang.

Such is a rough description of the men who speak this jargon; and simple and ridiculous as the vulgar scheme of a Rhyming Slang may appear, it must always be regarded as a curious fact in linguistic history. In order that the reader's patience may not be too much taxed, only a selection of rhyming words has been given in the Glossary,—and these for the most part, as in the case of the Back Slang, are the terms of every-day life, as used by this order of tramps and hucksters.

It must not be supposed, however, that the chaunter or patterer confines himself entirely to this Slang when conveying secret intelligence. On the contrary, although he speaks not a "leash of languages," yet is he master of the beggars' Cant, and is thoroughly "up" in street Slang. The following letter, written by a chaunter

* The famous printers and publishers of sheet songs and last dying speeches thirty years ago.

to a gentleman who took an interest in his welfare, will shew his capabilities in this line :—

Dear Friend,*

Excuse the liberty, since i saw you last i have not earned a thickun, we have had such a Dowry of Parny that it completely Stumped or Coopered Drory the Bossman's Patter therefore i am broke up and not having another friend but you i wish to know if you would lend me the price of 2 Gross of Tops, Dies, or Croaks, which is 7 shillings, of the above-mentioned worthy and Sarah Chesham the Essex Burick for the Poisoning job, they are both to be topped at Springfield Sturaban on Tuesday next. i hope you will oblige me if you can for it will be the means of putting a Quid or a James in my Clye. i will call at your Carser on Sunday Evening next for an answer, for i want a Speel on the Drum as soon as possible. hoping you and the family are All Square,

I remain Your obedient Servant,

The numerous allusions in the Glossary to well-known places in London, shew that this rude speech was mainly concocted in the metropolis. The police have made themselves partially acquainted with the BACK SLANG, but they are still profoundly ignorant of the Rhyming Slang.

* The writer, a street chaunter of ballads and last dying speeches, alludes in his letter to two celebrated criminals—Thos. Drory, the murderer of Jael Denny, and Sarah Chesham, who poisoned her husband, accounts of whose trials and "horrid deeds" he had been selling. I give a glossary of the Cant words :—

Thickun, a crown-piece.
Dowry of Parny, a lot of rain.
Stumped, bankrupt.
Coopered, spoilt.
Bossman, a farmer.
   ⁎ Drory was a farmer.
Patter, trial.
Tops, last dying speeches.
Dies,   *ib.*
Croaks,   *ib.*

Burick, a woman.
Topped, hung.
Sturaban, a prison.
Quid, a sovereign.
James,   *ib.*
Clye, a pocket.
Carser, a house or residence.
Speel on the Drum, to be off to the country.
All Square, all right, or quite well.

GLOSSARY OF THE RHYMING SLANG.

ABRAHAM'S WILLING, a shilling.
ALACOMPAIN, rain.
ALL AFLOAT, a coat.
ANY RACKET, a penny faggot.
APPLES AND PEARS, stairs.
ARTFUL DODGER, a lodger.
ARTICHOKE RIPE, smoke a pipe.
BABY PAPS, caps.
BARNET FAIR, hair.
BATTLE OF THE NILE, a tile—vulgar term for a hat.
BEN FLAKE, a steak.
BILLY BUTTON, mutton.
BIRCH BROOM, a room.
BIRD-LIME, time.
BOB, MY PAL, a gal,—vulgar pronunciation of *girl*.
BONNETS SO BLUE, Irish stew.
BOTTLE OF SPRUCE, a deuce,—Slang for twopence.
BOWL THE HOOP, soup.
BRIAN O'LINN, gin.
BROWN BESS, yes—the affirmative.
BROWN JOE, no—the negative.
BULL AND COW, a row.
BUSHY PARK, a lark.
BUTTER FLAP, a cap.
CAIN AND ABEL, a table.
CAMDEN TOWN, a brown,—vulgar term for a halfpenny.
CASTLE RAG, a flag,—Cant term for fourpence.
CAT AND MOUSE, a house.
CHALK FARM, the arm.
CHARING CROSS, a horse.
CHARLEY LANCASTER, a handkercher,—vulgar pronunciation of handkerchief.
CHARLEY PRESCOTT, waistcoat.
CHERRY RIPE, a pipe.
CHEVY CHASE, the face.
CHUMP (or CHUNK) OF WOOD, no good.
COW AND CALF, to laugh.

COVENT GARDEN, a farden,—Cockney pronunciation of farthing.
COWS AND KISSES, mistress or missus—referring to the ladies.
CURRANTS AND PLUMS, thrums,—Slang for threepence.
DAISY RECROOTS, (so spelt by my informant of Seven Dials; he means, doubtless, *recruits*,) a pair of boots
DAN TUCKER, butter.
DING DONG, a song.
DRY LAND, you understand.
DUKE OF YORK, take a walk.
EAST AND SOUTH, the mouth.
EAT A FIG, to "crack a crib," to break into a house, or commit a burglary.
EGYPTIAN HALL, a ball.
ELEPHANT'S TRUNK, drunk.
EPSOM RACES, a pair of braces.
EVERTON TOFFEE, coffee.
FANNY BLAIR, the hair.
FILLET OF VEAL, the treadwheel, house of correction.
FINGER AND THUMB, rum.
FLAG UNFURLED, a man of the world.
FLEA AND LOUSE, a bad house.
FLOUNDER AND DAB, (two kinds of flat fish,) a cab.
FLY MY KITE, a light.
FROG AND TOAD, the main road.
GARDEN GATE, a magistrate.
GERMAN FLUTES, a pair of boots.
GIRL AND BOY, a saveloy,—a penny sausage.
GLORIOUS SINNER, a dinner.
GODDESS DIANA, (pronounced DIANER,) a tanner,—sixpence.
GOOSEBERRY PUDDING, (*vulgo* PUDDEN,) a woman.
HANG BLUFF, snuff.
HOD OF MORTAR, a pot of porter.
HOUNSLOW HEATH, teeth.
I DESIRE, a fire.
I'M AFLOAT, a boat.
ISLE OF FRANCE, a dance.
ISABELLER, (vulgar pronunciation of ISABELLA,) an umbrella.
I SUPPOSE, the nose.
JACK DANDY, brandy.
JACK RANDALL, (a noted pugilist,) a candle.
JENNY LINDER, a winder,—vulgar pronunciation of window.

JOE SAVAGE, a cabbage.
LATH AND PLASTER, a master
LEAN AND LURCH, a church.
LEAN AND FAT, a hat.
LINENDRAPER, paper.
LIVE EELS, fields.
LOAD OF HAY, a day.
LONG ACRE, a baker.
LONG ACRE, a newspaper.—*See* the preceding.
LORD JOHN RUSSELL, a bustle.
LORD LOVEL, a shovel.
LUMP OF COKE, a bloak,—vulgar term for a man.
LUMP OF LEAD, the head.
MACARONI, a pony.
MAIDS A DAWNING, (I suppose my informant means *maids adorning*,) the morning.
MAIDSTONE JAILOR, a tailor.
MINCE PIES, the eyes.
MOTHER AND DARTER, (daughter,) water.
MUFFIN BAKER, a Quaker,—an unlawful sir-reverence.
NAVIGATORS, taturs,—vulgar pronunciation of potatoes
NAVIGATOR SCOT, baked potatoes all hot.
NEEDLE AND THREAD, bread.
NEVER FEAR, a pint of beer.
NIGHT AND DAY, go to the play.
NOSE AND CHIN, a winn,—*ancient Cant* for a penny.
NOSE-MY, backy,—vulgar pronunciation of tobacco.
OATS AND BARLEY, Charley.
OATS AND CHAFF, a footpath.
ORINOKO, (pronounced ORINOKER,) a poker.
OVER THE STILE, sent for trial.
PADDY QUICK, thick; or, a stick.
PEN AND INK, a stink.
PITCH AND FILL, Bill,—vulgar shortening for William.
PLATE OF MEAT, a street.
PLOUGH THE DEEP, to go to sleep.
PUDDINGS AND PIES, the eyes.
READ OF TRIPE, (?) transported for life.
READ AND WRITE, to fight.
READ AND WRITE, flight.—*See* preceding.

RIVER LEA, tea.
ROGUE AND VILLAIN, a shillin,—common pronunciation of shilling.
RORY O'MORE, the floor.
ROUND THE HOUSES, trouses,—vulgar pronunciation of trousers.
SALMON TROUT, the mouth.
SCOTCH PEG, a leg.
SHIP IN FULL SAIL, a pot of ale.
SIR WALTER SCOTT, a pot,—of beer
SLOOP OF WAR, a whore.
SNAKE IN THE GRASS, a looking-glass.
SORROWFUL TALE, three months in jail.
SPLIT ASUNDER, a costermonger.
SPLIT PEA, tea.
SPORT AND WIN, Jim.
STEAM-PACKET, a jacket.
ST MARTINS-LE-GRAND, the hand.
STOP THIEF, beef.
SUGAR AND HONEY, money.
SUGAR-CANDY, brandy.
TAKE A FRIGHT, night.
THREE-QUARTERS OF A PECK, the neck,—in writing, expressed by the simple "$\frac{3}{4}$."
THROW ME IN THE DIRT, a shirt.
TOMMY O'RANN, scran,—vulgar term for food.
TOM TRIPE, a pipe.
TOM RIGHT, night.
TOP JINT, (vulgar pronunciation of joint,) a pint,—of beer.
TOP OF ROME, home.
TURTLE DOVES, a pair of gloves.
TWO-FOOT RULE, a fool.
WIND DO TWIRL, a fine girl.

THE BIBLIOGRAPHY

OF

SLANG, CANT, AND VULGAR LANGUAGE;

OR,

A LIST OF THE BOOKS WHICH HAVE BEEN CONSULTED IN COMPILING THIS WORK,

COMPRISING NEARLY EVERY KNOWN TREATISE UPON THE SUBJECT.

SLANG has a literary history, the same as authorised language. More than one hundred works have treated upon the subject in one form or other,—a few devoting but a chapter, whilst many have given up their entire pages to expounding its history and use. Old Harman, a worthy man, who interested himself in suppressing and exposing vagabondism in the days of good Queen Bess, was the first to write upon the subject. Decker followed fifty years afterwards, but helped himself, evidently, to his predecessor's labours. Shakspeare, Beaumont and Fletcher, Ben Jonson, and Brome, each employed beggars' Cant as part of the machinery of their plays. Then came Head (who wrote *The English Rogue*, in 1680) with a glossary of Cant words "used by the Gipsies." But it was only a reprint of what Decker had given sixty years before. About this time authorised dictionaries began to insert vulgar words, labelling them "Cant." The Jack Sheppards and Dick Turpins of the early and middle part of the last century made Cant popular, and many small works were published upon the subject. But it was Grose, burly, facetious Grose, who, in the year 1785, collected the scattered glossaries of Cant and secret words, and formed one large work, adding to it all the vulgar words and Slang terms used in his own day. I am aware that the indelicacy and extreme vulgarity of the work renders it a disgrace to its compiler, still we must admit that it is by far the most important work which has ever appeared on street or popular language ; indeed, from its pages every succeeding work has, up to the present time, drawn its contents. The great fault of Grose's book consists in the author not contenting himself with Slang and Cant terms, but inserting every "smutty" and offensive word that could be raked out of the gutters of the streets. However, Harman and Grose are, after all, the only authors who have as yet treated the subject in an original manner, or have written on it from personal inquiry.

AINSWORTH'S (William Harrison) Novels and Ballads. *London*, V. D.
> Some of this author's novels, such as *Rookwood* and *Jack Sheppard*, abound in Cant words, placed in the mouths of the highwaymen. The author's ballads (especially "Nix my dolly, pals, fake away") have long been popular favourites.

ANDREWS' (George) Dictionary of the Slang and Cant Languages, Ancient and Modern, 12mo. *London*, 1809.
> A sixpenny pamphlet, with a coloured frontispiece representing a beggar's carnival.

A NEW DICTIONARY OF THE JAUNTING CREW, 12mo. N. D.
> Mentioned by John Bee in the Introduction to his *Sportsman's Slang Dictionary*.

ASH'S (John, LL.D.) New and Complete Dictionary of the English Language, 2 vols. 8vo. 1775.
> Contains a great number of Cant words and phrases.

BACCHUS AND VENUS; or, A Select Collection of near Two Hundred of the most Witty and Diverting Songs and Catches in Love and Gallantry, with Songs in the Canting Dialect, with a DICTIONARY, *explaining all Burlesque and Canting Terms*, 12mo. 1738.
> Prefixed is a curious woodcut frontispiece of a *Boozing-Ken*. This work is scarce, and much prized by collectors. The Canting Dictionary appeared before, about 1710, with the initials B. E. on the title. It also came out afterwards, in the year 1751, under the title of the *Scoundrel's Dictionary*, —a mere reprint of the two former impressions.

BAILEY'S (Nath.) Etymological English Dictionary, 2 vols. 8vo. 1737.
> Contains a great many Cant and Vulgar words;—indeed, Bailey does not appear to have been very particular what words he inserted, so long as they were actually in use. A *Collection of Ancient and Modern Cant Words* appears as an appendix to vol. ii. of this edition, (third.)

BANG-UP DICTIONARY; or, The Lounger and Sportsman's Vade Mecum, containing a copious and correct Glossary of the Language of the

Whips, illustrated by a great variety of original and curious Anecdotes, 8vo. 1812.

>A vulgar performance, consisting of pilferings from Grose, and made-up words with meanings of a degraded character.

BARTLETT'S Dictionary of Americanisms; a Glossary of Words and Phrases colloquially used in the United States, 8vo. *New York*, 1859

> It is a curious fact connected with Slang that a great number of vulgar words common in England are equally common in the United States; and when we remember that America began to people two centuries ago, and that these colloquialisms must have crossed the sea with the first emigrants, we can form some idea of the antiquity of popular or street language. Many words, owing to the caprices of fashion or society, have wholly disappeared in the parent country, whilst in the colonies they are yet heard. The words SKINK, to serve drink in company, and the old term MICHING or MEECHING, skulking or playing truant, for instance, are still in use in the United States, although nearly, if not quite, obsolete here.

BEAUMONT and FLETCHER'S Comedy of *The Beggar's Bush*, 4to, 1661, or any edition.

> Contains numerous Cant words.

BEE'S (Jon.) Dictionary of the Turf, the Ring, the Chase, the Pit, the Bon Ton, and the Varieties of Life, forming the completest and most authentic Lexicon Balatronicum hitherto offered to the notice of the Sporting World, by John Bee, [*i.e.*, John Badcock,] Esq., Editor of the *Fancy, Fancy Gazette, Living Picture of London*, and the like of that, 12mo. 1823.

> This author published books on Stable Economy under the name of Hinds. He was the sporting rival of Pierce Egan. Professor Wilson, in an amusing article in *Blackwood's Magazine*, reviewed this work.

BEE'S (Jon.) Living Picture of London for 1828, and Stranger's Guide through the Streets of the Metropolis; shewing the Frauds, the Arts, Snares, and Wiles of all descriptions of Rogues that everywhere abound, 12mo. 1828.

> Professes to be a guide to society, high and low, in London, and to give an insight into the language of the streets.

BEE'S (Jon.) Sportsman's Slang; a New Dictionary of Terms used in the Affairs of the Turf, the Ring, the Chase, and the Cockpit; with those of Bon Ton and the Varieties of Life, forming a *Lexicon Balatronicum et Macaronicum*, &c., 12mo, *plate*. *For the Author*, 1825.

> The same as the preceding, only with an altered title. Both wretched performances, filled with miserable attempts at wit.

BLACKGUARDIANA; or, Dictionary of Rogues, Bawds, &c., 8vo, WITH PORTRAITS, [by *James Caulfield*.] 1795.

> This work, with a long and very vulgar title, is nothing but a reprint of *Grose*, with a few anecdotes of pirates, odd persons, &c., and some curious portraits inserted. It was concocted by Caulfield as a speculation, and published at *one guinea* per copy; and, owing to the remarkable title, and the notification at the bottom that "only a few copies were printed," soon became scarce. For philological purposes it is not worth so much as any edition of Grose.

BOOK OF VAGABONDS.—*See* under LIBER VAGATORUM.

BOXIANA; or, Sketches of Modern Pugilism, by Pierce Egan, (an account of the prize-ring,) 3 vols. 8vo.   1820.
    Gives more particularly the Cant terms of pugilism, but contains numerous (what were then styled) "flash" words.

BRANDON. Poverty, Mendicity, and Crime; or, The Facts, Examinations, &c., upon which the Report was founded, presented to the House of Lords by W. A. Miles, Esq., to which is added a *Dictionary of the Flash or Cant Language, known to every Thief and Beggar*, edited by H. Brandon, Esq., 8vo.   1839.
    A very wretched performance.

BROME'S (Rich.) Joviall Crew; or, The Merry Beggars. Presented in a Comedie at the Cockpit, in Drury Lane, in the Year (4to)   1652.
    Contains many Cant words similar to those given by Decker,—from whose works they were doubtless obtained.

BROWN'S (Rev. Hugh Stowell) Lecture on Manliness, 12mo.   1857.
    Contains a few modern Slang words.

BRYDGES' (Sir Egerton) British Bibliographer, 4 vols. 8vo.   1810-14.
    Vol. ii., p. 521, gives a list of Cant words.

BULWER'S (Sir Edward Lytton) Paul Clifford.   V. D.
    Contains numerous Cant words.

BULWER'S (Sir Edward Lytton) Pelham.   V. D.
    Contains a few Cant terms.

BUTLER'S Hudibras, with Dr Grey's Annotations, 3 vols. 8vo.   1819.
    Abounding in colloquial terms and phrases.

CAMBRIDGE. Gradus ad Cantabrigiam; or, A Dictionary of Terms, Academical and Colloquial, or Cant, which are used at the University, *with Illustrations*, 12mo.   Camb., 1803.

CANTING ACADEMY; or, Villanies Discovered, wherein are shewn the Mysterious and Villanous Practices of that Wicked Crew—Hectors, Trapanners, Gilts, &c., with several new Catches and Songs; also Compleat Canting Dictionary, 12mo, *frontispiece*.   1674.
    Compiled by Richard Head.

CANTING: a Poem, interspersed with Tales and Additional Scraps, post 8vo.   1814.
    A few street words may be gleaned from this rather dull poem.

CANTING DICTIONARY; comprehending all the Terms, Antient and Modern, used in the several Tribes of Gypsies, Beggars, Shoplifters, Highwaymen, Foot-Pads, and all other Clans of Cheats and Villains, with Proverbs, Phrases, Figurative Speeches, &c., to which is added a complete Collection of Songs in the Canting Dialect, 12mo.   1725.
    The title is by far the most interesting part of the work. A mere make-up of earlier attempts.

CAREW. Life and Adventures of Bamfylde Moore Carew, the King of
the Beggars, *with Canting Dictionary, portrait,* 8vo. 1791.
> There are numerous editions of this singular biography. The Canting Dictionary is nothing more than a filch from earlier books.

CHARACTERISMS, or the Modern Age Displayed; being an Attempt to
Expose the Pretended Virtues of Both Sexes, 12mo, (part i., Ladies;
part ii., Gentlemen,) *E. Owen.* 1750.
> An anonymous work, from which some curious matter may be obtained.

CONYBEARE'S (Dean) Essay on Church Parties, reprinted from the
Edinburgh Review, No. CC., October 1853, 12mo. 1858.
> Several curious instances of religious or pulpit Slang are given in this exceedingly interesting little volume.

CORCORON, (Peter.) The Fancy, a Poem, 12mo. 182-.
> Abounding in Slang words and the terms of the prize-ring. Written in imitation of Moore's *Tom Crib's Memorial,* by one of the authors of *The Rejected Addresses.*

COTTON'S (Charles) Genuine Poetical Works, 12mo. 1771.
> "Scarronides, or Virgil Travestie, being the first and fourth Books of Virgil's Æneis, in English burlesque," 8vo, 1672, and other works by this author, contain numerous vulgar words now known as Slang.

DECKER'S (Thomas) The Bellman of London; bringing to light the most
notorious villanies that are now practised in the Kingdom, 4to, black
letter. London, 1608.
> Watt says this is the first book which professes to give an account of the Canting language of thieves and vagabonds. But this is wrong, as will have been seen from the remarks on Harman, who collected the words of the vagabond crew half a century before.

DECKER'S (Thomas) Lanthorne and Candle-light, or the Bellman's Second
Night's Walke, in which he brings to light a brood of more strange
villanies than ever were to this year discovered, 4to. London, 1608-9.
> This is a continuation of the former work, and contains the *Canter's Dictionary,* and has a frontispiece of the London Watchman with his staff broken.

DECKER'S (Thomas) Gulls' Hornbook, 4to. 1609.
> "This work affords a greater insight into the fashionable follies and vulgar habits of Queen Elizabeth's day than perhaps any other extant."

DECKER'S (Thomas) O per se O, or a new Cryer of Lanthorne and
Candle-light, an Addition of the Bellman's Second Night's Walke, 4to,
black letter. 1612.
> A lively description of London. Contains a Canter's Dictionary, every word in which appears to have been taken from Harman without acknowledgment. This is the first work that gives the Canting Song, a verse of which is inserted at page 20 of the Introduction. This Canting Song has since been inserted in nearly all Dictionaries of Cant.

DECKER'S (Thomas) Villanies discovered by Lanthorne and Candle-light,
and the Helpe of a new Cryer called O per se O, 4to. 1616.
> "With Canting Songs never before printed."

DECKER'S (Thomas) English Villanies, eight several times prest to Dea
  by the Printers, but still reviving again, are now the eighth time
  at the first) discovered by Lanthorne and Candle-light, &c., 4to. 16..
    The eighth edition of the "*Lanthorne and Candle-light.*"

DICTIONARY of all the Cant and Flash Languages, both Ancient a
  Modern, 18mo. *Bailey,* 17(

DICTIONARY of all the Cant and Flash Languages, 12mo. *London,* 17(

DICTIONARY of the Canting Crew, (Ancient and Modern,) of Gypsi
  Beggars, Thieves, &c., 12mo. N. D. [170(

DICTIONNAIRE des Halle, 12mo. *Bruxelles,* 16(
    This curious Slang Dictionary sold in the Stanley sale for £4, 16s.

DUCANGE ANGLICUS.—The Vulgar Tongue: comprising Two Gl(
  saries of Slang, Cant, and Flash Words and Phrases used in Lond
  at the present day, 12mo. 18(
    A silly and childish preformance, full of blunders and contradictions
    second edition appeared during the past year.

DUNCOMBE'S Flash Dictionary of the Cant Words, Queer Sayings, a
  Crack Terms now in use in Flash Cribb Society, 32mo, *coloured pri*
  18.

DUNTON'S Ladies' Dictionary, 8vo. *London,* 16(
    Contains a few Cant and vulgar words.

EGAN. Grose's Classical Dictionary of the Vulgar Tongue, with t
  addition of numerous Slang Phrases, edited by Pierce Egan, 8vo. 18.
    The best edition of Grose, with many additions, including a Life of this ce
    brated antiquary.

EGAN'S (Pierce) Life in London, 2 vols. thick 8vo, *with coloured plates*
  Geo. Cruikshank, representing high and low life. 18-
    Contains numerous Cant, Slang, sporting, and vulgar words, supposed by t
    author to form the basis of conversation in life, high and low, in Lond(

ELWYN'S (Alfred L.) Glossary of supposed *Americanisms*—Vulgar a
  Slang Words used in the United States, small 8vo. 18(

GENTLEMAN'S MAGAZINE, 8vo. N.
    "In a very early volume of this parent magazine were given a few pages,
    way of sample, of a Slang Vocabulary, then termed Cant. If, as
    suspect, this part of the Magazine fell to the share of Dr Johnson, w
    was then its editor, we have to lament that he did not proceed with t
    design."—*John Bee, in the Introduction to his Slang Dictionary,* 1825.

GENTLEMAN'S MAGAZINE, vol. xcii., p. 520.
    Mention made of Slang.

GLOSSARIES of County Dialects. V.
    Many of these will repay examination, as they contain Cant and Slang wor
    wrongly inserted as provincial or old terms.

GOLDEN CABINET (The) of Secrets opened for Youth's delightful P:
  time, in 7 parts, the last being the "City and Country Jester;" wi
  a Canting Dictionary, by Dr Surwan, 12mo. *London,* N. D. (173(
    Contains some curious woodcuts.

GREENE'S (Robert) Notable Discovery of Coosnage, now daily practised by sundry lewd persons called Conie-catchers and Crosse-biters. Plainly laying open those pernitious sleights that hath brought many ignorant men to confusion. Written for the general benefit of all Gentlemen, Citizens, Apprentices, Country Farmers, and Yeomen, that may hap to fall into the company of such cooseuing companions. With a delightful discourse of the coosnage of Colliers, 4to, *with woodcuts*. *Printed by John Wolfe*, 1591.

> The *first edition*. A copy of another edition, supposed to be *unique*, is dated 1592. It was sold at the Heber sale.

GREENE'S (Robert) Groundworke of Conny-Catching, the manner of their PEDLERS' FRENCH, and the meanes to understand the same, with the cunning sleights of the Conterfeit Cranke. Done by a Justice of the Peace of great Authoritie, 4to, *with woodcuts*. 1592.

> Usually enumerated among Greene's works, but it is only a reprint, with variations, of *Harman's Caveat*, and of which Rowland complains in his Martin Markall. The *second* and *third* parts of this curious work were published in the same year. Two other very rare volumes by Greene were published—*The Defence of Cony-Catching*, 4to, in 1592, and THE BLACK BOOKES MESSENGER, in 1595. They both treat on the same subjects.

GROSE'S (Francis, generally styled *Captain*) Classical Dictionary of the Vulgar Tongue, 8vo. 178—.

> The much-sought-after FIRST EDITION, but containing nothing, as far as I have examined, which is not to be found in the *second* and *third* editions. As respects indecency, I find all the editions equally disgraceful. The Museum copy of the *First Edition* is, I suspect, Grose's own copy, as it contains numerous manuscript additions which afterwards went to form the second edition. Excepting the obscenities, it is really an extraordinary book, and displays great industry, if we cannot speak much of its morality. It is the well from which all the other authors—Duncombe, Caulfield, Clarke, Egan, &c. &c.—drew their vulgar outpourings, without in the least purifying what they had stolen.

HAGGART. Life of David Haggart, alias John Wilson, alias Barney M'Coul, written by himself while under sentence of Death, *curious frontispiece of the Prisoner in Irons*, intermixed with all the Slang and Cant Words of the Day, to which is added a Glossary of the same, 12mo. 1821.

HALL'S (B. H.) Collection of College Words and Customs, 12mo. *Cambridge, (U. S.,)* 1856.

> Very complete. The illustrative examples are excellent.

HALLIWELL'S Archaic Dictionary, 2 vols. 8vo. 1855.

> An invaluable work, giving the Cant words used by Decker, Brome, and a few of those mentioned by Grose.

HARLEQUIN Jack Shepherd, with a Night Scene in Grotesque Characters, 8vo. (*About* 1736.)

> Contains Songs in the *Canting* dialect.

HARMAN'S (Thomas, Esq.) Caveat or Warening for Common Cursetors, vulgarly called Vagabones, set forth for the utilitie and profit of his naturall countrey, augmented and inlarged by the first author thereof;

whereunto is added the tale of the second taking of the counterf
Crank, with the true report of his behaviour and also his punishme
for his so dissembling, most marvellous to the hearer or reader there
newly imprinted, 4to. *Imprinted at London, by H. Middleton,* 15

> Contains the earliest Dictionary of the Cant language. Four editions w
> printed— William Griffith, 1566
> 1567
> 1567
> Henry Middleton, 1573
> What *Grose's Dictionary of the Vulgar Tongue* was to the authors of t
> earlier part of the present century, Harman's was to the Deckers, a
> Bromes, and Heads of the seventeenth.

HARRISON'S (William) Description of the Island of Britain, (prefixed
Holinshed's Chronicle,) 2 vols. folio. 15

> Contains an account of English vagabonds.

HAZLITT'S (William) Table Talk, 12mo, (vol. ii. contains a chapter
Familiar Style, with a notice on *Slang Terms*.) v.

HEAD'S (Richard) English Rogue, described in the Life of Merit
Latroon, a Witty Extravagant, 4 vols. 12mo.
Frans. Kirkman, 1671–

> Contains a list of Cant words, evidently copied from Decker.

HELL UPON EARTH, or the most pleasant and delectable History
Whittington's Colledge, otherwise vulgarly called Newgate, 12mo.
17

HENLEY'S (John, *better known as* ORATOR HENLEY) Various Sermons a
Orations. 1719–

> Contains numerous vulgarisms and Slang phrases.

[HITCHING'S (Charles, *formerly City Marshal, now a Prisoner in Newgat*
Regulator; or, a Discovery of the Thieves, Thief-Takers, and Loc
alias Receivers of Stolen Goods in and about the City of London, a
an Account of all the FLASH WORDS *now in vogue amongst the Thie*
&c., 8vo., VERY RARE, *with a curious woodcut.* 17

> A violent attack upon Jonathan Wild.

HOUSEHOLD WORDS, No. 183, September 24.

> Gives an interesting but badly-digested article on Slang; many of the
> amples are wrong.

JOHNSON'S (Dr Samuel) Dictionary, (the earlier editions.) v.

> Contains a great number of words italicised as *Cant*, low, or barbarous.

JONSON'S (Ben.) Bartholomew Fair, ii., 6.

> Several Cant words are placed in the mouths of the characters.

JONSON'S (Ben.) Masque of the Gipsies Metamorphosed, 4to. 16

> Contains numerous Cant words.

KENT'S (E.) Modern Flash Dictionary, containing all the Cant Wor
Slang Terms, and Flash Phrases now in Vogue, 18mo, *coloured fron
piece.* 18

L'ESTRANGE'S (Sir Roger) Works, (principally translations.) v.

> Abound in vulgar and Slang phrases.

LEXICON Balatronicum; a Dictionary of Buckish Slang, University Wit, and Pickpocket Eloquence, by a Member of the Whip Club, assisted by Hell-fire Dick, 8vo. 1811.

> One of the many reprints of *Grose's* second edition, put forth under a fresh, and what was then considered a more attractive title. It was given out in advertisements, &c., as a piece of puff, that it was edited by a Dr H. Clarke, but it contains scarcely a line more than Grose.

LIBER VAGATORUM: Der Betler Orden, 4to. Recently translated: The Book of Vagabonds and Beggars, (Liber Vagatorum: *Der Betler Orden,*) with a vocabulary of their Language, (*Rotwelsche Sprach;*) edited, with preface, by Martin Luther, in the year 1528. Now first Translated into English, with Notes, by John Camden Hotten; 4to, *with woodcuts.* 1859.

> The first edition of this book appears to have been printed at Augsburg, by Erhard Oglin, or Ocellus, about 1514,—a small quarto of twelve leaves. It was frequently reprinted at other places in Germany; and in 1528 there appeared an edition at Wirtemberg, with a preface by Martin Luther, who says that the "Rotwelsche Sprach," the Cant language of the beggars, comes from the Jews, as it contains many Hebrew words, as any one who understands that language may perceive. This book is divided into three parts, or sections; the first gives a special account of the several orders of the "Fraternity of Vagabonds;" the second, sundry "*notabilia*" relating to the different classes of beggars previously described; and the third consists of a "Rotwelsche Vocabulary," or "Canting Dictionary." There is a long notice of the "Liber Vagatorum" in the "Wiemarisches Jahrbuch," 10te, Band, 1856. Mayhew, in his *London Labour*, states that many of our Cant words are derived from the Jew fences. It is singular that a similar statement should have been made by Martin Luther more than three centuries before.

LIFE IN ST GEORGE'S FIELDS; or, The Rambles and Adventures of Disconsolate William. Esq., and his Surrey Friend, Flash Dick, with Songs and a FLASH DICTIONARY, 8vo. 1821.

MAGINN (Dr.,) wrote Slang Songs in *Blackwood's Magazine.* 1827.

MAYHEW'S (Henry) London Labour and the London Poor, 4 vols. 1851-61.

> An invaluable work to the inquirer into popular or street language.

MAYHEW'S (Henry) Great World of London, 8vo. 1857.

> An unfinished work, but containing several examples of the use and application of Cant and Slang words.

MIDDLETON (Thomas) and DECKER'S (Thomas) Roaring Girl; or Moll Cut Purse, 4to. 1611.

> The conversation in one scene is entirely in the so-called Pedlar's French. It is given in *Dodsley's Old Plays.*

MODERN FLASH DICTIONARY, 48mo. 1825.

> The smallest Slang Dictionary ever printed; intended for the waistcoat-pockets of the "BLOODS" of the Prince Regent's time.

MONCRIEFF'S Tom and Jerry, or Life in London, a Farce in Three Acts, 12mo. 1820.

> An excellent exponent of the false and forced "high life" which was so popular during the minority of George IV. The farce had a run of a hundred nights, or more, and was a general favourite for years. It abounds in Cant, and the language of "gig," as it was then often termed.

MORNINGS AT BOW STREET, by T. Wright, 12mo, *with Illustrations by George Cruikshank.* Tegg, 1838.
> In this work a few etymologies of Slang words are attempted.

NEW CANTING DICTIONARY, 12mo. N. D.
> A copy of this work is described in *Rodd's Catalogue of Elegant Literature*, 1845, part iv., No. 2128, with manuscript notes and additions in the autograph of Isaac Reed, price £1, 8s.

NEW DICTIONARY of the Terms, Ancient and Modern, of the Canting Crew in its several tribes of Gypsies, Beggars, Thieves, Cheats, &c., with an addition of some *Proverbs, Phrases, Figurative Speeches, &c.*, by B. E., GENT., 12mo. N. D. [1710.]
> Afterwards issued under the title of *Bacchus and Venus*, 1737, and in 1754 as the *Scoundrel's Dictionary*.

NEW DICTIONARY of all the Cant and Flash Languages used by every class of offenders, from a Lully Prigger to a High Tober Gloak, small 8vo., pp. 62. 179—.
> Mentioned by John Bee.

NOTES AND QUERIES. The invaluable Index to this most useful periodical may be consulted with advantage by the seeker after etymologies of Slang and Cant words.

PARKER. High and Low Life, A View of Society in, being the Adventures in England, Ireland, &c., of Mr G. Parker, a *Stage Itinerant*, 2 vols. in 1, thick 12mo. *Printed for the Author*, 1781.
> A curious work, containing many Cant words, with 100 orders of rogues and swindlers.

PARKER'S (Geo.) Life's Painter of Variegated Characters, with a Dictionary of Cant Language and Flash Songs, to which is added a Dissertation on Freemasonry, *portrait*, 8vo. 1789.

PEGGE'S (Samuel) Anecdotes of the English Language, chiefly regarding the Local Dialect of London and Environs, 8vo. 1803–41.

PERRY'S (William) London Guide and Stranger's Safeguard, against Cheats, Swindlers, and Pickpockets, by a Gentleman who has made the Police of the Metropolis an object of inquiry twenty-two years, (no wonder when the author was in prison a good portion of that time!) 1818.
> Contains a dictionary of Slang and Cant words.

PHILLIP'S New World of Words, folio. 1696.

PICKERING'S (F.) Vocabulary, or Collection of Words and Phrases which have been supposed to be peculiar to the United States of America, to which is prefixed an Essay on the present state of the English Language in the United States, 8vo. Boston, 1816.
> The remark made upon *Bartlett's Americanisms* applies equally to this work.

PICTURE OF THE FANCY, 12mo. 18—.
> Contains numerous Slang terms.

POTTER'S (H. T., of *Clay, Worcestershire*) New Dictionary of all the Cant and Flash Languages, both ancient and modern, 8vo., pp. 62. 1790.

POULTER. The Discoveries of John Poulter, alias Baxter, 8vo, 48 pages.
(1770?)
> At pages 42, 43, there is an explanation of the "Language of Thieves, commonly called Cant."

PRISON-BREAKER, The, or the Adventures of John Shepherd, a Farce, 8vo. London, 1725.
> Contains a Canting song, &c.

PUNCH, or the London Charivari,
> Often points out Slang, vulgar, or abused words. It also, occasionally, employs them in jokes, or sketches of character.

QUARTERLY REVIEW, vol. x., p. 528.
> Gives a paper on Americanisms and Slang phrases.

RANDALL'S (Jack, *the Pugilist*, formerly of the "*Hole in the Wall*," Chancery Lane) Diary of Proceedings at the House of Call for Genius, edited by Mr Breakwindow, to which are added several of Mr B.'s minor pieces, 12mo. 1820.
> Believed to have been written by Thomas Moore. The verses are mostly parodies of popular authors, and abound in the Slang of pugilism, and the phraseology of the fast life of the period.

RANDALL (Jack) a Few Selections from his Scrap Book; to which are added Poems on the late Fight for the Championship, 12mo. 1822.
> Frequently quoted by Moore in *Tom Crib's Memorial*.

SCOUNDREL'S DICTIONARY, or an Explanation of the Cant Words used by Thieves, Housebreakers, Street-robbers, and Pickpockets about Town, with some curious dissertations on the Art of Wheedling, &c., *the whole printed from a copy taken on one of their gang, in the late scuffle between the watchman and a party of them on Clerkenwell green*, 8vo. 1754.
> A reprint of *Bacchus and Venus*, 1737.

SHARP (Jeremy) The Life of an English Rogue, 12mo. 1740.
> Includes a "Vocabulary of the Gypsies' Cant."

SHERWOOD'S Gazetteer of Georgia, U.S., 8vo.
> Contains a glossary of words, Slang and vulgar, peculiar to the Southern States.

SMITH'S (Capt.) Compleat History of the Lives and Robberies of the most Notorious Highwaymen, Foot-pads, Shop-lifters, and Cheats, of both Sexes, in and about London and Westminster, 12mo, vol. i. 1719.
> This volume contains "THE THIEVES' NEW CANTING DICTIONARY OF THE WORDS, PROVERBS, &c., USED BY THIEVES."

SMITH (Capt. Alexander) The Thieves' Grammar, 12mo., p. 28. 17—.
> A copy of this work is in the collection formed by Prince Lucien Bonaparte

SMITH'S (Capt.) Thieves' Dictionary, 12mo. 1724.

SNOWDEN'S Magistrate's Assistant, and Constable's Guide, thick small 8vo. 1852.
> Gives a description of the various orders of cadgers, beggars, and swindlers, together with a *Glossary of the Flash Language*.

SPORTMAN'S DICTIONARY, 4to. 17—.
: By an anonymous author. Contains some low sporting terms.

STANLEY'S Remedy, or the Way how to Reform Wandring Beggars, Thieves, &c., wherein is shewed that Sodomes Sin of Idleness is the Poverty and the Misery of this Kingdome, 4to. 1646.
: This work has an engraving on wood which is said to be the veritable original of Jim Crow.

SWIFT'S coarser pieces abound in Vulgarities and Slang expressions.

THE TRIUMPH OF WIT, or Ingenuity displayed in its Perfection, being the Newest and most Useful Academy, Songs, Art of Love, *and the Mystery and Art of Canting, with Poems, Songs, &c., in the Canting Language*, 16mo. *J. Clarke*, 1735.
: What is generally termed a shilling *Chap Book*.

THE TRIUMPH OF WIT, or the Canting Dictionary, being the Newest and most Useful Academy, containing the Mystery and Art of Canting, with the original and present management thereof, and the ends to which it serves and is employed, illustrated with Poems, Songs, and various Intrigues in the Canting Language, with the Explanations, &c., 12mo. *Dublin*, N. D.
: A Chap Book of 32 pages, *circa* 1760.

THOMAS (I.) My Thought Book, 8vo. 1825.
: Contains a chapter on Slang.

THE WHOLE ART OF THIEVING and Defrauding Discovered: being a Caution to all Housekeepers, Shopkeepers, Salesmen, and others, to guard against Robbers of both Sexes, and the best Methods to prevent their Villanies; to which is added an Explanation of most of the Cant terms in the Thieving Language, 8vo, pp. 46. 1786.

TOM CRIB'S Memorial to Congress, with a Preface, Notes, and Appendix *by one of the Fancy* [Tom Moore, the poet,] 12mo. 1819.
: A humorous poem, abounding in Slang and pugilistic terms, with a burlesque essay on the classic origin of Slang.

VACABONDES, the Fraternatye of, as well of ruflyng Vacabones, as of beggerly, of Women as of Men, of Gyrles as of Boyes, with their proper Names and Qualities, with a Description of the Crafty Company of Cousoners and Shifters, also the XXV. Orders of Knaves; otherwyse called a Quartern of Knaves, confirmed by Cocke Lorell, 8vo. *Imprinted at London by John Awdeley, dwellyng in little Britayne streete without Aldersgate*. 1575.
: It is stated in *Ames' Typog. Antiq.*, vol ii., p 885, that an edition bearing the date 1565 is in existence, and that the compiler was no other than old John Audley, the printer, himself. This conjecture, however, is very doubtful. As stated by Watt, it is more than probable that it was written by Harman, or was taken from his works, in MS. or print.

VAUX'S (Count de, *a swindler and pickpocket*) Life, written by himself, 2 vols., 12mo, *to which is added a Canting Dictionary*. 1819.
: These Memoirs were suppressed on account of the scandalous passages contained in them.

WEBSTER'S (Noah) Letter to the Hon. John Pickering, on the Subject of his Vocabulary, or Collection of Words and Phrases supposed to be peculiar to the United States, 8vo, pp. 69. *Boston*, 1817.

WILD (Jonathan)—History of the Lives and Actions of Jonathan Wild, Thieftaker, Joseph Blake, *alias* Blueskin, Footpad, and John Sheppard, Housebreaker; together with A CANTING DICTIONARY BY JONATHAN WILD, *woodcuts*, 12mo. 1750.

WILSON (Professor) contributed various Slang pieces to *Blackwood's Magazine;* including a Review of Bee's Dictionary.

WITHERSPOON'S (Dr of America) Essays on Americanisms, Perversions of Language in the United States, *Cant* phrases, &c., 8vo., in the 4th vol. of his Works. *Philadelphia*, 1801.

> The earliest work on American vulgarisms. Originally published as a series of Essays, entitled the *Druid*, which appeared in a periodical in 1761.

THE END.

Books on Language.

Preparing, in 2 Vols. 8vo,

A DICTIONARY OF COLLOQUIAL ENGLISH:

THE WORDS AND PHRASES IN CURRENT USE COMMONLY CALLED "SLANG" AND "VULGAR."

Their Origin and Etymology traced, and their Use Illustrated by Examples drawn from the genteelest Authors.

THE notorious incompleteness of even the best of our English dictionaries can only be attributed to the manifest impossibility of any one man's registering and authenticating by an apposite example every word which is even common and current in printed literature. This difficulty is immeasurably increased when the words sought to be recorded are, in many instances, at present purely colloquial, and, if printed at all, imbedded in literature which is essentially fugitive,—such as the bulk of our plays and novels and the columns of our newspapers. Johnsonianism, if much at a discount in our literature, has certainly departed altogether from our daily speech, which every year seems to become more and more idiomatical, nay—with reverence be it spoken—*slangy*; and the Editor believes that unless the colloquialisms of this generation be registered, our descendants will have a very colourless picture of the conversation and manners of their

fathers, of all ranks of society. There is surely nothing trivia
an attempt to do this thoroughly and systematically,—a like w
being done for our county dialects and obsolete literature
the first philologists in Europe, necessarily in an imperfect man
and with immense labour. And the Editor hopes that those i
whose hands this falls will kindly render him assistance in fil
up the deficiencies of this third edition, and in illustrating
newer and more uncommon words by extracts from our literat
It will be endeavoured to select such illustrations as shall be
only valuable as such, but interesting in themselves. All con
butions in aid of this work,—suggestions on origin and ety
logy, unregistered words, definitions, and illustrative example
will be thankfully received and acknowledged by the publisl
Mr CAMDEN HOTTEN, Piccadilly, London.

JUNE 4, 1864.

☞ *It is the Editor's intention, also, to give in this work*
FRENCH SLANG EQUIVALENTS *for our own vulgar terms o*
neologisms. As the task is a difficult one—the every-day spe
of Paris being much more changeable than that of Londor
the Editor will be thankful for any assistance rendered.

BY PERMISSION OF H.I.H. PRINCE LUCIEN BONAPARTE.

Preparing, in 1 small vol., sq. 24mo, exquisitely printed,

The Song of Solomon in the North-Derbyshire Dialect.

Edited, with Notes, &c., by THOMAS HALLAM, Esq.

⁎ Uniform with the other small books on Dialect issued by H.I.H. the Prince Lucien Bonaparte. This is the first time the NORTH-DERBYSHIRE DIALECT has been specially treated of.

BY PERMISSION OF H.I.H. PRINCE LUCIEN BONAPARTE.

Preparing, in 1 small vol., sq. 24mo, exquisitely printed,

The Gipsy Vocabulary; or, List of Words taken down from the Mouths of Gipsies in Somersetshire, by a Clergyman resident there in 1780. Edited, with Notes, Introduction, &c., by W. PINKERTON, Esq., F.L.S.

⁎ Uniform with the other small books on Language issued by H.I.H. Prince Lucien Bonaparte. The value of this Vocabulary consists in the fact that the words were written down on occasions of ACTUAL CONVERSATIONS WITH GIPSIES, and that it was not compiled from Grellman or any of the Continental works.

WINCHESTER WORDS AND PHRASES.

In preparation, 8vo,

Glossary of all the Words, Phrases, Customs, peculiar to Winchester College.

⁎ See *School Life at Winchester College*, which will be shortly published.

In preparation, 1 vol., small 8vo,

The School and College Slang of England; or, Glossaries

the Words and Phrases peculiar to the Six great Educatio[nal] Establishments of the Country.

DICTIONARY OF AMERICANISMS.

Thick 8vo, published at £1, 5s., only 12s. 6d.,

Glossary of Words and Phrases usually regarded

peculiar to the United States. By JOHN RUSSELL BA[RT]-LETT. THIRD and BEST EDITION.

⁎ The work extends to 560 pages, and presents to the Eng[lish] reader a body of admirably-selected extracts from the humorous dialectical literature of the United States. *The work is offered at [the] lowest cash price, and must be applied for* DIRECT, *as no discount ca[n be] allowed to any agent.*

It is a curious fact connected with Slang that a great numbe[r of] vulgar words common in England are equally common in the Un[ited] States; and when we remember that America began to people [two] centuries ago, and that these colloquialisms must have crossed the [sea] with the first emigrants, we can form some idea of the antiquity [of] popular or street language. Many words, owing to the caprice[s of] fashion or society, have wholly disappeared in the parent coun[try,] whilst in the colonies they are yet heard. The words SKINK, to s[erve] drink in company, and the old term MICHING or MEECHING, skulk[ing] or playing truant, for instance, are still in use in the United Sta[tes,] although nearly, if not quite, obsolete here.

Now ready, only a few Copies for sale, original price 5s.,
now offered at 2s. 6d.,

A Dictionary of the Oldest Words in the English Language, from the Semi-Saxon Period of A.D. 1250 to 1300; consisting of an Alphabetical Inventory of every Word found in the printed English Literature of the Thirteenth Century. By the late HERBERT COLERIDGE, Secretary to the Philological Society. 8vo, neat.

An invaluable work to historical students and those interested in linguistic pursuits. "The present publication may be considered as the foundation-stone of the Historical and Literary Portion" of the great ENGLISH DICTIONARY now in preparation by the Philological Society. "Explanatory and etymological matter has been added, which, it is hoped, may render the work more generally interesting and useful than could otherwise have been the case."

☞ *The Publisher will be glad to receive the names of gentlemen who may desire to secure Copies of any of the above works. Of three of them only a very limited number will be printed.*

VERY IMPORTANT NEW BOOKS.

Special List for 1869.

⁎ NOTE.—*In order to ensure the correct delivery of the actual Works, or Particular Editions, specified in this List, the name of the Publisher should be distinctly given. Stamps or a Post Office Order may be remitted direct to the Publisher, who will forward per return.*

A TRULY MAGNIFICENT WORK.—"LIVES OF THE SAINTS." Enriched with Fifty-one exquisite Full-page Miniatures, in gold and colours. Every page of the Text within Engraved Borders of Beautiful Design. In thick 4to, sumptuously printed, £7, bound in silk velvet, enriched with gold, preserved in a case.

☞ THIS VERY IMPORTANT WORK, commenced three years since, has at length been completed, and fully justifies the high expectations formed of it during its progress through the press. Taking the text of the Rev. Alban Butler as his guide, the Editor has, wherever practicable, carefully verified the references of that eminent divine. The delicacy and finish of the beautiful miniatures have never before been approached in any similar work in this country. They exhibit a beauty and exquisite softness of colour which have hitherto only been realised by the most expensive miniature paintings. The work must be seen to be appreciated, as it is like no other of the kind. The preparation has been so costly and slow that the book is never likely to decrease in value.

A VERY SPLENDID VOLUME.—SAINT URSULA, PRINCESS OF BRITAIN, AND HER COMPANIONS. With Twenty-five Full-page 4to Illuminated Miniatures from the Pictures of Cologne, and exquisitely designed Woodcut Borders. In crown 4to, beautifully bound in silk and gold, £3 10s.

⁎ The finest Book-Paintings of the kind ever published. The artist obtained the Gold Prize at the Paris Exposition.

☞ THE BOOK MUST BE SEEN TO BE APPRECIATED. The illustrations are exact reproductions of the exquisite paintings of the Van Eyck school, and in finish and beauty are far above any similar book-paintings issued in this country. As the preparation of the work has been so costly and slow it is never likely to decrease in value.

Exquisite Miniatures and Illuminations.—"Golden Verses from the New Testament," with 50 Illuminations and Miniatures from celebrated MISSALS and BOOKS OF HOURS of 14th and 15th centuries in GOLD and COLOURS. The text very beautifully printed in letters of gold on fine ivory paper. 4to, in a very handsome cloth case with silk ribbons, 30s.; or bound in a volume, morocco, gilt edges, £2 5s.

John Camden Hotten, 74 and 75, Piccadilly, W.

VERY IMPORTANT NEW BOOKS.

Pictorial description of Abyssinia.
DEDICATED TO HER MAJESTY THE QUEEN BY ROYAL COMMAND.

Views in Central Abyssinia. With Portraits of
Natives of the Galla Tribes, taken in Pen and Ink under circumstances of peculiar difficulty, by T. Zender. With letterpress description by SOPHIE F. VEITCH, daughter of the Chaplain to the Bishop of Jerusalem. 4to, price 12s.

⁎ A book of peculiar interest at the present moment, as it gives a marvellously faithful panorama of the country, about which so much has recently been said. The soiled worn volume from which these facsimiles were taken is quite a curiosity, having been constantly secreted about the person of the draughtsman, fearing the observation of the native chiefs, who do not allow drawings to be made.

Mary Lamb's Poems and Letters; with Inedited
Remains of CHARLES LAMB. Now first collected, with numerous illustrations of Lamb's favourite haunts in London and the suburbs. *Facsimiles on old paper of the title-pages of the rare first editions of Lamb and Coleridge's works. Facsimile of a page of the original MS. "Essay on Roast Pig," Hancock's admirable Portrait of the essayist now first correctly reproduced, and many other relics of the delightful essayist.* Crown 8vo, price 10s. 6d.

FAIR ROSAMOND'S COTTAGE.

The Collector. Choice Essays on Books, Authors,
Newspapers, Pictures, Inns, Doctors, Holidays, &c. Introduction by Dr. DORAN. A Choice Book, on toned paper, half morocco, 6s.

⁎ A charming volume of delightful Essays, with exquisitely-engraved Vignette of an Old Book Collector busily engaged at his favourite pursuit of book-hunting. The work is a companion volume to Disraeli's "Curiosities of Literature," and to the more recently published "Book-Hunter," by Mr. John Hill Burton.

"A comely and suitably named volume. His humour and reading are considerable, and whilst he displays the latter with the frankness of a collector not ashamed of his function, he exercises the former with unflagging spirit and excellent effect."—*Athenæum.*

John Camden Hotten, 74 and 75, Piccadilly, W.

VERY IMPORTANT NEW BOOKS.

John Ruskin and **George Cruikshank.** — "**German** Popular Stories.**" Collected by the Brothers GRIMM, from Oral Tradition, and Translated by EDGAR TAYLOR. Edited by JOHN RUSKIN. WITH TWENTY-TWO ILLUSTRATIONS AFTER THE INIMITABLE DESIGNS OF GEORGE CRUIKSHANK. Both series complete in 1 vol. Very choicely printed, in small 4to, price 6s.

*** These are the designs which Mr. Ruskin has praised so highly, placing them far above all Cruikshank's other works of a similar character. So rare had the original book (published in 1823-1826) become, that £5 to £6 per copy was an ordinary price. By the consent of Mr. Taylor's family a new Edition is now issued, under the care and superintendence of the printers who issued the originals forty years ago. The Illustrations are considered amongst the most extraordinary examples of successful reproduction ever published. A very few copies on LARGE PAPER, 21s.; or with proofs of plates on INDIA PAPER, price 31s. 6d.

"'Grimm's German Stories' was so well adapted to the genius of Cruikshank, that it has suggested one of the very best of all his etchings. The two elves, especially the nearer one, who is putting on his breeches, are drawn with a point at once so precise and vivacious, so full of keen fun and inimitably happy invention, that I have not found their equals in comic etching anywhere. It is said that these elves are regarded with peculiar affection by the great master who created them; it is only natural, for he has a right to be proud of them."—*Hammerton's Etching and Etchers.*

Hood's "Whims and Oddities," 1826. A New and very Cheap Edition of this well-known Book, with the Author's 40 inimitably funny Woodcuts. Square 12mo, price 1s. 6d. stiff cover; or cloth neat, 2s.

*** Christopher North once remarked of this book that "it contained more wit, more fun and humour, than any other work of its size."

Hawthorne's Note Book. A new and most interesting volume of Autobiographical Reminiscences, Ideas, and Suggestions by this delightful author, selected from his private Note Books. Square 12mo, stiff cover, 1s. 6d.; or cloth neat, 2s.

☞ The poet Longfellow thus anticipates this charming book:—" Live ever, sweet, sweet book. It comes from the hand of a man of genius. Everything about it has the freshness of morning and May."

John Camden Hotten, 74 and 75, Piccadilly, W.

VERY IMPORTANT NEW BOOKS.

Price to Subscribers, 27s., afterwards to be raised to 36s.

Life and Newly-Discovered Writings of Daniel Defo[e]
Comprising Several Hundred Important Essays, Pamphlets, and oth[er] Writings, now first brought to light, after many years' diligent searc[h]. By WILLIAM LEE, Esq. With Facsimiles and Illustrations.

*** For many years it has been well known in literary circles tha[t] the gentleman to whom the public is indebted for this valuable additi[on] to the knowledge of Defoe's Life and Works has been an indefatigab[le] collector of everything relating to the subject, and that such collecti[on] had reference to a more full and correct Memoir than had yet been give[n] to the world. In 3 vols., uniform with "Macaulay's History of England.

Vol. I.—A NEW MEMOIR OF DEFOE.
Vols. II. and III.—HITHERTO UNKNOWN WRITINGS.

*** *This will be a most valuable contribution to English History an[d] English Literature.*

The Best Handbook of Heraldry. Profusely Illus[-]trated with Plates and Woodcuts. By JOHN E. CUSSANS. In crow[n] 8vo, pp. 360, in *emblazoned gold cover*, with copious Index, 7s. 6d.

*** *This volume, beautifully printed on toned paper, contains not onl[y] the ordinary matter to be found in the best books on the science [of] Armory, but several other subjects hitherto unnoticed. Amongst thes[e] may be mentioned:*—1. DIRECTIONS FOR TRACING PEDIGREES. 2. D[E]CIPHERING ANCIENT MSS., ILLUSTRATED BY ALPHABETS AND FACSIMILE[S]. 3. THE APPOINTMENT OF LIVERIES. 4. CONTINENTAL AND AMERICA[N] HERALDRY, &c.

Michael Faraday. Philosopher and Christian. B[y] The Rev. SAMUEL MARTIN, of Westminster. Toned paper, Portrait, 6[d.]
*** An admirable *résumé*—designed for popular reading—of this great man's life.

VERY IMPORTANT NEW BOOKS.

THE NEW "PUNIANA SERIES" OF
CHOICE ILLUSTRATED WORKS OF HUMOUR.

Elegantly printed on toned paper, full gilt, gilt edges, for the Drawing Room, price 6s. each:—

1. **Carols of Cockayne. By Henry S. Leigh.** Vers de Société, and charming Verses descriptive of London life. With numerous exquisite little designs by ALFRED CONCANEN and the late JOHN LEECH. Small 4to, elegant, uniform with "Puniana," 6s.

2. **The "Bab Ballads."** New Illustrated Book of HUMOUR; OR, A GREAT DEAL OF RHYME WITH VERY LITTLE REASON. BY W. S. GILBERT. WITH A MOST LAUGHABLE ILLUSTRATION ON NEARLY EVERY PAGE, DRAWN BY THE AUTHOR. On toned paper, gilt edges, price 6s.

"An awfully Jolly Book for Parties."

3. **Puniana. Best Book of Riddles and Puns ever** formed. Thoughts Wise—and Otherwise. With nearly 100 exquisitely fanciful drawings. Contains nearly 3,000 of the best Riddles and 10,000 most outrageous Puns, and is one of the most popular books ever issued. New edition, uniform with the "Bab Ballads," price 6s.

Why did Du Chaillu get so angry when he was chaffed about the Gorilla? Why? we ask.
Why is a chrysalis like a hot roll? You will doubtless remark, "Because it's the grub that makes the butter fly!" But see "Puniana."
Why is a wide-awake hat so called? Because it never had a nap, and never wants one.

The *Saturday Review* says of this most amusing work—"Enormous burlesque—unapproachable and pre-eminent. We venture to think that this very queer volume will be a favourite. It deserves to be so: and we should suggest that, to a dull person desirous to get credit with the young holiday people, it would be good policy to invest in the book, and dole it out by instalments."

John Camden Hotten, 74 and 75, Piccadilly, W.

VERY IMPORTANT NEW BOOKS.

Popular Shilling Books of Humour.
ARTEMUS WARD: HIS BOOK.
ARTEMUS WARD AMONG THE MORMONS.
BIGLOW PAPERS.
ORPHEUS C. KERR PAPERS.
JOSH BILLINGS.
HOOD'S VERE VEREKER.
HOLMES' WIT AND HUMOUR.
NEVER CAUGHT.
CHIPS FROM A ROUGH LOG.
MR. SPROUTS: HIS OPINIONS.

Yankee Drolleries. Edited by George Augustus Sala,
Containing Artemus Ward; Biglow Papers; Orpheus C. Kerr; Major Jack Downing; and Nasby Papers. One of the cheapest books ever published. New Edition, on toned paper, cloth extra, 700 pages, 3s. 6d.

Orpheus C. Kerr Papers. The Original American
Edition, Three Series, complete. 3 vols. 8vo, cloth; sells at £1 2s. 6d., now specially offered at 15s.

∗ A most mirth-provoking work. It was first introduced into this country by the English officers who were quartered during the late war on the Canadian frontier. They found it one of the drollest pieces of composition they had ever met with, and so brought copies over for the delectation of their friends.

A Keepsake for Smokers.—"The Smoker's Text-
Book." By J. HAMER, F.R.S.L. This day, exquisitely printed from "silver-faced" type, cloth, very neat, gilt edges, 2s. 6d., post free.

> 18
>
> THE TRUE CONSOLER.
>
> HE who doth not smoke hath either known no great griefs, or refuseth himself the softest consolation, next to that which comes from heaven "What, softer than woman?" whispers the young reader. Young reader, woman teases as well as consoles. Woman makes half the sorrows which she boasts the privilege to soothe. Woman consoles us, it is true, while we are young and handsome; when we are old and ugly, woman scolds and scolds us. On the whole, then, woman is this scale, the weed in that, Jupiter, hang out thy balance, and weigh them both; and if thou give the preference to woman, all I can say is, the next time Juno ruffles thee—O Jupiter: try the weed.
> BULWER's—"What will he do with it?"

"A pipe is a great comforter, a pleasant soother. The man who smokes thinks like a sage, and acts like a Samaritan."—*Bulwer.*

"A tiny volume, dedicated to the votaries of the weed; beautifully printed on toned paper in, we believe, the smallest type ever made (cast especially for show at the Great Exhibition in Hyde Park), but very clear notwithstanding its minuteness. . . . The pages sing in various styles the praises of tobacco. Amongst the writers laid under contribution are Bulwer, Kingsley, Charles Lamb, Thackeray, Isaac Browne, Cowper, and Byron."—*The Field.*

Laughing Philosopher (The), consisting of several
Thousand of the best JOKES, WITTICISMS, PUNS, EPIGRAMS, HUMOROUS STORIES, and Witty Compositions in the English Language; intended as "Fun for the Million." Square 12mo, nearly 800 pages, frontispiece, half morocco neat, 5s. 6d.

VERY IMPORTANT NEW BOOKS.

AARON PENLEY'S Sketching in Water Colours, for 21s. By AARON PENLEY, Author of "The English School of Painting in Water-Colours," &c. ILLUSTRATED WITH TWENTY-ONE BEAUTIFUL CHROMO-LITHOGRAPHS, produced with the utmost care to resemble original WATER-COLOUR DRAWINGS. Small folio, the text tastefully printed, in handsome binding, gilt edges, suitable for the drawing-room table, price 21s.

*** It has long been felt that the magnificent work of the great English master of painting in water-colours, published at £4 4s., was too dear for general circulation. The above embodies all the instructions of the distinguished author, with twenty-one beautiful specimens of water-colour painting.

A Clever and Brilliant Book (*Companion to the "Bon Gaultier Ballads"*) **PUCK ON PEGASUS.** By H. CHOLMONDELEY PENNELL.

☞ *This most amusing work has already passed through* FIVE EDITIONS, *receiving everywhere the highest praise as "a clever and brilliant book."* TO NO OTHER WORK OF THE PRESENT DAY HAVE SO MANY DISTINGUISHED ARTISTS CONTRIBUTED ILLUSTRATIONS. To the designs of GEORGE CRUIKSHANK, JOHN LEECH, JULIAN PORTCH, "PHIZ," and other artists, SIR NOEL PATON, MILLAIS, JOHN TENNIEL, RICHARD DOYLE, and M. ELLEN EDWARDS *have now contributed several exquisite pictures, thus making the new edition—which is* TWICE THE SIZE OF THE OLD ONE, *and contains irresistibly funny pieces*—THE BEST BOOK FOR THE DRAWING-ROOM TABLE NOW PUBLISHED.

In 4to, *printed within an india-paper tone, and elegantly bound, gilt, gilt edges, price* 10s. 6d. *only.*

VERY IMPORTANT NEW BOOKS.

UNIFORM WITH MR. RUSKIN'S EDITION OF "GERMAN POPULAR STORIES."

New Book of Delightful Tales.—"Family Fairy Tales;" or, Glimpses of Elfland at Heatherston Hall." Edited by CHOLMONDELEY PENNELL, Author of "Puck on Pegasus," &c., adorned with beautiful pictures of "My Lord Lion," "King Uggermugger," and other great folks. Handsomely printed on toned paper, in cloth, green and gold, price 3s. 6d. plain, 4s. 6d. coloured.

₊ This charming volume has been univer...lly praised by the critical press.

Popular Romances of the West of England; or, the Drolls of Old Cornwall. Collected and edited by ROBERT HUNT, F.R.S. This day, in 2 vols. 8vo, very handsomely printed, price 16s.

☞ *Only a few copies of this very interesting work now remain, and* COPIES WILL SOON BECOME SCARCE.

₊ Many of the stories are remarkable for their wild poetic beauty; others surprise us by their quaintness; whilst others, again, show forth a tragic force which can only be associated with those rude ages which existed long before the period of authentic history. Mr. George Cruikshank has supplied two wonderful pictures to the work. One is a portrait of Giant Bolster, a personage twelve miles high.

Gustave Dore's Favourite Pencil Sketches.—Historical Cartoons; or, Rough Pencillings of the World's History from the First to the Nineteenth Century. By GUSTAVE DORE. With admirable letterpress descriptions by THOMAS WRIGHT, F.S.A. Oblong 4to, handsome table book, 7s. 6d.

₊ A new book of daring and inimitable designs, which will excite considerable attention, and doubtless command a wide circulation.

Captain Castagnette. His Surprising, almost Incredible Adventures. 4to, with GUSTAVE DORE'S Illustrations. 1s. 9d. (sells at 5s.)

DIRECT APPLICATION *must be made to Mr. Hotten for this book.*

Cent. per Cent. A Story written upon a Bill Stamp. By BLANCHARD JERROLD. With numerous coloured illustrations in the style of the late Mr. Leech's charming designs. [*Immediately.*

₊ A Story of "The Vampires of London," as they were pithily termed in a recent notorious case, and one of undoubted interest.

VERY IMPORTANT NEW BOOKS.

Seymour's Sketches. A Companion Volume to
"Leech's Pictures." The Book of Cockney Sports, Whims, and Oddities. Nearly 200 highly amusing Illustrations. Oblong 4to, a handsome volume, half morocco, price 12s.

*** A re-issue of the famous pictorial comicalities which were so popular thirty years ago. The volume is admirably adapted for a table-book, and the pictures will doubtless again meet with that popularity which was extended towards them when the artist projected with Mr. Dickens the famous "Pickwick Papers."

The Famous "DOCTOR SYNTAX'S" Three Tours.
One of the most Amusing and Laughable Books ever published. With the whole of Rowlandson's very droll full-page illustrations, *in colours, after the original drawings*. Comprising the well-known TOURS:—

1. In Search of the Picturesque.
2. In Search of Consolation.
3. In Search of a Wife.

The three series complete and unabridged from the original editions in one handsome volume, with a Life of this industrious Author—the English Le Sage—now first written by John Camden Hotten.

*** It is not a little surprising that the most voluminous and popular English writer since the days of Defoe should never before have received the small honour of a biography. *This Edition contains the whole of the original, hitherto sold for £1 11s. 6d., but which is now published at* **7s. 6d. only.**

A VERY USEFUL BOOK. In folio, half morocco, cloth sides, 7s. 6d.
Literary Scraps, Cuttings from Newspapers, Extracts, Miscellanea, &c. *A FOLIO SCRAP-BOOK OF 340 COLUMNS*, formed for the reception of Cuttings, &c., with guards.

☞ *Authors and literary men have thanked the publisher for this useful book.*

*** A most useful volume, and one of the cheapest ever sold. The book is sure to be appreciated, and to become popular.

Hone's Scrap Book. A Supplementary Volume to
the "Every-Day Book," the "Year-Book," and the "Table-Book." From the MSS. of the late WILLIAM HONE, with upwards of One Hundred and Fifty engravings of curious or eccentric objects. Thick 8vo, uniform with "Year-Book," pp. 800.   [*In preparation.*

John Camden Hotten, 74 and 75, Piccadilly, W.

VERY IMPORTANT NEW BOOKS.

Sets of "Punch," 1841—1860. Mr. Hotten has
purchased from the Messrs. Virtue and Co. their ENTIRE REMAINDER of this important set of books, which contains, among its 12,000 Illustrations and Contributions from the most noted Wits of the time, the WHOLE OF LEECH'S SKETCHES, 4 vols.; LEECH'S PENCILLINGS, 2 vols.; TENNIEL'S CARTOONS; DOYLE'S MR. PIP'S HYS DIARY; MANNERS AND CUSTOMS OF THE ENGLISH; BROWN, JONES, AND ROBINSON; Punch's Almanacks, 1 vol.; Thackeray's Miscellanies, 4 vols.; The Caudle Lectures; Story of a Feather; &c., &c. 39 half-yearly vols. bound in 20 vols., cloth gilt, gilt edges, published at £16 10s., to be obtained of Mr. Hotten for £6 10s. ONLY.

The Standard Work on Diamonds and Precious Stones;
their History, Value, and Properties, with Simple Tests for Ascertaining their Reality. By HARRY EMANUEL, F.R.G.S. With numerous Illustrations, tinted and plain. New Edition, Prices brought down to Present Time, full gilt, 12s. 6d.

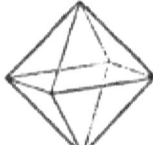 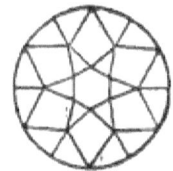 

"Will be acceptable to many readers."—*Times.*
"An invaluable work for buyers and sellers."—*Spectator.*
See the *Times'* Review of three columns.

⁎ *This new edition is greatly superior to the previous one. It gives the latest market value for Diamonds and Precious Stones of every size.*

The Young Botanist: A Popular Guide to Elementary
Botany. By T. S. RALPH, of the Linnæan Society. In 1 vol., with 300 Drawings from Nature, 2s. 6d. plain, 4s. 6d. coloured by hand.

⁎ An excellent book for the young beginner. The objects selected as illustrations are either easy of access as specimens of wild plants, or are common in gardens.

Gunter's Modern Confectioner. The Best Book on
Confectionery and Desserts. An Entirely New Edition of this Standard Work on the Preparation of Confectionery and the Arrangement of Desserts. Adapted for private families or large establishments. By WILLIAM JEANES, Chief Confectioner at Messrs. Gunter's (Confectioners to Her Majesty), Berkeley-square. With Plates, post 8vo, cloth, 6s. 6d.

"All housekeepers should have it."—*Daily Telegraph.*

⁎ *This work has won for itself the reputation of being the Standard English Book on the preparation of all kinds of Confectionery, and on the arrangement of Desserts.*

John Camden Hotten, 74 and 75, Piccadilly, W.

VERY IMPORTANT NEW BOOKS.

MOST AMUSING NEW BOOK.

Caricature History of the Georges (House of Hanover).

Very entertaining book of 640 pages, with 400 Pictures, Caricatures, Squibs, Broadsides, Window Pictures. By T. WRIGHT, F.S.A. 7s. 6d.

*** Companion Volume to "History of Signboards." Reviewed in almost every English journal with highest approbation.

"A set of caricatures such as we have in Mr. Wright's volume brings the surface of the age before us with a vividness that no prose writer, even of the highest power, could emulate. Macaulay's most brilliant sentence is weak by the side of the little woodcut from Gillray wich gives us Burke and Fox."—*Saturday Review.*

"A more amusing work of its kind never issued from the press."—*Art Journal.*

"This is one of the most agreeable and interesting books of the season."—*Public Opinion.*

"It seems superfluous to say that this is an entertaining book. It is indeed one of the most entertaining books we have read for a long time. It is history teaching by caricature. There is hardly an event of note, hardly a personage of mark, hardly a social whimsey worth a moment notice, which is not satirised and illustrated in these pages. We have here the caricaturists from Hogarth to Gillray, and from Gillray to Cruikshank."—*Morning Star.*

"It is emphatically one of the liveliest of books, as also one of the most interesting. It has the twofold merit of being at once amusing and edifying. The 600 odd pages which make up the goodly volume are doubly enhanced by some 400 illustrations, of which a dozen are full-page engravings."—*Morning Post.*

"Mr. Thomas Wright is so ripe a scholar, and is so rich in historical reminiscences, that he cannot fail to make an interesting book on any subject he undertakes to illustrate. He has achieved a success on the present occasion."—*Press.*

Notice.—Large-paper Edition. 4to, only 100 printed,

on extra fine paper, wide margins for the lovers of choice books, with extra Portraits, half-morocco (a capital book to illustrate), 30s.

Romance of the Rod: an Anecdotal History of the

Birch in Ancient and Modern Times. With some quaint illustrations. Crown 8vo, handsomely printed.   [*In preparation.*

John Camden Hotten, 74 and 75, Piccadilly, W.

VERY IMPORTANT NEW BOOKS.

NEW BOOK BY THE AUTHOR OF "A NIGHT IN A WORK-HOUSE."

Preparing, in crown 8vo, handsomely printed,

The Wilds of London: with a Full Account of the Natives. By the Amateur "Lambeth Casual," Mr. JAMES GREENWOOD, of the *Pall Mall Gazette*.

"Mr. James Greenwood, the brother of the editor of the *Pall Mall Gazette*, who wrote such a spirited account of his workhouse experiences for this journal, has just commenced a series of 'descriptive sketches, from the personal observations and experiences of the writer, of remarkable scenes, people, and places in London.'"—*London Review*.

The Thames from Oxford to London. Forty Exquisite Photographs. Royal 4to. Both series complete in a neat French morocco folio, with flaps, gilt side, £3 10s.

LIST OF PHOTOGRAPHS.—FIRST SERIES.

Oxford.
Barges at Oxford.
Ifley Mill.
Bridge at Nuneham.
Day's Lock.
Shellingford.
Wallingford Bridge.
Near Goring.

Pangbourne (3 views).
Boat House, Park Place.
Henley-on-Thames.
Medmenham Abbey.
New Lock, Hurley.
Marlow.

Great Marlow Lock.
Boulter's Lock, Maidenhead.
Maidenhead Railway Bridge.
Water Oakley, near Windsor.

SECOND SERIES.

Windsor (4 views).
Eton College.
Halliford.
Garrick's Villa, Hampton.

Moulsey.
Hampton Court (2 views).
Twickenham (3 views).
Eel-pie Island.

Duke of Buccleuch's.
Richmond (2 views).
Kew (2 views).
Westminster Palace and Bridge.

∗ This is an admirable collection of Views of the most charmingly picturesque spots on the River Thames, in the very highest style of Landscape Photography.

A Tour in Crete, during the Insurrections of the Cretans, 1867. By ED. POSTLETHWAITE, Author of "The Fortunes of a Colonist," "Pilgrimage over the Prairies," "Diary of George Dern," "Poems by Tristam," &c. This day, cloth neat, price 2s. 6d.

Letters from Greece, written in 1867. By Ed. POSTLETHWAITE, Author of "A Tour in Crete," &c. With Three Photographs, cloth, 4s. 6d.

FOLK-LORE, LEGENDS, PROVERBS OF ICELAND.

Now ready, Cheap Edition, with Map and Tinted Illustrations, 2s. 6d.

Oxonian in Iceland; with Icelandic Folk-Lore and Sagas. By the Rev. FRED METCALFE, M.A.

Tom Marchmont: a Novel. Just out, 3 vols. 8vo, cloth, 31s. 6d.

"A story of English life, with a hero who is not depicted in accordance with the conventional rules for masculine perfection framed by modern society."

John Camden Hotten, 74 and 75, Piccadilly, W.

VERY IMPORTANT NEW BOOKS.

The History of Advertising in all Ages and Countries.
A Companion to the "HISTORY OF SIGNBOARDS." With many very amusing Anecdotes and Examples of Successful Advertisers. By Messrs. LARWOOD and HOTTEN. [*In preparation.*

Signboards: their History. With Anecdotes of Famous
Taverns and remarkable Characters. By JACOB LARWOOD and JOHN CAMDEN HOTTEN. "A book which will delight all."—*Spectator*. This day, Fourth Edition, pages 580, price 7s. 6d. only.

From the " Times."
"It is not fair on the part of a reviewer to pick out the plums of an author's book, thus filching away his cream, and leaving little but skim-milk remaining; but, even if we were ever so maliciously inclined,

From the " Times."
we could not in the present instance pick out all Messrs. Larwood and Hotten's plums, because the good things are so numerous as to defy the most wholesale depredation."—*Review of three columns.*

BULL AND MOUTH.
(Angel St., St Martin's-le-Grand, circa 1800.)

⁎ Nearly 100 most curious illustrations on wood are given, showing the various old signs which were formerly hung from taverns and other houses. The frontispiece represents the famous sign of "The Man loaded with Mischief," in the colours of the original painting said to have been executed by Hogarth.

Notice.—"Large-paper Edition," with Seventy-Two
extra Illustrations (not given in the small edition), showing Old London in the days when Signboards hung from almost every house. In 4to, half-morocco neat, 30s.

⁎ Only a small number printed on extra fine paper with wide margins for the lover of fine books.

The Parks of London. Their History and Asso-
ciations from the Earliest Times. By JACOB LARWOOD. WITH ILLUSTRATIONS BY THE AUTHOR. [*In the Press.*

AN EXTRAORDINARY BOOK.

Hotten's Edition of "Contes Drolatiques" (Droll
Tales collected from the Abbeys of Loraine). Par BALZAC. With Four Hundred and Twenty-five Marvellous, Extravagant, and Fantastic Woodcuts by GUSTAVE DORÉ. Beautifully printed, thick 8vo, half morocco, Roxburghe, 12s. 6d.

⁎ The most singular designs ever attempted by any artist. This book is a fund of amusement. So crammed is it with pictures that even the contents are adorned with thirty-three illustrations.

Direct application must be made to Mr. Hotten for this work.

John Camden Hotten, 74 and 75, Piccadilly, W.

VERY IMPORTANT NEW BOOKS.

Common Prayer. Illustrated by Holbein and Albert Durer. With Wood Engravings of the Dance of Death, a singularly curious series after Holbein, with Scriptural Quotations and Proverbs in the Margin. 8vo, exquisitely printed on tinted paper, 8s. 6d.; in dark morocco, Elizabethan style, gilt edges, 16s. 6d.
Apply DIRECT *for this exquisite volume.*

AN APPROPRIATE BOOK TO ILLUMINATE.

⁎ The attention of those who practise the beautiful art of Illuminating is requested to the following sumptuous volume.

The Presentation Book of Common Prayer. Illus-trated with Elegant Ornamental Borders in red and black, from "Books of Hours" and Illuminated Missals. By GEOFFREY TORY. One of the most tasteful and beautiful books ever printed. May now be seen at all booksellers,

Although the price is only a few shillings (7s. 6d. in plain cloth; 8s. 6d. antique do.; 14s. 6d. morocco extra), this edition is so prized by artists that at the South Kensington and other important Art Schools copies are kept for the use of students.

English Church Furniture, Ornaments, and Decora-tions, at the Period of the Reformation. Edited by ED. PEACOCK, F.S.A. *MOST INTERESTING BOOK ON ANGLICAN CHURCH ORNAMENTS.* Thick 8vo, with illustrations, 15s.

"Very curious as showing what articles of church furniture were in those days considered to be idolatrous or unnecessary. The work, of which only a limited number has been printed, is of the highest interest to those who take part in the present Ritual discussion."—*See Religious Journals.*

NEW BOOK BY PROFESSOR RENAN'S ASSOCIATE.

Apollonius of Tyana: the Pagan or False Christ of the Third Century. An Essay. By ALBERT REVILLE, Pastor of the Walloon Church at Rotterdam. Authorised translation. Price 3s. 6d.

⁎ A most curious account of an attempt to revive Paganism in the third century by means of a false Christ. Strange to say, the principal events in the life of Apollonius are almost identical with the Gospel narrative.

Carlyle on the Choice of Books. Address by Thomas CARLYLE, with Memoir, Anecdotes, Two Portraits, and View of his House in Chelsea. This day, elegantly printed, pp. 96, cloth 2s.

⁎ The leader in *Daily Telegraph,* April 25th, largely quotes from above "Memoir."

Smiles's (Saml.) Story of the Life of George Stephen-son; a Companion Volume to "Self-Help." Sells at 6s. A few copies only at 3s. 9d. *Apply to Mr. Hotten* DIRECT *for this book.*

Malone's (Ed.) Life. By Sir James Prior, with his Manuscript Anecdotes, "Maloniana," &c. A handsome library vol., with fine portrait. Sells at 14s. Cloth new, 4s. 3d.
Apply to Mr. Hotten DIRECT *for this book.*

John Camden Hotten, 74 and 75, Piccadilly, W.

VERY IMPORTANT NEW BOOKS.

NEW BOOK BY THE "ENGLISH GUSTAVE DORE."—
COMPANION TO THE "HATCHET THROWERS."

Legends of Savage Life. By James Greenwood, the famous Author of "A Night in a Workhouse." With 36 inimitably droll illustrations, drawn and coloured by ERNEST GRISET, the "English Gustave Doré." 4to, coloured, 7s. 6d.; plain, 5s.

⁎ Readers who found amusement in the "Hatchet-Throwers" will not regret any acquaintance they may form with this comical work. The pictures are among the most surprising which have come from this artist's pencil.

"A Munchausen sort of book. The drawings by M. Griset are very powerful and eccentric."—*Saturday Review.*

School Life at Winchester College; or, the Reminiscences of a Winchester Junior. By the Author of "The Log of the Water Lily," and "The Water Lily on the Danube." Second edition, revised, coloured plates, 7s. 6d. [*In preparation.*

⁎ This book does for Winchester what "Tom Brown's School Days" did for Rugby.

Log of the "Water Lily" (Thames Gig), during Two Cruises in the Summers of 1851-52, on the Rhine, Neckar, Main, Moselle, Danube, and other Streams of Germany. By R. B. MANSFIELD, B.A., of University College, Oxford, and illustrated by ALFRED THOMPSON, B.A., of Trinity College, Cambridge. [*In preparation.*

⁎ This was the earliest boat excursion of the kind ever made on the Continental rivers. Very recently the subject has been revived again in the exploits of Mr. MacGregor in his "Rob Roy Canoe." The volume will be found most interesting to those who propose taking a similar trip, whether on the Continent or elsewhere.

The Hatchet-Throwers. With Thirty-six Illustrations, coloured after the Inimitably Grotesque Drawings of ERNEST GRISET. The English Gustave Doré. 4to, cloth gilt, 7s. 6d.; plates, uncoloured, 5s.

⁎ Comprises the astonishing adventures of Three Ancient Mariners the Brothers Brass or Bristol, Mr. Corker, and Mungo Midge.

Melchior Gorles. By Henry Aitchenbie. 3 vols. 8vo, £1 11s. 6d.

⁎ The New Novel, illustrative of "Mesmeric Influence," or whatever else we may choose to term that strange power which some persons exercise over others.

John Camden Hotten, 74 and 75, Piccadilly, W.

VERY IMPORTANT NEW BOOKS.

AN INTERESTING VOLUME TO ANTIQUARIES.
Army Lists of the Roundheads and Cavaliers in the
Civil War, 1642. 4to, half morocco, handsomely printed, price 7s. 6d.

*** These most curious Lists show on which side the gentlemen of England were to be found during the great conflict between the King and the Parliament. Only a very few copies have been most carefully reprinted on paper that will gladden the heart of the lover of choice books.

Magna Charta. An Exact Facsimile of the Original
Document preserved in the British Museum, very carefully drawn, and printed on fine plate paper, nearly 3 feet long by 2 feet wide, with the Arms and Seals of the Barons elaborately emblazoned in gold and colours. A.D. 1215. Price 5s.; by post, on roller, 5s. 4d. Handsomely framed and glazed, in carved oak of an antique pattern, 22s. 6d.

*** Copied by express permission, and the only correct drawing of the Great Charter ever taken. It is uniform with the "Roll of Battle Abbey." A full translation, with Notes, has just been prepared, price 6d.

UNIFORM WITH "MAGNA CHARTA."
Roll of Battle Abbey; or, a List of the Principal
Warriors who came over from Normandy with William the Conqueror and settled in this country, A.D. 1066-7, from Authentic Documents, very carefully drawn, with the Arms of the principal Barons elaborately emblazoned in gold and colours, price 5s.; by post, on roller, 5s. 4d. Handsomely framed and glazed, in carved oak of an antique pattern, price 22s. 6d.

Illuminated Charter-Roll of Waterford, Temp.
Richard II. In 1 vol. 4to, with 19 large and most curious Plates in facsimile, coloured by hand, including an ancient View of the City of Waterford. Subscribers, 20s.; Non-subscribers, 30s. [*Preparing*.

*** Of the very limited impression proposed, more than 150 copies have already been subscribed for. An ancient Illuminated Roll, of great interest and beauty, comprising all the early Charters and Grants to the City of Waterford, from the time of Henry II. to Richard II. Full-length Portraits of each King adorn the margin, varying from eight to nine inches in length.

The Oldest Heraldic Roll.—"The Roll of Cærlaver-
lock," with the Arms of the Earls, Barons, and Knights who were present at the Siege of this Castle in Scotland, 26 Edward I., A.D. 1300; including the Original Anglo-Norman Poem, and an English Translation of the MS. in the British Museum. By THOMAS WRIGHT, Esq., M.A., F.S.A. *THE ARMS SPLENDIDLY EMBLAZONED IN GOLD AND COLOURS.* In 4to, very handsomely printed, extra gold cloth, 18s.; or crimson morocco extra, the sides and back covered in rich fleur-de-lys, gold tooling, 55s.

*** A very handsome volume, and a delightful one to lovers of Heraldry, as it is the earliest blazon of arms known to exist.

Now publishing in monthly parts, price 1s.
A New and Complete Parochial History of Cornwall,
Compiled from the Best Authorities, and Corrected and Improved from Actual Survey; with Illustrations of the Principal Objects of Interest. Volume I. now ready, price 16s.

---

16   *John Camden Hotten, 74 and 75, Piccadilly, W.*

VERY IMPORTANT NEW BOOKS.

MR. SWINBURNE'S NEW BOOK.

*** "*A wonderful literary performance.*"—"*Splendour of style and majestic beauty of diction never surpassed.*"—WILLIAM BLAKE: A CRITICAL ESSAY. With facsimile Paintings, coloured by hand, from the original drawings painted by Blake and his wife. Thick 8vo, pp. 350, 16s.

"An extraordinary work: violent, extravagant, perverse, calculated to startle, to shock, and to alarm many readers, but abounding in beauty, and characterised by intellectual grasp. . . . . His power of word-painting is often truly wonderful—sometimes, it must be admitted, in excess, but always full of matter, form, and colour, and instinct with a sense of vitality."—*Daily News*, Feb. 12, 1868.

"It is in every way worthy of Mr. Swinburne's high fame. In no prose work can be found passages of keener poetry or more finished grace, or more impressive harmony. Strong, vigorous, and musical, the style sweeps on like a river."—*Sunday Times*, Jan. 12, 1868.

Mr. Swinburne's New Poem. — A Song of Italy.
Fcap. 8vo, toned paper, cloth, price 3s. 6d.

*** The *Athenæum* remarks of this poem—"Seldom has such a chant been heard so full of glow, strength, and colour."

Mr. Swinburne's Poems and Ballads. Third Edition.
Price 9s.

Mr. Swinburne's Notes on his Poems, and on the Reviews which have appeared upon them, is now ready, price 1s.

Mr. Swinburne's Atalanta in Calydon. New Edition, fcap. 8vo, price 6s.

Mr. Swinburne's Chastelard. A Tragedy. New Edition. Price 7s.

Mr. Swinburne's Queen Mother and Rosamond. New Edition, fcap. 8vo, price 5s.

Mr. Swinburne's Bothwell. *A NEW POEM.*
[*In preparation.*

John Camden Hotten, 74 and 75, Piccadilly, W.

VERY IMPORTANT NEW BOOKS.

Original Edition of Blake's Works.

NOTICE.—Mr. Hotten has in preparation a few facsimile copies (*exact as to paper, printing—the water-colour drawings being filled in by an artist*) of the ORIGINAL EDITIONS of the Books written and Illustrated by WILLIAM BLAKE. As it is only intended to produce—with utmost care—a few examples of each work, Mr. Hotten will be glad to hear from any gentleman who may desire to secure copies of these wonderful books. The first volume, "MARRIAGE OF HEAVEN AND HELL," 4to, is now being issued, price 30s., half morocco.

"Blake is a real name, I assure you, and a most extraordinary man he is, if he still be living. He is the Blake whose wild designs accompany a splendid edition of 'Blair's Grave.' He paints in water-colours marvellous strange pictures—visions of his brain—which he asserts he has seen. They have great merit. I must look upon him as one of the most extraordinary persons of the age."—CHARLES LAMB.

George Chapman's Plays, from the Original Texts.

Edited, with Notes and an Introduction, by ALGERNON CHARLES SWINBURNE. 4 vols., tastefully printed, uniform with Wm. Pickering's Editions of the "Old Dramatists." [*In preparation.*

UNIFORM WITH MR. SWINBURNE'S POEMS.
Fcap. 8vo, 450 pages, Fine Portrait and Autograph, 7s. 6d.

Walt Whitman's Poems. (Leaves of Grass, Drum-Taps, &c.) Selected and Edited by WILLIAM MICHAEL ROSSETTI.

"Whitman is a poet who bears and needs to be read as a whole, and then the volume and torrent of his power carry the disfigurements along with it and away.—He is really a fine fellow."—*Chambers's Journal*, in a very long Notice, July 4th, 1868.

☞ A great deal of prejudice in this country has been shown against this very remarkable author. His work should be read by independent minds, and an opinion formed totally apart from the attacks that have been made upon him.

Rossetti's Criticisms on Swinburne's Poems. Price 3s. 6d.

The Prometheus Bound of Æschylus. Translated in the Original Metres by C. B. CAYLEY, B.A. Cloth, price 3s. 6d.

SECOND EDITION.—Now ready, 4to, 10s. 6d., on toned paper, very elegant.

Bianca. Poems and Ballads. By Edward Brennan.

VERY IMPORTANT NEW BOOKS.

Fair Rosamond, and other Poems. By B. Mont-
GOMERIE RANKING (of the Inner Temple). Fcap. 8vo, price 6s.

Strawberry Hill, and other Poems. By Colburn
MAYNE, Esq. In strawberry binding, fcap. 8vo, 7s. 6d.

"It is a bright, clever little book, in which we find a great deal of good rhyme, and some genuine and pleasing poetry. There are several charming pictures of the historic group, which we know from Horace Walpole's letters and Sir Joshua's paintings."—*Morning Star.*

Infelicia. Poems by Adah Isaacs Menken. Illustrated with NUMEROUS GRACEFULLY PENCILLED DESIGNS DRAWN ON WOOD, BY ALFRED CONCANEN. Dedicated, by permission, to CHARLES DICKENS, with photographic facsimile of his letter, and a very beautifully engraved portrait of the Authoress. In green and gold, 5s. 6d.

"A pathetic little volume exquisitely got up."—*Sun.*

"It is full of pathos and sentiment, displays a keen appreciation of beauty, and has remarkable earnestness and passion."—*Globe.*

"A loving and delicate care has been bestowed on perhaps the daintiest pages of verse that have been issued for many years."—*Lloyd's News.*

"Few, if any, could have guessed the power and beauty of the thoughts that possessed her soul, and found expression in language at once pure and melodious. . . . . Who shall say Menken was not a poet? Throughout her verse there runs a golden thread of rich and pure poetry."—*Press.*

"There is a passionate richness about many of the poems which is almost startling."—*Sunday Times.*

"What can we say of this gifted and wayward woman, the existence of whose better nature will be suggested for the first time to many by the posthumous disclosure of this book? We do not envy the man who, reading it, has only a sneer for its writer; nor the woman who finds it in her heart to turn away with averted face."—*New York Round Table.*

"An amazing little book, unhappily posthumous, which a distinguished woman has left as a legacy to mankind and the ages."—*Saturday Review.*

Anacreon in English. Attempted in the Metres of
the Original. By THOMAS J. ARNOLD. A choice little volume, price 4s.

The Village on the Forth, and other Poems. By
PHILIP LATIMER. Just published, elegantly printed, price 3s. 6d.

"Chips from a Rough Log; or, Extracts from a
Journal kept on board the good ship "Parisian," by HAMILTON D. GUNDRY. Fcap. 8vo, price 3s. 6d., cloth neat.

John Camden Hotten, 74 and 75, Piccadilly, W.

VERY IMPORTANT NEW BOOKS.

Poems from the Greek Mythology, and Miscellaneous Poems. By EDMUND OLLIER. This day, cloth neat, 5s.

"What he has written is enough, and more than enough, to give him a high rank amongst the most successful cultivators of the English Muse."—*Globe.*

Poems. Characteristic, Itinerary, and Miscellaneous.

By P. F. ROE. Part I.—Rythmical Etchings of Character. II.—Tracings of Travel. III.—Minor Poems. IV.—Translations. Price 7s. 6d.

Facts and Fancies from the Farm. Poems by James

DAWSON. Fcap. 8vo, neatly printed, 2s. 6d.

"Here we have some very pretty and readable poetry—some of it so much above the average as to warrant expectations of something far better, and we shall look forward with interest to the next volume from the same hand."—*Globe.*

The Idolatress, and other Poems. By Dr. James

Wills, Author of "Dramatic Scenes," "The Disembodied," and of various Poetical Contributions to "Blackwood's Magazine." Price 6s.

"One great merit of the 'Idolatress' is to be found in the ability with which the writer has contrasted a spiritual faith and its claims on the conscience, with a material faith that captivates the imagination through the senses."—*Athenæum,* July 11th, 1868.

Lyrics and Bucolics. The Eclogues of Virgil, a

Selection from the Odes of Horace, and the Legend of the Sibyll. Translated by HERBERT NOYES, Esq. An elegant little volume, bound in blue and gold, carmine edges, price 4s. 6d.

By the same Author.—An Idyll of the Weald. With

other Lays and Legends. By HERBERT NOYES, Esq. In uniform binding, price 9s.

The New Poetical Satire.—Horse and Foot; or,

Pilgrims to Parnassus. By RICHARD CRAWLEY. "I'll not march through Coventry with them, that's flat." Price 3s. 6d.

☞ The "*Pall Mall Gazette*" *has just given two columns of satisfactory criticism upon this work.*

Wit and Humour. By the "Autocrat of the Break-

fast Table." In crown 8vo, toned paper, elegant, price 3s. 6d.

⁎⁎ A volume of delightfully humorous Poems, very similar to the mirthful verses of Tom Hood. Readers will not be disappointed with this work.

Songs of the Nativity. — Old English Religious

Ballads and Carols. An entirely new collection of Old Carols, including some never before given in any collection. With Music to the more popular. Edited by W. H. HUSK, Librarian to the Sacred Harmonic Society. In small 4to, with very beautiful floriated borders, in the Renaissance style, cloth gilt, price 12s. 6d.

VERY IMPORTANT NEW BOOKS.

Lost Beauties of the English Language. Revived

and Revivable in England and America. An Appeal to Authors, Poets, Clergymen, and Public Speakers. By CHARLES MACKAY, LL.D. In crown 8vo, uniform with the "Slang Dictionary," price 6s. 6d.

[*In preparation.*

Captain Grose's Dictionary of the Vulgar Tongue,

1785. A genuine unmutilated Reprint of the First Edition, price 6s.

*** Only a small number of copies of this very vulgar, but very curious, book have been printed for the Collectors of "Street Words" and Colloquialisms, on fine toned paper, half-bound morocco, gilt top.

Slang Dictionary; or, the Vulgar Words, Street

PHRASES, and "FAST" EXPRESSIONS OF HIGH AND LOW SOCIETY; many with their Etymology, and a few with their History traced. WITH CURIOUS ILLUSTRATIONS. A New Dictionary of Colloquial English. Pp. 328, in 8vo, price 6s. 6d., by post, 7s.

See TWO UPON TEN, *in the Dictionary*, p. 264.

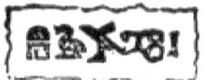

Egyptian Hieroglyphic verb, to be drunk, showing the amputation of a man's leg. See under BREAKY LEG (viz. *Strong Drink*) *in the Dictionary,* p. 81.

☞ One hundred and forty newspapers in this country alone have reviewed with approbation this Dictionary of Colloquial English. "It may be doubted if there exists a more amusing volume in the English language."—SPECTATOR. "Valuable as a work of reference."—SATURDAY REVIEW. "All classes of society will find amusement and instruction in its pages."—TIMES.

Original Edition of the Famous Joe Miller's Jests;

or, the Wit's Vade-Mecum; a Collection of the most brilliant Jests, politest Repartees, most elegant Bons-Mots, and most pleasant short Stories in the English Language. London: printed by T. Read, 1739. An interesting specimen of remarkable facsimile, 8vo, half morocco, price 9s. 6d.

*** *ONLY A VERY FEW COPIES OF THIS HUMOROUS AND RACY OLD BOOK HAVE BEEN REPRODUCED.*

John Camden Hotten, 74 and 75, Piccadilly, W.

VERY IMPORTANT NEW BOOKS.

In preparation, an entirely
New Book by the late Artemus Ward. Edited by
his executors, T. W. Robertson and E. P. Hingston. Illustrated with 35 pictures, taken from his world-renowned Panorama.

Immediately, cloth, very neat, 2s. 6d.
The Works of Charles F. Browne, better known as
"ARTEMUS WARD." Portrait by Geflowski, the Sculptor, and fac-similes, &c.

History of Playing Cards. With Anecdotes, Ancient
and Modern Games, Conjuring, Fortune-Telling, and Card-Sharping. With Sixty curious illustrations. Skill and Sleight-of-Hand; Gambling

and Calculation; Cartomancy and Cheating; Old Games and Gaming-Houses; Card Revels and Blind Hookey; Piquet and Vingt-et-un; Whist and Cribbage; Old-Fashioned Tricks. Pp. 550, price 7s. 6d.
"A highly-interesting volume."—*Morning Post*.

Cruikshank's Comic Almanack. A complete set, as
published in the original numbers from 1835 to 1853. 19 vols., neatly bound in 5 vols., half-morocco, Roxburgh style, £3 3s. Containing MERRY TALES, JESTS, HUMOROUS POETRY, WHIMS, ODDITIES, &c., by THACKERAY, THOMAS HOOD, ALBERT SMITH, and other well-known comic writers. Illustrated with nearly ONE THOUSAND WOODCUTS AND STEEL ENGRAVINGS by the *inimitable* GEORGE CRUIKSHANK and other Artists. *Very scarce.*

Mr. Sprouts his Opinions. The New and Genuine
Book of Humour. Uniform with "Artemus Ward." By RICHARD WHITEING. New Shilling Edition now ready.

VERY IMPORTANT NEW BOOKS.

Wright's (Thomas, M.A.) History of Domestic

Manners and Sentiments in England during the Middle Ages. 1862. Thick small 4to. Illustrated with a great profusion of most interesting woodcuts, drawn and engraved by Fairholt, from the illuminations in contemporary MSS. and other sources. Cloth, bevelled boards, red edges. Sells at 21s. New, 10s. 6d. only.

DIRECT APPLICATION *must be made to Mr. Hotten for this Work.*

Caxton's Statutes of Henry VII., 1489. Edited,

with Notes and Introduction, by JOHN RAE, Esq., Fellow of the Royal Institution. In remarkable facsimile, from the rare original, small folio.

The earliest known volume of Printed Statutes, and remarkable as being in English. It contains some very curious and primitive Legislation on Trade and Domestic Matters, such as:—

Price of Hats and Caps	Giving of Livery	Correcting Priests
French Wines	Concerning Customs	Against Hunters
Act for Peopling Isle of Wight	Fires in London	Marrying a Woman against her Will, &c.
Against Butchers	Rebels in the Field	

Genealogical Collections concerning the Sir-Name of

Baird, and the Families of Auchmedden, Newbyth, and Sauchton Hall in particular. With copies of old letters and papers worth preserving, and account of several transactions in this country during the last two centuries. Reprinted from the original MS. in the Advocates' Library, Edinburgh. Price to Subscribers, 10s. 6d. [*Preparing.*

*** The present edition will include an appendix containing a large amount of fresh genealogical information. The work is one possessing general interest, foreign to most Family Histories. No pains will be spared to make the work an accurate and beautiful one. As the impression will be limited strictly to 100 copies, early application must be made to secure them.

ANECDOTES OF THE "LONG PARLIAMENT" OF 1645.

The Mysteries of the Good Old Cause: Sarcastic

Notices of those Members of the Long Parliament that held places, both Civil and Military, contrary to the Self-denying Ordinance of April 3, 1645; with the sums of money and lands they divided among themselves. In 4to, half morocco, choicely printed, price 7s. 6d.

Warrant to Execute Charles I. An Exact Facsimile

of this Important Document in the House of Lords, with the Fifty-nine Signatures of the Regicides, and Corresponding Seals, admirably executed on paper made to imitate the Original Document, 22 in. by 14 in. Price 2s.; by post, 2s. 4d. Handsomely framed and glazed, in carved oak of an antique pattern, 14s. 6d.

Warrant to Execute Mary Queen of Scots. The

Exact Facsimile of this Important Document, including the Signature of Queen Elizabeth and Facsimile of the Great Seal. Safe on roller, 2s.; by post, 2s. 4d. Handsomely framed and glazed, in carved oak of an antique pattern, 14s. 6d.

VERY IMPORTANT NEW BOOKS

Best Guide to Reading Old MSS., Records, &c.—
"Wright's Court Hand Restored; or, Student's Assistant in Reading Old Deeds, Charters, Records, &c." Half morocco, 10s. 6d.

☞ *A New Edition, corrected, of* AN INVALUABLE WORK TO ALL WHO HAVE OCCASION TO CONSULT OLD MSS., DEEDS, CHARTERS, &c. *It contains a series of Facsimiles of old MSS. from the time of the Conqueror, Tables of Contractions and Abbreviations, Ancient Surnames, &c.*

Handbook of Family History of the English Counties:
Descriptive Account of 20,000 most Curious and Rare Books, Old Tracts, Ancient Manuscripts, Engravings, and Privately-printed Family Papers, relating to the History of almost every Landed Estate and Old English Family in the Country; interspersed with nearly Two Thousand Original Anecdotes, Topographical and Antiquarian Notes. By JOHN CAMDEN HOTTEN. Nearly 350 pages, very neat, price 5s.

⁎ By far the largest collection of English and Welsh Topography and Family History ever formed. Each article has a small price affixed for the convenience of those who may desire to possess any book or tract that interests them.

Higgins' (Godfrey) Celtic Druids; or, an attempt to
show that the Druids were the Priests of Oriental Colonies, the introducers of the first or Cadmean System of Letters, the Builders of Stonehenge, of Carnac, and other Cyclopean Works in Asia and Europe. 4to, numerous plates of Druid monuments, rare, 32s.

⁎ The most philosophical digest of the existing information upon the origin of Druidical Worship. Copies have been sold for £7. At the above price the book is ridiculously cheap, compared with the sums of money that have been paid for it very recently. Large paper copy, boards, 45s., very scarce.

DIRECT APPLICATION *must be made to procure at these reduced prices.*

Esholt in Airedale, Yorkshire: the Cistercian Priory
of St. Leonard, Account of, with View of Esholt Hall. Small 4to, 1s. 6d.

London Directory for 1667, the Earliest Known
List of the London Merchants. 12mo, very choicely printed, price 6s. 6d. See Review in the *Times*, Jan. 22.

⁎ This curious little volume has been reprinted verbatim from one of the only two copies known to be in existence. It contains an Introduction pointing out some of the principal persons mentioned in the list.

For historical and genealogical purposes the little book is of the greatest value.

EXACT FACSIMILE, LETTER FOR LETTER, OF THE EXCESSIVELY RARE ORIGINAL,

Much Adoe about Nothing. As it hath been sundrie
times publikely acted by the Right Honourable the Lord Chamberlaine his seruants. Written by WILLIAM SHAKESPEARE, 1600.

⁎ Small quarto, on fine toned paper, half-bound morocco, Roxburghe style, only 4s. 6d. (Original price, 10s. 6d.)

www.ingramcontent.com/pod-product-compliance
Lightning Source LLC
Chambersburg PA
CBHW030745250426
43672CB00028B/617